06

007

08

1 2 MAY 2009
-1 FEB 2010

Advanced Database Technology and Design

For a listing of related titles from *Artech House Computing Library,*
turn to the back of this book.

Advanced Database Technology and Design

Mario Piattini
Oscar Díaz
Editors

Artech House
Boston • London
www.artechhouse.com

Library of Congress Cataloging-in-Publication Data
Advanced database technology and design / Mario G. Piattini, Oscar Díaz, editors.
    p.   cm. — (Artech House computing library)
    Includes bibliographical references and index.
    ISBN 0-89006-395-8 (alk. paper)
    1. Database management.   2. Database design.   I. Piattini, Mario, 1966–
II. Díaz, Oscar.   III. Series.
QA76.9.D3 A3435   2000
005.74—dc21
                                                         00-055842
                                                         CIP

British Library Cataloguing in Publication Data
Advanced database technology and design. — (Artech House computing library)
    1. Databases   2. Database design
    I. Piattini, Mario G.   II. Díaz, Oscar
    005.7'4

    ISBN 0-89006-395-8

Cover design by Igor Valdman

© 2000 ARTECH HOUSE, INC.
685 Canton Street
Norwood, MA 02062

International Standard Book Number: 0-89006-395-8
Library of Congress Catalog Card Number: 00-055842

10 9 8 7 6 5 4 3 2 1

Contents

Preface — — — — — — — — — — — — — — — — — — — *xv*

Part I: Fundamentals — — — — — — — — — — — — — 1

1   Evolution and Trends of Database Technology   3

1.1   Introduction   3

1.2   Database Evolution   4

1.2.1   Historical Overview: First and Second DB Generations   4

1.2.2   Evolution of DB Design Methodologies   8

1.3   The New DB Generation   10

1.3.1   Problems of Current DBs   11

1.3.2   Changes in Organizations and in Computers:
The Impact on DBs   11

1.3.3   Nontraditional Applications   13

1.4   Research and Market Trends   15

1.4.1   Performance   16

1.4.2   Distribution and Integration   17

1.4.3   Functionality and Intelligence   18

1.5   Maturity of DB Technology   20

References   22

Selected Bibliography   23

2	**An Introduction to Conceptual Modeling of Information Systems**	**25**
2.1	The Functions of an Information System	25
2.1.1	The Memory Function	28
2.1.2	The Informative Function	28
2.1.3	The Active Function	30
2.1.4	Examples of ISs	31
2.2	Conceptual Modeling	33
2.2.1	Conceptual Schema of the State	34
2.2.2	Information Base	38
2.2.3	Conceptual Schema of the Behavior	39
2.2.4	Integrity Constraints	43
2.2.5	Derivation Rules	45
2.3	Abstract Architecture of an IS	46
2.4	Requirements Engineering	51
2.5	Desirable Properties of Conceptual Schemas	53
	References	56
	Selected Bibliography	57

	Part II: Advanced Technologies	**59**

3	**Active Databases**	**61**
3.1	Introduction	61
3.2	Example: University Database	63
3.3	Analysis	64
3.3.1	Recovering Business Policies	64
3.3.2	Causal Business Policies	67
3.4	Design	69
3.4.1	Active Rules	69
3.4.2	Supporting Recovering Business Policies Through Active Rules	69
3.4.3	Supporting Causal Business Policies Through Active Rules	73
3.4.4	Active Behavior	76
3.5	Implementation Issues	78

3.5.1	Active Rules in Oracle	79
3.5.2	Active Rules in Use	81
3.5.3	Standardizing Active Behavior in SQL: 1999	85
3.6	Rule Maintenance	85
3.7	Summary	87
	References	88
	Selected Bibliography	89

4	**Deductive Databases**	**91**
4.1	Introduction	91
4.2	Basic Concepts of Deductive Databases	93
4.2.1	Definition of a Deductive Database	93
4.2.2	Semantics of Deductive Databases	96
4.2.3	Advantages Provided by Views and Integrity Constraints	98
4.2.4	Deductive Versus Relational Databases	100
4.3	Query Processing	102
4.3.1	Bottom-Up Query Evaluation	103
4.3.2	Top-Down Query Evaluation	105
4.3.3	Magic Sets	107
4.4	Update Processing	108
4.4.1	Change Computation	109
4.4.2	View Updating	114
4.4.3	Integrity Constraint Enforcement	117
4.4.4	A Common Framework for Database Updating Problems	119
4.5	Deductive Database System Prototypes	128
4.6	Summary	130
	References	131
	Selected Bibliography	136

5	**Temporal Database Systems**	**137**
5.1	Introduction	137
5.2	Temporal Data	140
5.2.1	Some Basic Concepts and Questions	142

5.3	What's the Problem?	146
5.3.1	"Semitemporalizing" Suppliers and Parts	147
5.3.2	Fully Temporalizing Suppliers and Parts	149
5.4	Intervals	154
5.5	Interval Types	156
5.6	Scalar Operators on Intervals	159
5.7	Aggregate Operators on Intervals	160
5.8	Relational Operators Involving Intervals	162
5.9	Constraints Involving Intervals	170
5.10	Update Operators Involving Intervals	174
5.11	Database Design Considerations	176
5.11.1	"Horizontal" Decomposition	177
5.11.2	"Vertical" Decomposition	179
5.12	Further Points	181
5.13	Summary	182
	References	184
	Selected Bibliography	184
6	**Object-Relational Database Systems**	**189**
6.1	Introduction	189
6.2	A Quick Look at Relational and Object-Oriented Databases	191
6.3	Contrasting the Major Features of Pure Relational and Object-Oriented Databases	192
6.4	Drawbacks of Pure Relational and Object-Oriented Databases	193
6.5	Technology Issues: Enabling Object Functionality in the Relational World	195
6.5.1	Behavior	196
6.5.2	Collection Types	196
6.5.3	Encapsulation	197
6.5.4	Polymorphism	197
6.5.5	Inheritance	197
6.6	ORDBMS: A Closer Look at Characteristics in the Physical Implementation	198

6.7	Design Issues: Capturing the Essence of the Object-Relational Paradigm	201
6.8	An Object-Relational Example	203
6.9	The ABC Corporation Example	207
6.10	Summary	208
	Selected Bibliography	208
7	**Object-Oriented Database Systems**	**211**
7.1	Introduction and Motivation	211
7.2	Basic Concepts of the Object-Oriented Data Model	212
7.2.1	Objects and Object Identifiers	214
7.2.2	Aggregation	216
7.2.3	Methods	217
7.2.4	Classes and Instantiation Mechanisms	218
7.2.5	Inheritance	219
7.3	Graphical Notation and Example	220
7.4	ODMG Standard	221
7.4.1	Objects and Literals	222
7.4.2	Types: Classes and Interfaces	222
7.4.3	Subtypes and Inheritance	223
7.4.4	Extents	223
7.4.5	Keys	224
7.4.6	Collection and Structured Types	224
7.5	Technology	225
7.5.1	GemStone	225
7.5.2	ObjectStore	227
7.5.3	POET	229
7.6	Object-Oriented Database Design	230
7.6.1	Conceptual Design	232
7.6.2	Standard Schema Design	233
7.6.3	Implementation Schema Design	242
7.7	Summary	246
	References	248
	Selected Bibliography	249
	Web Sites	250

8	**Multimedia Database Management Systems**	**251**
8.1	Introduction	251
8.1.1	Diverse Nature of Media Objects	251
8.1.2	Complexity and Multidimensionality	252
8.2	A Sample IMD	254
8.3	Design of an MM-DBMS for IMDs	256
8.3.1	Modeling IMDs	256
8.3.2	IMD Retrieval Issues	266
8.4	Conclusions	274
8.4.1	Main Achievements of MM-DBMS Technology	274
8.4.2	Commercial Products and Research Prototypes	280
8.4.3	Further Directions and Trends	282
	References	286
	Selected Bibliography	289
9	**Distributed Databases**	**291**
9.1	Introduction	291
9.2	Distributed Database Architecture	293
9.2.1	Five-Level Model for Heterogeneous Multi-DBMS	296
9.2.2	Four-Level Model for Homogeneous Multi-DBMS	298
9.2.3	Three-Level Model for Single-DBMS	298
9.2.4	Physical Database Connectivity	298
9.2.5	Distributed Data Independence	299
9.2.6	Other Decentralized Database Architectures	300
9.3	Distributed Database Design	301
9.3.1	Data Fragmentation and Replication in Relational DDBs	301
9.3.2	Top-Down Design of Relational DDBs	304
9.3.3	Bottom-Up Design of Heterogeneous DDBs	307
9.4	Distributed Query Processing	310
9.4.1	Query Processing in Relational DDBs	310
9.4.2	Query Processing in Heterogeneous DDBs	314
9.5	Distributed Transaction Management	315
9.5.1	Distributed Concurrency Control	316
9.5.2	Distributed Commit	319

9.5.3	Distributed Recovery	322
9.5.4	Transaction Management in Heterogeneous DDBs	322
9.6	Current Trends and Challenges	323
9.6.1	Alternative Transaction Models	323
9.6.2	Mediator Architectures	324
9.6.3	Databases and the World Wide Web	325
	References	325
	Selected Bibliography	327

10	**Mobile Computing: Data Management Issues**	**329**
10.1	Introduction	329
10.2	Motivation	331
10.3	Architecture	332
10.4	Technological Aspects: Wireless Networks	334
10.4.1	Analog Cellular Networks	334
10.4.2	Digital Cellular Networks	334
10.4.3	Wireless Wide-Area Networks	335
10.4.4	Wireless Local-Area Networks	335
10.4.5	Satellite Networks	335
10.4.6	The Future	336
10.5	Special Issues for Consideration	336
10.5.1	Mobility	336
10.5.2	Wireless Medium	336
10.5.3	Portability of Mobile Elements	337
10.6	Impact of Mobile Computing on Data Management	338
10.6.1	Transactions	338
10.6.2	Data Dissemination by Broadcasting	339
10.6.3	Query Processing	340
10.6.4	Caching	341
10.6.5	Database Interfaces	341
10.7	Communication Models and Agents	342
10.7.1	Communication Models	342
10.7.2	Agents	343
10.8	Mobile Computer Design Features for Accessing Data Services	344

10.9	Summary	347
	References	347
	Selected Bibliography	351

11	**Secure Database Systems**	**353**
11.1	Introduction	353
11.2	Access Control: Concepts and Policies	354
11.2.1	Basic Concepts	354
11.2.2	Access Control Policies	355
11.2.3	Administration Policies	360
11.3	Discretionary Access Control Models and Systems	362
11.3.1	Authorization Models for Relational DBMSs	363
11.3.2	Authorization Models for Object DBMSs	366
11.3.3	Authorization Models for Active DBMSs	369
11.3.4	Comparative Analysis of Authorization Models	370
11.3.5	Discretionary Access Control in Commercial DBMSs	370
11.4	Multilevel Security in Database Systems	375
11.4.1	Multilevel Relational Data Model	375
11.4.2	Architectures	376
11.4.3	Prototypes	380
11.4.4	Commercial Products	384
11.4.5	Multilevel Object Data Models	387
11.5	Design Issues	392
11.6	Some Research Trends	393
11.6.1	Digital Libraries	394
11.6.2	Data Protection for Workflow Management Systems	396
11.6.3	Data Protection for the World Wide Web	397
11.7	Summary	398
	References	399
	Selected Bibliography	402

12	**Component Database Systems**	**403**
12.1	Introduction	403
12.2	Motivation	405
12.3	Principles of Component DBMSs	409

12.3.1   DBMS Architecture   409
12.3.2   Components and DBMS Architecture   412
12.3.3   Typology of Component DBMSs   413
12.4   Component Database Models   416
12.4.1   Plug-In Components   417
12.4.2   Middleware DBMS   419
12.4.3   Service-Oriented DBMSs   422
12.4.4   Configurable DBMSs   423
12.4.5   Categories of Component DBMS Models   424
12.5   Development of Component DBMSs and Their
         Applications   424
12.5.1   Database Design for CDBMSs   426
12.5.2   Development of CDBMS Components   427
12.6   Related Work: The Roots of CDBMSs   428
12.7   Summary   430
         References   431

Part III: Advanced Design Issues   437

**13   CASE Tools: Computer Support for Conceptual
           Modeling   439**
13.1   Introduction to CASE Tools   439
13.1.1   Functional Classification of CASE Tools   440
13.1.2   Communication Between CASE Tools   444
13.2   A CASE Framework for Database Design   445
13.3   Conceptual Design Tools   447
13.3.1   The Choice of the Conceptual Model   448
13.3.2   Conceptual Modeling Tools   449
13.3.3   Verification and Validation Tools   455
13.3.4   Conceptual Design by Schema Integration   463
13.3.5   Conceptual Design Based Upon Reusable
         Components   467
13.3.6   Conclusion on the Conceptual Level   468
13.4   Logical Design Tools   469
13.4.1   Fundamentals of Relational Design   469
13.4.2   Functional Dependency Acquisition   470

13.4.3	Mapping From Conceptual Schema to Logical Schema	473
13.4.4	Concluding Remarks on the Logical Design	479
13.5	Summary	479
	References	480
	Selected Bibliography	482

14	**Database Quality**	**485**
14.1	Introduction	485
14.2	Data Model Quality	488
14.2.1	Quality Factors	490
14.2.2	Stakeholders	490
14.2.3	Quality Concepts	492
14.2.4	Improvement Strategies	493
14.2.5	Quality Metrics	493
14.2.6	Weighting	500
14.3	Data Quality	501
14.3.1	Management Issues	502
14.3.2	Design Issues	504
14.4	Summary	505
	References	506
	Selected Bibliography	509

About the Authors	**511**

Index	**517**

Preface

Since computers were introduced to automate organization management, information system evolution has influenced data management considerably. Applications demand more and more services from information stored in computing systems. These new services impose more stringent conditions on the currently prevailing client/server architectures and relational database management systems (DBMSs). For the purpose of this book, those demands can be arranged along three aspects, namely:

Enhancements on the structural side. The tabular representation of data has proved to be suitable for applications, such as insurance and banking, that have to process large volumes of well-formatted data. However, newer applications such as computer-aided manufacturing or geographic information systems have a tough job attempting to fit more elaborate structures into flat records. Moreover, the SQL'92 types are clearly insufficient to tackle time or multimedia concerns.

Improvements on the behavioral side. Data are no longer the only aspect to be shared. Code can, and must, be shared. DBMS providers are striving to make their products evolve from data servers to code servers. The introduction of rules to support active and deductive capabilities and the inclusion of user-defined data types are now part of that trend.

Architectural issues. New applications need access to heterogeneous and distributed data, require a higher throughoutput (e.g., large number of transactions in e-commerce applications), or need to share code. The client/server architecture cannot always meet those new demands.

This book aims to provide a gentle and application-oriented introduction to those topics. Motivation and application-development considerations, rather than state-of-the-art research, are the main focus. Examples are extensively used in the text, and a brief selected reading section appears at the end of each chapter for readers who want more information. Special attention is given to the design issues raised by the new trends.

The book is structured as follows:

Part I: Fundamentals

Chapter 1 gives an overview of the evolution of DBMS and how its history has been a continuous effort to meet the increasing demands of the applications. Chapter 2 provides a gentle introduction to the key concepts of conceptual modeling.

Part II: Advanced Technologies

This part presents technological and design issues that we need to face to address new application requirements. The first two chapters deal with rule management, Chapter 3 covers active database systems, and Chapter 4 deductive ones. Chapter 5 examines the concepts of temporal databases and the problems of time management. Chapters 6 and 7 discuss two different ways of introducing object orientation in database technology: the more evolutionary one (object-relational DBMSs) and the more revolutionary one (object-oriented DBMSs). Chapter 8 discusses the issues related to multimedia databases and their management. Chapters 9 and 10 present distributed and mobile DBMSs, respectively. Chapter 11 focuses on security concerns by discussing secure DBMSs. Chapter 12 introduces a new approach to DBMS implementation: component DBMSs.

Part III: Advanced Design Issues

Part III looks at two topics that are necessary for obtaining databases of a certain level of quality. Chapter 13 examines various concepts associated with computer-aided database design that claim to be an effective way to improve database design. Chapter 14 concentrates on considering quality issues in database design and implementation.

As for the audience, the book is targeted to senior undergraduates and graduate students. Thus, it is mainly a textbook. However, database professional and application developers can also find a gentle introduction to these topics and useful hints for their job. The prerequisites for understanding the book are a basic knowledge of relational databases and software engineering. Some knowledge of object-oriented technology and networks is desirable.

We would like to thank Artech House, especially Viki Williams, and Marcela Genero of UCLM for their support during the preparation of this book.

It is our hope that the efforts made by the distinct authors to provide a friendly introduction to their respective areas of expertise will make the reader's journey along the database landscape more pleasant.

Mario Piattini
Oscar Díaz
August 2000

Part I:
Fundamentals

1

Evolution and Trends of Database Technology

Adoración de Miguel, Mario Piattini, and Paloma Martínez

1.1 Introduction

The history of database (DB) dates from the mid-1960s. DB has proved to be exceptionally productive and of great economic impact. In fact, today, the DB market exceeds $8 billion, with an 8% annual growth rate (IDC forecast). Databases have become a first-order strategic product as the basis of Information Systems (IS), and support management and decision making.

This chapter studies from a global perspective the current problems that led to the next generation of DBs.[1] The next four sections examine the past, that is, the evolution of DB (Section 1.2); the troubles and challenges facing current DBs, including changes in the organizations and changes in the type of applications (Section 1.3); the current research and market trends based on the performance, functionality, and distribution dimensions (Section 1.4); and the maturity level of the technology (Section 1.5).

---

1. Development and tendencies in DB technology are too complicated to sum up in a few pages. This chapter presents one approach, but the authors are aware that some aspects that are important to us may not be significant to other experts and vice versa. In spite of that, we think it would be interesting for the reader to have a global view of the emergence and development of DB, the problems that have to be solved, and DB trends.

1.2 Database Evolution

In the initial stages of computing, data were stored in files systems. The problems (redundancy, maintenance, security, the great dependence between data and applications, and, mainly, rigidity) associated with the use of such systems gave rise to new technology for the management of stored data: *databases*. The first generation of DB management systems (DBMSs) evolved over time, and some of the problems with files were solved. Other problems, however, persisted, and the relational model was proposed to correct them. With that model, the second generation of DBs was born. The difficulties in designing the DBs effectively brought about design methodologies based on data models.

1.2.1 Historical Overview: First and Second DB Generations

Ever since computers were introduced to automate organization management, IS evolution has considerably influenced data management. IS demands more and more services from information stored in computing systems. Gradually, the focus of computing, which had previously concentrated on processing, shifted from process-oriented to data-oriented systems, where data play an important role for software engineers. Today, many IS design problems center around data modeling and structuring.

After the rigid files systems in the initial stages of computing, in the 1960s and early 1970s, the first generation of DB products was born. Database systems can be considered intermediaries between the physical devices where data are stored and the users (human beings) of the data. DBMSs are the software tools that enable the management (definition, creation, maintenance, and use) of large amounts of interrelated data stored in computer-accessible media. The early DBMSs, which were based on hierarchical and network (Codasyl) models, provided logical organization of data in trees and graphs. IBM's IMS, General Electric's IDS, (after Bull's), Univac's DMS 1100, Cincom's Total, MRI's System 2000, and Cullinet's (now Computer Associates) IDMS are some of the well-known representatives of this generation. Although efficient, this type of product used procedural languages, did not have real physical or logical independence, and was very limited in its flexibility. In spite of that, DBMSs were an important advance compared to the files systems.

IBM's addition of data communication facilities to its IMS software gave rise to the first large-scale database/data communication (DB/DC) system, in which many users access the DB through a communication network.

Since then, access to DBs through communication networks has been offered by commercially available DBMSs.

C. W. Bachman played a pioneering role in the development of network DB systems (IDS product and Codasyl DataBase Task Group, or DBTG, proposals). In his paper "The Programmer as Navigator" (Bachman's lecture on the occasion of his receiving the 1973 Turing award), Bachman describes the process of traveling through the DB; the programmer has to follow explicit paths in search of one piece of data going from record to record [1].

The DBTG model is based on the data structure diagrams [2], which are also known as Bachman's diagrams. In the model, the links between record types, called Codasyl sets, are always one occurrence of one record type to many, that is, a functional link. In its 1978 specifications [3], Codasyl also proposed a data definition language (DDL) at three levels (schema DDL, subschema DDL, and internal DDL) and a procedural (prescriptive) data manipulation language (DML).

Hierarchical links and Codasyl sets are physically implemented via pointers. That implementation, together with the functional constraints of those links and sets, is the cause of their principal weaknesses (little flexibility of such physical structures, data/application dependence, and complexity of their navigational languages) of the systems based on those models. Nevertheless, those same pointers are precisely the reason for their efficiency, one of the great strengths of the products.

In 1969–1970, Dr. E. F. Codd proposed the relational model [4], which was considered an "elegant mathematical theory" (a "toy" for certain experts) without any possibility of efficient implementation in commercial products. In 1970, few people imagined that, in the 1980s, the relational model would become mandatory (a "decoy") for the promotion of DBMSs. Relational products like Oracle, DB2, Ingres, Informix, Sybase, and so on are considered the second generation of DBs. These products have more physical and logical independence, greater flexibility, and declarative query languages (users indicate what they want without describing how to get it) that deal with sets of records, and they can be automatically optimized, although their DML and host language are not integrated. With relational DBMSs (RDBMSs), organizations have more facilities for data distribution. RDBMSs provide not only better usability but also a more solid theoretical foundation.

Unlike network models, the relational model is value-oriented and does not support object identity. (There is an important tradeoff between object identity and declarativeness.) As a result of Codasyl DBTG and IMS support object identity, some authors introduced them in the object-oriented DB class. As Ullman asserts: "Many would disagree with our use of the term 'object-oriented' when applied to the first two languages: the Codasyl DBTG language, which was the origin of the network model, and IMS, an early database system using the hierarchical model. However, these languages support object identity, and thus present significant problems and significant advantages when compared with relational languages" [5].

After initial resistance to relational systems, mainly due to performance problems, these products have now achieved such wide acceptance that the network products have almost disappeared from the market. In spite of the advantages of the relational model, it must be recognized that the relational products are not exempt from difficulties. Perhaps one of the greatest demands on RDBMSs is the support of increasingly complex data types; also, null values, recursive queries, and scarce support for integrity rules and for domains (or abstract data types) are now other weaknesses of relational systems. Some of those problems probably will be solved in the next version of Structured Query Language (SQL), SQL: 1999 (previously SQL3) [6].

In the 1970s, the great debate on the relative merits of Codasyl and relational models served to compare both classes of models and to obtain a better understanding of their strengths and weaknesses.

During the late 1970s and in the 1980s, research work (and, later, industrial applications) focused on query optimization, high-level languages, the normalization theory, physical structures for stored relations, buffer and memory management algorithms, indexing techniques (variations of B-trees), distributed systems, data dictionaries, transaction management, and so on. That work allowed efficient and secure on-line transactional processing (OLTP) environments (in the first DB generation, DBMSs were oriented toward batch processing). In the 1980s, the SQL language was also standardized (SQL/ANS 86 was approved by the American National Standard Institute (ANSI) and the International Standard Organization (ISO) in 1986), and today, every RDBMS offers SQL.

Many of the DB technology advances at that time were founded on two elements: reference models and data models (see Figure 1.1) [7]. ISO and ANSI proposals on reference models [8–10] have positively influenced not only theoretical researches but also practical applications, especially in DB development methodologies. In most of those reference models, two main concepts can be found: the well-known three-level architecture (external, logical, and internal layers), also proposed by Codasyl in 1978, and the recursive data description. The separation between logical description of data and physical implementation (data application independence) devices

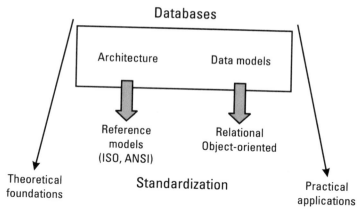

Figure 1.1 Foundations of DB advances.

was always an important objective in DB evolution, and the three-level architecture, together with the relational data model, was a major step in that direction.

In terms of data models, the relational model has influenced research agendas for many years and is supported by most of the current products. Recently, other DBMSs have appeared that implement other models, most of which are based on object-oriented principles.[2]

Three key factors can be identified in the evolution of DBs: theoretical basis (resulting from researchers' work), products (developed by vendors), and practical applications (requested by users). Those three factors have been present throughout the history of DB, but the equilibrium among them has changed. What began as a product technology demanded by users' needs in the 1960s became a vendor industry during the 1970s and 1980s. In the 1970s, the relational model marked the consideration of DB as a research technology, a consideration that still persists. In general, users' needs have always influenced the evolution of DB technology, but especially so in the last decade.

Today, we are witnessing an extraordinary development of DB technology. Areas that were exclusive of research laboratories and centers are appearing in DBMSs' latest releases: World Wide Web, multimedia, active, object-oriented, secure, temporal, parallel, and multidimensional DBs.

---

2. An IDC forecast in 1997 denoted that object-oriented DBMSs would not overcome 5% of the whole DB market.

Table 1.1 summarizes the history of DBs (years are approximate because of the big gaps that sometimes existed between theoretical research, the appearance of the resulting prototypes, and when the corresponding products were offered in the market).

1.2.2 Evolution of DB Design Methodologies[3]

DB modeling is a complex problem that deals with the conception, comprehension, structure, and description of the real world (universe of discourse),

Table 1.1
Database Evolution

1960	First DB products (DBOM, IMS, IDS, Total, IDMS) Codasyl standards
1970	Relational model RDBMS prototypes Relational theoretical works Three-level architecture (ANSI and Codasyl) E/R model First relational market products
1980	Distributed DBs CASE tools SQL standard (ANSI, ISO) Object-oriented DB manifesto
1990	Third-generation DB manifesto Client/server architecture (two-tier architecture) First object DB products Reference models (ISO/ANSI) SQL 92 ODMG consortium (OO standards) Data warehouses SQL: 1999 (previously SQL3)
2000	Three-tier architecture Object relational model Databases and the World Wide Web Mobile DBs SQL/MM

---

3. In considering the contents of this book and the significance of DB design, we thought it appropriate to dedicate a part of this first chapter to presenting the evolution of DB design.

through the creation of schemata, based on the abstraction processes and models. The use of methodologies that guide the designer in the process of obtaining the different schemata is essential. Some methodologies offer only vague indications or are limited to proposing some heuristics. Other methodologies establish well-defined stages (e.g., the schemata transformation process from entity relationship (E/R) model to relational model [11–13]) and even formalize theories (e.g., the normalization process introduced by Codd in 1970 [4] and developed in many other published papers.[4]

Database design also evolved according to the evolution of DBMSs and data models. When data models with more expressive power were born, DBMSs were capable of incorporating more semantics, and physical and logical designs started distinguishing one from the other as well. With the appearance of the relational model, DB design focused, especially in the academic field, on the normalization theory. ANSI architecture, with its three levels, also had a considerable influence on the evolution of design methodologies. It helped to differentiate the phases of DB design. In 1976, the E/R model proposed by Chen [14, 15] introduced a new phase in DB design: conceptual modeling (discussed in Chapters 2 and 14). This stage constitutes the most abstract level, closer to the universe of discourse than to its computer implementation and independent of the DBMSs. In conceptual modeling, the semantics of the universe of discourse have to be understood and represented in the DB schema through the facilities the model provides. As Saltor [16] said, a greater semantic level helps to solve different problems, such as federated IS engineering, workflow, transaction management, concurrency control, security, confidentiality, and schemata evolution.

Database design is usually divided into three stages: conceptual design, logical design, and physical design.

- The objective of conceptual design is to obtain a good representation of the enterprise data resources, independent of the implementation level as well as the specific needs of each user or application. It is based on conceptual or object-oriented models.

---

4. The normalization theory (or dependency theory) has greatly expanded over the past years, and there are a lot of published works on the subject. For that reason, we refer only to the first paper by Codd introducing the first three normal forms. Readers who want to get into the subject should consult Kent's work "A Simple Guide to Five Normal Forms in Relational Database Theory" (*CACM*, 26 (2), 1983), which presents a simple, intuitive characterization of the normal forms.

- The objective of logical design is to transform the conceptual schema by adapting it to the data model that implements the DBMS to be used (usually relational). In this stage, a logical schema and the most important users' views are obtained.
- The objective of physical design is to achieve the most efficient implementation of the logical schema in the physical devices of the computer.

During the last few years, there have been many attempts to offer a more systematic approach to solving design problems. In the mid-1980s, one of those attempts was design automatization through the use of computer-aided software/system engineering (CASE) tools (see Chapter 13). CASE tools contributed to spreading the applications of conceptual modeling and relaunching DB design methodologies. While it is true that some CASE tools adopted more advanced approaches, many continued to be simple drawing tools. At times, they do not even have a methodological support or are not strict enough in their application. As a result, designers cannot find the correct path to do their job [17]. Furthermore, the models the tools generally support are logical models that usually include too many physical aspects, in spite of the fact that the graphic notation used is a subset of the E/R model.

New (object-oriented) analysis and design techniques, which at first focused on programming language and recently on DBs [18, 19], have appeared in the last decade. Those methodologies—Booch method, object-oriented software engineering (OOSE), object modeling technique (OMT), unified method, fusion method, Shlaer-Mellor method, and Coad-Yourdon method, to name some important examples—are mainly distinguished by the life cycle phase in which they are more focused and the approach adopted in each phase (object-oriented or functional) [20]. A common characteristic is that they generally are event driven.

The IDEA methodology [21], as a recent methodological approach, is an innovative object-oriented methodology driven by DB technology. It takes a data-centered approach, in which the data design is performed first, followed by the application design.

1.3 The New DB Generation

Many nontraditional applications still do not use DB technology because of the special requirements for such a category of applications. The current

DBMSs cannot provide the answers to those requirements, and almost all the vendors have started adding new facilities to their products to provide solutions to the problem. At the same time, the advances in computers (hardware and software) and the organizational changes in enterprises are forcing the birth of a new DB generation.

1.3.1 Problems of Current DBs

Although one might think that DB technology has reached its maturity, the new DB generation has demonstrated that we still ignore the solutions to some of the problems of the new millennium. In spite of the success of this technology, different "preoccupation signals" must be taken into account [22]:

- Current DBMSs are monolithic; they offer all kinds of services and functionalities in a single "package," regardless of the users' needs, at a very high cost, and with a loss of efficiency.
- There are more data in spreadsheets than in DBMSs.
- Fifty percent of the production data are in legacy systems.
- Workflow management (WFM) systems are not based on DB technology; they simply access DBs through application programming interfaces (APIs).
- Replication services do not escalate over 10,000 nodes.
- It is difficult to combine structured data with nonstructured data (e.g., data from DBs with data from electronic mail).

1.3.2 Changes in Organizations and in Computers: The Impact on DBs

DBMSs must also take into account the changes enterprises are going through. In today's society, with its ever increasing competitive pressure, organizations must be "open," that is, supporting flexible structures and capable of rapid changes. They also must be ready to cooperate with other organizations and integrate their data and processes consistently. Modern companies are competing to satisfy their clients' needs by offering services and products with the best quality-to-price ratio in the least time possible.

In that context, the alignment of IS architectures and corporate strategies becomes essential. IS must be an effective tool to achieving flexible organizations and contributing to business process redesign. For example, teleworking is beginning to gain more and more importance in companies and is becoming strategic for some of them. As a result, the DB technology required (such as DB access through mobile devices) will be essential in teleworking environments.

DBs considered as the IS kernel are influenced by those changes and must offer adequate support (flexibility, lower response times, robustness, extensibility, uncertainty management, etc.) to the new organizations. The integration of structured and nonstructured data is extremely essential to organizations, and future DBMSs must meet that demand. An increasing trend is globalization and international competition. That trend rebounds on technology, which must provide connectivity between geographically distributed DBs, be able to quickly integrate separate DBs (interoperable protocols, data distribution, federation, etc.), and offer 100% availability (24 hours a day, 7 days a week, 365 days a year). The new DB products must assist customers in locating distributed data as well as connecting PC-based applications to DBs (local and remote).

Besides changes in enterprises, advances in hardware have a great impact on DBs as well. The reduction in the price of both main and disk memory has provided more powerful equipment at lower costs. That factor is changing some DBMSs algorithms, allowing large volumes of data to be stored in the main memory. Likewise, new kinds of hardware including parallel architectures, such as symmetric multiprocessing (SMP) and massively parallel processing (MPP), offer DBMSs the possibility of executing a process in multiple processors (e.g., parallelism is essential for data warehouses). Other technologies that are influencing those changes are compression/decompression techniques, audio and video digitizers, optical storage media, magnetic disks, and hierarchical storage media.

Nomadic computing, that is, personal computers, personal digital assistants (PDA), palmtops, and laptops, allows access to information anywhere and at any time. That poses connectivity problems and also affects DB distribution.

The client/server model had a great influence on DBs in the 1980s, with the introduction of two-tier architecture. Middleware and transaction processing (TP) monitors developed during that decade have contributed to three-tier architecture, where interface, application, and data layers are separated and can reside in different platforms.

This architecture can be easily combined with the Internet and intranets for clients with browser technology and Java applets. Products that implement Object Management Group's (OMG) Common Object Request Broker Architecture (CORBA) or Microsoft's Distributed Common Object Model (DCOM) can also be accommodated in these new architectures.

Finally, high-speed networks, such as Fast Ethernet, AnyLan, fiber distributed data interface (FDDI), distributed queue dual bus (DQDB), and frame relay, are also changing the communication layer where DBs are situated.

In summary, enterprises demand technological changes because of special needs. In relation to their organizational structure, the need for open organizations requires distributed, federated, and Web DBMSs; the need for strategic information gives rise to data warehouse and OLAP technologies, and the increasing need for data requires very large DBs.

1.3.3 Nontraditional Applications

First-generation DB products provided solutions to administrative problems (personnel management, seat reservations, etc.), but they were inadequate for other applications that dealt with unexpected queries (such as decision support systems demand), due to the lack of data/application independence, low-level interfaces, navigational data languages not oriented to final users, and so on.

That changed with the arrival of relational products, and the application of DBs in different areas grew considerably. However, there are important cultural, scientific, and industrial areas where DB technology is hardly represented because of the special requirements of those kinds of applications (very large volumes of data, complex data types, triggers and alerts for management, security concerns, management of temporal and spatial data, complex and long transactions, etc.). The following are some of the most important nontraditional applications that DB technology has hardly embraced.

- *Computer-aided software/system engineering (CASE)*. CASE requires managing information sets associated with all the IS life cycle: planning, analysis, design, programming, maintenance, and so on. To meet those requirements, DBMSs must provide version control, triggers, matrix and diagram storage, and so on.

- *Computer-aided design (CAD)/computer-aided manufacturing (CAM)/ computer-integrated manufacturing (CIM)*. CAD/CAM/CIM requires the introduction of alerters, procedures, and triggers in DBMSs to manage all the data relative to the different stages of the production operation.

- *Geographical information systems (GISs).* GISs manage geographical/spatial data (e.g., maps) for environmental and military research, city planning, and so on.

- *Textual information.* Textual information management was executed by special software (information retrieval systems), but the integration of structured and textual data is now in demand.

- *Scientific applications.* Both in the microcosmos (e.g., Genome project) and in the macrocosmos (e.g., NASA's earth-observing systems), new kinds of information must be managed. In addition, a larger quantity of information ("petabytes") must be stored.

- *Medical systems.* Health personnel need different types of information about their patients. Such information could be distributed to different medical centers. Security concerns are also high in this type of IS.

- *Digital publication.* The publishing sector is going through big changes due to the development of electronic books, which combine text with audio, video, and images.

- *Education and training.* In distance learning processes, multimedia courses require data in real time and in an Internet or intranet environment.

- *Statistical systems.* Statistical systems have to deal with considerable data volumes with expensive cleaning and aggregation processes, handling time, and spatial dimensions. These systems are also a grave security concern.

- *Electronic commerce.* The Internet Society estimates that more than 200 million people will use the Internet in 2000. The applications linked to the Internet (video on demand, electronic shopping, etc.) are increasing every day. The tendency is to put all the information into cyberspace, thus making it accessible to more and more people.

- *Enterprise resource planning packages.* These packages, such as SAP, Baan, Peoplesoft, and Oracle, demand support for thousands of concurrent users and have high scalability and availability requirements.

- *On-line analytical processing (OLAP) and data warehousing (DW).* DW is generally accepted as a good approach to providing the framework for accessing the sources of data needed for decision making in business. Even though vendors now offer many DW servers and OLAP tools, the very large multidimensional DBs required for this type of applications have many problems, and some of them are still unsolved.

The new (third) DB generation must help to overcome the difficulties associated with the applications in the preceding list. For example, the need for richer data types requires multimedia and object-oriented DBMSs, and the need for reactiveness and timeliness requires other types of functionalities, such as active and real-time DBMSs, respectively. The third generation is characterized by its capacity to provide data management capabilities that allow large quantities of data to be shared (like their predecessors, although to a greater extent). Nevertheless, it must also offer object management (more complex data types, multimedia objects, etc.) and knowledge management (supporting rules for automatic inference and data integrity) [23].

1.4 Research and Market Trends

In addition to the factors that encouraged DBMS evolution, the dimensions along which research and market trends are evolving are performance, distribution, and functionality (see Figure 1.2).

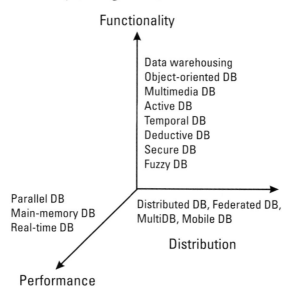

Figure 1.2 Dimensions in the evolution of DB technology.

An issue related to those three dimensions is the separation of the functionalities of the DBMS into different components. Nowadays, DBMSs are monolithic in the sense that they offer all the services in one package (persistence, query language, security, etc.). In the future, component DB systems will be available, whereby different services could be combined and used according to the user's needs (see Chapter 12).

1.4.1 Performance

In the next five years, data stored in DBs will be 10 times more capable. Like gas, data expand to fill all the space available. Ten years ago, a DB of 1 Gb (10^9) would have been considered as a very large database (VLDB). Today, some companies have several terabytes (10^{12}) of data, and DBs (data warehouses) of pentabytes (10^{15}) are beginning to appear.

To cope with the increasing volume, DBs are taking advantage of new hardware. Since the mid-1980s, different parallel DBs (shared memory, shared disk, shared nothing) have been implemented, exploiting parallelism as well as interquery (several queries executed independently in various processors) and intraquery (independent parts of a query executed in different processors).

Performance is also important in a given set of applications where response time is critical (e.g., control systems). The ability to respond is of vital importance because it is not so much rapid response as guaranteed response in a specific time, be it real-time or not. Real-time DBMSs, conceived with that objective in mind, set priorities for transactions.

Hardware performance-to-price ratio also allows the DB (or part of it) to be stored in the main memory during its execution. Therefore, we can distinguish between new main-memory DBs and traditional disk-resident DBs. In main-memory DBs, several concepts, such as index structures, clustering, locks, and transactions, must be restated.

In general, all the query-processing algorithms and even the classical transaction properties of atomicity, consistency, isolation, and durability (ACID) must be adapted to new-generation DBs and, especially, to complex object management. Concurrency control and recovery in object database management systems (ODMS) require research into new techniques (long transactions that may last for days and long-term checkout of object versions). Traditional logging and locking techniques perform poorly for long transactions and the use of optimistic locking techniques as well as variations of known techniques (such as shadow paging) may help to remedy the lock and log file problems [24].

To facilitate the effective use of the DB hardware and software resources, the DB administrator (DBA) is necessary. This person (or group of persons) has a fundamental role in the performance of the global DB system. The DBA is also responsible for protecting the DB as a resource shared by all the users. Among other duties, the DBA must carry out backup, recovery, and reorganization; provide DB standards and documentation; enforce data activity policy; control redundancy; maintain configuration control; tune the DB system; and generate and analyze DB performance reports. Physical design and performance tuning are key aspects and essential to the success of a DB project. The changes in the performance dimension also oblige the introduction of important transformations in the DBA functions [25]. The role of the DBA in the future will be increasingly difficult, and DBMS products will have to offer, increasingly, facilities to help the DBA in DB administration functions.

1.4.2   Distribution and Integration

In the last decade, the first distributed DBMSs appeared on the market and have been an important focus of DB research and marketing. Some achievements of the early distributed products were two-phase commit, replication, and query optimization.

Distributed DBs (see Chapter 9) can be classified into three areas: distribution, heterogeneity, and autonomy [26]. In the last area, federated DBs (semiautonomous DBs) and multidatabases (completely autonomous) can be found. A higher degree of distribution is offered by mobile DBs (see Chapter 10), which can be considered distributed systems in which links between nodes change dynamically.

From that point of view, we must also emphasize the integration of DBs and the Internet and the World Wide Web. The Web adds new components to DBs, including a new technology for the graphical user interface (GUI), a new client/server model (the hypertext transfer protocol, HTTP), and a hyperlink mechanism between DBs [27].

New architectures capable of connecting different software components and allowing the interoperation between them are needed. Database architectures must provide extensibility for distributed environments, allow the integration of legacy mainframe systems, client/server environments, Web-based applications, and so on.

Vendors now offer enough of the integration facilities required to access distributed DBs from all types of devices (personal computers, PDAs, palmtops, laptops, etc.) and some support for Internet data. However, vendors still do not offer complete integration between DBs and Internet data. More research and development work are needed in this area.

1.4.3 Functionality and Intelligence

In this dimension, the evolution of IS can be summarized as the "functionality migration" from programs to DB. From the inception of DBs, we have seen the consolidation of a trend toward transferring all possible semantics from programs to the DB dictionary-catalog so as to store it together with the data. The migration in semantics and other functionalities have evident advantages, insofar as its centralization releases the applications from having to check integrity constraints and prevents their verification from being repeated in the different application programs. Thus, all the programs can share the data without having to worry about several concerns the DBMS keeps unified by forcing their verification, regardless of the program that accesses the DB.

At a first glance, in a process-oriented IS based on files, there are only data in the "DB" (file); all the information on the data, constraints, control, and process was in the program (Figure 1.3). The location of that information in programs contributes to the classical problems of redundancy, maintenance, and security of this kind of IS.

Earlier DBMSs represented a second approach in which description of data was stored with the data in the DB catalog or dictionary. However, in

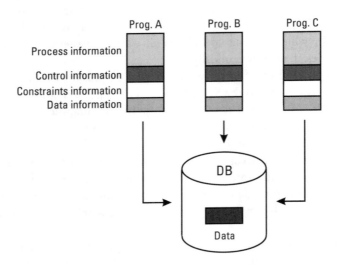

Figure 1.3 Process-oriented systems.

the DBMSs of the 1980s, programs were responsible for the verification of constraints (until the 1990s relational products did not support, e.g., referential integrity or check constraints). Later, with the improvement of the performance-to-cost ratio and optimizers, products incorporated more and more information on constraints in the DBMS catalog, becoming *semantic DBs*. In the early 1990s, *active DBs* appeared (see Chapter 3). In those DBMSs, besides the description of the data and the constraints, part of the control information is stored in the DB. Active DBs can run applications without the user's intervention by supporting triggers, rules, alerts, daemons, and so on.

Finally, we are witnessing the appearance of *object-oriented* (see Chapter 7) and *object-relational* (see Chapter 6) DBMSs, which allow the definition and management of objects (encapsulating structure and behavior). Objects stored in DBs can be of any type: images, audio, video, and so on. Then, there are *multimedia* DBs (see Chapter 8), which could be the last step in the evolution of DBs along the functionality dimension (Figure 1.4).

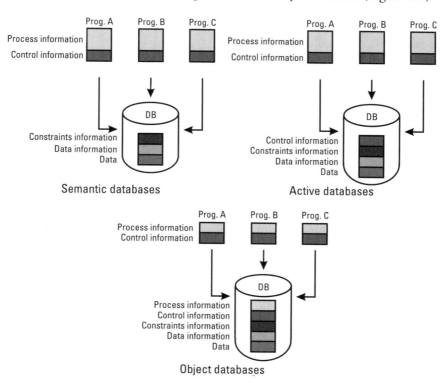

Figure 1.4 Semantic, active, and object DB systems.

Future DBMSs must manage in an integrated way, not only different types of data and objects but also knowledge. In that respect, research into *deductive* DBMSs has been carried out (see Chapter 4).

Two other important aspects of modern IS that are being incorporated into DBs are time (*temporal DBs;* see Chapter 5) and uncertainty (*fuzzy DBs*). Both aspects are crucial in decision-making. Decision support systems (DSS) and executive information systems (EIS) are being integrated in wider data warehousing/data mining environments in which DB technology plays a decisive role.

Another important concern for IS managers is security. The so-called *secure* or *multilevel DBs* (see Chapter 11) now on the market provide mandatory access control that is more secure than traditional discretionary access control.

1.5   Maturity of DB Technology

Some experts believe we are in a transition period, moving from centralized relational DBs to the adoption of a new generation of advanced DBs: more semantics, more intelligent, more distributed, and more efficient. In practice, however, changes seem to be slower, and centralized relational DBs still dominate the DB market landscape.

In the 1980s (and well into the 1990s), we underwent the transition from network to relational products. Even today, this technology has not matured enough. As a result of the adoption of an immature technology, the transfer process became complicated and the risks increased. However, it can offer opportunities for organizations to have a greater competitive advantage with an incipient technology, which can be more productive and capable of delivering better quality products with cost savings. We must not, however, forget the risks, such as the shortage of qualified personnel, the lack of standards, insufficient guarantee on the investment returns, instability of the products with little competition among vendors, and so on, associated with opting for a technology too soon.

In fact, not all the technologies are mature. The maturity level of a technology can be measured in three ways (Figure 1.5):

- Scientific, that is, research dedicated to the technology;
- Industrial, that is, product development by vendors;
- Commercial, that is, market acceptance of the technology and its utilization by users.

Table 1.2 indicates the maturity level (ranging from 1 to 5) in each dimension for different DB technologies.

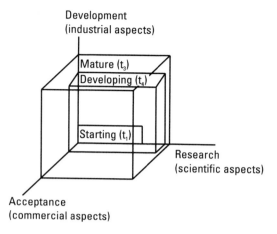

Figure 1.5 Dimensions in technology maturity.

Table 1.2
Maturity Level of Different DB Technologies

Technology	Scientific	Industrial	Commercial
Relational DBs	5	5	5
Parallel DBs	4	3	3
Real-time DBs	3	2	1
Main-memory DBs	3	2	1
Active DBs	4	3	2
Deductive DBs	4	2	1
Object-oriented DBs	4	3	1
Multimedia DBs	4	3	3
Web DBs	3	2	2
Spatiotemporal DBs	3	1	1
Secure DBs	3	3	1
Fuzzy DBs	2	1	0
Distributed DBs	4	3	2
Federated DBs/multidatabases	3	2	1
Mobile DBs	2	2	1
Component DBs	2	1	0
Data warehouses	2	3	2

Synergy among technologies also must be considered. For example, fuzzy and deductive DBs can use the same logical language; both temporal and real-time DBs deal with the management of time; real-time and main-memory DBs can use analogous techniques for memory management; multimedia DBs explore parallel capabilities; parallel and distributed DBs can take advantage of the same techniques for intra- and interquery parallelism; and parallelism is also needed for DW.

To respond to the challenges that the new applications present, it is absolutely necessary that managers and technicians be well informed and that they comprehend the basic aspects of the new-generation DB systems.

References

[1]   Bachman, C. W., "The Programmer as Navigator," *Comm. ACM*, Vol. 16, No. 11, 1973, pp. 653–658.

[2]   Bachman, C. W., "Data Structure Diagrams," *Data Base*, Vol. 1, No. 2, 1969.

[3]   Codasyl DDL, "Data Description Language," *J. Development*, U.S. Government Printing Office, Vol. 3, No. 4, 1978, pp. 147–320.

[4]   Codd, E. F., "A Relational Model of Data for Large Shared Data Banks," *Comm. ACM*, Vol. 13, No. 6, 1970, pp. 377–387.

[5]   Ullman, J. D., *Database and Knowledge-Base Systems*, Rockville, MD: Computer Science Press, 1988.

[6]   Eisenberg, A., and J. Melton, "Standards—SQL: 1999 (Formerly Known as SQL3)," *SIGMOD Record*, Vol. 28, No. 1, 1999, pp. 131–138.

[7]   De Miguel, A., and M. Piattini, *Concepción y Diseño de Bases de Datos: Del Modelo E/R al Modelo Relacional*, Wilmington, DE: Addison-Wesley Iberoamericana, 1993.

[8]   ANSI, "Reference Model for DBMS Standardization: Report of the DAFTG of the ANSI/X3/SPARC Database Study Group," *SIGMOD Record*, Vol. 15, No. 1, 1986.

[9]   ANSI, "Reference Model for DBMS User Facility: Report by the UFTG of the ANSI/X3/SPARC Database Study Group," *SIGMOD Record*, Vol. 17, No. 2, 1988.

[10]   ISO, "Reference Model of Data Management," *ISO/IEC IS 10032*, 1993.

[11]   Batini, C., S. Ceri, and S. B. Navathe, *Conceptual Database Design: An Entity-Relationship Approach*, Redwood City, CA: Benjamin/Cummings, 1992.

[12]   Teorey, T. J., D. Yang, and J. P. Fry, "A Logical Design Methodology for Relational Databases Using the Extended Entity-Relationship Model," *ACM Computing Surveys*, Vol. 18, No. 2, 1986, pp. 197–222.

[13] Cuadra, D., et al., "Control de restricciones de cardinalidad en una metodología de desarrollo de bases de datos relacionales," *Novatica*, No. 140, 1999, pp. 28–33.

[14] Chen, P. P., "The Entity/Relationship Model: Toward a Unified View," *ACM Trans. on Database Systems*, Vol. 1, No. 1, Mar. 1976, pp. 9–36.

[15] Chen, P. P., "The Entity/Relationship Model: A Basis for the Enterprise View of Data," *AFIPS Conference Proc.*, Vol. 46, 1977.

[16] Saltor, F., "Sobre la evolución reciente de las bases de datos," *Novatica*, No. 140, July/Aug. 1999, pp. 5–6.

[17] Atkins, C., "Prescription or Description: Some Observations on the Conceptual Modeling Process," *Proc. Intl. Conf. Software Engineering: Education and Practice*, 1996.

[18] Blaha, M., and W. Premerlani, *Object-Oriented Modeling and Design for Database Applications*, Upper Saddle River, NJ: Prentice-Hall, 1998.

[19] Graham, I., B. Henderson-Sellers, and H. Younessi, *The OPEN Process Specification*, New York: ACM Press, 1997.

[20] Graham, I., *Object-Oriented Methods*, Reading, MA: Addison-Wesley, 1991.

[21] Ceri, S., and P. Fraternali, *Designing Database Applications With Objects and Rules: The IDEA Methodology*, Reading, MA: Addison-Wesley, 1997.

[22] Buchmann, A., "Bases de datos: QUO VADIS," *Conference in the I Jornadas de Investigación y Docencia en Bases de Datos*, Brisaboa et al. (eds.), A Coruña, June 26–28, 1996.

[23] Cattell, R. G. G., "What Are Next-Generation Database Systems?" *Comm. ACM*, Vol. 34, No. 10, 1991, pp. 31–33.

[24] Cattell, R. G. G., *Object Data Management: Object-Oriented and Extended Relational Database Systems*, Reading, MA: Addison-Wesley, 1991.

[25] Downgiallo, E., et al., "DBA for the Future," *Database Programming & Design*, Vol. 10, No. 6, 1997, pp. 32–41.

[26] Özsu, M. T., and P. Valduriez, "Distributed Database Systems: Where Are We Now?" *IEEE Computer*, Aug. 1991, pp. 68–78.

[27] Bancilhon, F., "The Magic Encounter of Object Database Technology and the Web," *O2 Technology*, Palo Alto, CA, 1996.

Selected Bibliography

Berstein, P., et al., "The Asilomar Report on Database Research," *SIGMOD Record*, Vol. 27, No. 4, 1998, pp. 74–80.

This report remarks that "the database research community should embrace a broader research agenda," covering the content of the Web and other data stores. The authors recommend a 10-year goal for the DB community: "The Information Utility: Make it easy for everyone to store, organize, access, and analyze the majority of human information online."

Silberschatz, A., M. Stonebraker, and J. Ullman (eds.), "Database Research: Achievements and Opportunities into the 21st Century," *SIGMOD Record,* Vol. 25, No. 1, 1996, pp. 52–63.

This report reflects the main conclusions from a workshop held in May 1995, where the prospects for DB research were considered. The two major themes dealt with in the report are the new demands placed on DB systems and the need of transferring research ideas to practical use.

2

An Introduction to Conceptual Modeling of Information Systems

Antoni Olivé

2.1 The Functions of an Information System

The concept *information system* began to emerge around 1960. Even though it may be considered an old concept, it is still difficult to define what an IS is. Part of that difficulty is because ISs can be analyzed in at least three distinct and complementary perspectives [1]:

- The contribution they provide;
- Their structure and behavior;
- The functions they perform.

From the first perspective, ISs are defined as means for wider systems to achieve their objectives. That kind of definition emphasizes that ISs are sub-systems of wider systems, to which they contribute. An IS does not exist for itself. Examples of that kind of definition would be: "An IS is a system designed to support operations, management, and decision-making in an organization" or "An IS is a system that facilitates communication among its users."

For our purposes, the main problem with that kind of definition is that it does not give a clear characterization of ISs. The wider system of which an IS is part may require means that are not ISs to achieve its objectives. Furthermore, other things can provide the same type of contribution, without being an IS. For example, there are various ways to facilitate communication among users, including working physically close to each other or participating in meetings.

Even if it is difficult to define ISs in terms of the contribution they provide, it is important to realize that this perspective is essential during their development. The requirements of an IS are determined from the objectives of the organization for which the system is designed and built.

From the second perspective, definitions emphasize the structure and the behavior of the physical and abstract elements that make up an IS. Both structure and behavior can be characterized at different levels of detail.

For the purposes of conceptual modeling, the most useful definitions are those based on the functions performed by ISs, that is, definitions that emphasize what ISs do, abstracting from why and how they do it.

Within this third perspective, the classical definition says that "an IS is a system that collects, stores, processes, and distributes information." That definition is commonly accepted for both its simplicity and its generality. However, some comments may be in order to make it more precise.

First, in IS engineering, we should restrict the definition to designed systems, that is, systems an engineer designs and builds [2]. The restriction is needed because natural systems that perform information-processing functions are beyond the scope of our study. For example, in cognitive science the human mind is viewed as a complex system that receives, stores, processes, and distributes information.

Second, the definition is too general with respect to the kind of information an IS may deal with. In fact, the definition poses no constraint on the kind of information, with the result that it encompasses systems that many people would not consider ISs. For example, a fax could be considered an IS according to that definition, because it can be seen as a system that receives documents (which contain data representing some information), stores them (even if only for a short time), translates them (i.e., changes the representation of the information), and sends the result through the phone.

The usual constraint on the kind of information handled by an IS is that it must be about the state of some domain (also called object system or universe of discourse). The nature of this domain is irrelevant to the definition of IS. For many systems, its domain is an organization, but the definition does not exclude other, different domains, such as a vehicle, the atmosphere, or a chess game. According to that definition, a fax machine is not an IS. A fax does not consider the documents it sends as information about the state of some domain. To a fax, documents are just uninterpreted data.

Thus, we define an IS as a designed system that collects, stores, processes, and distributes information about the state of a domain. It is easy to agree on those functions, but the problem is that they are too general and are not related to the purpose for which the IS exists. For those reasons, many authors prefer a more specific definition of the functions, one that captures more neatly the nature of ISs.

To that end, it is considered that an IS has three main functions (Figure 2.1) [3]:

1. *Memory function,* to maintain a representation of the state of a domain;

2. *Informative function,* to provide information about the state of a domain;

3. *Active function,* to perform actions that change the state of a domain.

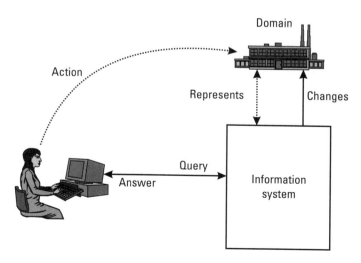

Figure 2.1 The functions of an IS.

2.1.1   The Memory Function

The memory function is needed by the other two functions. Its objective is to maintain internally a representation of the state of the domain. Moreover, the representation must be correct and complete [4].

The memory function can be performed in two execution modes: *on request* or *autonomously*. In the first mode, the system memorizes the state because a user explicitly tells the system the state and orders (normally implicitly) the system to memorize it. For example, a system knows customers' addresses because any time a customer changes addresses, a user tells the IS the new address and expects the system to remember it. The IS has no way to know customers' addresses except by a user explicitly telling it that information.

In the second mode, *autonomously*, the system memorizes the state of the domain without an explicit request from a user. This mode has two variants. In the first variant, the system is able to observe autonomously the state, for example, a system that periodically reads a device that gives the temperature of a building. In that case, the system can maintain a representation of the temperature because it gets it directly from the environment. The second variant is related to the active function and will be described later.

The memory function is considered to be passive, in the sense that it does not perform anything that directly affects users or the domain. However, it is required by the other functions and constrains what they can perform.

2.1.2   The Informative Function

With the informative function, the system provides users with information about the state of the domain. Often, the state of the domain is observable directly in the domain, and at the same time it is represented in the IS. For example, the quantity of a given product in the shelves of a retail store may be observed when necessary, and at the same time it can be represented in the IS. In those cases there is a redundancy, but it is a desired one, because it may be easier to ask the system than to observe the domain.

In other cases, the state is represented only in the IS, and it is not possible (or difficult) to observe it directly in the domain. For example, in a retail store it is not possible to observe how many units of some product have been sold up to a given moment. As another example, in the banking domain, consider balances of accounts. The balance of an account at a given instant cannot be known by observation of the owner of the account or the bank office where the account was created. The only place where balances are represented is inside the IS. In those cases, the IS is the only source of information about the state, and the system becomes indispensable to its users.

To perform the informative function, the system needs an inference capability, allowing it to infer the required information from the memory. In the most frequent case, users pose a query, and the system answers it. Both query and answer are in a language understood by the users and by the system.

Queries may be extensional (the most frequent case) or intensional. An extensional query asks information about the state of the domain (either the current state or some previous one), and the system gives an extensional or intensional answer. An extensional answer, which is the usual case, consists of more or less elaborated information about the state of the domain. Examples of simple extensional answers are:

- Joan takes the Algebra course.

- Eighty students take the Programming course.

Some extensional answers must be much more elaborated and may require a statistical analysis, a simulation or the execution of a decisional model. Examples of such answers are:

- Ninety percent of customers that buy books also buy CDs.

- No customer has bought more than 200 books.

Less frequently, the answer to an extensional query may be intensional. An intensional answer characterizes the state of the domain, but it does not describe the state explicitly [5]. For example, to the question "Who earns more than $100,000?" the system might answer, "The managers."

Intensional queries ask about the kinds of information the system knows, rather than particular information [6], for example,

- What do you know about students?

- What is the maximum number of courses a student may take simultaneously?

- What is a student?

The informative function also admits the two execution modes. The most frequent case is the *on request* mode: Users get information when they ask it explicitly. In contrast, in the mode *autonomously*, users define a condition on the state of the domain and order the system to inform them when that condition is satisfied. For example, the condition might be "the temperature is over 40°C" and users expect that the system will issue some signal when that condition is satisfied.

The informative function does not change the state of the domain. The system merely provides the information requested by users. It is the users who will take actions that change the domain, if they want to do so.

2.1.3 The Active Function

With the active function, the system performs actions that modify the state of the domain. To perform the active function, the system must know the actions it can take, when those actions can be taken, and their effect on the state of the domain.

The active function also has the two execution modes. In the *on request* mode, users delegate to the system the taking of some action that may modify the state of the domain. For example, users may ask the system to calculate the interests to be paid to bank accounts and charge them to the accounts' balances.

In the mode *autonomously*, users delegate to the system the taking of some action that may modify the state of the domain, when some condition is satisfied. The system will monitor the state of the domain, and when the condition is fulfilled, it will perform the delegated action.

The nature of actions that may be delegated to the system (in both execution modes) are varied. It may be a simple and well-defined action or one for which only the objectives are defined, leaving autonomy to the system on how to achieve those objectives.

The classical example of active function, with mode *autonomously*, is the automatic replenishment of a store. Users define, for each product, a reorder point and a quantity to order. The system maintains the quantity on hand of each product, and users delegate to it to issue orders to suppliers when the quantity on hand is below the reorder point. It is assumed that orders to suppliers are part of the domain and, thus, the state of the domain changes when a new order is issued.

It is interesting to note that, in the preceding example, if the orders were not part of the domain, then the automatic replenishment would not be an example of the active function. It would be an example of the informative action. Outputs from the system could be a requirement for action to the users, but the state of the domain would not be altered.

Given that the active function may change the state of the domain without the direct intervention of users, it is a function that calls the memory function, in the execution mode *autonomously*.

Table 2.1 summarizes the examples of the three functions and the two execution modes.

2.1.4   Examples of ISs

All conventional ISs perform a memory function and some informative function. We will not describe any concrete examples, since they are well known, and identification of the functions they perform is simple. However, it may be worthwhile to comment on some particular classes of systems and to see that, even if one might doubt whether they are ISs, they in fact perform the functions we have seen in this section.

Example 2.1

Assume a chess-playing system that can play against either a human or a machine. We are going to see that this system may be considered an IS.

The domain consists of the board, the pieces and their position on the board, the player, and the rules of the game. At any moment, the domain is in some state, which is time varying. The rules of the game, however, are fixed. The system has to maintain a representation of the state of the domain; otherwise, it would not be able to play. When a move is completed, the system must somehow know that in order to update the state representation. This is a simple example of the memory function of an IS.

The system has to visualize on the screen the state of the game continuously. When a game starts, the system shows the initial distribution of pieces.

Table 2.1
Examples of Functions and Execution Modes

Functions	Execution Modes	
	On request	Autonomously
Memory	Change of a customer's address	Reading of temperature
Informative	Courses a student takes	Signal when temperature is over 40°C
Active	Pay interests to accounts	Automatic replenishment

After every move, the system must show the new distribution. It is therefore an example of the informative function, in the mode *autonomously*.

Once the player has made a move, it is expected that the system will think about the available alternatives to achieve its objective (using the current state of the game and the knowledge the system may have) and that, after a while, it will make its own move. In making the move, the system changes the state of the domain. Therefore, this is a complex example of the active function.

If the system were naive enough to offer sincere advice on the next move to the player, that would be an example of the informative function, in the mode *on request*.

Example 2.2

Let us consider an e-mail system. The domain consists of users, who can send or receive messages, distribution lists, active messages, folders created by users to organize their active messages, and so on. Each message has a content, a subject, a sender, a date, and one or more receivers. Normally, the content and the subject of a message are uninterpreted data for the system.

The memory function consists of maintaining a representation of the state of the domain. The main part of the state will be represented only within the system, and it is not directly observable in the domain. The state changes when a user issues a message, receives a message, creates or deletes a folder, puts a message in a folder (or removes a message from it), and so on.

Among other things, the informative function allows users to visualize their active messages (at different levels of detail), as well as the contents of their folders.

The active function consists of sending messages issued by users to their receivers. The effect is that the sent message is put in the input folder of each receiver. This function is performed in the mode *on request*.

Example 2.3

This last example is not a concrete system, but a class of systems: real-time systems. There is not a consensus on what real-time systems are, but they tend to be identified by means of a set of common characteristics [7].

First, a real-time system monitors and controls an environment (i.e., it issues controlling commands that change the environment). Using our terminology, monitoring the environment is a memory function, and controlling it is an active function. Second, real-time systems interact with users for whom they perform a needed function. Such functions may be either informative or active. Real-time systems frequently have various sensors and intersystem interfaces that provide continuous or periodic input. These are the mechanisms by which the system knows the state of the environment, for the memory function. Finally, a real-time system has a set of actuators or intersystem interfaces that must be driven periodically. They correspond to the mechanisms by which the system sends to the environment the output form, the active function.

A real-time system has other characteristics that do not refer to the essential functions that must be performed but to how they must be performed, for example, sampling intervals of sensors, response time, concurrent processing of multiple inputs, high reliability, resource (main or secondary memory, processor capacity, etc.) limitations, and so on. These characteristics are important, but they do not change the fact that real-time systems may be seen as ISs.

2.2 Conceptual Modeling

Section 2.1 reviewed the main functions of an IS. To be able to perform those functions, an IS requires some knowledge about its domain. The main objective of conceptual modeling is the elicitation and formal definition of the general knowledge about a domain that an IS needs to know to perform the required functions.

This section describes the kinds of knowledge required by most ISs. The line of reasoning we will follow is this:

- If the memory function of an IS has to maintain a representation of the state of the domain, then we must define which is the concrete state that must be represented.

- The state of most domains is time varying, which requires defining the causes of changes and the effects of those changes on the state.

- The representation of the state in the IS must be consistent; therefore, it is necessary to define what it means to be a consistent representation.

- Many times, answering queries posed by users requires some inference capability on the part of the IS. This capability uses derivation rules, which must be defined.

This section develops that line of reasoning. Along the way, we introduce informally the terminology and give an intuitive idea of the basic concepts.

2.2.1 Conceptual Schema of the State

The objective of the memory function of an IS is to maintain a consistent representation of the state of its domain. The state of a domain consists of a set of relevant properties.

The question of which exactly are the relevant properties of the domain of an IS depends on the purpose for which the IS is built. We have already mentioned that an IS is always a means for a wider system to achieve its objectives. The relevant properties are determined by the functions of those objectives and of the expected contribution of the IS to them. We focus here on what are relevant properties rather than how to determine them. That, of course, does not mean that the latter aspect is less important than the former one.

In the IS field, we make the fundamental assumption that a domain consists of objects and the relationships between those objects, which are classified into concepts. The state of a particular domain, at a given time, consists, then, of a set of objects, a set of relationships, and a set of concepts into which those objects and relationships are classified. For example, in the domain of a company, we may have the concepts of *Customer, Product,* and *Sale.* Those concepts are usually stable. On the other hand, at a given instant, we have objects classified as customers, objects classified as products, and relationships between customers and products classified as sales.

That fundamental assumption is also shared by disciplines such as linguistics, (first-order) logic, and cognitive science. Unfortunately, those disciplines have not yet arrived at an agreement in the terminology, the definitions, the concepts, and the mechanisms to distinguish among objects and relationships in a domain. The result is that we do not have at our disposal a solid theoretical basis, and, as is often the case in the IS field, we must adopt a humble and eclectic attitude.

The assumption that a domain consists of objects, relationships, and concepts is a specific way to view the world (domain). At first sight, it seems an evident assumption. Reality, however, is far from that. Other views are possible, views that may be more adequate in other fields. As a simple and well-known example in propositional logic, one assumes that domains consist of facts, which may be either true or false. The study of the nature and the organization of the real world is the subject of the branch of philosophy called *ontology*.

When we assume that a domain consists of objects, relationships, and concepts, we commit ourselves to a specific way of observing domains. The term used in ontology to designate such commitments is *ontological commitment*. In the IS field, the term *conceptual model* is the commitment corresponding to viewing domains in a particular way. In principle, the same conceptual model can be applied to many different domains, and several conceptual models could be applied to the same domain.

The set of concepts used in a particular domain is a *conceptualization* of that domain. The specification of that conceptualization, in some language, is called an *ontology* of that domain [8, 9]. There may be several conceptualizations for a given domain and, thus, several ontologies. An ontology is also a concrete view of a particular domain. Therefore, it is also an ontological commitment for the persons that observe and act on that domain. In the IS field, ontologies are called *conceptual schemas*, and the languages in which they are written are called *conceptual modeling languages*.

As we will see, conceptual models of ISs are much more complex than simply assuming that a domain consists of objects and relationships. A conceptual model assumes that a domain includes other "things," and also that objects, relationships, and concepts have several properties that must be distinguished. On the other hand, a conceptual model includes a view of how a domain changes.

There is a great diversity in conceptual models, which make them more or less useful in particular situations or for particular purposes. However, all of them share the fundamental assumption we have mentioned and that we will make precise.

We begin trying to establish the distinction between concept and object. According to the dictionaries, a *concept* is "an abstract or generic idea generalized from particular instances" or "an idea or mental picture of a group or class of objects formed by combining all their aspects."

Those definitions fit our purpose. A concept, then, is something that we have formed in our mind through generalization from some instances. A concept has an extension and an intension. The extension of a concept is the set of its possible instances, while the intension is the property shared by all its instances.

As human beings, we use the concepts we have to structure our perception of a domain. In that sense, concepts are like eyeglasses with which we observe a domain. Concepts allow us to classify the things we perceive as exemplars of concepts we have. In other words, what we observe depends on the concepts we use in the observation.

Classification is the operation that associates an object with a concept. The inverse operation, *instantiation*, gives an instance of a concept. The set of objects that are an instance of a concept at some time is called the *population* of that concept at that time.

An *entity type* is a concept whose instances are individual and identifiable objects. Objects that are instances of an entity type are called *entities*. Figure 2.2 shows a simple example of entity and entity type.

All entities are instances of some entity type, but an entity may be an instance of more than one entity type. For example, in Figure 2.2 the entity shown could also be an instance of *Doctor*.

If there is a "thing" in which we are interested, but we are not able to classify it in any of the concepts we have, then we have to form a new concept of which that "thing" could be an instance. In contrast, there may be concepts without instances in the usual domains. The typical example is *Unicorn*. In conceptual modeling, we do not show interest in concepts without instances.

Some concepts are associative, in the sense that their instances relate two or more entities. *Relationship types* are concepts whose instances are *relationships*. Figure 2.3 shows an example of relationship type *Reads* between *Person* and *Book*.

A particular case of relationship is the *reference relationship*. In principle, each entity in the domain must have at least one name that allows us to distinguish among entities. A name is a linguistic object that we use to refer to an entity. Names are also entities and, therefore, instances of some entity

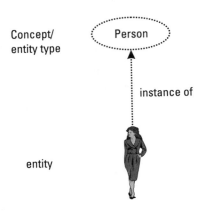

Figure 2.2 Entities as instances of concepts.

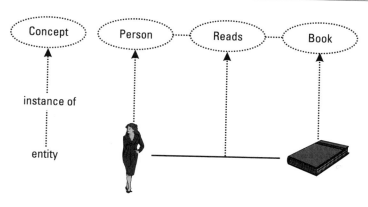

Figure 2.3 Relationships as instances of concepts.

type, that we call lexical entity types. Examples of lexical entity types are *String, Number, Bar code, ISBN code.*

The correspondence between an entity and its name is established by means of a relationship. That relationship is also an instance of some relationship type, sometimes called a reference relationship type. There may be more than one reference relationship type, for example,

- The relationship type between *Person* and *String;*
- The relationship type between *Book* and *ISBN code;*
- The relationship type between *Book* and *Number* (in a library).

The set of entity and relationship types used to observe the state of a domain is the conceptualization of that state. The description, in some language, of that conceptualization, as well as other elements we will see in a moment, is called the ontology of the state, or the *conceptual schema of the state.* The set formed by the conceptual schema of the state and the conceptual schema of the behavior, which will be described later, is called the *conceptual schema.* Languages used to define conceptual schemas are called conceptual modeling languages.

Not all entities and relationships in a domain need to be represented in the IS. That leads us to distinguish between conceptual schema of a domain and conceptual schema of an IS. The former describes the conceptualization of the domain, without regard to which entities and relationships will be represented in the IS. In contrast, the latter describes only the fragment of the conceptualization such that its entities and relationships are represented in the IS.

2.2.2 Information Base

An *information base* is a description of the entities and relationships of a domain that are represented in the IS [10]. In principle, this description could be done in any language, but usually it is done in a logic-based language. Sometimes, the description of an entity or a relationship is called a fact, and we say that the information base contains the facts about a domain.

For example, if we use the language of first-order logic as the modeling language, we could have a schema formed by predicates *Person*, *Book*, and *Reads*, which represent entity types *Person* and *Book* and relationship type *Reads*. The information base might contain, at some time, the facts *Person(A)*, *Book(B)*, and *Reads(A,B)*.

Figure 2.4 illustrates the relationship between a conceptual schema and an information base. The conceptual schema of the domain includes the concepts from Figure 2.3 and two other concepts, *Town* and *Lives*. However, we want to represent in the IS only the entities and relationships shown in the conceptual schema of Figure 2.3. The conceptual schema is described in a graphical language, in which rectangles correspond to entity types and lines to relationship types. The information base contains three facts, described in the language of first-order logic. Predicates correspond to entity and relationship types.

The information base does not exist physically. It is only an abstract description we use to reason about a schema and to exemplify particular situations in a domain. Naturally, the IS must maintain an internal

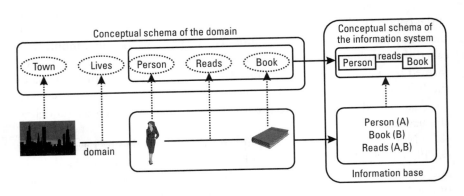

Figure 2.4 Conceptual schema and information base.

description (e.g., in a DB) of the entities and relationships in a domain, but this description is at a very low level in order to be efficiently processable by the processors used. The information base is a description close to the conceptual schema and is not meant to be an internal description.

Unfortunately, the term *conceptual model* is not always used with the same meaning in the literature. Besides the meaning we have given to it, other meanings we may find are these:

- Conceptual model = conceptual schema
- Conceptual model = conceptual schema + information base

We have chosen to use three distinct terms (*conceptual model, conceptual schema, information base*) to distinguish three different concepts. The same distinction is well established in the DB field, where we distinguish clearly among data model (for instance, relational data model), DB schema (in some data models), and DB (instance of a schema).[1]

2.2.3   Conceptual Schema of the Behavior

Most IS domains change through time, at two levels: conceptual schema and state. Changes at the conceptual schema level are less frequent than those at the state level, and their origin is due to changes in users' interests: For whatever reason, users lose interest in the representation of some entities and relationships or they want other entities and relationships to be represented in the IS.

The most frequent changes (and the only ones we consider here) occur at the state level. It is easily observable that the state of most IS domains changes through time. In consequence, if the information base is a truthful representation of that state, then the facts of the information base will need to change through time.

---

1. The term *information base* may be confused with the term *knowledge base*, used in the deductive DB's field, as well as in artificial intelligence. A knowledge base is a set of representations of knowledge about a domain [11]. Normally, the language used to represent this knowledge is the language of first-order logic. The knowledge may be simple facts, which are represented as atomic formulas, or general knowledge about a domain, which is represented as complex formulas. In conceptual modeling, the general knowledge about a domain is represented in the conceptual schema, while simple facts are represented in the information base. Therefore, the correspondence is knowledge base = conceptual schema + information base.

We say that there is a change in the state of the domain at time t if the entities or relationships that exist at t are different from those existing at the previous time. In other words, a state change is a change in the population or one or more entity or relationship types between two states: the new state (corresponding to t), and the old state (corresponding to $t-1$).

Any change in the population of an entity (relationship) type can always be decomposed into a set of one or more elementary changes of the following types:

- Insertion of entity (relationship). This change happens when there is an entity (relationship) in the new state that did not exist in the old state.

- Deletion of entity (relationship). This change happens when there was an entity (relationship) in the old state that does not exist in the new state.

The causes of the changes are the *events* [3, 12]. A domain does not change its state if no event happens. An event is any circumstance that happens at a given instant and whose effect is a change in the domain state. Normally, these circumstances are actions (or decisions) performed by human beings that act on a domain (e.g., hiring an employee or making a move in a chess game), but they also may be the result of physical processes (e.g., dropping some amount of liquid into a tank or the rising of the sun).

It is usually assumed that events are instantaneous, that is, they do not have duration. It is also assumed that an event causes a transition in the domain, from an old state to a new one, without any noticeable intermediate state. In many cases, those assumptions do not pose any particular problems. For example, the process of hiring a new employee takes some time, but it is likely that we are interested only in the outcome of that process: From that moment on, the person will be an employee, which he or she was not at the previous time.

In some cases, however, events have duration. To handle those cases in conceptual models that require instantaneous events, it may be necessary to refine the conceptual schema of the domain or the event itself. For example, assume the domain includes the relationship type *Is at* between persons and places. In principle, it seems natural to consider that persons are at some place at any moment. Let us consider now the event corresponding to the move of a person from an origin to a target. If we assume that the event is instantaneous, then the person will continue to be at some place at any moment. But if we assume that a move is not instantaneous, then there will be a temporal interval during which we will not know where a person is. If we want to take into account that fact, we will need to do the following:

- Refine the conceptual schema of the domain: now there will be some times when we do not know where a person is.

- Transform the move event into two events: the beginning and the end of a move.

- Consider that the effect of the beginning of a move is that we enter a state in which we do not know where the moving person is.

- Consider that the effect of the end of a move is that there is a relationship between the moving person and the target place.

For the designer, it is important to distinguish between external and generated events. An event is external if it occurs independently of the IS. If the IS is computer-based, external events happen even if the system is out of service. Such events are called external because they happen outside the control of the system. The system will need to be notified of the events (to update its information base), but the system itself has not produced the events. Many events are external, for example, the hiring of an employee or the sunrise.

A system may know external events either by direct observation or by users' communication:

- In direct observation, the system has some mechanism that allows it to detect the occurrence of events. For example, a system may have a sensor that detects the arrival of a car in a toll station.

- In users' communication, the users tell the system of the events when they occur. For example, when a company changes the price of a product, the system is also notified of the change.

As mentioned in Section 2.1, an IS may also have an active function. In the active function, the users may delegate to the system the generation of some events that change the state of the domain when some conditions hold. A generated event is an event induced directly by the IS. Without the participation of the system, the event would not be generated, and, therefore, the domain would not change. The system may generate an event as a response to an explicit request from users, when it detects that the state of the domain satisfies some condition, or because it considers the event necessary to achieve an objective defined by the users.

Example 2.4

Assume an IS that controls an elevator. At each floor there is a button that users can press to request the elevator. Pressing one of the buttons is an external event. The system responds immediately by turning on the light associated with the button (to inform users that the system is aware of their request). Turning on and off light buttons are generated events. Taking into account the current position of the elevator, as well as the pending requests, the system issues several commands to start or stop the motor. Those commands are also generated events.

Events, either external or generated, are also instances of concepts. An *event type* is a concept whose instances are events. Events may have relationships with other entities. In particular, all events have a relationship with an entity that is a time instant, which corresponds to the time when the event happens. Figure 2.5 shows an example of the event type *change of residence*. Events of this type are related with a person (who changes), a town (new residence), and a date (occurrence time).

The set of event types that exist in a domain is part of the conceptual schema of events. The description, in some language, of that schema, as well as other elements described next, is called the *conceptual schema of the behavior.*

To be able to update the information base, the IS must know not only the events that have happened but also their effect on the information base.

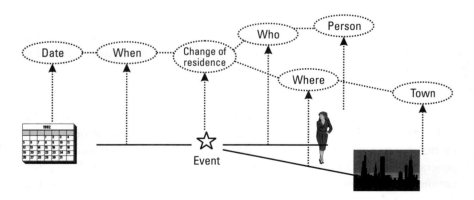

Figure 2.5 Event type and instance.

The definition of that effect, in some language, is also part of the conceptual schema of the behavior.

In conceptual modeling, there are several distinct ways to define the effect of events. The most usual way consists of defining, for each event type, an effect function that gives the new state for any old state and any instance of the event type. For example, the effect function corresponding to the event type *change of residence*, shown in Figure 2.5, might be (informally)

> If an event of type *change of residence*, of person *p* and town *c*, occurs on date *d*, then in the new state, corresponding to date *d*, person *p* will not live any longer where she lived before, and she will be living in town *c*.

In the example, the effect of the event is quite limited, and the effect function is simple. In practice, however, it is not so easy to define the effect, because there are many event types, and some of them have a complex effect function.

For generated events, the conceptual schema of the behavior includes the definition of the generating conditions, that is, when the events must be generated.

Example 2.5

Assume an IS that monitors the level of water in a tank. The system has a sensor that detects the level of water at any time. It is expected that the system will keep the input valve open when the water level is below a desired minimum and closed when the level is above a desired maximum. Generated event types are the opening and the closing of the valve. The generation condition of the former could be "when the current level is below the minimum and the valve is not open already" and that of the latter, "when the current level is above the maximum and the valve is not closed."

2.2.4 Integrity Constraints

The information base is a representation of the state of the domain. An IS obtains and updates the information base from messages received through the input interface or by direct observation of the domain.

In a perfect world, the information base would be an exact representation of the domain. Input messages would always be correct, and the system would receive all relevant messages. Furthermore, the direct observation of the domain would always be faithful. In a perfect world, the representation would always be correct (or valid) and complete.

Unfortunately, in the real world it is likely that some received messages are incorrect, in the sense that they communicate something that is not true. Also, the direct observation of the domain may be distorted. In such cases, some of the facts in the information base may not be valid. It is also likely that the system does not receive all relevant messages; then the information base may not be complete.

Validity and completeness are the two components of the integrity of an information base [13]. We say that an information base has integrity when all its facts are valid and it contains all relevant facts. Integrity is an important property of an information base. Lack of integrity normally has negative consequences, which in some cases may be serious.

In most systems, total integrity can be achieved only by human intervention. In many cases, it is necessary to check the facts in the information base against the domain. For example, many retail stores need to check periodically that the products they have on shelves correspond to their records in the IS. It is not difficult to see that in some cases the cost of integrity is high and hardly avoidable.

However, it is possible to build mechanisms in the IS that automatically guarantee some level of integrity. We can define conditions on the information base such that, if satisfied, we can have some level of confidence on its integrity. These conditions, called *integrity constraints*, are defined in the conceptual schema. An integrity constraint is a condition that might not be satisfied under some circumstances, but it is understood that the IS will include mechanisms to guarantee its satisfaction at any time.

Example 2.6

Assume that a conceptual schema has a relationship type *Assigned to*, involving entity types *Employee* and *Project*. Suppose that in the domain all employees are always assigned to one or more projects. An integrity constraint might be "all employees are assigned to some project." Once defined in the conceptual schema, we can assume that all states of the information base will contain for each known employee at least one relationship with a project. The constraint, however, does not guarantee total integrity (e.g., the information base could have wrong assignments), but its satisfaction is a necessary condition.

We say that an information base is *consistent* if it satisfies all defined integrity constraints. We also say that a constraint is violated when the information base does not satisfy it. When a constraint is violated, the system must produce some response to maintain consistency. The most frequent case is when a violation is caused by the arrival of some erroneous message, and the response is usually the rejection of the message, asking for its correction.

Most integrity constraints refer to facts of the information base, and then they are part of the conceptual schema of the state. Some constraints, however, refer to events; then they are part of the conceptual schema of the behavior. An example of the latter, which refers to events of type *Birth*, could be "a person cannot be parent of himself."

2.2.5   Derivation Rules

By means of the informative function, an IS provides information about the state of the domain to users, either when they request it or under predefined circumstances.

If an IS does not have any inference capability, it can provide only information collected from the environment. In some cases, that may be all that is required, but in most cases users expect that systems have some capability to infer new facts from the ones they know. A simple example is totaling. If we give to the system a sequence of numbers, we normally assume the system will at least be able to compute their total.

Most ISs have some inference capability, which requires two main components: derivation rules and an inference mechanism. Derivation rules are defined in the conceptual schema. The inference mechanism uses derivation rules to infer new information. How the inference mechanism works may vary from one IS to another, and it is considered to be part of the internal structure of the system; therefore, it is not specified in the conceptual schema.

A *derivation rule* is an expression that defines how new facts may be inferred from others. The concrete form of this expression depends on the conceptual modeling language used. Often, the expressions are formulas in a logic style, but nothing prevents the use of conventional algorithms. For example, assume we want to define the derivation rule corresponding to the concept *grandparent* from the concept *parent*. An expression in logic style would be "a person *gp* is grandparent of person *gc* if *gp* is a parent of a person *p* and *p* is a parent of *gc*."

An equivalent algorithmic expression that gets the four grandparents of person *gc* could be:

1. Get the two parents *p1* and *p2* of *gc*.
2. Get the two parents *gp1* and *gp2* of *p1*.

3. Get the two parents *gp3* and *gp4* of *p2*.

4. The grandparents of *gc* are *gp1*, *gp2*, *gp3*, and *gp4*.

Derivation rules may be specific of a given domain (e.g., a bank), applicable to all domains of a certain class (e.g., banking), or domain independent (e.g., statistical concepts). The conceptual schema must include all derivation rules that can be used in a particular system, but we should explicitly define only those rules that are specific to our domain. The other derivation rules could be shared by all conceptual schemas for domains of the same class or by all conceptual schemas.

In practice, most derivation rules infer new facts of the information base, and then the rules are included as part of the conceptual schema of the state. However, nothing prevents the inference of events from other events, and then the corresponding derivation rules are part of the conceptual schema of the behavior. For example, a derivation rule referring to events of type *Travel* could define *Long travels* as those travels such that the distance traveled is greater than 1000 km.

2.3 Abstract Architecture of an IS

Section 2.2 presented conceptual schemas. This section shows the essential role these schemas play in the architecture of ISs. By architecture, we mean the main components and their relationships. In principle, there are many possible architectures, and choosing the most convenient for a particular IS depends on many factors, including the preferred architectural style and the hardware and software platform on top of which it must work. However, we do not need to take such diversity into account here. For our purposes, it will suffice to consider the ANSI/SPARC abstract architecture proposed in the ISO report [10] (Figure 2.6).

To illustrate this architecture and the role played by conceptual schemas in it, we will use the example of a chess-playing system that can play with persons or with other systems.

The conventional representation of the state of a chess game is a drawing like the one shown in Figure 2.7. However, not everybody uses exactly the same representation; different icons can be used to denote the same piece. Some users may prefer other graphical representations (e.g., the three-dimensional view), and in some cases text-based representations may be preferred (e.g., in machine-machine communication).

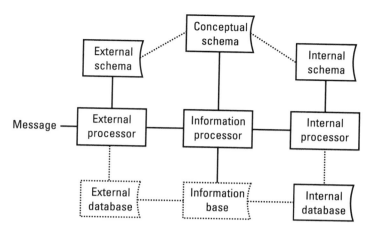

Figure 2.6 ANSI/SPARC architecture.

Figure 2.7 A representation of the state of a chess game.

An external schema is a form of representation of the state of the domain used in the domain, and an external DB is the representation of the state of the domain in that external schema. Figure 2.7 can be considered an external DB. External DBs are virtual, in the sense that they do not have a physical and persistent existence within the system.

Besides a form of representation, external schemas also include aspects of manipulation of this form, like the language used to ask queries or to communicate external events. In the example, we again find some diversity. There are several textual (official) and graphical ways to represent a move (e.g., as a string, like the string "D71," or by dragging a piece to the desired place).

The result is that in general there are several external schemas for a given domain and it is not possible to single out one that satisfies all possible users and all possible uses. Therefore, the system must deal with several external schemas. To do that, the system needs to know the meaning of the representations used and the meaning of the allowed manipulations.

Figure 2.8 shows a simplified conceptual schema of the example. In the figure, entity types are represented by rectangles and relationship types by lines connecting the involved entity types. The name of the relationship type is placed near the line, with a small filled triangle that shows the way to read the name.

Each piece is of some type (king, queen, bishop, etc.), has a color (black or white), and is located at some square. Squares also have a color. For clarity, we will call board square (or just square) to a square that is part of the board, and representation square to a square drawn in the representation of the board (external schema). A board square is located at a row and a column,

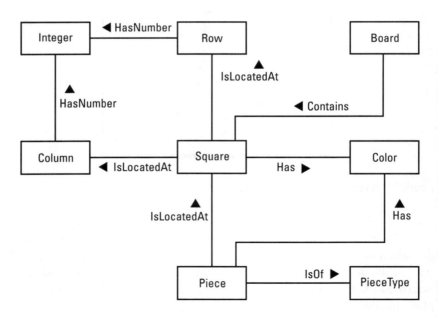

Figure 2.8 Conceptual schema of the chess-playing example.

which define its position in the board. Rows and columns have a number (integer).

The conceptual schema might also include a derivation rule defining that a board square is *free* if there is not a piece located at it; otherwise, it is *occupied.*

There is a single conceptual schema and there may be one or more external schemas. External schemas are defined in terms of the conceptual schema. For instance, the correspondence between the conceptual schema in Figure 2.8 and the external schema used in Figure 2.7 is as follows:

- The board is represented by a (large) square, subdivided into 64 smaller representation squares corresponding to the board squares.
- Representation squares are painted with the same color as the corresponding board squares.
- Each piece has a different icon, depending on its type and color.
- If a piece p is located at a board square s, then the icon corresponding to p is put over the representation square corresponding to s.

The correspondence between manipulations and the external events is defined similarly. For example, when the user drags a piece to a representation square, the conceptual meaning is a move of that piece to the board square where it is released.

The *external processor* is the architectural component that interacts with users. In principle, there is an external processor for each external schema. The external processors receive the messages from users (in the language of the external schema), translate them into the language of the conceptual schema, and forward them to the information processor.

The *information processor* is the component that handles the (conceptual) messages originated by the users and performs the active function that may be delegated to the system. In particular, if a message communicates an external event, then the information processor has to apply the corresponding effect function and check that the resulting state is consistent. In the case of the example, if a new move is received, the information processor has to check whether the move is valid and, if so, to update the state of the game.

To perform those tasks, the information processor needs to access and manipulate the state of the domain. It cannot use an external representation because, in general, they may be partial, and, on the other hand, they include aspects that do not have any relationship with the nature of the domain.

For example, if the system had to use the representation shown in Figure 2.7 to check whether the move of the black queen to column 1, row 5 is valid, the information processor should check, among other things, that the representation square in column 2 and row 6 does not have any icon over it. Neither "representation square" nor "icon" is a relevant concept in the domain. It is much better that the information processor may ask questions like "Is the board square of column 6 and row 2 free?" where both *board square* and *free* are defined in the conceptual schema. For similar reasons, which will be explained, the information processor cannot use an internal representation.

What is most natural for the information processor is to use a representation based on the conceptual schema, which is the information base. However, the information base is virtual, because it does not exist physically within the system. When the information processor asks itself questions like "Is the board square in column 6 and row 2 free?" it behaves as if the information base really existed. In reality the question will be sent to the internal processor, which will answer it using the physical DB.

The representation of the state that the system has to maintain internally must allow, among other things, an efficient execution. That means the design of the internal representation must take into account technical factors. We call *internal schema* the representation form of the state of the domain used internally by the system, and *internal DB* the state representation in that schema. The internal DB is the only one that has a physical existence. The internal schema also includes the set of operations that can be invoked on the DB.

An internal schema for the system example that would be almost optimal from the point of view of the amount of space used (although not from other technical points of view) could be a file with the following record structure:

PieceType, Color, Row, Column

where PieceType could use one character (with a K for king, Q for queen, R for rook, etc.), Color one bit (0: white, 1: black), and Row and Column a single byte (number 1...8). Internal schemas, like the external ones, are defined with respect to the conceptual schema. In the example, the correspondence might be:

- The file has a record for each piece that is on the board.
- The first field indicates the piece type, the second its color, the third the row number of the board square where the piece is located, and the fourth the column number.

- The color of the board square is not represented explicitly. The external processor may infer it by adding the numbers of the row and the column: If the result is even, the board square is black; otherwise, it is white.

Using that internal schema, the partial contents of the internal DB corresponding to Figure 2.7 would be

R	1	8	2
R	1	8	4
K	1	8	7
Q	1	7	3

......

The internal processor receives the commands issued by the information processor and executes them, possibly accessing the internal DB. For example, if the internal processor receives the command (or, as in this case, question) "Is the board square of column 6 and row 2 free?" it will check whether there is a record, in the above file, such that Row = 2 and Column = 6. If there is not such a record, the answer to the question will be positive, and negative otherwise. To perform its task, the internal processor needs to know the internal schema, including its correspondence with the conceptual schema.

Modern architectures of ISs are layered, with three logical layers: presentation, domain, and data management. The equivalent to the external processors is located in the presentation layer, the information processor in the domain layer, and the internal processor in the data management layer.

2.4   Requirements Engineering

Section 2.3 discussed the role of conceptual schemas in the architecture of ISs. Now, we are going to see their role in the development of the systems.

Conceptual schemas are the common base for external and internal schemas, as well as for their processors. Therefore, it is clear that it is not possible to design the architecture of an IS without the conceptual schema. Conceptual modeling must precede system design.

It is important to realize that it is impossible to design a system without knowing its conceptual schema. The only available options are either to define explicitly the schema or to have it in the minds of the designers. Unfortunately, sometimes the latter option is taken.

The stage that precedes system design is called *requirements engineering* [14]. Its objective is to capture the requirements that must be satisfied by the system. Normally, requirements engineering is a complex process, because the many persons (users, designers, managers, etc.) involved in it may have different views, needs, and interests.

Requirements engineering consists of three main phases, which can be performed iteratively:

- Requirements determination;
- Requirements specification;
- Requirements validation.

During *requirements determination,* the future users of the system and the designers analyze the problems, the needs, and the domain characteristics. On the basis of that analysis, they decide the changes to be introduced in the domain and the functions that should be performed by a new IS. Requirements determination is a crucial phase, because it determines a significant part of the final success or failure of the whole project. In this phase, it is decided how the future system will be, and an error in the decision often implies that users eventually will get an inadequate system.

During this phase, a conceptual schema of the existing domain may be elaborated, if it is considered necessary to achieve a common understanding of the domain. A conceptual schema of the desired domain can also be elaborated, without determining yet the part that will correspond to the new IS.

In the *requirements specification* phase, the functional and nonfunctional requirements of the new system are defined. The result is a set of documents (called specifications) that describe exactly the system that the users want and that the designers have to design and build. Functional requirements describe what the system must do, while nonfunctional requirements describe global properties of the system, like, for example, response time or portability.

The conceptual schema of an IS is the specification of the functional requirements of the system. The conceptual schema specifies all functions (memory, informative, and active) that must be performed by the system and, together with the nonfunctional requirement specification, corresponds to the system specification.

During *requirements validation*, specifications are checked with respect to users' needs. In this phase, it must be ensured that users get a complete understanding of how the future system will be before it is built. This is also a crucial phase that can be done well only if requirements have been described explicitly.

Validation can be performed in two main ways:

- By presenting the conceptual schema and in general the specifications in a language and form that is easily understood by users. If the conceptual modeling language used is not completely understandable by the users, it will be necessary to provide either some help for its interpretation or translation to more familiar languages (not excluding natural language). When the conceptual schema is large, as is often the case, its structuring in fragments or views may be mandatory.

- By building (partial) prototypes of the system. If the conceptual modeling language used is formal, then prototypes may be generated automatically. This form of validation is usually more effective than the other form, but in general it is more expensive.

In summary, conceptual schemas are elaborated during the requirements engineering stage and are the basis for the next stage, system design.

For further details on how these activities can be facilitated by computers, see Chapter 13.

2.5 Desirable Properties of Conceptual Schemas

Now that we have seen what the conceptual schemas are and their role in the architecture of the system and during the development process, this section describes which properties should have these schemas in order to play those roles effectively [15–17].

A well-known property of conceptual schemas is the *100% principle*, or *completeness*, which states that

> All relevant general static and dynamic aspects, i.e., all rules, laws, etc.,
> of the universe of discourse should be described in the conceptual

schema. The information system cannot be held responsible for not meeting those described elsewhere, including in particular those in application programs [10].

The justification for the 100% principle is that a conceptual schema is the definition of the general domain knowledge the IS needs to perform its functions; therefore, the conceptual schema must include all required knowledge. If we had a "compiler" able to generate a system from the conceptual schema, then it would be obvious that the system could not contain anything not included in the schema. A conceptual schema is complete if it satisfies this property.

An important conclusion from the 100% principle is that the conceptual modeling language used must allow the description of all relevant aspects of a domain.

The *correctness* property is complementary to the completeness property: A conceptual schema is correct if the knowledge that defines it is true in the domain and relevant to the functions the IS must perform. For example, in our chess-playing system the fact that players have an address is probably irrelevant.

The Venn diagram in Figure 2.9 shows graphically the relationship between completeness and correctness. The left circle, A, represents the domain knowledge the IS needs to know to perform its functions. The right circle, C, represents the knowledge defined in the conceptual schema. In a complete conceptual schema, A is a subset of C. In a correct conceptual schema, C is a subset of A. In a complete and correct conceptual schema, A = C.

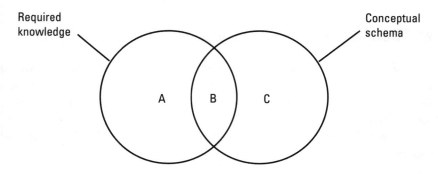

Figure 2.9 Completeness and correctness.

Correctness and completeness of a conceptual schema are checked during the requirements validation phase.

Another property that has become popular is the *principle of conceptualization*, which states that

> A conceptual model should only include conceptually relevant aspects, both static and dynamic, of the universe of discourse, thus excluding all aspects of (external or internal) data representation, physical data organization and access as well as aspects of particular external user representation such as message formats, data structures, etc. [10].

The justification is similar to the previous one: If a conceptual schema is the basis for system design, then it should not include any design aspect, thus leaving freedom to designers to decide on all those aspects. On the other hand, when a schema focuses only on conceptual aspects, it is simpler and, therefore, easier to be understood by users. A conceptual schema that satisfies this principle is called *design independent.*

Conceptual schemas are described in some conceptual modeling language. This language will have a set of rules that must be respected. A conceptual schema is *syntactically valid* (or just valid) if it respects all the rules of the language in which it is written. Syntactic correctness of a schema is independent of the domain.

Sometimes, the same piece of knowledge about a domain may be expressed in two or more ways in a given language. The property of *simplicity* states that simple schemas must be preferred, that is, schemas that use fewer language constructs or less complex constructs.

Closely related to the simplicity property is the property of *ease of understanding*. A conceptual schema should be easily understandable by the persons involved in the development of the IS, particularly its future users. Section 2.4 mentioned the importance of this property during requirements validation.

Finally, we mention the property of *stability*, also called flexibility, extensibility, or modifiability. A conceptual schema is stable if small changes in the properties of the domain or in the users' requirements do not imply large changes in the schema.

There are some proposals of metrics for evaluating these properties in a conceptual schema (see Chapter 14). A representative example is [18]. However, this is an issue where more work needs to be done to be fully practical.

References

[1] Langefors, B., "Information Systems," *Proc. IFIP '74*, North Holland, 1974, pp. 937–945.

[2] Checkland, P., *Systems Thinking, Systems Practice*, New York: Wiley, 1981.

[3] Boman, M., et al., *Conceptual Modelling*, New York: Prentice-Hall, 1997.

[4] Wand, Y., and R. Weber, "An Ontological Analysis of Some Fundamental Information Systems Concepts," *Proc. 9th. Intl. Conf. on Information Systems*, Minneapolis, MN, Dec. 1988, pp. 213–225.

[5] Motro, A., "Intensional Answers to Database Queries," *IEEE Trans. on Knowledge and Data Engineering*, Vol. 6, No. 3, June 1994, pp. 444–454.

[6] Papazoglou, M. P., "Unraveling the Semantics of Conceptual Schemas," *Comm. ACM*, Vol. 38, No. 9, Sept. 1995, pp. 80–94.

[7] Ellis, J. R., *Objectifying Real-Time Systems*, New York: SIGS Books, 1994.

[8] Uschold, M., and M. Gruninger, "Ontologies: Principles, Methods, and Applications," *Knowledge Engineering Review*, Vol. 11, No. 2, 1996, pp. 93–136.

[9] Mylopoulos, J., "Information Modeling in the Time of the Revolution," *Information Systems*, Vol. 23, No. 3/4, 1998, pp. 127–155.

[10] ISO/TC97/SC5/WG3, *Concepts and Terminology for the Conceptual Schema and the Information Base*, J. J. Van Griethuysen (ed.), Mar. 1982.

[11] Russell, S., and P. Norvig, *Artificial Intelligence: A Modern Approach*, Englewood Cliffs, NJ: Prentice-Hall, 1995.

[12] Cook, S., and J. Daniels, *Designing Object Systems: Object-Oriented Modelling With Syntropy*, New York: Prentice-Hall, 1994.

[13] Motro, A., "Integrity = Validity + Completeness," *ACM Trans. Database Systems*, Vol. 14, No. 4, 1989, pp. 480–502.

[14] Loucopoulos, P., and V. Karakostas, *System Requirements Engineering*, New York: McGraw-Hill, 1995.

[15] Bubenko, J. A., Jr., "Validity and Verification Aspects of Information Modeling," *Third Intl. Conf. on VLDB*, Tokyo, Oct. 1977, pp. 556–565.

[16] Davis, A. M., *Software Requirements: Objects, Functions, and States*, Englewood Cliffs, NJ: Prentice-Hall, 1993.

[17] Lindland, O. I., G. Sindre, and A. Solvberg, "Understanding Quality in Conceptual Modeling," *IEEE Software*, Mar. 1994, pp. 42–49.

[18] Moody, D. L., "Metrics for Evaluating the Quality of Entity Relationship Models," *Proc. 17th Intl. Conf. on Conceptual Modeling*, Singapore, Nov. 1998, LNCS 1507, Springer, pp. 211–225.

Selected Bibliography

Batini, C., S. Ceri, and S. B. Navathe, *Conceptual Database Design: An Entity-Relationship Approach*, Redwood City, CA: Benjamin/Cummings, 1992.

This book is devoted to conceptual modeling but focuses on DBs.

Nijssen, G. M., and T. A. Halpin, *Conceptual Schema and Relational Database Design*, New York: Prentice-Hall, 1989.

Chapter 2 of this book (along with Chapter 4 of [14]) is an appropriate general introduction to conceptual modeling.

Borgida, A., S. Greenspan, and J. Mylopoulos, "Knowledge Representation as the Basis for Requirements Specifications," *IEEE Computer*, Apr. 1985, pp. 82–91.

This article emphasizes principles with reference to languages.

Loucopoulos, P., "Conceptual Modeling," in *Conceptual Modeling, Databases, and CASE: An Integrated View of Information Systems Development*, P. Loucopoulos and R. Zicari (eds.), New York: Wiley, 1992, pp. 1–26, and Rolland, C., and C. Cauvet, "Trends and Perspectives in Conceptual Modeling," pp. 27–48 in the same book, provide a complete picture of conceptual models and conceptual modeling languages, including many references.

Falkenberg et al., "A Framework of Information System Concepts: The FRISCO Report," IFIP WG 8.1 Task Group FRISCO, Dec. 1996.

This report is a recent in-depth treatment of IS concepts.

Boman, M., et al., *Conceptual Modeling*, Upper Saddle River, NJ: Prentice-Hall, 1997.

This is one of the very few books that deals entirely with conceptual modeling of information systems.

Mylopolous, J., "Information Modeling in the Time of the Revolution," *Information Systems*, Vol. 23, No. 3/4, 1998, pp. 127–155.

This article gives a modern view of the field.

Part II:
Advanced Technologies

3

Active Databases

Oscar Díaz and Norman Paton

3.1 Introduction

DBMSs are at the heart of current IS technology. They provide reliable, efficient, and effective mechanisms for storing and managing large volumes of information in a multiuser environment. In recent years, there has been a trend in DB research and practice toward increasing the proportion of the semantics of an application that is supported within the DB system itself. Temporal DBs, spatial DBs, multimedia DBs, and DB programming languages are examples of that trend. Active DBs can be considered part of this trend, where the semantics that are supported reflect the reactive behavior of the domain.

Traditional DBMSs are passive in the sense that commands are executed by the DB (e.g., query, update, delete) as and when requested by the user or the application program. However, some situations cannot be modeled effectively by that pattern. As an example, consider a university DB where data are stored about students, lecturers, timetables, bus schedules, and so on and which is accessed by different terminals. As new students join the school (i.e., a new tuple is inserted in the *student* table), the bus should stop at new students' addresses. Two options are available to the administrator of a passive DB system who is seeking to support such a requirement. One is to add the additional monitoring functionality to all enrollment programs so the situation is checked for each time a student is added. However, that approach leads to the semantics of the monitoring task being distributed, replicated, and hidden among different application programs. The second approach relies on a polling mechanism that periodically checks the addresses of the students. Unlike the first approach, here the semantics of the application are represented in a single place, but the difficulty stems from ascertaining the most appropriate polling frequency. If too high, there is a cost penalty. If too low, the reaction may be too late (e.g., the students are left on the pavement until the polling program is run again).

An active DB would support the application by moving the reactive behavior from the application (or polling mechanism) into the DBMS. Active DBs are thus able to monitor and react to specific circumstances of relevance to an application. The reactive semantics are both centralized and handled in a timely manner.

The advantages that can be drawn from this migration are numerous [1]. First, it promotes code reusability. Rather than replicating code in distinct applications, the code resides in a single place from which it is implicitly invoked. Such centralization accounts for increasing consistency because no application can bypass the policy, and maintenance is eased as changes to the policy are localized in a single piece of code. Moreover, in a client/server environment, centralized reactive behavior reduces network traffic, as the reaction associated with the event is executed locally as the single implicit invocation arises. By contrast, if the reaction were embedded within the application, the distinct SQL statements would have been executed across the net.

The rest of this chapter is structured as follows. Section 3.2 introduces an example that will be used to illustrate distinct aspects of reactive behavior through the rest of the chapter. Reactive behavior is generally supported using rules. Rules can be seen as an implementation mechanism, but implementation must be preceded by analysis and design. Thus, Section 3.3 provides some insights on how rules can be ascertained from business policies during analysis. At design time, rules need to be described and their behavior understood. Section 3.4 illustrates the subtleties of rule behavior through distinct examples and presents graphical notations for rule description. Section 3.5 addresses implementation issues, illustrating features using the rule system of Oracle. Finally, Section 3.6 tackles the maintenance of rule sets.

3.2 Example: University Database

This section outlines the DB that will be used later in the chapter to illustrate the utility of active functionality. The DB stores details of a training company that provides consultancy and courses. The E/R diagram for the DB is depicted in Figure 3.1, and the SQL *create table* commands for the corresponding tables are provided in Figure 3.2.

Each of the entity types in the DB is represented using a table in SQL. Because each attendee can take many courses and each course can be taken

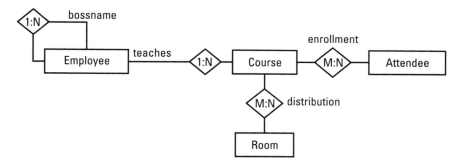

Figure 3.1 E/R schema for the example.

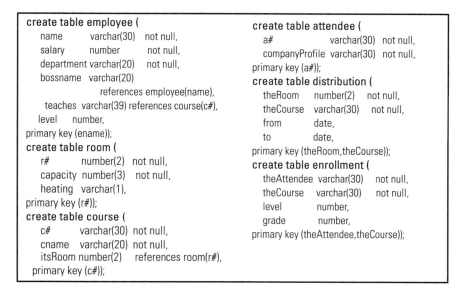

```
create table employee (                     create table attendee (
    name        varchar(30)   not null,        a#              varchar(30)  not null,
    salary      number        not null,        companyProfile  varchar(30)  not null,
    department varchar(20)    not null,     primary key (a#));
    bossname  varchar(20)                   create table distribution (
              references employee(name),       theRoom     number(2)    not null,
    teaches varchar(39) references course(c#),  theCourse   varchar(30)   not null,
    level    number,                            from        date,
primary key (ename));                           to          date,
create table room (                          primary key (theRoom,theCourse));
    r#         number(2)   not null,         create table enrollment (
    capacity number(3)    not null,            theAttendee  varchar(30)    not null,
    heating   varchar(1),                       theCourse    varchar(30)    not null,
primary key (r#));                              level             number,
create table course (                           grade            number,
    c#         varchar(30)  not null,        primary key (theAttendee,theCourse));
    cname    varchar(20)  not null,
    itsRoom number(2)    references room(r#),
primary key (c#));
```

Figure 3.2 Tables for the example.

by many attendees, the relationship between attendees and courses is represented using a distinct table, namely, *enrollment*, which has *grade* and *level* as its attributes. Moreover, the distribution table supports the relationship between courses and the rooms where they are taught. Finally, an employee has a boss and teaches only a course at a given level. The *bossname* and *teaches* attributes, respectively, realize such links.

3.3 Analysis

Analysis refers to the process of identifying and capturing application requirements from the user's point of view. The developer should focus on the semantics of the application rather than the characteristics of the final system. The result is a consistent description (conceptual model) of the expectations the user has about system functionality. Since DBs traditionally store raw data, the main concern of these models used to be the structural aspects of the domain. However, that is no longer true. Most commercial DBMSs are able to manage code in the form of store procedures, packages, and triggers. Thus, we need to extend previous methods so they also capture the behavioral aspects of the domain. Here, we focus on those aspects that eventually will be supported as triggers.

The first step is requirements elicitation, that is, how to ascertain the functional requirements of the system to be built. As far as active behavior is concerned, a good starting point is to look at business policies. Policies are explicit statements of constraints placed on the business that concern both structural features (i.e., asserting the description of essential concepts, relationships, or states) and behavioral characteristics (i.e., describing the procedures that govern or regulate how the business operates). For the purpose of this chapter, we will focus on the elicitation and description of two types of business policies: recovering business policies and causal business policies.

3.3.1 Recovering Business Policies

DB people traditionally have focused on the structural side of the domain, paying special attention to what is known as *integrity constraints*. Integrity constraints express conditions that hold in the domain. For instance, the constraint *the number of students enrolled in a course cannot go above the capacity of the course's room* expresses a condition that is always true in the domain, and so it should be preserved in the DB. However, integrity constraints may be violated when data are modified. For instance, the *number of students* constraint can be violated when a new student is enrolled or when the course is moved to a different room.

It is generally considered that it is not so important how integrity constraints are preserved as long as the system guarantees that the consistency is preserved. For that reason, most systems just reject those updates that cause a constraint to be violated. However, a businessperson's perspective can be quite different. As stated in [2], the user is very interested in how the integrity constraint is enforced and may have invested a lot of time in determining what are considered to be the optimal procedures for ensuring that violations never occur or are dealt with properly should they occur. As an example, consider an attempt to enroll a new student in an already complete course. The previous constraint will be violated, and an option is to reject the update straight away. However, that is a stringent and unrealistic way to preserve most of the constraints. A more realistic situation could be to split the course into two groups and distribute the students evenly. That ends up with two groups, both of them obeying the constraint. The substantial part is not only the integrity constraint as such but the procedure to be followed should the constraint be violated. Indeed, these recovering procedures, rather than the constraints themselves, reflect more accurately the essence and idiosyncrasies of the business. It is common for distinct businesses to share the same constraints but to have distinct procedures for restoring the same constraint. Think about the overdraft constraint (i.e., when an account goes into the red). Although most banks do not allow negative balances, the action to be taken when an overdraft occurs can be diverse. These procedures constitute one of the main hallmarks of the business, and their importance cannot be underestimated.

It is worth noticing that the constraint is frequently hidden and difficult to ascertain, as businesspeople are not always aware of the constraints behind the procedures they follow. Domain users prefer to express themselves in terms of "doing" rather than "knowing," and it is the task of the analyst to dig out and elicit the behind-the-scenes constraint.

An additional difficulty is that recovery procedures for the same integrity constraint can vary among the departments of the enterprise. Take again the room's capacity threshold constraint. During the elicitation phase, distinct stakeholders are interviewed. Those from the computing department indicate that when the course registration is overbooked, the students are split across two rooms; however, the engineering department follows a distinct approach: *when overbooking arises, the course is moved to a new place with enough room for all the students.* Notice that the underlying constraint is the same, but the procedures are different. On building a common repository not only of data but also of the procedures of the organization, the analyst should be aware of those differences.

The process, then, begins by an unambiguous description of the constraint. Next, the analyst should ascertain whether the violation of the constraint is always restricted. In the former case, the constraint should be supported declaratively using the SQL-supported *check* construct wherever possible. Otherwise, a procedural approach is followed that eventually will be implemented as triggers. The obtaining of policies starts by identifying the structural operations that can violate the constraint either directly or indirectly. However, some of those operations might be prevented from happening due to other constraints (e.g., the updating of some attributes is restricted) or interface validation. For those operations that can be performed, the context and compensating action that restore the validity must be stated.

As an example, consider the *room's capacity threshold* constraint. Table 3.1 shows some of the distinct structural operations that can violate that constraint. Some updates are prevented from happening by other constraints. Only new enrollments and the assignment of a room to an already available course need to be monitored. The table also shows the distinct compensating actions that follow the violation of the policy, which depends on the cause: If a new enrollment overflows the capacity of the current

Table 3.1
Recovering Business Policy From the Room's Capacity Threshold Constraint

Structural Operation	Possible?	Reaction	Name
Update of capacity on classroom	No	—	No
Insert on enrollment	Yes	Find a bigger classroom	Enrollment overflow policy
Update of *theStudent* on enrollment	No	—	—
Update of *theCourse* on enrollment	No	—	No
Insert on distribution	Yes	Reject the update	Room inadequacy policy
Update of *theClassroom* on distribution	No	—	—
Update of *theCourse* on distribution	No	—	—

classroom, the system attempts to find another classroom with enough room for everybody; if a classroom is assigned that cannot lodge the already enrolled students, the insertion is rejected straightaway.

3.3.2 Causal Business Policies

Besides those policies whose rationale is restoring integrity constraint validity, other policies have to be found in the business's way of working. Rather than looking at the structural side of the domain, such policies are found in the behavioral realm of the enterprise; they reflect the procedural aspects of the organization. Elicitation of those policies is not an easy task and frequently involves some reengineering, because policies are hard-coded within programs or business procedures.

During the elicitation process, a good starting point is to look at state transition diagrams (STD). STDs are the final result of the behavioral analysis phase that represents the allowable sequence of events for each entity. An STD is represented as a network where nodes represent states, and arcs are labeled with the events that allow transitions between states. The transitions can be restricted to the satisfaction of certain conditions. Most of the information in the STD will finally be supported as part of the operations that realize the events.

An example of an STD for the *course* entity is shown in Figure 3.3: The course begins by being approved by the department. Next, students can register for the course, but the course is not set until at least 20 students have enrolled. Once the course is set, a classroom is assigned and the course starts. Eventually, the course terminates.

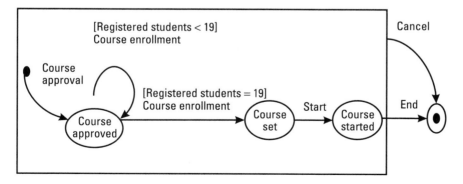

Figure 3.3 Course's state transition diagram.

STD can help the analyst dig out hidden business policies. Three elementary questions can be posed to discover those policies (see Table 3.2):

- Can any of the events that appear in the STD be caused by other events? For instance, the analyst may be intrigued to know what causes a course to start. Distinct alternatives are possible, depending on the organization's policy: The course can start at an established date or once the number of students surpasses a given threshold. In the latter case, the enrollment of a new student causes the beginning of the course.

- Can an event cause other events to happen?

- What if an event does not happen? Does it matter? For instance, what if not enough students (i.e., the threshold number of students set for the course to take place) are registered in a reasonable period of time? Is the course cancelled or postponed? What happens with the already enrolled students? The analyst should address all those questions and find the answers from the stakeholders.

This situation leads to the so-called *nonevents* [3]. The effect of one event, such as *enrollment,* may prepare the environment for the next expected event. Hence, when a course is approved, the system sets up a window of expectation (e.g., a month) for the students to register, and then the course begins. However, there is no guarantee that that will happen. That is, the required number of *enrollment* events may not occur. Nonevents are often overlooked and omitted, but they represent the clue to ascertaining important business policies.

Table 3.2
Causal Business Policies

Effect	Cause	Kind of Cause
A course starts when...	the number of students is above 20.	State condition
A student is reassigned when...	the student's course is cancelled.	Operational event
A course is cancelled when...	fewer than 20 enrollments are produced in a month since the course was approved.	Composite event

3.4 Design

Once relevant policies have been identified, the next step is to describe them using active rules, the basic components of which are presented in Section 3.4.1. Next, we address how both recovering and causal business policies can be mapped into active rules in Sections 3.4.2 and 3.4.3, respectively. Those rules can, however, give rise to complex run-time behavior, which is considered in Section 3.4.4.

3.4.1 Active Rules

Active rules have up to three components: an event, a condition, and an action (hence, active rules are also known as ECA rules). The basic computational model of an active rule is that it lies dormant until an event takes place that corresponds to the rule's event definition. When the event has taken place, the rule's condition is evaluated, and if it is true, the action is executed. The following descriptions make these notions more precise:

- *Event definition.* The event definition describes the happening to which the rule may have to respond. The happening is most often some operation within the DB, such as the insertion, update, or deletion of a tuple.

- *Condition.* The condition is a boolean expression or a query that examines the context in which the event has taken place. The fact that the event has taken place may not be enough in itself to require that the action be carried out.

- *Action.* The action is the program block that specifies the response required to the event that has taken place, given that the condition has evaluated to true. The action often carries out some update operation on the DB or communicates information to the user of the DB.

3.4.2 Supporting Recovering Business Policies Through Active Rules

Recovering business policies express ways to overcome the unfulfillment of integrity constraints. Because constraints are representations of structural conditions that hold in the domain, violations of constraints are due to structural events, that is, events that directly handle the structure of the schema. As for the relational model, that means that insert, delete, and update are the operations that put in motion a recovering business policy.

As an example, consider the integrity constraint that states that no employee should be paid more than his or her boss. This integrity constraint can be violated by distinct structural events, leading to different recovering business policies (see Table 3.3).

The following is an example of a rule that monitors the insertion of new tuples into the employee table:

```
after insert on employee
if   new.salary > (select B.salary
     from employee B
     where B.name = new.bossname)
do   rollback
```

That rule definition, in an imaginary rule language based on SQL, illustrates a range of features of active rule languages that need some explanation.

The event definition *after insert on employee* describes what may trigger the rule. A rule is triggered when an event that matches its event definition has taken place. In this case, the rule is triggered every time a new *employee* tuple is inserted into the DB.

The condition is described in the *if* clause. The condition compares the value of the *salary* attribute of the newly inserted employee with the salary of the boss of the employee. Information on the newly inserted tuple is referred to using the reserved word *new*. Thus, *new.salary* is the salary of the newly inserted tuple, and *new.bossname* is the value of the *bossname* attribute of the newly inserted tuple. The condition compares the salary of the newly

Table 3.3
Recovering Business Policy From the Constraint on Salary

Event	Condition	Action
Insert on employee	Salary of employee bigger than salary of employee's boss	Increase salary of boss
Update of salary on employee	Salary of employee bigger than salary of employee's boss	Increase salary of boss
Update of salary on employee (boss)	New salary of boss below higher salary among subordinates	Set salary of highest paid employee to salary of new boss
Update of bossname on employee	Salary of new boss below salary of previous boss	Reject update

inserted employee with the salary of the boss of the employee by retrieving the latter using a nested query.

The action is described in the *do* clause. The action in this case is straightforward: The transaction in which the employee was inserted is rolled back. The update violated the integrity constraint and, as a result, was blocked by the active rule. It is not difficult, however, to identify ways of fixing the constraint, as an alternative to blocking the update. For example, the following revised version of the rule maintains the constraint by increasing the salary of the boss of the newly inserted employee:

```
after insert on employee
if   new.salary  (select B.salary
     from employee B
     where B.name = new.bossname)
do   update employee
     set salary = new.salary
     where name = new.bossname
```

A less generous policy might involve reducing the salary of the newly inserted employee to that of the boss.

To provide complete enforcement of the constraint, it is also necessary to define active rules that react to changes in the salaries of existing employees or changes to the boss of an existing employee. For example, the following rule responds to increases in the salary of the employee:

```
after update of salary on employee
if   new.salary > old.salary  and
     new.salary > (select B.salary
         from employee B
         where B.name = new.bossname)
do   update employee
     set salary = new.salary
     where name = new.bossname
```

The event definition means that the rule is triggered by any modification to the salary of an existing employee. The condition of the rule first checks to see if the new value of the salary (i.e., the one after the update) is greater than the old value of the salary (i.e., the one before the update). If so, the constraint can be violated by an employee who used to be paid less than the boss now being paid more than the boss. The second part of the rule's condition performs this test. If the employee is indeed paid more than the boss, then the salary of the boss is increased.

However, that is not the only way in which the constraint can be violated by salary changes. Any reduction to the salary of a boss could cause the boss to be paid less than (one or more) of the boss's subordinates. This situation can be handled by the following rule:

```
after update of salary on employee
if  (new.salary < old.salary  and
     new.salary < (select max(S.salary)
        from employee S
        where S.bossname = new.name))
do   update employee
     set salary = new.salary
     where bossname = new.name and salary
     > old.salary
```

That rule implements a less generous policy than some of the earlier ones, in that it reduces the salary of all better paid subordinates to the salary of the now not-so-well-paid boss.

The other update operation that must be monitored is a change to the boss of an employee, which can be addressed by the following rule:

```
after update of bossname on employee
if  new.salary < (select B.salary
     from employee B
     where B.name = old.bossname)
do   rollback
```

That example illustrates rule support for a recovering business policy.

As is probably evident from these examples, writing active rules is by no means straightforward. Even in this none-too-complex example, identifying the events that are able to violate the integrity constraint is not trivial, and ensuring that appropriate responses are made to similar but different happenings (e.g., salary increases must be responded to differently from salary decreases) can be quite involved. Overall, active rules can be seen as being quite powerful, in that a range of tasks can be supported by active rules that would be much more difficult without them. However, writing correct rules is a skilled task.

3.4.2.1 Graphical Representation

Once rules have been elicited, graphical notations can promote user inter-action. Tools that support a graphical representation make the specification more comprehensible and appealing to the end user, thereby easing model validation. Here, we present the extension to the E/R model presented in [4], known as the *(ER)² model.*

As an example, consider the *increase employee's salary policy.* This situation could be reflected using the $(ER)^2$ notation as shown in Figure 3.4. The regulation is modeled as an update on the employee's salary, which in turn could lead to updating the corresponding boss's salary, if his or her salary is below the employee's. Arc labels indicate the operation to be applied to the entity (e.g., *m* for modification), whereas circles and polygons stand for events and rules, respectively. As for rules, they have a primitive event, a condition over the DB state, and an action that is described as a list of DB operations or external actions. Conditions and actions are described separately from the diagram, using textual descriptions displayed through windows when circles or polygons are clicked on, thus avoiding cluttering of the diagrammatic representation [4].

3.4.3 Supporting Causal Business Policies Through Active Rules

Causal business policies concern the behavioral side of the domain. Unlike recovering policies, now the relevant aspects to be tracked are not only state conditions but also behavior invocation.

Let's consider the policies outlined in Section 3.3.2 and shown in Table 3.2. The circumstances to which a policy may respond can be diverse, namely,

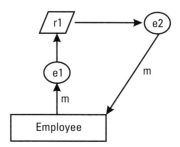

Figure 3.4 An $(ER)^2$ schema.

1. A condition on the DB state (e.g., *the number of students is above 20*);

2. The invocation of a structural operation (e.g., *the assignment of a room to a course* can be realized as an insertion on the distribution table);

3. The invocation of a domain operation (e.g., *a course is cancelled*);

4. A complex history of previous operations within an interval (e.g., *fewer than 20 enrollments within a month of a course being approved*). It is worth noticing that the cause is not that 20 students are currently registered, but that the operation *enrollment* has been invoked 20 times in a given time frame, that is, it is not a condition on the DB state but on the history of the event flow.

The first two cases can be supported with active rules using a similar approach to the one presented in the preceding section. However, policies caused by domain operations need some further explanation.

Although data are the traditional asset of DBMSs, currently most of the systems also support the description of domain operations within the realm of the system through stored procedures. As an example, consider a course cancellation, which affects distinct tables: tuple deletion in the distribution table, tuple deletion on the enrollment table, tuple modification on the course table, and so on. All those low-level structural operations can be grouped into a domain-meaningful operation through a cancellation stored procedure. The benefits include modularity, maintainability, and reduction in network traffic as the whole set of structural operations is executed locally after a single invocation of the procedure.

Let's go back to the cancellation policy, which states that before cancelling a course, if there are already some attendees enrolled, they should be moved to a related course (e.g., the same course but taught at a different time). The question is whether the policy should be supported as an independent active rule or within a stored procedure. The former approach implies the definition of rules such as

```
before   cancellation(C: course)
if   (select count(E.theAttendee)
     from enrollment E
     where E.theCourse = C) > 0
do   .....
```

An alternative would be to embed this policy in the stored procedure that implements *cancellation*. Which is best? In [5], the notion of stability is proposed as a criterion: If the policy is likely to evolve in the future, use an active rule approach; otherwise, consider embedding it in the procedure. Active rules involve an indirection that makes them less efficient than stored procedures; on the other hand, they enhance system modularity, traceability, and maintainability as they are described as separate chunks of code, without being intertwined with other supporting aspects.

However, the use of stored procedures is not always viable. When the cause is described as a composite combination of distinct operations, active rules with composite events will be the direct approach.

3.4.3.1   Graphical Representation

$(ER)^2$ diagrams are well suited for depicting simple rules with structural events. However, as rules become more complicated with composite and operation-based events, the use of the $(ER)^2$ notation can lead to cluttered diagrams with structural and behavioral features jointly described. In this context, some authors advocate separate description of rules. As a case in point, here the notation presented in [5] is introduced.

To illustrate this notation, consider the policy whereby courses in computing are cancelled if fewer than 20 enrollments take place in a month since the course was approved. The policy applies only if the average number of courses taught by the employee who appears as the instructor is above 3. Figure 3.5 depicts the policy. Simple events are denoted through black triangles (e.g., *course_approval, course_enrollment*); simple events participate in the

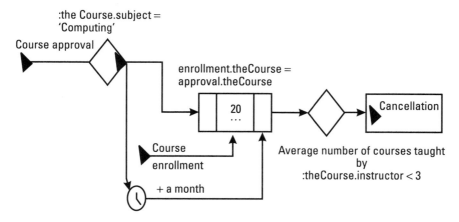

Figure 3.5 A graphical notation for the course cancellation policy.

definition of composite events: Figure 3.5 shows a *times* event within the interval delimited by a month since the approval of the course. A rule's condition is split into two kinds of predicates: predicates on the event parameters (represented as a rhombus with a black angle) and predicates on the state of the DB (depicted as a white rhombus). Finally, a rule's action is denoted as a rectangle where further black triangles are enclosed that stand for the policy's effect.

3.4.4   Active Behavior

Section 3.4.3 focused on the syntax of rules. Just as important is the run-time behavior of sets of rules, which can be complex.

The run-time behavior of a collection of rules is determined by the execution model of the rule system supporting the rules. There are two principal issues: (1) when rules are processed and (2) how multiple event occurrences are handled.

3.4.4.1   When Rules Are Processed

When an event takes place that matches the definition of a rule, the rule is triggered. It is possible that as soon as a rule is triggered, the transaction that raised the event is suspended, and the rule's condition and (if the condition is true) the rule's action are evaluated to completion right away.

However, that may not be the desired behavior. For example, consider the following situation. Employee *Tom* has the salary *1000* and the boss *Sally*. Employee *Sally* has the salary *1050*. The following program is run:

```
update employee
set salary = salary * 1.10
```

What are the resulting salaries of *Tom* and *Sally*, given the rules defined in Section 3.4.1? The answer is that it depends on the order in which the tuples are updated in the *employee* table.

If *Tom* is processed before *Sally*, then the increase in *Tom's* salary by 10% to *1100* will violate the integrity constraint and trigger the rule that monitors updates to salaries. That in turn will cause *Sally's* salary to be increased to *1100*, thereby reinstating the constraint. However, after that the update program will perform a further change to *Sally's* salary, making it 1100 * 1.10, or *1210*. That probably was *not* the intention of the person who wrote the update request.

If *Sally* is processed before *Tom*, the constraint is never violated, no rule actions are executed, and both *Sally* and *Tom* receive a 10% raise in salary.

In this case, the basic problem arises from the fact that the integrity constraint is enforced too eagerly, in the middle of a collection of updates. It is often the case that programmers are happy to allow some temporary violation of constraints within a transaction but require that the collection of operations that constitute the transaction leave the DB in a consistent state. That means the checking of constraints can be deferred until the end of the transaction.

The notion of when an active rule is evaluated relative to its triggering event is captured by *coupling modes*. The two most common coupling modes are *immediate* and *deferred*. When a rule with an immediate coupling mode is triggered, the triggering transaction is suspended, and the rule's condition and (if necessary) action are evaluated right away. If the immediate rule *r1* triggers another immediate rule *r2*, then the processing of *r1* is suspended until *r2* has been processed to completion. When a rule with a deferred coupling mode is triggered, it is added to a queue of triggered rules. The queue of triggered rules is processed at some later time, typically the end of the transaction. When deferred rules are being processed, if a deferred rule triggers an immediate rule, then the deferred rule is suspended and the immediate rule is processed to completion. If a deferred rule triggers a deferred rule, then the recently triggered rule is added to the queue, and the original rule continues to be processed.

In practice, systems differ in their support for coupling modes and in the ways they avoid problems such as that of the nondeterministic outcome of rule processing described for the salaries integrity constraint. Some systems avoid the problem by preventing rules from changing tables that are involved in the triggering process (e.g., this is the behavior supported in Oracle8).

3.4.4.2 How Multiple Event Occurrences Are Handled

In immediate rule processing, a rule is triggered as soon as a single event corresponding to the rule's event definition takes place. However, with deferred rule processing, multiple events may have taken place that match a single rule's condition before the rule is scheduled for processing. There are two ways in which that can be handled:

- Every time a deferred rule is triggered, a (*rule name, event instance*) pair is added to the queue of deferred rules waiting to be processed. When the rules come to be processed, there may be several entries in the queue corresponding to the same rule, and they are removed for processing one at a time. The information about the event that is passed to the rule is the information about a single event.

- Every time a deferred rule is triggered, a (*rule name, set of event instances*) pair is added to the queue of deferred rules that is waiting to be processed. When the rules come to be processed, there can be at most one entry in the queue corresponding to a single rule. When the rule is removed from the queue for processing, the information about the event that is passed to the rule is the description of the complete set of events.

When a rule is evaluated in the context of a single event instance, it is said to have a *transition granularity* of *tuple*. When a rule is evaluated in the context of a collection of triggering event instances, it is said to have a *transition granularity* of *set*.

3.5 Implementation Issues

Now that the basic structural and behavioral features of active rules have been introduced, it is possible to look at how rules are supported in concrete systems. Most of the systems follow an event-condition-action approach for the description of triggers. However, variations can be found in the following aspects:

- *Language expressiveness.* Rule systems differ in the range of things that can be said within the event definition, condition, and action of a rule.

- *Information passing.* It is common for one part of a rule to need access to information from another part. In particular, information about the event is often central to the definitions of conditions and actions. Event information is accessed in the above examples using *new* and *old.* Values for both *new* and *old* are available in rules monitoring update events, while only *new* is defined for *insert* events, and only *old* is defined for *delete* events.

- *Execution model.* How rules are handled at execution time is far from straightforward. Indeed, whereas most systems follow an event-condition-action approach to rule description, there is a great diversity on how rules are treated at run time.

This section addresses the support for active rules in Oracle8, describes how the Oracle8 rule system can be applied to the example application from Section 3.2, and addresses the relationship between the Oracle rule language and the emerging SQL: 1999 industry standard.

3.5.1 Active Rules in Oracle

This section describes the Oracle active rule language, illustrating its features using examples based on the application from Section 3.2.

The following is a simple example of an Oracle active rule, which, every time someone from a computing company registers, stores in the *enrollment* table a tuple to indicate that the new attendee takes the course *CS0*. This is an example of a causal business policy.

```
create or replace trigger addCS0
after insert on attendee
for each row
when (new.company = 'Computing')
begin
    insert into enrollment values
    (:new.a#, 'CS0', NULL);
end;
```

This command uses a significant range of features of the Oracle rule language:

1. Active rules are known as *triggers* in Oracle, and every trigger has a name (in this case, *addCS0*).
2. The event is declared using the same syntax as in Section 3.4.1. Events can monitor *insert*, *delete*, or *update* operations on tables. Stored procedure invocations cannot be monitored by event definitions.
3. The *for each row* clause indicates that this is a trigger with *tuple-level transition granularity* that has an *immediate coupling mode*.
4. The condition is declared in the *when* clause. The condition is a boolean expression—it is not possible to embed complete SQL queries in the *when* clause. The condition can refer to values associated with the event using *old* and/or *new*. If an action contains functionality, the execution of which needs to be conditional on information stored in the DB, the conditionality needs to be captured in the action itself.

5. The action of an Oracle trigger is a PL/SQL block. PL/SQL is the programming language extension of SQL provided with Oracle. PL/SQL blocks are delimited by *begin* and *end*. In this case, the only statement in the block inserts a new tuple into the *enrollment* table. The action can refer to values associated with the event using *:old* and *:new*.

The above example is known as a *row trigger* because of the tuple-level transition granularity. The other form of trigger is known as a *statement trigger* because the rule is triggered once in response to an SQL modification statement (i.e., *insert, delete, update*). A statement trigger can thus be seen as having set level transition granularity, because a single modification statement may modify several tuples. However, the trigger is processed as soon as the statement that triggered it starts (for *before* events) or finishes (for *after* events), rather than at some point less strongly linked to the triggering operation.

The following is an example of a statement trigger that blocks attempts to update the enrollment table at weekends:

```
create or replace trigger weekends
before delete or insert or update on enrollment
declare
    not_at_weekends exception;
begin
    if (to_char(sysdate,'DY') = 'SAT' or
    to_char(sysdate,'DY') = 'SUN') then
        raise not_at_weekends;
    end if;
exception
    when not_at_weekends
    then raise_application_error(-20225,
    'Cannot change grade at weekends');
end;
```

This command also illustrates a range of features:

1. The event definition in this case is a *before* event, which means that the rule is processed (immediately) before the operation that has triggered the rule is executed.

2. The event definition is *composite*. Before this, every event definition shown has been *primitive*—it has had a single component. The event definition for this rule is composite, because the complete definition has several parts linked using *or*. This rule is triggered by events of any of the types named in the event definition. The only composite event construction operator in Oracle is *or*.

3. There is no *for each row* clause, which indicates that it is a *statement trigger*.

4. There is no *when* clause because the *when* clause is not supported for statement triggers.

5. The *declare* clause introduces variables local to the adjacent PL/SQL block.

6. The action responds to the attempt to update the *enrollment* table at the weekend by raising an exception, which has the effect of rolling back the triggering statement.

A further characteristic of statement triggers is that there is no access from statement triggers to event information using *new* or *old*. One reason for that is that *new* and *old* only provide a way of obtaining information about a single event, and statement triggers may be responding to multiple events. Proposals have been made that allow triggers with set transition granularities to access information about their events using transition tables [6], but such facilities are not provided in Oracle.[1]

3.5.2 Active Rules in Use

This section shows how active behavior can be supported using the Oracle rule system. Examples have been given of the use of rules for both integrity maintenance and authorization. This section deals with auditing and view maintenance.

3.5.2.1 Auditing

DB systems often come with some mechanism for monitoring changes made to the DB. However, the facilities provided, like those for integrity maintenance, are limited in their scope and are not programmable in the way that

---

1. Other DBMSs, such as SQL-Server, provide a set of temporal tables (inserted, deleted) that hold the whole set of tuples affected during the statement.

triggers are. The following is a simple example of how triggers can be used for auditing. The table *enrollment_log* is used to store modifications to the enrollment table:

```
create table enrollment_log (
     who   varchar(20)  not null,
     when  date  not null,
     theAttendee varchar(5)  not null,
     theCoursevarchar(5)  not null,
     old_grade  number,
     new_grade  number);
```

```
create or replace trigger enrollment_log
after insert or update on enrollment
for each row
begin
     if inserting then
          insert into enrollment_log values
(USER,SYSDATE,:new.theAttendee,:new.theCourse,
NULL,:new.grade);
     else /* updating */
          insert into enrollment_log values
          (USER,SYSDATE,:new.theAttendee,:new.the
          Course,:old.grade,:new.grade);
     end if;
end;
```

This trigger uses a number of facilities not shown before. The rule's action is able to test for the sort of event that is being monitored using *inserting,* which is true if the event that triggered the rule was an insert (analogous facilities exist for delete and update events). The values for the variables USER and SYSDATE are updated automatically by the system for use in PL/SQL programs. They provide the user name of the current user and the date/time, respectively.

3.5.2.2 View Materialization

A view is a table, the contents of which are computed from values already stored in the DB. For example, the following is an SQL view definition:

```
create view maximums as
select theCourse, max(grade) as maximum
from enrollment
group by theCourse;
```

The view *maximums* associates the *theCourse* of any course with the maximum grade of any student taking the course.

A materialized view is a view for which the computed value of the view is stored in the DB. It can be beneficial to materialize a view if it is used regularly and is expensive to compute. The following trigger could be used to materialize the view in the table *maximums*:

```
create table maximums (
    theCourse  varchar(5)  not null,
    maxval  number);

create or replace trigger materialize1
after delete or insert or update of grade on
enrollment
begin
    delete from maximums;
    insert into maximums
        select theCourse, max(grade)
        from enrollment
        group by theCourse;
end;
```

This statement-level trigger materializes the view by recomputing the view every time the table *enrollment* is modified, which gives the anticipated functionality but is likely to be quite inefficient. That is because most statements that modify *enrollment* will make only a few changes to the table and thus are likely to imply few, if any, changes to the materialized view. Despite that, the view is recomputed whenever *enrollment* is modified.

A better solution would be to support incremental maintenance of the view. That involves propagating individual updates on the underlying enrollment table to the materialized view as soon as the update takes place. For example, the following rule handles the insertion of new data into *enrollment*:

```
create or replace trigger materialize2
after insert on enrollment
for each row
declare
    themax number;
begin
    select maxval into themax
    from maximums
    where theCourse = :new.theCourse;

    if (:new.grade > themax) then
        update maximums
        set maxval = :new.grade
        where theCourse = :new.theCourse;
    end if;
exception
        when NO_DATA_FOUND
        then insert into maximums values
        (:new.theCourse, :new.grade);
end;
```

This rule is triggered by updates on *enrollment* such as *insert into enrollment values ('S4', 'CS1', 66)*. The rule must allow for two circumstances when handling this update:

1. There is already a tuple in *maximums* for the course with *c#* equal to *CS1*. If there is, and *66* is greater than the previous maximum grade on *CS1*, then the tuple for *CS1* in maximums must be updated. This functionality is handled in the trigger by retrieving the current value for the maximum grade into *themax* and then comparing *themax* with *:new.grade*.

2. There is no tuple in *maximums* for the course with *c#* equal to *CS1*. This functionality is handled in the trigger using the exception mechanism. If there is no tuple for *CS1* in *maximums*, then a *NO_DATA_FOUND* exception will be raised when the trigger tries to obtain a value for *themax*. This exception is trapped by the exception clause, which responds by inserting a new tuple into *maximums* based on the newly inserted values.

Performing incremental view maintenance for *update* and *delete* is not so straightforward. Row triggers handling those operations may have to read from the enrollment table to compute values for use in *maximums*, but that is illegal in Oracle, because accessing the *enrollment* table while that table is being modified leads to nondeterministic results of the form outlined in Section 3.4.4.1. That leaves the user with two options: (1) using a statement trigger to recompute *maximums* for deletes and updates or (2) storing information about the changes to *enrollment* temporarily in a table using a *row trigger* for subsequent processing using a *statement trigger*.

It thus can be seen that triggers do provide support for incremental materialized view maintenance, but that for some views this is quite involved, requiring careful construction of the relevant triggers.

3.5.3 Standardizing Active Behavior in SQL: 1999

Most of the principal relational DB vendors include active features in their products. For a survey, see [7]. However, although these generally are quite similar in their facilities and syntax, it is certainly not the case that rules written for one product are likely to run on another. To address that problem, triggers are included as part of the SQL: 1999 standard [8]. The principal differences between the SQL: 1999 triggers and Oracle triggers are as follows:

1. SQL: 1999 triggers allow SQL queries in rule conditions, whereas Oracle only allows boolean expressions.

2. SQL: 1999 statement triggers are able to access information about events by accessing *OLD_TABLE* and *NEW_TABLE* transition tables, which capture the state of the tuples affected by the triggering statement before and after the execution of the statement.

3. The execution model of SQL: 1999 has been designed to reduce the risks of nondeterministic behavior resulting from rule processing. In Oracle, nondeterminism is avoided by strict run-time monitoring; in SQL: 1999 the interleaving of updates with trigger processing has been reduced by slightly deferring processing of row triggers.

The syntax of triggers in SQL: 1999 is similar to that in Oracle.

3.6 Rule Maintenance

Once in use, the rule set may need to be changed for different reasons: to overcome a failure to realize user requirements (*corrective maintenance*); to enhance system tuning but without affecting its basic functionality; and to evolve requirements leading to a change in the system's underlying functionality (*adaptive maintenance*) [9]. At a first glance, explicit capturing of business policies through triggers will certainly help the maintenance of corporate regulations in the DB system. Triggers support chunks of expertise that are self-contained, isolated units that can be enlarged, removed, or updated more easily than when they were previously coded in application programs. However, that is not the end of the story.

Maintenance of large rule sets can be difficult, and ascertaining the effects of rule removal or addition is far from straightforward. It is the insidious ways in which rules can interact that makes addition or removal of a single rule whose code looks perfectly satisfactory such a complicated task. A previously correct rule set can stop enjoying this property after addition or removal of a rule. Evolution-support tools are required to ease migration and to determine the impact of additions and deletions.

To illustrate the difficulty of writing correct triggers, consider a policy whereby when an employee who is teaching a course moves to the next level, all his or her students should be moved accordingly. On the assumption that only one class at each level can be under way, a first attempt to support this policy can lead to the following trigger:

```
create or replace trigger levelChange
after update of level on employee
for each row
begin
    update enrollment
    set level = :new.level
    where theCourse = 'Computing' and level =
    :old.level
end;
```

If we look carefully at how that rule behaves at run time, we will realize that the behavior is not as expected. Let's consider that

John follows course 'Computing', level 1, taught by Employee1

Anne follows course 'Computing', level 2, taught by Employee2

Employee1 teaches course 'Computing', level 1

Employee2 teaches course 'Computing', level 2

Computing courses last for a week, so at the end of the week, the next instruction is issued:

```
update employee
set level = level + 1
where teaches = 'Computing';
```

Once *employee1* is updated, the row trigger fires, updating the level of *John* to *2*. The next employee to be updated is *employee2*. The trigger is fired again and updates all tuples in enrollment whose level is *2*. However, now not only is *Anne* following level *2*, but so is *John* after the previous update. That will lead to both *Anne* and *John* being moved to level *3*. Even worse, the final result will depend on the order in which tuples are arranged in the table! If *Anne* were taken first, *John* would not have been upgraded yet, and so the final result would look correct.

As this example points out, it is necessary to be extremely careful when writing triggers. Unfortunately, few tools are available to help designers debug, trace, and maintain triggers. The only functionality available in current systems is the possibility to temporarily deactivate a trigger: A trigger can be tracked alone without other triggers being fired simultaneously. However, the difficulty of the task lies not in debugging a single trigger but in understanding how a set of triggers influences the final behavior.

3.7 Summary

Active DBs extend the behavior representation facilities of a DB system with mechanisms that support reactive behavior. This reactive behavior can be used to implement a range of different functionalities, including business rules, integrity constraints, auditing, and view materialization.

Active extensions to DBs provide implementation mechanisms that are not supported in conventional DB schema design frameworks. The identification of reactive aspects of an application may imply the use of more comprehensive modeling facilities, as well as changes in the way that DB designers work. This chapter identified two different kinds of business policy that can be supported using reactive facilities, namely, recovering business policies and causal business policies. It also showed how examples of such policies can be captured in advanced modeling methods for DB design.

The identification of reactive functionality in applications is by no means the end of the story. The implementation of reactive behavior as active DB rules is itself a skilled task, because rules may interact with each other in unanticipated ways, and the semantics of rule evaluation systems is often difficult to understand fully. However, active facilities are now supported in most commercial relational DB systems, and this chapter gave examples of how the Oracle trigger system can handle a range of different kinds of functionality. Active rule systems provide a coherent framework for the expression of behavioral requirements that would be difficult to capture in their absence. However, although active rules provide powerful, self-contained behavioral units, their presence in a broader context in which there can be many complex responses taking place to the same event means that developing and maintaining a large rule base must be approached with care.

References

[1]   Mullins, R. S., "The Procedural DBA," *J. Database Programming & Design,* Vol. 8, No. 12, 1995, pp. 40–45.

[2]   Moriarty, T., "A Businessperson's Perspective," *J. Database Programing & Design,* Vol. 1, No. 8, 1998, pp. 40–45.

[3]   Ruble, D. A., *Practical Analysis and Design for Client/Server and GUI Systems,* Yourdon Press Computing Series, Upper Saddle River, NJ: Prentice-Hall, 1997.

[4]   Tanaka, A. K., et al., "ER-R: An Enhanced ER Model With Situation-Action Rules To Capture Application Semantics," *Proc. 10th Intl. Conf. on Entity Relationship Approach,* 1991, pp. 59–75.

[5]   Díaz, O., J. Iturrioz, and M. G. Piattini, "Promoting Business Rules in Object-Oriented Methods," *J. Systems and Software,* Vol. 41, No. 2, 1998, pp. 105–115.

[6]   Widom, J., and S. J. Finkelstein, "Set-Oriented Production Rules in Relational Database Systems," *Proc. ACM SIGMOD,* 1990, pp. 259–270.

[7]   Widom, J., and S. Ceri (eds.), *Active Database Systems,* San Francisco, CA: Morgan Kaufmann, 1996.

[8]   Fortier, S., *SQL3: Implementing the SQL Foundation Standards,* New York: McGraw-Hill, 1999.

[9]   Lientz, B., E. B. Swanson, and G. E. Tompkins, "Characteristics of Applications Software Maintenance," *Comm. ACM,* Vol. 21, 1978, pp. 466–471.

Selected Bibliography

Paton, N., and O. Díaz, "Active Database Systems," *ACM Computing Surveys*, Vol. 31, No. 1, 1999, pp. 63–103.

This article provides an in-depth view of distinct topics currently being investigated in the area of active DBMSs. It examines several research prototypes that address open problems in the area and describes triggers in SQL: 1999.

Ceri, S., and P. Fraternalli, *Designing Database Applications With Objects and Rules*, Reading, MA: Addison-Wesley, 1997.

This book covers several stages during DB application development (analysis, design, and implementation) where an object-oriented approach is followed. Examples are given using Chimera, a conceptual model and language for active DBMSs developed by the authors. This book also describes a tool environment that assists in the use of Chimera in the design of active DB application.

Owens, K. T., *Building Intelligent Databases With Oracle PL/SQL, Triggers, and Stored Procedures*, 2nd ed., Upper Saddle River, NJ: Prentice-Hall, 1998.

This book provides real examples of the complexity of handling triggers in a commercial system such as Oracle and the combined use of triggers and stored procedures. An interesting trigger methodology is presented that is biased toward Oracle.

4

Deductive Databases

Ernest Teniente

4.1 Introduction

Database technology has evolved quickly since the first DBMS appeared around 1960. Nowadays, DBMSs play an important role in the ISs in manufacturing, banking, and public administration, among other industries. A common feature of all the systems is their ability to manage large volumes of data, although they usually perform simple operations to manipulate the data.

On the other hand, and parallel to the development of DBMSs, expert systems were developed to support the process of decision-making within narrow domains in particular contexts. The main feature of these systems is to provide reasoning capabilities to help decision-making, but they usually are not able to manage large volumes of information. Figure 4.1 illustrates the parallel evolution of DBs and expert systems and states their main features.

Deductive DBs were proposed as an attempt to overcome the limitations of traditional DB systems by incorporating, somehow, the distinguishing features provided by expert systems. Therefore, deductive DBs could be seen as an integration of *data* (as in a DBMS) and *knowledge* (as in an expert system).

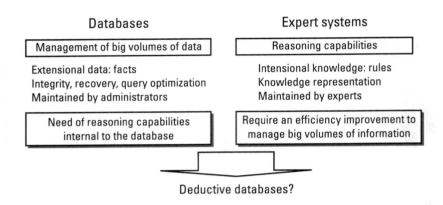

Figure 4.1 Parallel evolution of DBs and expert systems.

Data are represented by means of extensions of DB predicates (i.e., facts), while knowledge is represented by the intension of DB predicates. Knowledge, or intensional information, is defined by means of rules that allow us to deduce new information from that explicitly stored in the DB. Two kinds of rules are usually considered: *deductive rules*, which allow us to define new facts (view or derived facts) from stored facts, and *integrity constraints*, which state conditions to be satisfied by the DB.

Deductive DBs are able to manage most of the current applications, being specially suited for those applications that are characterized by the need to perform more complex manipulations on the data rather than just querying or updating base facts [1]. Deductive rules and integrity constraints, together with reasoning capabilities, ease the sharing of common knowledge within more complex application domains, thus facilitating knowledge reusability.

Deductive DBs also can be understood as the result of the application of logic (and artificial intelligence (AI) aspects) in the traditional DB field since they use Datalog, a language derived from logic programming, as a representation language, to define the contents and the structure of the information stored in the DB. Datalog is a declarative, nonprocedural language, uniform and set oriented. The impact of logic in deductive DBs is widely discussed in [2, 3].

From a historical perspective, deductive DBs can be seen as extensions of the relational ones as well, mainly because the expressive power of their data definition language is greater than that of relational DBs. This important issue is not so clear at the present moment and will deserve further discussion in Section 4.2.

In fact, it has been shown how relational DBs can be seen as special theories of first-order logic [4]. Thus, they could be interpreted as deductive DBs. By carrying out this "logical reconstruction," it is possible to formally validate query evaluation or update processing algorithms, which is hard to address in the context of relational DBs.

This chapter provides an overview of the main features of deductive DBs and illustrates the main problems encountered when dealing with intensional information. Our presentation is based on giving an intuitive idea of those problems and providing several examples. For that reason, we sometimes omit certain details that are not possible to cover without a more formal explanation. There are various places where these details can be found. Several books are devoted, entirely or in part, to deductive DBs [1, 5–15]. We also provide references to relevant papers when presenting problems not sufficiently addressed by those books.

Section 4.2 defines basic concepts of deductive DBs and compares them to relational DBs. Section 4.3 presents the main approaches to query processing. Section 4.4 describes the main problems present in update processing and the main achievements in this area. Section 4.5 examines the main functionalities provided by existing prototypes of deductive DBs.

4.2 Basic Concepts of Deductive Databases

This section presents the basic notions needed to understand the problems behind deductive DBs. More precisely, it provides a formal definition of deductive DBs, a brief overview of their semantics, a discussion of the advantages provided by the intensional information and a comparison of the expressive powers of relational and deductive DBs. The language used to define deductive DBs is usually called Datalog. For that reason, deductive DBs are sometimes known as Datalog programs.

4.2.1 Definition of a Deductive Database

A deductive DB consists of three finite sets: a set of facts, a set of deductive rules, and a set of integrity constraints. Facts state basic information that is known to be true in the DB. Deductive rules allow the derivation of new facts from other facts stored in the DB. Integrity constraints correspond to conditions that each state of the DB should satisfy.

To formally define those concepts, we need to introduce the following terminology. A *term* is either a variable or a constant. If P is a predicate symbol and $t_1, \ldots, t_n$ are terms, then $P(t_1, \ldots, t_n)$ is an *atom*. The atom is *ground* if all terms t_i are constants. A *literal* is either an atom or a negated atom.

Facts, deductive rules, and integrity constraints are represented as clauses of the general form:

$$A_0 \leftarrow L_1 \wedge \ldots \wedge L_n \quad \text{with } n \geq 0$$

where A_0 is an atom denoting the *conclusion* and each L_i is a literal, representing a *condition*. A_0 is called the *head* and $L_1 \wedge \ldots \wedge L_n$ the *body*. Variables in the conclusion and in the conditions are assumed as universally quantified over the whole formula. For that reason, quantifiers are always omitted.

Facts are represented by means of clauses with an empty body, that is, atoms. For instance, a fact stating that Mary is the mother of Bob would be represented as Mother(Mary, Bob). A deductive DB contains only ground facts.

Deductive rules define intensional information, that is, information that is not explicitly stored in the DB. That intensional information is gathered by means of facts about derived predicates. The definition of a derived predicate P is the set of all deductive rules that have P in their head. For example, the rules "if x is the mother of y, then x is a parent of y" and "if x is the father of y, then x is a parent of y" define the derived predicate Parent(x,y), which corresponds to the classical notion of parent. That can be represented as:

$$\text{Parent}(x,y) \leftarrow \text{Mother}(x,y)$$
$$\text{Parent}(x,y) \leftarrow \text{Father}(x,y)$$

Integrity constraints are usually represented by means of clauses with an empty head, also called *denials*. A denial has the following form:

$$\leftarrow L_1 \wedge \ldots \wedge L_n \quad \text{with } n \geq 1$$

and states that $L_1 \wedge \ldots \wedge L_n$ may never hold in a DB containing that integrity constraint. Representation by denials entails no loss of generality because any integrity constraint expressed as a general first-order formula can be transformed into an equivalent set of clauses containing, at least, an integrity constraint in denial form [16].

For the sake of uniformity, the head of each integrity constraint usually contains an inconsistency predicate ICn, which is just a possible name given to that constraint. This is useful for information purposes because ICn allows the identification of the constraint to which it refers. If a fact ICi is true in a certain DB state, then the corresponding integrity constraint is violated in that state. For instance, an integrity constraint stating that nobody may be father and mother at the same time could be represented as *IC2* ← Parent(x,y) ∧ Mother(x,z).

A deductive DB D is a triple $D = (F, DR, IC)$, where F is a finite set of ground facts, DR a finite set of deductive rules, and IC a finite set of integrity constraints. The set F of facts is called the extensional part of the DB (EDB), and the sets DR and IC together form the so-called intensional part (IDB).

Database predicates are traditionally partitioned into base and derived predicates, also called *views*. A base predicate appears in the EDB and, possibly, in the body of deductive rules and integrity constraints. A derived (or view) predicate appears only in the IDB and is defined by means of some deductive rule. In other words, facts about derived predicates are not explicitly stored in the DB and can only be derived by means of deductive rules. Every deductive DB can be defined in this form [17].

Example 4.1

This example is of a deductive DB describing familiar relationships.

Facts

Father(John, Tony)   Mother(Mary, Bob)
Father(Peter, Mary)

Deductive Rules

Parent(x,y) ← Father(x,y)
Parent(x,y) ← Mother(x,y)
GrandMother(x,y) ← Mother(x,z) ∧ Parent(z,y)
Ancestor(x,y) ← Parent(x,y)
Ancestor(x,y) ← Parent(x,z) ∧ Ancestor(z,y)
Nondirect-anc(x,y) ← Ancestor(x,y) ∧ ¬Parent(x,y)

Integrity Constraints

IC1(x) ← Parent(x,x)
IC2(x) ← Father(x,y) ∧ Mother(x,z)

The deductive DB in this example contains three facts stating extensional data about *fathers* and *mothers*, six deductive rules defining the intensional notions of *parent*, *grandmother*, and *ancestor*, with their meaning being hopefully self-explanatory, and *nondirect-anc*, which defines nondirect ancestors as those ancestors that do not report a direct parent relationship. Two integrity constraints state that nobody can be the parent of himself or herself and that nobody can be father and mother at the same time.

Note that inconsistency predicates may also contain variables that allow the identification of the individuals that violate a certain integrity constraint. For instance, the evaluation of IC2(x) would give as a result the different values of x that violate that constraint.

4.2.2   Semantics of Deductive Databases

A semantic is required to define the information that holds true in a particular deductive DB. This is needed, for instance, to be able to answer queries requested on that DB. In the absence of negative literals in the body of deductive rules, the semantics of a deductive DB can be defined as follows [18].

An *interpretation*, in the context of deductive DBs, consists of an assignment of a concrete meaning to constant and predicate symbols. A certain clause can be interpreted in several different ways, and it may be true under a given interpretation and false under another. If a clause C is true under an interpretation, we say that the interpretation satisfies C. A fact F follows from a set S of clauses; each interpretation satisfying every clause of S also satisfies F.

The Herbrand base (HB) is the set of all facts that can be expressed in the language of a deductive DB, that is, all facts of the form $P(c_1, \ldots, c_n)$ such that all c_i are constants. A *Herbrand interpretation* is a subset ϑ of HB that contains all ground facts that are true under this interpretation. A ground fact $P(c_1, \ldots, c_n)$ is true under the interpretation ϑ if $P(c_1, \ldots, c_n) \in \vartheta$. A rule of the form $A_0 \leftarrow L_1 \wedge \ldots \wedge L_n$ is true under ϑ if for each substitution θ that replaces variables by constants, whenever $L_1 \theta \in \vartheta \wedge \ldots \wedge L_n \theta \in \vartheta$, then it also holds that $A_0 \theta \in \vartheta$.

A Herbrand interpretation that satisfies a set S of clauses is called a Herbrand model of S. The least Herbrand model of S is the intersection of all possible Herbrand models of S. Intuitively, it contains the smaller set of facts required to satisfy S. The least Herbrand model of a deductive DB D defines exactly the facts that are satisfied by D.

For instance, it is not difficult to see that the Herbrand interpretation {Father(John,Tony), Father(Peter,Mary), Mother(Mary,Bob), Parent(John,

Tony)} is not a Herbrand model of the DB in Example 4.1. Instead, the interpretation {Father(John,Tony), Father(Peter,Mary), Mother(Mary,Bob), Parent(John,Tony), Parent(Peter,Mary), Parent(Mary,Bob), Ancestor(John, Tony), Ancestor(Peter,Mary), Ancestor(Mary,Bob), Ancestor(Peter,Bob)} is a Herbrand model. In particular, it is the least Herbrand model of that DB.

Several problems arise if semantics of deductive DBs are extended to try to care for negative information. In the presence of negative literals, the semantics are given by means of the *closed world assumption* (CWA) [19], which considers as false all information that cannot be proved to be true. For instance, given a fact $R(a)$, the CWA would conclude that $\neg R(a)$ is true if $R(a)$ does not belong to the EDB and if it is not derived by means of any deductive rule, that is, if $R(a)$ is not satisfied by the clauses in the deductive DB.

This poses a first problem regarding negation. Given a predicate $Q(x)$, there is a finite number of values x for which $Q(x)$ is true. However, that is not the case for negative literals, where infinite values may exist. For instance, values x for which $\neg Q(x)$ is true will be all possible values of x except those for which $Q(x)$ is true.

To ensure that negative information can be fully instantiated before being evaluated and, thus, to guarantee that only a finite set of values is considered for negative literals, deductive DBs are restricted to be *allowed*. That is, any variable that occurs in a deductive rule or in an integrity constraint has an occurrence in a positive literal of that rule. For example, the rule $P(x) \leftarrow Q(x) \wedge \neg R(x)$ is allowed, while $P(x) \leftarrow S(x) \wedge \neg T(x,y)$ is not. Nonallowed rules can be transformed into allowed ones as described in [16]. For instance, the last rule is equivalent to this set of allowed rules: {$P(x) \leftarrow S(x) \wedge \neg aux\text{-}T(x)$, $aux\text{-}T(x) \leftarrow T(x,y)$}.

To define the semantics of deductive DBs with negation, the Herbrand interpretation must be generalized to be applicable also to negative literals. Now, given a Herbrand interpretation ϑ, a positive fact F will be satisfied in ϑ if $F \in \vartheta$, while a negative fact will be satisfied in ϑ if $\neg F \notin \vartheta$. The notion of Herbrand model is defined as before.

Another important problem related to the semantics of negation is that a deductive DB may, in general, allow several different interpretations. As an example, consider this DB:

$R(a)$

$P(x) \leftarrow R(x) \wedge \neg Q(x)$

$Q(x) \leftarrow R(x) \wedge \neg P(x)$

This DB allows to consider as true either {$R(a)$, $Q(a)$} or {$R(a)$, $P(a)$}. $R(a)$ is always true because it belongs to the EDB, while $P(a)$ or $Q(a)$ is true depending on the truth value of the other. Therefore, it is not possible to agree on unique semantics for this DB.

To avoid that problem, deductive DBs usually are restricted to being *stratified.* A deductive DB is stratified if derived predicates can be assigned to different strata in such a way that a derived predicate that appears negatively on the body of some rule can be computed by the use of only predicates in lower strata. Stratification allows the definition of recursive predicates, but it restricts the way negation appears in those predicates. Roughly, semantics of stratified DBs are provided by the application of CWA strata by strata [14]. Given a stratified deductive DB D, the evaluation strata by strata always produces a minimal Herbrand model of D [20].

For instance, the preceding example is not stratifiable, while the DB of Example 4.1 is stratifiable, with this possible stratification: S_1 = {Father, Mother, Parent, GrandMother, Ancestor} and S_2 = {Nondirect-anc}.

Determining whether a deductive DB is stratifiable is a decidable problem and can be performed in polynomial time [6]. In general, several stratifications may exist. However, all possible stratifications of a deductive DB are equivalent because they yield the same semantics [5].

A deeper discussion of the implications of possible semantics of deductive DBs can be found in almost all books explaining deductive DBs (see, for instance, [5, 6, 8, 9, 11, 14]). Semantics for negation (stratified or not) is discussed in depth in [5, 21]. Several procedures for computing the least Herbrand model of a deductive DB are also described in those references. We will describe the main features of these procedures when dealing with query evaluation in Section 4.3.

4.2.3   Advantages Provided by Views and Integrity Constraints

The concept of *view* is used in DBs to delimit the DB content relevant to each group of users. A view is a virtual data structure, derived from base facts or other views by means of a definition function. Therefore, the extension of a view does not have an independent existence because it is completely defined by the application of the definition function to the extension of the DB. In deductive DBs, views correspond to derived predicates and are defined by means of deductive rules. Views provide the following advantages.

- Views simplify the user interface, because users can ignore the data that are not relevant to them. For instance, the view

GrandMother(x,y) in Example 4.1 provides only information about the grandmother x and the grandson or granddaughter y. However, the information about the parent of y is hidden by the view definition.

- Views favor logical data independence, because they allow changing the logical data structure of the DB without having to perform corresponding changes to other rules. For instance, assume that the base predicate Father(x,y) must be replaced by two different predicates Father1(x,y) and Father2(x,y), each of which contains a subset of the occurrences of Father(x,y). In this case, if we consider Father(x,y) as a view predicate and define it as

$$\text{Father}(x,y) \leftarrow \text{Father1}(x,y)$$
$$\text{Father}(x,y) \leftarrow \text{Father2}(x,y)$$

we do not need to change the rules that refer to the original base predicate Father.

- Views make certain queries easier or more natural to define, since by means of them we can refer directly to the concepts instead of having to provide their definition. For instance, if we want to ask about the ancestors of Bob, we do not need to define what we mean by ancestor since we can use the view Ancestor to obtain the answers.

- Views provide a protection measure, because they prevent users from accessing data external to their view. Users authorized to access only GrandMother do not know the information about parents.

Real DB applications use many views. However, the power of views can be exploited only if a user does not distinguish a view from a base fact. That implies the need to perform query and update operations on the views, in addition to the same operations on the base facts.

Integrity constraints correspond to requirements to be satisfied by the DB. In that sense, they impose conditions on the allowable data in addition to the simple structure and type restrictions imposed by the basic schema definitions. Integrity constraints are useful, for instance, for caching data-entry errors, as a correctness criterion when writing DB updates, or to enforce consistency across data in the DB.

When an update is performed, some integrity constraint may be violated. That is, if applied, the update, together with the current content of the

DB, may falsify some integrity constraint. There are several possible ways of resolving such a conflict [22].

- Reject the update.
- Apply the update and make additional changes in the extensional DB to make it obey the integrity constraints.
- Apply the update and ignore the temporary inconsistency.
- Change the intensional part of the knowledge base (deductive rules and/or integrity constraints) so that violated constraints are satisfied.

All those policies may be reasonable, and the correct choice of a policy for a particular integrity constraint depends on the precise semantics of the constraint and of the DB.

Integrity constraints facilitate program development if the conditions they state are directly enforced by the DBMS, instead of being handled by external applications. Therefore, deductive DBMSs should also include some capability to deal with integrity constraints.

4.2.4   Deductive Versus Relational Databases

Deductive DBs appeared as an extension of the relational ones, since they made extensive use of intensional information in the form of views and integrity constraints. However, current relational DBs also allow defining views and constraints. So exactly what is the difference nowadays between a deductive DB and a relational one?

An important difference relies on the different data definition language (DDL) used: Datalog in deductive DBs or SQL [23] in most relational DBs. We do not want to raise here the discussion about which language is more natural or easier to use. That is a matter of taste and personal background. It is important, however, to clarify whether Datalog or SQL can define concepts that cannot be defined by the other language. This section compares the expressive power of Datalog, as defined in Section 4.2.1, with that of the SQL2 standard. We must note that, in the absence of recursive views, Datalog is known to be equivalent to relational algebra (see, for instance, [5, 7, 14]).

Base predicates in deductive DBs correspond to relations. Therefore, base facts correspond to tuples in relational DBs. In that way, it is not difficult to see the clear correspondence between the EDB of a deductive DB and the logical contents of a relational one.

Deductive DBs allow the definition of derived predicates, but SQL2 also allows the definition of views. For instance, predicate GrandMother in Example 4.1 could be defined in SQL2 as

```
CREATE VIEW grandmother AS
    SELECT mother.x, parent.y
    FROM mother, parent
    WHERE mother.z=parent.z
```

Negative literals appearing in deductive rules can be defined by means of the NOT EXISTS operator from SQL2. Moreover, views defined by more than one rule can be expressed by the UNION operator from SQL2.

SQL2 also allows the definition of integrity constraints, either at the level of table definition or as assertions representing conditions to be satisfied by the DB. For instance, the second integrity constraint in Example 4.1 could be defined as

```
CREATE ASSERTION ic2 CHECK
    (NOT EXISTS (
        SELECT father.x
        FROM father, mother
        WHERE father.x=mother.x ))
```

On the other hand, key and referential integrity constraints and exclusion dependencies, which are defined at the level of table definition in SQL2, can also be defined as inconsistency predicates in deductive DBs.

Although SQL2 can define views and constraints, it does not provide a mechanism to define recursive views. Thus, for instance, the derived predicate Ancestor could not be defined in SQL2. In contrast, Datalog is able to define recursive views, as we saw in Example 4.1. In fact, that is the main difference between the expressive power of Datalog and that of SQL2, a limitation to be overcome by SQL3, which will also allow the definition of recursive views by means of a Datalog-like language.

Commercial relational DBs do not yet provide the full expressive power of SQL2. That limitation probably will be overcome in the next few years; perhaps then commercial products will tend to provide SQL3. If that is achieved, there will be no significant difference between the expressive power of Datalog and that of commercial relational DBs.

Despite these minor differences, all problems studied so far in the context of deductive DBs have to be solved by commercial relational DBMSs since they also provide the ability to define (nonrecursive) views and constraints. In particular, problems related to query and update processing in the presence of views and integrity constraints will be always encountered, independently of the language used to define them. That is true for relational DBs and also for most kinds of DBs (like object-relational or object-oriented) that provide some mechanism for defining intensional information.

4.3 Query Processing

Deductive DBMSs must provide a query-processing system able to answer queries specified in terms of views as well as in terms of base predicates. The subject of query processing deals with finding answers to queries requested on a certain DB. A query evaluation procedure finds answers to queries according to the DB semantics.

In Datalog syntax, a query requested on a deductive DB has the form *?-W(x)*, where *x* is a vector of variables and constants, and *W(x)* is a conjunction of literals. The answer to the query is the set of instances of *x* such that *W(x)* is true according to the EDB and to the IDB. Following are several examples.

> *?- Ancestor(John, Mary)* returns true if John is ancestor of Mary and false otherwise.

> *?- Ancestor(John, x)* returns as a result all persons *x* that have John as ancestor.

> *?- Ancestor(y, Mary)* returns as a result all persons *y* that are ancestors of Mary.

> *?- Ancestor(y, Mary) ∧ Ancestor(y, Joe)* returns all common ancestors *y* of Mary and Joe.

Two basic approaches compute the answers of a query *Q:*

- *Bottom-up (forward chaining).* The query evaluation procedure starts from the base facts and applies all deductive rules until no new consequences can be deduced. The requested query is then evaluated against the whole set of deduced consequences, which is treated as if it was base information.

- *Top-down (backward chaining)*. The query evaluation procedure starts from a query Q and applies deductive rules backward by trying to deduce new conditions required to make Q true. The conditions are expressed in terms of predicates that define Q, and they can be understood as simple subqueries that, appropriately combined, provide the same answers as Q. The process is repeated until conditions only in terms of base facts are achieved.

Sections 4.3.1 and 4.3.2 present a query evaluation procedure that follows each approach and comments on the advantages and drawbacks. Section 4.3.3 explains magic sets, which is a mixed approach aimed at achieving the advantages of the other two procedures. We present the main ideas of each approach, illustrate them by means of an example, and then discuss their main contributions. A more exhaustive explanation of previous work in query processing and several optimization techniques behind each approach can be found in most books on deductive DBs (see, for instance, [1, 8, 9, 24]).

The following example will be used to illustrate the differences among the three basic approaches.

Example 4.2

Consider a subset of the rules in Example 4.1, with some additional facts:

Father(Anthony, John)   Mother(Susan, Anthony)

Father(Anthony, Mary)   Mother(Susan, Rose)

Father(Jack, Anthony)   Mother(Rose, Jennifer)

Father(Jack, Rose)   Mother(Jennifer, Monica)

Parent(x,y) ← Father(x,y)   (rule R1)

Parent(x,y) ← Mother(x,y)   (rule R2)

GrandMother(x,y) ← Mother(x,z) ∧ Parent(z,y)   (rule R3)

4.3.1 Bottom-Up Query Evaluation

The naive procedure for evaluating queries bottom-up consists of two steps. The first step is aimed at computing all facts that are a logical consequence of the deductive rules, that is, to obtain the minimal Herbrand model of the deductive DB. That is achieved by iteratively considering each deductive rule until no more facts are deduced. In the second step, the query is solved against the set of facts computed by the first step, since that set contains all the information deducible from the DB.

Example 4.3

A bottom-up approach would proceed as follows to answer the query *?-GrandMother(x, Mary)*, that is, to obtain all grandmothers *x* of *Mary*:

1. All the information that can be deduced from the DB in Example 4.2 is computed by the following iterations:

    a. Iteration 0: All base facts are deduced.

    b. Iteration 1: Applying rule R1 to the result of iteration 0, we get

       Parent(Anthony, John)   Parent(Jack, Anthony)

       Parent(Anthony, Mary)   Parent(Jack, Rose)

    c. Iteration 2: Applying rule R2 to the results of iterations 0 and 1, we also get

       Parent(Susan, Anthony)   Parent(Rose, Jennifer)

       Parent(Susan, Rose)   Parent(Jennifer, Monica)

    d. Iteration 3: Applying rule R3 to the results of iterations 0 to 2, we further get

       GrandMother(Rose, Monica)   GrandMother(Susan, Mary)

       GrandMother(Susan, Jennifer) GrandMother(Susan, John)

    e. Iteration 4: The first step is over since no more new consequences are deduced when rules R1, R2, and R3 are applied to the result of previous iterations.

2. The query *?-GrandMother(x, Mary)* is applied against the set containing the 20 facts deduced during iterations 1 to 4. Because the fact GrandMother(Susan, Mary) belongs to this set, the obtained result is *x* = Susan, which means that Susan is the only grandmother of Mary known by the DB.

    Bottom-up methods can naturally be applied in a set-oriented fashion, that is, by taking as input the entire extensions of DB predicates. Despite this important feature, bottom-up query evaluation presents several drawbacks.

   - *It deduces consequences that are not relevant to the requested query.* In the preceding example, the procedure has computed several data about parents and grandmothers that are not needed to compute the query, for instance, Parent(Jennifer, Monica), Parent(Rose, Jennifer), Parent(Jack, Anthony), or GrandMother (Susan, Jennifer).

- *The order of selection of rules is relevant to evaluate queries efficiently.* Computing the answers to a certain query must be performed as efficiently as possible. In that sense, the order of taking rules into account during query processing is important for achieving maximum efficiency. For instance, if we had considered rule R3 instead of rule R1 in the first iteration of the previous example, no consequence would have been derived, and R3 should have been applied again after R1.

- *Computing negative information must be performed stratifiedly.* Negative information is handled by means of the CWA, which assumes as false all information that cannot be shown to be true. Therefore, if negative derived predicates appear in the body of deductive rules, we must first apply the rules that define those predicates to ensure that the CWA is applied successfully. That is, the computation must be performed strata by strata.

4.3.2 Top-Down Query Evaluation

Given a certain query Q, the naive procedure to evaluate Q top-down is aimed at obtaining a set of subqueries Q_i such that Q's answer is just the union of the answers of each subquery Q_i. To obtain those subqueries, each derived predicate P in Q must be replaced by the body of the deductive rules that define P. Because we only replace predicates in Q by their definition, the evaluation of the resulting queries is equivalent to the evaluation of Q, when appropriately combined. Therefore, the obtained subqueries are "simpler," in some sense, because they are defined by predicates "closer" to the base predicates.

Substituting queries by subqueries is repeated several times until we get queries that contain only base predicates. When those queries are reached, they are evaluated against the EDB to provide the desired result. Constants of the initial query Q are used during the process because they point out to the base facts that are relevant to the computation.

Example 4.4

The top-down approach to compute *?-GrandMother(x, Mary)* works as follows:

1. The query is reduced to *Q1*: *?- Mother(x,z)* ∧ *Parent(z, Mary)* by using rule R3.

2. *Q1* is reduced to two subqueries, by using either R1 or R2:

   Q2a: *?- Mother(x, z)* ∧ *Father(z, Mary)*

   Q2b: *?- Mother(x, z)* ∧ *Mother(z, Mary)*

3. Query *Q2a* is reduced to *Q3*: *?- Mother(x, Anthony)* because the DB contains the fact Father(Anthony, Mary).

4. Query *Q2b* does not provide any answer because no fact matches Mother(*z*, Mary).

5. Query *Q3* is evaluated against the EDB and gives *x* = Susan as a result.

At first glance, the top-down approach might seem preferable to the bottom-up approach, because it takes into account the constants in the initial query during the evaluation process. For that reason, the top-down approach does not take into account all possible consequences of the DB but only those that are relevant to perform the computation. However, the top-down approach also presents several inconveniences:

- *Top-down methods are usually one tuple at a time.* Instead of reasoning on the entire extension of DB predicates, as the bottom-up method does, the top-down approach considers base facts one by one as soon as they appear in the definition of a certain subquery. For that reason, top-down methods used to be less efficient.

- *Top-down may not terminate.* In the presence of recursive rules, a top-down evaluation method could enter an infinite loop and never terminate its execution. That would happen, for instance, if we consider the derived predicate Ancestor in Example 4.1 and we assume that a top-down computation starts always by reducing a query about Ancestor to queries about Ancestors again.

- *It is not possible to determine always, at definition time, whether a top-down algorithm terminates.* Thus, in a top-down approach we do not know whether the method will finish its execution if it is taking too much time to get the answer.

- *Repetitive subqueries.* During the process of reducing the original query to simpler subqueries that provide the same result, a certain subquery may be requested several times. In some cases, that may cause reevaluation of the subquery, thus reducing efficiency of the whole evaluation.

4.3.3 Magic Sets

The magic sets approach is a combination of the previous approaches, aimed at providing the advantages of the top-down approach when a set of deductive rules is evaluated bottom-up. Given a deductive DB D and a query Q on a derived predicate P, this method is aimed at rewriting the rules of D into an equivalent DB D' by taking Q into account. The goal of rule rewriting is to introduce the simulation of top-down into D' in such a way that a bottom-up evaluation of rules in D' will compute only the information necessary to answer Q. Moreover, the result of evaluating Q on D' is equivalent to querying Q on D.

Intuitively, this is performed by expressing the information of Q as extensional information and by rewriting the deductive rules of D used during the evaluation of Q. Rule rewriting is performed by incorporating the information of Q in the body of the rewritten rules.

Example 4.5

Consider again Example 4.2 and assume now that it also contains the following deductive rules defining the derived predicate Ancestor:

$$\text{Ancestor}(x,y) \leftarrow \text{Parent}(x,y)$$
$$\text{Ancestor}(x,y) \leftarrow \text{Parent}(x,z) \land \text{Ancestor}(z,y)$$

Rewritten "magic" rules for evaluating bottom-up the query *?-Ancestor(Rose,x)* are as follows:

$$\text{Magic\_Anc}(\text{Rose})$$

$\text{Ancestor}(x,y) \leftarrow \text{Magic\_Anc}(x) \land \text{Parent}(x,y)$	(rule R1)
$\text{Magic\_Anc}(z) \leftarrow \text{Magic\_Anc}(x) \land \text{Parent}(x,z)$	(rule R2)
$\text{Ancestor}(x,y) \leftarrow \text{Magic\_Anc}(x) \land \text{Parent}(x,z) \land \text{Ancestor}(z,y)$	(rule R3)

Assuming that all facts about Parent are already computed, in particular, Parent(Rose, Jennifer) and Parent(Jennifer, Monica), a naive bottom-up evaluation of the rewritten rules would proceed as follows:

1. The first step consists of seven iterations.

    a. Iteration 1: Ancestor(Rose, Jennifer) is deduced by applying R1.

    b. Iteration 2: Magic_Anc(Jennifer) is deduced by applying R2.

    c. Iteration 3: No new consequences are deduced by applying R3.

    d. Iteration 4: Ancestor(Jennifer, Monica) is deduced by applying R1.

    e. Iteration 5: Magic_Anc(Monica) is deduced by applying R2.

    f. Iteration 6: Ancestor(Rose, Monica) is deduced by R3.

    g. Iteration 7: No new consequences are deduced by applying R1, R2, and R3.

2. The obtained result is {Ancestor(Rose, Jennifer), Ancestor(Rose, Monica)}.

Note that by computing rewritten rules bottom-up, we only deduce the information relevant to the requested query. That is achieved by means of the Magic_Anc predicate, which is included in the body of all rules, and by the fact Magic_Anc(Rose), which allows us to compute only Rose's descendants.

4.4 Update Processing

Deductive DBMSs must also provide an update processing system able to handle updates specified in terms of base and view predicates. The objective of update processing is to perform the work required to apply the requested update, by taking into account the intensional information provided by views and integrity constraints.

This section reviews the most important problems related to update processing: change computation, view updating, and integrity constraint enforcement. We also describe a framework for classifying and specifying all of those problems. The following example will be used throughout this presentation.

Example 4.6

The following deductive DB provides information about employees.

Emp(John, Sales)	Mgr(Sales, Mary)	Work_age(John)
Emp(Albert, Marketing)	Mgr(Marketing, Anne)	Work_age(Albert)
Emp(Peter, Marketing)		Work_age(Peter)

Edm(e,d,m) ← Emp(e,d) ∧ Mgr(d,m)   Work_age(Jack)

Works(e) ← Emp(e,d)

Unemployed(e) ← Work_age(e) ∧ ¬Works(e)

IC1(d,m1,m2) ← Mgr(d,m1) ∧ Mgr(d,m2) ∧ m1 ≠ m2

IC2(e) ← Works(e) ∧ ¬Work_age(e)

The DB contains three base predicates: *Emp*, *Mgr*, and *Work_age*, stating employees that work in departments, departments with their managers, and persons who are of working age. It also contains three derived predicates: *Edm*, which defines employees with the department for which they work and the corresponding managers; *Works*, which defines persons who work as those assigned to some department; and *Unemployed*, which defines persons unemployed as those who are of working age but do not work. Finally, there are two integrity constraints: *IC1*, which states that departments may only have one manager, and *IC2*, which states that workers must be of working age.

4.4.1 Change Computation

4.4.1.1 Definition of the Problem

A deductive DB can be updated through the application of a given *transaction*, that is, a set of updates of base facts. Due to the presence of deductive rules and integrity constraints, the application of a transaction may also induce several changes on the intensional information, that is, on views and integrity constraints. Given a transaction, change computation refers to the process of computing the changes on the extension of the derived predicates induced by changes on the base facts specified by that transaction.

Example 4.7

The content of the intensional information about *Edm* and *Works* in the DB in Example 4.6 is the following.

Edm			Works
Employee	Department	Manager	Employee
John	Sales	Mary	John
Albert	Marketing	Anne	Albert
Peter	Marketing	Anne	Peter

The application of a transaction T={insert(Emp(Jack,Sales))} will induce the insertion of new information about *Edm* and *Works*. In particular, after the application of *T*, the contents of *Edm* and *Works* would be the following:

Edm			Works
Employee	Department	Manager	Employee
John	Sales	Mary	John
Albert	Marketing	Anne	Albert
Peter	Marketing	Anne	Peter
Jack	Sales	Mary	Jack

That is, the insertion of Emp(Jack, Sales) also induces the insertion of the intensional information Edm(Jack, Sales, Mary) and Works(Jack).

There is a simple way to perform change computation. First, we compute the extension of the derived predicates *before* applying the transaction. Second, we compute the extension of the derived predicates *after* applying the transaction. Finally, we compute the differences between the computed extensions of the derived predicates before and after applying the transaction. This approach is sound, in the sense that the computed changes correspond to those induced by the transaction, but inefficient, because, in general, we will have to compute the extension of information that is not affected by the update. Therefore, the change computation problem consists of efficiently computing the changes on derived predicates induced by a given transaction.

4.4.1.2   Aspects Related to Change Computation

We have seen that there is a naive but inefficient way to perform the process of change computation. For that reason, the main efforts in this field have been devoted to providing efficient methods to perform the calculation. Several aspects have to be taken into account when trying to define an efficient method.

- *Efficiency can be achieved only by taking the transaction into account.* The naive way of computing changes on the intensional information is inefficient because we have to compute a lot of information that does not change. Therefore, an efficient method must start by considering the transaction and computing only those changes that it may induce.

- *A transaction can induce multiple changes.* Due to the presence of several views and integrity constraints, even the simplest transactions consisting on a single base fact update may induce several updates on the intensional information. That was illustrated in Example 4.7, where the insertion of Emp(Jack, Sales) induced the insertions of Edm(Jack, Sales, Mary) and Works(Jack).

- *Change computation is nonmonotonic.* In the presence of negative literals, the process of change computation is nonmonotonic, that is, the insertion of base facts may induce deletions of derived information, while the deletion of base facts may induce the insertion of derived information. Nonmonotonicity is important because it makes it more difficult to incrementally determine the changes induced by a given transaction. For instance, applying the transaction $T = \{delete(Emp(John, Sales))\}$ to Example 4.6 would induce the set of changes $S = \{delete(Edm(John, Sales, Mary)),$ delete(Works(John)), and insert(Unemployed(John))\}$. Note that the insertion of Unemployed(John) is induced because the deletion of Works(John) is also induced.

- *Treatment of multiple transactions.* A transaction consists of a set of base fact updates to be applied to the DB. Therefore, we could think of computing the changes induced by each single base update independently and to provide as a result the union of all computed changes. However, that is not always a sound approach because the computed result may not correspond to the changes really induced. As an example, assume that $T = \{delete(Emp(John, Sales)),$ delete(Work_age (John))\}$ is applied to Example 4.6. The first update in T induces $S_1 = \{delete (Edm(John, Sales, Mary)),$ delete(Works(John)), insert(Unemployed(John))\}$, as we have just seen, while the second update does not induce any change. Therefore, we could think that S_1 defines exactly the changes induced by T. However, that is not the case because the deletion of Work_age(John) prevents the insertion of Unemployed(John) to be induced, being $S_T = \{delete(Edm(John, Sales, Mary)), delete(Works (John))\}$ the exact changes induced by T.

4.4.1.3 Applications of Change Computation

We have explained up to this point the process of change computation as that of computing changes on intentional information without giving a concrete semantics to this intensional information. Recall that deductive DBs define intensional information as views and integrity constraints. Considering change computation in each of those cases defines a different application of the problem. Moreover, change computation is also used in active DBs to compute the changes on the condition part of an active rule induced by an update.

- *Materialized view maintenance.* A view is materialized if its extension is physically stored in the DB. This is useful, for instance, to improve the performance of query processing because we can make use of the stored information (thus treating a view as a base predicate) instead of having to compute its extension. However, the extension of a view does not have an independent existence because it is completely defined by the deductive rules. Therefore, when a change is performed to the DB, the new extension of the materialized views must be recomputed. Instead of applying again the deductive rules that define each materialized view, this is better performed by means of change computation.

  Given a DB that contains some materialized views and a transaction, materialized view maintenance consists of incrementally determining which changes are needed to update all materialized views accordingly.

- *Integrity constraint checking.* Integrity constraints state conditions to be satisfied by each state of the DB. Therefore, a deductive DBMS must provide a way to guarantee that no integrity constraint is violated when a transaction is applied. We saw in Section 4.2.3 that there are several ways to resolve this conflict. The best known approach, usually known as integrity constraint checking, is the rejection of the transaction when some integrity constraint is to be violated. That could be done by querying the contents of the inconsistency predicates after applying the transaction, but, again, this is an inefficient approach that can be drastically improved by change computation techniques.

  Given a consistent DB, that is, a DB in which all integrity constraints are satisfied, and a transaction, integrity constraint checking consists of incrementally determining whether this update violates some integrity constraint.

- *Condition monitoring in active databases.* A DB is called active, as opposed to passive, when a transaction not only can be applied externally by the user but also internally because some condition of the DB is satisfied. Active behavior is usually specified by means of condition-action (CA) or event-condition-action (ECA) rules. The following is an example of a possible ECA rule for the DB in Example 4.6:

Event:	insert(Emp(e,d))
Condition:	Emp(e,d) and Mgr(d,Mary)
Action:	"execute transaction T"

That is, when an employee *e* is assigned to a department *d*, the transaction *T* must be executed if *d* has Mary as a manager. Note that the condition is a subcase of the deductive rule that defines the view *Edm*. Condition monitoring refers to the process of computing the changes in the condition to determine whether a CA or ECA rule must be executed. Therefore, performing condition monitoring efficiently is similar to computing changes on the view.

Given a set of conditions to monitor and a given transaction, condition monitoring consists of incrementally determining the changes induced by the transaction in the set of conditions.

4.4.1.4 Methods for Change Computation

Unfortunately, there is no survey that summarizes previous research in the area of change computation, although a comparison among early methods is provided in [25]. For that reason, we briefly point out the most relevant literature to provide, at least, a reference guide for the interested reader. Although some methods can handle all the applications of change computation, references are provided for each single application.

- *Integrity checking.* Reference [26] presents a comparison and synthesis of some of the methods proposed up to 1994. Interesting work not covered by this synthesis was also reported in [27–30]. More recent proposals, which also cover additional aspects not considered here, are [31–33].

- *Materialized view maintenance.* This is the only area of change computation covered by recent surveys that describe and compare previous research [34, 35]. A classification of the methods along some relevant features is also provided by these surveys. The application of view maintenance techniques to DWs [36] has motivated an increasing amount of research in this area during recent years.

- *Condition monitoring.* Because of the different nature of active and deductive DBs, the approach taken to condition monitoring in the field of active DBs is not always directly applicable to the approach for deductive DBs. Therefore, it is difficult to provide a complete list of references that deal with this problem as we have presented it. To get an idea of the field, we refer to [37–40], and to the references therein. Additional references can be found in Chapter 3.

4.4.2   View Updating

The advantages provided by views can be achieved only if a user does not distinguish a view from a base fact. Therefore, a deductive update processing system must also provide the ability to request updates on the derived facts, in addition to updates on base facts. Because the view extension is completely defined by the application of the deductive rules to the EDB, changes requested on a view must be translated to changes on the EDB. This problem is known as *view updating*.

4.4.2.1   Definition of the Problem

A view update request, that is, a request for changing the extension of a derived predicate, must always be translated into changes of base facts. Once the changes are applied, the new state of the DB will induce a new state of the view. The goal of view updating is to ensure that the new state of the view is as close as possible to the application of the request directly to the original view. In particular, it must guarantee that the requested view update is satisfied. This process is described in Figure 4.2 [41].

The EDB corresponds to the extensional DB where the view that we want to update, V(EDB), is defined according to a view definition function V (i.e., a set of deductive rules). When the user requests an update U on

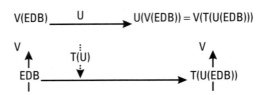

Figure 4.2 The process of view updating.

V(EDB), the request must be translated into a set of base fact updates T(U). These modifications lead to the new extensional DB T(U(EDB)), when applied to the EDB. Then, the application of V to T(U(EDB)) should report to the new extension of the view U(V(EDB)) that satisfies the requested update.

Given a deductive DB and a view update request U that specifies desired changes on derived facts, the view update problem consists of appropriately translating U into a set of updates of the underlying base facts. The obtained set of base fact updates is called the *translation* of a view update request. Note that translations correspond to transactions that could be applied to the DB to satisfy the view update request.

Example 4.8

The view update request U_1 = {delete(Works(Peter))} is satisfied by the translation T_1 = {delete(Emp(Peter, Marketing))}, in the DB in Example 4.6.

As opposed to the problem of change computation, there is no simple procedure to obtain the translations that satisfy a view update request. For that reason, the work performed so far in view updating has been concerned more with effectiveness issues, like obtaining translations that really satisfy the request or obtaining all possible translations, rather than with efficiency issues.

4.4.2.2   Aspects Related to View Updating

We briefly summarize the main aspects that make the problem of view updating a difficult one and that explain why there is not yet an agreement on how to incorporate existing view updating technology into commercial products. All the examples refer to the DB in Example 4.6.

Multiple Translations

In general, there exist multiple translations that satisfy a view update request. For instance, the request U = {delete(Edm(Peter, Marketing, Anne))} can be satisfied by either T_1 = {delete(Emp(Peter, Marketing))} or T_2 = {delete(Mgr (Marketing, Anne))}.

The existence of multiple translations poses two different requirements to methods for view updating. First, the need to be able to obtain all possible translations (otherwise, if a method fails to obtain a translation, it is not possible to know whether there is no translation or there is one but the method is not able to find it). Second, criteria are needed to choose the best solution, because only one translation needs to be applied to the DB.

Side Effects

The application of a given translation may induce additional nonrequested updates on the view where the update is requested or on other views, that is, it may happen that $U(V(EDB)) \neq V(T(U(EDB)))$. These additional updates, known as *side effects*, are usually hidden to the user. As an example, the application of the previous translation T_1 would induce the side effects $S_1 = \{delete(Works(Peter)), insert(Unemployed(Peter))\}$ and T_2 would induce $S_2 = \{delete(Edm(Albert, Marketing, Anne))\}$.

View Updating Is Nonmonotonic

In the presence of negative literals, the process of view updating is nonmonotonic, that is, the insertion of derived facts may be satisfied by deleting base facts, while the deletion of derived facts may be satisfied by inserting base facts. For instance, the view update request $U = \{insert(Unemployed(John))\}$ is satisfied by the translation $T = \{delete(Emp(John, Sales))\}$.

Treatment of Multiple-View Updates

When the user requests the update of more than one derived fact at the same time, we could think of translating each single view update isolatedly and to provide as a result the combination of the obtained translations. However, that is not always a sound approach because the obtained translations may not satisfy the requested multiple view update. The main reason is that the translation of a request may be inconsistent with an already translated request.

Assume the view update $U = \{insert(Unemployed(John)), delete(Work\_age(John))\}$ is requested. The first request in U is satisfied by the translation $T_1 = \{delete(Emp(John, Sales))\}$, while the second by $T_2 = \{delete(Work\_age(John))\}$. Then, we could think that the translation $T = S_1 \cup S_2 = \{delete(Emp(John, Sales)), delete(Work\_age (John))\}$ satisfies U. However, that is not the case, because the deletion of Work_age(John) does not allow John to be unemployed anymore.

Translation of Existential Deductive Rules

The body of a deductive rule may contain variables that do not appear in the head. These rules usually are known as *existential rules*. When a view update is requested on a derived predicate defined by means of some existential rule, there are many possible ways to satisfy the request, in particular, one way for each possible value that can be assigned to the existential variables. The problem is that, if we consider infinite domains, an infinite number of translations may exist.

Possible translations to U = {insert(Works(Tony))} are T_1 = {insert (Emp(Tony, Sales))}, T_2 = {insert(Emp(Tony, Marketing))}, ..., T_k = {insert (Emp(Tony, Accounting))}. Note that we have as many alternatives as possible for values of the departments' domain.

4.4.2.3 Methods for View Updating

As it happens for change computation, there is not yet any survey on view updating that helps to clarify the achievements in this area and the contribution of the various methods that have been proposed. Such a survey would be necessary to stress the problems to be addressed to convert view updating into a practical technology or to show possible limitations of handling this problem in practical applications.

View updating was originally addressed in the context of relational DBs [41–44], usually by restricting the kind of views that could be handled. This research opened the door to methods defined for deductive DBs [45–52]. A comparison of some of these methods is provided in [51]. A different approach aimed at dealing with view updating through transaction synthesis is investigated in [53]. A different approach to transactions and updates in deductive DBs is provided in [54].

4.4.3 Integrity Constraint Enforcement

4.4.3.1 Definition of the Problem

Integrity constraint enforcement refers to the problem of deciding the policy to be applied when some integrity constraint is violated due to the application of a certain transaction. Section 4.2.3 outlined several policies to deal with integrity constraints. The most conservative policy is that of *integrity constraint checking*, aimed at rejecting the transactions that violate some constraint, which is just a particular application of change computation, as discussed in Section 4.4.1.

An important problem with integrity constraint checking is the lack of information given to the user in case a transaction is rejected. Hence, the user may be completely lost regarding possible changes to be made to the transaction to guarantee that the constraints are satisfied. To overcome that limitation, an alternative policy is that of *integrity constraint maintenance*. If some constraint is violated, an attempt is made to find a repair, that is, an additional set of base fact updates to append to the original transaction, such that the resulting transaction satisfies all the integrity constraints. In general, several ways of repairing an integrity constraint may exist.

Example 4.9

Assume that the transaction T = {insert(Emp(Sara, Marketing))} is to be applied to our example DB. This transaction would be rejected by an integrity constraint checking policy because it would violate the constraint IC2. Note that T induces an insertion of Works(Sara) and, because Sara is not within labor age, IC2 is violated.

In contrast, an integrity constraint maintenance policy would realize that the repair insert(Work_age(Sara)) falsifies the violation of IC2. Therefore, it would provide as a result a final transaction T' = {insert(Emp (Sara, Marketing)), insert(Work_age(Sara))} that satisfies all the integrity constraints.

4.4.3.2   View Updating and Integrity Constraints Enforcement

In principle, view updating and integrity constraint enforcement might seem to be completely different problems. However, there exists a close relationship among them.

A Translation of a View Update Request May Violate Some Integrity Constraint

Clearly, translations of view updating correspond to transactions to be applied to the DB. Therefore, view updating must be followed by an integrity constraint enforcement process if we want to guarantee that the application of the translations does not lead to an inconsistent DB, that is, a DB where some integrity constraint is violated.

For instance, a translation that satisfies the view update request U = {insert(Works(Sara))} is T = {insert(Emp(Sara, Marketing))}. We saw in Example 4.9 that this translation would violate IC2, and, therefore, some integrity enforcement policy should be considered.

View updating and integrity constraint checking can be performed as two separate steps: We can first obtain all the translations, then check whether they violate some constraint, and reject those translations that would lead the DB to an inconsistent state.

In contrast, view updating and integrity constraint maintenance cannot be performed in two separate steps, as shown in [51], unless additional information other than the translations is provided by the method of view updating. Intuitively, the reason is that a repair could invalidate a previously satisfied view update. If we do not take that information into account during integrity maintenance, we cannot guarantee that the obtained transactions still satisfy the requested view updates.

Repairs of Integrity Constraints May Require View Updates

Because derived predicates may appear in the definition of integrity constraints, any mechanism that restores consistency needs to solve the view update problem to be able to deal with repairs on derived predicates.

For instance, consider the transaction T_i = {delete(Work_age(John))}. The application of this transaction would violate IC2 because John would work without being of working age. This violation can be repaired by considering the view update U = {delete(Works(John))}, and its translation leads to a final transaction T_f = {delete(Work_age(John)), delete(Emp(John, Sales))}, which does not violate any integrity constraint.

For those reasons, it becomes necessary to combine view updating and integrity constraint enforcement. This combination can be done either by considering the integrity constraint checking or maintenance approach. The result of the combined process is the subset of the translations obtained by view updating that, when extended by the required repairs if the maintenance approach is taken, would leave the DB consistent.

Research on integrity constraint maintenance suffered a strong impulse after [55]. A survey of the early methods on this subject is given in [56]. After this survey, several methods have been proposed that tackle the integrity constraint maintenance problem alone [57–61] or in combination with view updating [46, 49, 51, 52]. Again, there is no recent survey of previous research in this area.

4.4.4   A Common Framework for Database Updating Problems

Previous sections described the most important problems related to update processing in deductive DBs. We have also shown that the problems are not completely independent and that the aspects they must handle present certain relationships. However, up until now, the general approach of dealing with those problems has been to provide specific methods for solving particular problems. In this section, we show that it is possible to uniformly integrate several deductive DB updating problems into an update processing system, along the ideas proposed in [62].

Solving problems related to update processing always requires reasoning about the effect of an update on the DB. For that reason, all methods are explicitly or implicitly based on a set of rules that define the changes that occur in a transition from an old state of the DB to a new one, as a consequence of the application of a certain transaction. Therefore, any of these rules would provide the basis of a framework for classifying and specifying update problems. We consider the event rules [29] for such a basis.

4.4.4.1   Event Rules

Event rules explicitly define the differences between consecutive DB states, that is, they define the exact changes that occur in a DB as a consequence of the application of a certain transaction. The definitions of event rules depend only on the rules of the DB, being independent of the stored facts and of any particular transaction.

Event rules are based on the notion of *event*. Given a predicate P, two different kinds of events on P are distinguished: an insertion event, ιP, and a deletion event, δP. Events are formally defined as follows:

$$\forall \mathbf{x} \, (\iota P(\mathbf{x}) \leftrightarrow P^n(\mathbf{x}) \wedge \neg P(\mathbf{x}))$$

$$\forall \mathbf{x} \, (\delta P(\mathbf{x}) \leftrightarrow P(\mathbf{x}) \wedge \neg P^n(\mathbf{x}))$$

P and P^n refer to predicate P evaluated in the old and new states of the DB, respectively. These rules are called event rules and define the facts about P that are effectively inserted or deleted by a transaction.

If P is a base predicate, ιP and δP facts represent insertions and deletions of base facts. If P is a derived or an inconsistency predicate, ιP and δP facts represent induced insertions and induced deletions on P. In particular, if P is an inconsistency predicate, a fact ιP represents a violation of the corresponding integrity constraint.

Furthermore, a transition rule associated with each derived or inconsistency predicate P is also defined. The transition rule for P defines the extension of P in the new state of the DB (denoted by P^n), according to possible previous states of the DB and to the transactions that can be applied in each state.

Example 4.10

Consider the derived predicate Unemployed from the DB in Example 4.6. Event and transition rules associated with Unemployed are the following.

ιUnemployed(e) $\leftrightarrow$ Unemployed^n(e) $\wedge$ $\neg$Unemployed(e)

δUnemployed(e) $\leftrightarrow$ Unemployed(e) $\wedge$ $\neg$Unemployed^n(e)

Unemployed^n(e) $\leftrightarrow$ [(Work_age(e) $\wedge$ $\neg\delta$Work_age(e) $\wedge$ $\neg$Works(e) $\wedge$ $\neg\iota$Works(e)) $\vee$

(Work_age(e) $\wedge$ $\neg\delta$Work_age(e) $\wedge$ δWorks(e)) $\vee$

(ιWork_age(e) $\wedge$ $\neg$Works(e) $\wedge$ $\neg\iota$Works(e)) $\vee$

(ιWork_age(e) $\wedge$ δWorks(e))]

The previous transition rule defines all possible ways of satisfying a derived fact Unemployed(E) in the new state of the DB. For instance, the third disjunct states that Unemployed(E) will be true in the updated DB if Work_age(E) has been inserted, Works(E) was false in the old state of the DB, and it has not been inserted.

These rules can be intensively simplified, as described in [29, 30]. However, for the purposes of this presentation, it is enough to consider them as expressed before. The procedure for obtaining transition rules is given in [62].

4.4.4.2 Interpretations of Event Rules

Event rules can be interpreted in two different ways, according to the direction in which the equivalence is considered. The two interpretations are known as upward (or deductive) and downward (or abductive).

Upward Interpretation

Upward interpretation is provided by considering the left implication of the equivalence in the event and transition rules. It defines changes on derived predicates induced by changes on base predicates given by a transaction that consists of a set of base event facts.

In this interpretation, the event rules corresponding to Unemployed are expressed as

$$\iota \text{Unemployed}(e) \leftarrow \text{Unemployed}^n(e) \wedge \neg \text{Unemployed}(e)$$

$$\delta \text{Unemployed}(e) \leftarrow \text{Unemployed}(e) \wedge \neg \text{Unemployed}^n(e)$$

the intended meaning of which is that there will be an induced insertion (deletion) of a fact Unemp if the body of its corresponding event rule evaluates to true in the transition from the old to the new state of the DB.

The result of upward interpreting an event rule corresponding to a derived predicate P—succinctly, the upward interpretation of $\iota P(\mathbf{x})$ or $\delta P(\mathbf{x})$—is a set of derived event facts. Each of them corresponds to a change of a derived fact induced by the transaction. Note that the upward interpretation of an event rule always requires the upward interpretation of the transition rule of predicate P. To compute the upward interpretation, literals in the body of transition and event rules are interpreted as follows.

- An old DB literal ($P(\mathbf{x})$ or $\neg P(\mathbf{x})$) corresponds to a query that must be performed in the current state of the DB.

- A base event literal corresponds to a query that must be applied to the given transaction.

- A derived event literal is handled by upward interpreting its corresponding event rule. In the particular case of a negative derived event, for example, $\neg \iota P(x)$, its upward interpretation corresponds to a condition whose truth value is given by the result of the upward interpretation of $\iota P(x)$. This condition will be true if the latter result does not contain any derived event fact and false otherwise. The same holds for the downward interpretation of $\neg P^n(x)$.

Example 4.11 illustrates upward interpretation.

Example 4.11

Consider again the event and transition rules in Example 4.10 and assume a given transaction $T = \{\iota Work\_age(John)\}$ is requested with an empty EDB. Induced insertions on Unemployed are given by upward interpreting the literals in (Unemployed^n(e) $\wedge$ $\neg$Unemployed(e)). Then, we start by upward interpreting Unemployed^n.

Consider the third disjunctand of this rule: $\iota Work\_age(e) \wedge \neg Works(e) \wedge \neg \iota Works(e)$. The first literal, $\iota Work\_age(e)$, is a base event literal and, thus, corresponds to a query to the given transaction. The only answer to this query is $e = John$. Now, the second and third literals must be evaluated only for $e = John$. It is not difficult to see that the resulting queries associated to each of the literals hold. Therefore, the third disjunctand is true for $e = John$ and, thus, Unemployed^n(John) is also true.

The second literal in the insertion event rule is an old DB literal, $\neg$Unemployed(e), which holds in the current state for the value $e = John$. Therefore, the transaction T induces ιUnemployed(John). It can be similarly seen that this transaction does not induce any other change, mainly because the queries on the other disjunctands fail to produce an answer. Thus, upward interpretation of ιUnemployed(e) results in $\{\iota Unemployed(John)\}$.

Downward Interpretation

Downward interpretation is provided by considering the right implication of the equivalence in the event and transition rules. It defines changes on base predicates needed to satisfy changes on derived predicates given by a set of derived event facts. In general, several sets of changes on base predicates that satisfy changes on derived predicates may exist. Each possible set is a transaction that accomplishes the required changes on derived predicates.

In this interpretation, the event rules corresponding to unemployed are expressed as

$$\iota\text{Unemployed}(e) \rightarrow \text{Unemployed}^n(e) \wedge \neg\text{Unemployed}(e)$$
$$\delta\text{Unemployed}(e) \rightarrow \text{Unemployed}(e) \wedge \neg\text{Unemployed}^n(e)$$

the intended meaning of which is that to perform an insertion (deletion) of a fact Unemp it is required that the body of its corresponding event rule evaluates to true in the transition.

The result of downward interpreting an event rule corresponding to a derived predicate P with respect to a derived event fact $\iota P(X)$ or $\delta P(X)$ (succinctly, the downward interpretation of $\iota P(X)$ or $\delta P(X)$) is a disjunctive normal form, where each disjunctand defines a possible alternative to satisfy the change specified by the derived event fact. Each disjunctand may contain positive base event facts, which define a possible transaction to be applied, and negative base event facts, representing events that the transaction may not contain. To compute the downward interpretation, literals in the body of transition and event rules are interpreted as follows.

- An old DB literal corresponds to a query on the current state of the DB.
- A base event literal defines different alternatives of base fact updates to be performed, an alternative for each possible way to instantiate this event. Negative base event literals correspond to events that must not be performed.
- A derived event literal corresponds to possible changes on a derived predicate, one for each possible way to instantiate this event. It is handled by downward interpreting its corresponding event rule. The downward interpretation of a negative derived event or transition literal is defined as the disjunctive normal form of the logical negation of the result obtained by downward interpreting the corresponding positive derived literal.

The downward interpretation of a set of event facts is defined as the disjunctive normal form of the logical conjunction of the result of downward interpreting each event in the set. Example 4.12 illustrates the downward interpretation.

Example 4.12

Consider again the event and transition rules in Example 4.10 and assume now that the insertion of the fact Unemployed(John) is requested, that is, ιUnemployed(John). We are going to show how the downward interpretation of ιUnemployed(John) defines the changes on the EDB required to satisfy this request.

Changes on base predicates needed to satisfy ιUnemployed(John) are given by downward interpreting the literals in (Unemployed^n(John) $\wedge \neg$Unemployed(John)). Then, we start by downward interpreting the transition rule for Unemployed^n.

Consider the third disjunctand of this rule. The first literal, ιWork_age(e), is a base event literal and, thus, corresponds to a base fact update that must be performed. The second literal, $\neg$Works(John), is a DB literal that holds in the current state. The third literal, $\neg\iota$Works(John), is a negative base event and, thus, corresponds to a change that must not be performed. Therefore, from this disjunctand, we obtain the alternative (ιWork_age(John) $\wedge \neg\iota$Works(John)). In a similar way, it can be seen that no other alternatives are obtained by considering the other disjunctands.

Thus, the final result of downward interpreting ιUnemployed(John) is (ιWork_age(John) $\wedge \neg\iota$Works(John)). Therefore, the application of the transaction T = {ιWork_age(John)} to the current state of the DB will accomplish the insertion of Unemployed(John).

4.4.4.3 Classifying Database Updating Problems

We have seen in previous sections that views (materialized or not), integrity constraints, and conditions to be monitored can be expressed as derived predicates. In all cases, they are defined by a certain deductive rule, and the only difference among them is the precise semantics given to the predicate in the head of the rule. Thus, a predicate P defined by the rule $P(x) \leftarrow Q(x) \wedge \neg R(x)$, can be a view $View(x) \leftarrow Q(x) \wedge \neg R(x)$, an integrity constraint $IC(x) \leftarrow Q(x) \wedge \neg R(x)$, or a condition $Cond(x) \leftarrow Q(x) \wedge \neg R(x)$, by changing only the semantics given to P.

The upward and downward interpretations of the event rules corresponding to *View*, *IC*, and *Cond* allow us to classify deductive DB updating problems, in particular, change computation, view updating, integrity constraint enforcement, and several problems we have not yet described.

This is summarized in Table 4.1. Rows correspond to the particular interpretation to consider and to the relevant event P that must be interpreted.[1] Columns correspond to the precise semantics given to the event predicate. The first column assumes that P is a view, the second one that P is

---

1. *T* corresponds to a given transaction that is required sometimes for certain DB updating problems.

Table 4.1
Classification of Database Updating Problems

		View	IC	Condition
Upward interpretation of	ιP	Materialized view maintenance	IC checking	Condition monitoring
	δP		Checking consistency restoration	
Downward interpretation of	ιP	View updating	Redundancy of integrity constraints	Enforcing condition activation
	δP	View liveliness	Repairing inconsistent DB satisfiability checking	Condition validation
	$T \wedge \neg \iota P$	Preventing side effects	IC maintenance	Preventing condition
	$T \wedge \neg \delta P$		Maintaining DB inconsistency	Activation

an inconsistency predicate, and the third one that it is a condition. Each resulting cell refers to the DB updating problem resulting from the previous choices.

For instance, Table 4.1 states that integrity constraint checking and condition monitoring can be specified as the upward interpretation of ιIC and ιCond or δCond, respectively. View updating can also be specified as the downward interpretation of ιView, View being a derived given fact. Integrity maintenance is the downward interpretation of $T \wedge \neg \iota$IC, where T is a given transaction to be applied to the DB.

In this way, the upward and downward interpretations define a common framework for classifying and specifying deductive DB updating problems. A particular implementation of each interpretation would produce a particular method for update processing able to deal with all problems that fit naturally in that form of reasoning. Therefore, two methods should be enough to uniformly integrate DB updating problems into an update processing system.

The rest of this section briefly describes problems that have not been presented yet.

Satisfiability Checking

Intuitively, a DB schema is satisfiable [63, 64] if there is a state of the schema in which all integrity constraints are satisfied. Clearly, views and/or integrity constraints in a nonsatisfiable schema are ill-designed because any facts entered to the DB would give rise to constraint violations.

Example 4.13

Consider the following schema:

Some_Emp ← Emp(e,d)

Has_Mgr(d) ← Mgr(d,m)

Works_For(e,m) ← Emp(e,d) ∧ Mgr(d,m)

IC1 ← ¬Some_Emp

IC2 ← Emp(e,d) ∧ ¬Has_Mgr(d)

IC3 ← Mgr(d,m) ∧ ¬Emp(m,d)

IC4 ← ¬Works_For(e,e)

This schema is unsatisfiable in any state. IC1 requires the DB to have at least one employee working in a department, but IC2 enforces all departments to have managers, while IC3 obliges managers of a department to be employees of the same department. Since IC4 impedes nobody to work for himself or herself (i.e., to manage a department where he or she works), it is impossible to find a state of the DB that satisfies all four constraints.

Satisfiability checking is different from integrity constraint enforcement, because the former is independent of any state and any update, while the latter is not. Moreover, an unsatisfiable schema is repaired by changing the definition of views and/or integrity constraints, while an inconsistent DB is repaired by adding or removing facts that return the DB to a consistent state.

View Liveliness

A derived predicate P is lively if there is a consistent state of the DB schema in which at least one fact about P is true. Predicates that are not lively correspond to relations that are empty in each consistent state. Such predicates clearly are not useful and possibly ill-specified. As an example, neither the predicate Q nor S is lively in a DB {$Q(x)$ ← $R(x,y)$ ∧ $S(y)$, IC1(x) ← $S(x)$} because IC1 prevents any fact about them to be true. This definition of "liveliness" essentially coincides with the definition of "satisfiable" in [66].

Redundancy of Integrity Constraints

Intuitively, a constraint is redundant if integrity does not depend on it. Such a redundancy should be detected by schema validation and then be eliminated. Redundancy of a constraint may be due to several reasons: because the constraint definition itself states a contradiction (i.e., something that may never happen) or because it is enforced by the specifications of the other integrity constraints. Redundancy of constraints is similar to subsumption, as defined in [66] and discussed in the next section. As an example, consider the following schema:

$$P \leftarrow Q \qquad\qquad IC1 \leftarrow Q \wedge \neg P$$
$$P \leftarrow R \wedge S \qquad\qquad IC2 \leftarrow T \wedge S$$
$$IC3 \leftarrow T$$

IC1 is redundant because Q implies P; therefore, it is impossible to have Q and not to have P. IC2 is also redundant because it is entailed by the third one. Therefore, the previous schema allows the same consistent states than a schema containing only IC3.

Preventing Side Effects

Undesired updates, or side effects, may be induced on some derived predicate when a transaction is applied. The problem of preventing side effects is concerned with determining a set of base fact updates that, appended to a given transaction, ensures that the resulting transaction will not induce the undesired side effects.

Repairing Inconsistent Databases

It may be interesting sometimes to allow for intermediate inconsistent DB states (e.g., to avoid excessive integrity enforcement). In that case, the problem arises of repairing the inconsistent DB, which is concerned with obtaining a set of base fact updates that restores the DB to a consistent state, in which no integrity constraint is violated.

Maintaining Database Inconsistency

Given an inconsistent DB state and a transaction, the problem is to obtain an additional set of base fact updates to append to the transaction to guarantee that the resulting DB state remains inconsistent. Although there is no clear practical application of this problem, it can be naturally classified and specified in the previous framework.

Enforcing Condition Activation

This problem refers to obtaining a set of changes of base facts that would induce an activation of a given condition if applied to the current DB state.

Preventing Condition Activation

Given a transaction, the problem is to find an additional set of insertions and/or deletions of base facts to be appended to the original transaction such that it is guaranteed that no changes in the specified condition will occur.

More details about this framework can be found in [62]. Problems related to DB schema validation, like satisfiability checking, view liveliness, or redundancy of integrity constraints have been investigated in depth in [67]. Recently, [68] showed that query containment can also be reformulated as a view updating problem and, thus, can be also specified by means of the downward interpretation.

4.5   Deductive Database System Prototypes

Results from the large amount of theoretical research devoted to deductive DBs have both penetrated current relational DBMSs and inspired several extensions to the relational model. Furthermore, this research has materialized in some prototypes of deductive DBMSs [13, 69]. Among these developed systems are Aditi, CORAL, DECLARE, Glue-Nail (see [70] for descriptions and references), LDL [71], EKS-V1 [72, 73], XSB [74], Validity [75], FOLRE [76], and the two prototypes developed during the IDEA Project [77].

Table 4.2 summarizes some aspects of those systems. We have considered only the aspects directly related to the main topics addressed in this chapter, that is, deductive DB definition, query processing, and update processing. Table 4.2 is both an adaptation and an extension of [69], which provides a wider comparison for some of the considered aspects. Relevant issues considered for each aspect are the following.

- *Deductive database definition.* Deductive rules and integrity constraints are the key concepts of deductive DBs. All the systems allow the definition of recursive rules that may contain negative literals in the body, while only some of them allow the definition of integrity constraints.

- *Query processing.* Not all the systems provide the three basic approaches to query evaluation. We distinguish whether a system provides a top-down (TD), bottom-up (BU), or magic sets (MS) approach. Most of the systems incorporate additional optimizations during query evaluation, in addition to the general approaches considered in this chapter (see [69]).

Table 4.2
Summary of Deductive DBMS Prototypes

Deductive Prototypes	DB Definition		Query Processing	Update Processing			Storage
	Rules	Constraints		Updates	Change computation	IC enforcement	
Aditi	Negative, recursive	No	TD, BU, MS	No	None	None	EDB, IDB
CORAL	Negative, recursive	No	TD, BU, MS	Base	None	None	EDB, IDB
DECLARE	Negative, recursive	No	BU, MS	No	None	None	EDB
EKS-V1	Negative, recursive	Yes	TD	Base	MVM, ICC	ICC	EDB, IDB
FOLRE	Negative, recursive	Yes	TD	Base, view	MVM, ICC, CM	ICC, ICM	EDB, IDB
Glue-Nail	Negative, recursive	No	BU, MS	Base	None	None	EDB
IDEA Project	Negative, recursive	Yes	TD	Base	MVM, ICC, CM	ICC, ICM	EDB, IDB
LDL	Negative, recursive	No	TD, BU, MS	Base	None	None	EDB
XSB	Negative, recursive	No	TD	No	None	None	EDB, IDB

- *Update processing.* Three issues are relevant here: the kind of updates allowed by each system, that is, updates of base facts and/or view updates; the applications of change computation provided, that is, materialized view maintenance (MVM), integrity constraint checking (ICC), or condition monitoring (CM); and the integrity constraint enforcement policy, that is, ICC or integrity constraint maintenance (ICM).

- *Storage.* It states whether the EDB, the IDB, or both are kept on secondary storage.

As shown in Table 4.2, most deductive DBMSs have concentrated on providing efficient techniques for the storage and retrieval of large amounts of complex data. Thus, just a few current deductive DBMSs provide some mechanism for advanced data updating, other than updates of base facts. To our fair knowledge, only EKS-V1, FOLRE, and the two prototypes developed into the IDEA project incorporate advanced update capabilities. On the other hand, systems providing advanced update capabilities have deserved little attention to query processing issues and rely on a back end that fully provides the support for query evaluation needs, or they are not able to evaluate queries efficiently.

4.6 Summary

Deductive DBs contain intensional information, expressed as views and integrity constraints, in addition to extensional information. Therefore, they require a query and an update processing system able to deal with that kind of information. This chapter presented several problems encountered when dealing at run time with intensional information, like query processing, change computation, view updating, or integrity constraint enforcement, and provided an overview of previous research in this area.

While techniques developed as a result of the research in deductive DBs have been incorporated into current relational technology, there is no deductive DBMS in commercial use. A possible reason is that although most deductive prototypes provide efficient techniques for query processing, update processing has not been extensively considered. Therefore, the most distinguishing feature of deductive technology—the update and management of intensional information—is not fully provided by existing prototypes.

We believe the reason behind this situation is the isolated way in which update problems have been dealt with in the past and the impossibility of applying advanced update processing in practical applications (since it is not provided by major deductive systems).

We want to stress that the difficulties of dealing with intensional information are not unique to deductive DBs; they also appear in most kinds of DBs that provide some mechanism to define this information, like relational, object-relational, or object-oriented DBs. Hence, those DBs will also need to deal with some of the problems addressed in this chapter.

The design of deductive DBs to identify derived predicates and integrity constraints during conceptual modeling was not addressed in this chapter and is still an open field of research. Some ideas on this topic are presented in [15, 77].

References

[1] Gardarin, G., and P. Valduriez, *Relational Databases and Knowledge Bases*, Reading, MA: Addison-Wesley, 1989.

[2] Grant, J., and J. Minker, "The Impact of Logic Programming on Databases," *Comm. ACM*, Vol. 35, No. 3, 1992, pp. 66–81.

[3] Minker, J. (ed.), *Foundations of Deductive Databases and Logic Programming*, Los Altos, CA: Morgan Kaufmann, 1988.

[4] Reiter, R., "Towards a Logical Reconstruction of Relational Database Theory," in M. L. Brodie, J. Mylopoulos, and J. W. Schmidt (eds.), *On Conceptual Modeling*, New York: Springer-Verlag, 1984, pp. 191–233.

[5] Abiteboul, S., R. Hull, and V. Vianu, *Foundations of Databases*, Reading, MA: Addison-Wesley, 1995.

[6] Bidoit, N., *Bases de Données Déductives: Presentation de Datalog*, Armand Colin, Éditeur, 1992, (in French).

[7] Cacace, F., et al., "Logic Programming and Databases," in P. Loucopoulos and R. Zicari (eds.), *Conceptual Modeling, Databases, and CASE*, New York: Wiley, 1992, pp. 247–269.

[8] Ceri, S., G. Gottlob, and L. Tanca, *Logic Programming and Databases*, New York: Springer-Verlag, 1990.

[9] Das, S. K., *Deductive Databases and Logic Programming*, Reading, MA: Addison-Wesley, 1992.

[10] Date, C. J., *An Introduction to Database Systems*, 6th ed., Reading, MA: Addison-Wesley, 1995.

[11]   Elmasri, R., and S. B. Navathe, *Fundamentals of Database Systems*, 2nd ed., Redwood City, CA: Benjamin/Cummings, 1994.

[12]   Gallaire, H., J. Minker, and J. M. Nicolas, "Logic and Databases: A Deductive Approach," *ACM Computing Surveys*, Vol. 16, No. 2, 1984, pp. 153–185.

[13]   Minker, J., "Logic and Databases: A 20-Year Retrospective," *Proc. Intl. Workshop on Logic in Databases (LID)*, San Miniato, Italy, 1996, pp. 5–52.

[14]   Ullman, J. D., *Principles of Database and Knowledge-Base Systems*, Rockville, MD: Computer Science Press, 1988.

[15]   Wagner, G., *Foundations of Knowledge Systems: With Applications to Databases and Agents*, Boston, MA: Kluwer Academic Publishers, 1998.

[16]   Lloyd, J. W., and R. Topor, "Making Prolog More Expressive," *J. Logic Programming*, Vol. 1, No. 3, 1984, pp. 225–240.

[17]   Bancilhon, F., and R. Ramakrishnan, "An Amateur's Introduction to Recursive Query Processing," *Proc. 12th ACM SIGMOD Conf. on Management of Data*, Washington, DC, 1986, pp. 16–52.

[18]   Ceri, S., G. Gottlog, and L. Tanca, "What You Always Wanted to Know About Datalog (and Never Dared to Ask)," *IEEE Trans. on Knowledge and Data Engineering*, Vol. 1, No. 1, 1989, pp. 146–166.

[19]   Reiter, R., "On Closed World Databases," in H. Gallaire and J. Minker (eds.), *Logic and Databases*, New York: Plenum Press, 1978, pp. 56–76.

[20]   Przymusinski, T., "On the Semantics of Stratified Deductive Databases," *Proc. Workshop on Foundations of Deductive Databases and Logic Programming*, Washington, DC, 1986, pp. 433–443.

[21]   Bidoit, N., "Negation in Rule-Based Database Languages: A Survey," *Theoretical Computer Science*, Vol. 78, No. 1, 1991, pp. 3–84.

[22]   Winslett, M., *Updating Logical Databases*, Cambridge Tracts in Theoretical Computer Science 9, 1990.

[23]   Date, C. J., and H. Darwen, *A Guide to the SQL Standard*, 4th ed., Reading, MA: Addison-Wesley, 1997.

[24]   Ramakrishnan, R., *Database Management Systems*, Boston, MA: McGraw-Hill, 1998.

[25]   Urpí, T., *El Mètode dels Esdeveniments per al Càlcul de Canvis en Bases de Dades Deductives*, Ph.D. thesis, Universitat Politècnica de Catalunya, Barcelona, Spain, 1993 (in Catalan).

[26]   García, C., et al., "Comparing and Synthesizing Integrity Checking Methods for Deductive Databases," *Proc. 10th Intl. Conf. on Data Engineering (ICDE'94)*, Houston, TX, 1994, pp. 214–222.

[27]   Ceri, S., and J. Widom, "Deriving Production Rules for Constraint Maintenance," *Proc. 16th Intl. Conf. on Very Large Data Bases (VLDB'90)*, Brisbane, Australia, 1990, pp. 566–577.

[28]   Küchenhoff, V., "On the Efficient Computation of the Difference Between Consecutive Database States," *Proc. 2nd Intl. Conf. on Deductive and Object-Oriented Databases (DOOD'91)*, Munich, Germany, 1991, pp. 478–502.

[29]   Olivé, A., "Integrity Checking in Deductive Databases," *Proc. 17th Intl. Conf. on Very Large Data Bases (VLDB'91)*, Barcelona, Spain, 1991, pp. 513–523.

[30]   Urpí, T., and A. Olivé, "A Method for Change Computation in Deductive Databases," *Proc. 18th Intl. Conf. on Very Large Data Bases (VLDB'92)*, Vancouver, Canada, 1992, pp. 225–237.

[31]   Bertino, E., B. Catania, and S. Bressan, "Integrity Constraint Checking in Chimera," *2nd Intl. Workshop on Constraint Database Systems (CDB'97)*, Delphi, Greece, 1997, pp. 160–186.

[32]   Lee, S. Y., and T. W. Ling, "Further Improvements on Integrity Constraint Checking for Stratifiable Deductive Databases," *Proc. 22nd Intl. Conf. on Very Large Data Bases (VLDB'96)*, Bombay, India, 1996, pp. 495–505.

[33]   Seljee, R., "A New Method for Integrity Constraint Checking in Deductive Databases," *Data and Knowledge Engineering*, Vol. 15, No. 1, 1995, pp. 63–102.

[34]   Gupta, A., and I. S. Mumick, "Maintenance of Materialized Views: Problems, Techniques and Applications," *Data Engineering Bulletin*, Vol. 18, No. 2, 1995, pp. 3–18.

[35]   Roussopoulos, N., "Materialized Views and Data Warehouses," *SIGMOD Record*, Vol. 27, No. 1, 1998, pp. 21–26.

[36]   Ullman, J. D., "Efficient Implementation of Data Cubes Via Materialized Views," *Proc. 2nd Intl. Conf. on Knowledge Discovery and Data Mining (KDD-96)*, Portland, OR, 1996, pp. 386–388.

[37]   Baralis, E., S. Ceri, and S. Paraboschi, "Compile-Time and Run-Time Analysis of Active Behaviors," *Trans. of Knowledge and Data Engineering*, Vol. 10, No. 3, 1998, pp. 353–370.

[38]   Hanson, E. N., et al., "A Predicate Matching Algorithm for Database Rule Systems," *Proc. ACM SIGMOD Conf. on Management of Data*, Atlantic City, NJ, 1990, pp. 271–280.

[39]   Rosenthal, A., et al., "Situation Monitoring for Active Databases," *Proc. 15th Intl. Conf. on Very Large Data Bases (VLDB'89)*, Amsterdam, Netherlands, 1989, pp. 455–464.

[40]   Urpí, T., and A. Olivé, "Semantic Change Computation Optimization in Active Databases," *Proc. 4th Intl. Workshop on Research Issues on Data Engineering—Active Database Systems (RIDE-ADS'94)*, Houston, TX, 1994, pp. 19–27.

[41] Keller, A. M., "Algorithms for Translating View Updates to Database Updates for Views Involving Selection, Projections and Joins," *Proc. 4th Symp. on Principle of Database Systems (PODS'85)*, Portland, OR, 1985, pp. 154–163.

[42] Date, C. J., "Updating Views," in *Relational Database: Selected Writings*, Reading, MA: Addison-Wesley, 1986, pp. 367–395.

[43] Furtado, A. L., K. C. Sevcik, and C. S. Dos Santos, "Permitting Updates Through Views of Databases," *Information Systems*, 1979.

[44] Larson, J., and A. Sheth, "Updating Relational Views Using Knowledge at View Definition and View Update Time," *Information Systems*, Vol. 16, No. 2, 1991, pp. 145–168.

[45] Bry, F., "Intensional Updates: Abduction Via Deduction," *Proc. 7th Intl. Conf. on Logic Programming (ICLP'90)*, Jerusalem, Israel, 1990, pp. 561–575.

[46] Decker, H., "An Extension of SLD by Abduction and Integrity Maintenance for View Updating in Deductive Databases," *Proc. Joint Intl. Conf. and Symp. on Logic Programming (JICSLP'96)*, Bonn, Germany, 1996, pp. 157–169.

[47] Guessoum, A., and J. W. Lloyd, "Updating Knowledge Bases II," *New Generation Computing*, Vol. 10, 1991, pp. 73–100.

[48] Kakas, A., and P. Mancarella, "Database Updates Through Abduction," *Proc. 16th Intl. Conf. on Very Large Data Bases (VLDB'90)*, Brisbane, Australia, 1990, pp. 650–661.

[49] Lobo, J., and G. Trajcewski, "Minimal and Consistent Evolution of Knowledge Bases," *J. Applied Non-Classical Logics*, Vol. 7, No. 1–2, 1997, pp. 117–146.

[50] Teniente, E., and A. Olivé, "The Events Method for View Updating in Deductive Databases," *Proc. 3rd Intl. Conf. on Extending Database Technology (EDBT'92)*, Vienna, Austria, 1992, pp. 245–260.

[51] Teniente, E., and A. Olivé, "Updating Knowledge Bases While Maintaining Their Consistency," *VLDB J.*, Vol. 4, No. 2, 1995, pp. 193–241.

[52] Wüthrich, B., "On Updates and Inconsistency Repairing in Knowledge Bases," *Proc. 9th Intl. Conf. on Data Engineering (ICDE'93)*, Vienna, Austria, 1993, pp. 608–615.

[53] Pastor, J. A., and A. Olivé, "Supporting Transaction Design in Conceptual Modeling of Information Systems," *Proc. 7th. Intl. Conf. on Advanced Information Systems Engineering (CAISE'95)*, Jyväskylä, Finland, 1995, pp. 40–53.

[54] Montesi, D., E. Bertino, and M. Martelli, "Transactions and Updates in Deductive Databases," *IEEE Trans. on Knowledge and Data Engineering*, Vol. 9, No. 5, 1997, pp. 784–797.

[55] Moerkotte, G., and P. C. Lockemann, "Reactive Consistency Control in Deductive Databases," *ACM Trans. on Database Systems*, Vol. 16, No. 4, Dec. 1991, pp. 670–702.

[56] Fraternali, P., and S. Paraboschi, "A Review of Repairing Techniques for Integrity Maintenance," *Intl. Work. on Rules in Database Systems (RIDS'93)*, Edinburgh, Scotland, 1993, pp. 333–346.

[57] Ceri, S., et al., "Automatic Generation of Production Rules for Integrity Maintenance," *ACM Trans. on Database Systems*, Vol. 19, No. 3, 1994, pp. 367–422.

[58] Gertz, M., and U. W. Lipeck, "Deriving Integrity Maintaining Triggers From Transaction Graphs," *Proc. 9th Intl. Conf. on Data Engineering (ICDE'93)*, Vienna, Austria, 1993, pp. 22–29.

[59] Mayol, E., and E. Teniente, "Structuring the Process of Integrity Maintenance," *Proc. 8th Intl. Conf. on Database and Expert Systems Applications (DEXA'97)*, Toulouse, France, 1997, pp. 262–275.

[60] Qian, X., "The Deductive Synthesis of Database Transactions," *ACM Trans. on Database Systems*, Vol. 18, No. 4, 1993, pp. 626–677.

[61] Schewe, K. D., and B. Thalheim, "Achieving Consistency in Active Databases," *Proc. Intl. Work. on Research Issued in Data Engineering—Active Database Systems (RIDE-ADS'94)*, Houston, TX, 1994, pp. 71–76.

[62] Teniente, E., and T. Urpí, "A Common Framework for Classifying and Specifying Deductive Database Updating Problems," *Proc. 11th Intl. Conf. on Data Engineering (ICDE'95)*, Taipei, Taiwan, 1995, pp. 173–182.

[63] Bry, F., H. Decker, and R. Manthey, "A Uniform Approach to Constraints Satisfaction and Constraints Satisfiability in Deductive Databases," *Proc. 1st Intl. Conf. on Extending Database Technology (EDBT'88)*, Venezia, Italy, 1988, pp. 488–505.

[64] Inoue, K., M. Koshimura, and R. Hasegawa, "Embedding Negation as Failure Into a Model Generation Theorem Prover," *Proc. 11th Intl. Conf. on Automatic Deduction (CADE'92)*, Saratoga Springs, NY, 1992, pp. 400–415.

[65] Levy, A., and Y. Sagiv, "Semantic Query Optimization in Datalog Programs," *Proc. 14th Symp. on Principle of Database Systems (PODS'95)*, San Jose, CA, 1995, pp. 163–173.

[66] Gupta, A., et al., "Constraint Checking With Partial Information," *Proc. 13th Symp. on Principles of Database Systems (PODS'94)*, Minneapolis, MN, 1994, pp. 45–55.

[67] Decker, H., E. Teniente, and T. Urpí, "How To Tackle Schema Validation by View Updating," *Proc. 5th Intl. Conf. on Extending Database Technology (EDBT'96)*, Avignon, France, 1996, pp. 535–549.

[68] Farré, C., E. Teniente, and T. Urpí, "Query Containment as a View Updating Problem," *Proc. 9th Database and Expert Systems Applications (DEXA'98)*, Vienna, Austria, 1998, 310–321.

[69] Ramakrishnan, R., and J. Ullman, "A Survey of Research on Deductive Database Systems," *J. Logic Programming*, Vol. 23, No. 2, 1995, pp. 125–149.

[70] "Special Issue on Prototypes of Deductive Database Systems," *J. Very Large Databases*, Vol. 3, No. 2, 1994.

[71] Chimenti, D., et al., "The LDL System Prototype," *IEEE Trans. on Knowledge and Data Engineering*, Vol. 2, No. 1, 1990, pp. 76–90.

[72] Vieille, L., et al., "EKS-V1: A Short Overview," *AAAI'90 Workshop on KB Management Systems*, 1990.

[73] Vieille, L., et al., "An Overview of the EKS-V1 System," *ECRC Research Report*, 1991.

[74] Sagonas, K., T. Swift, and D. S. Warren, "XSB as an Efficient Deductive Database Engine," *Proc. ACM SIGMOD Conf. on Management of Data*, Minneapolis, MN, 1994, pp. 442–453.

[75] Friesen, O., A. Lefebvre, and L. Vieille, "Validity: Applications of a DOOD System," *Proc. 5th Intl. Conf. on Extending Database Technology (EDBT'96)*, Avignon, France, 1996, pp. 131–134.

[76] Mayol, E., et al., "FOLRE: A Deductive Database System for the Integrated Treatment of Updates," *Proc. 3rd Intl. Workshop on Rules in Database Systems (RIDS'97)*, Skövde, Sweden, 1997, pp. 35–50.

[77] Ceri, S., and P. Fraternali, *Designing Database Applications With Objects and Rules: The IDEA Methodology*, Reading, MA: Addison-Wesley, 1997.

Selected Bibliography

The main goal of this chapter was to provide a comprehensive summary of the main features of deductive DBs. A more detailed explanation of some of these features is provided in some of the references.

References [5, 6, 8, 9, 15] are devoted entirely to deductive DBs. Their main concern is to describe the semantics of deductive DBs and to explain the different approaches to query processing. Reference [9] has a chapter on integrity constraining checking, while [15] discusses deductive DB design and considers deductive DBs in the general context of knowledge systems.

Most books on DBs, for instance, [1, 10, 11, 14], include some chapters on deductive DBs. They address mainly issues behind the semantics of deductive DBs and query processing issues. Reference [14] also considers the problem of query containment checking.

Update processing is not broadly covered by any of the references. Relevant papers that have been cited in this chapter describe the different problems that need to be addressed.

5

Temporal Database Systems[1]

Hugh Darwen and C. J. Date

5.1 Introduction

Loosely speaking, a **temporal database** is one that contains historical data instead of, or as well as, current data. Such databases have been under active investigation since the mid-1970s. Some of those investigations adopt the extreme position that data in such a database are only inserted, never deleted or updated, in which case the database contains historical data only. The other extreme is a **snapshot** database, which contains current data only, and data are deleted or updated when the facts represented by those data cease to be true (in other words, a snapshot database is just a database as conventionally understood, not a temporal database at all).

By way of example, consider the suppliers and parts database of Table 5.1.

That database is, of course, a snapshot database, and it shows among other things that the status of supplier S1 is currently 20. A temporal version of that database, by contrast, might show not only that the status is currently

1. C. J. Date, *An Introduction to Database Systems*, 7th Edition, (Chapter 22), © 2000 Addison-Wesley Publishing Company, Inc. Reprinted by permission of Addison Wesley Longman.

Table 5.1
The Suppliers and Parts Database (Sample Values)—Current Snapshot Version
(Primary Key Attributes in All Examples Are Shown in Bold and Underlined)

S

S#	SNAME	STATUS	CITY
S1	Smith	20	London
S2	Jones	10	Paris
S3	Blake	30	Paris
S4	Clark	20	London
S5	Adams	30	Athens

SP

S#	P#
S1	P1
S1	P2
S1	P3
S1	P4
S1	P5
S1	P6
S2	P1
S2	P2
S3	P2
S4	P2
S4	P4
S4	P5

20, but also that it has been 20 ever since July 1, and perhaps that it was 15 from April 5 to June 30, and so on.

In a snapshot database, the time of the snapshot is usually taken to be "now" (that is, the time at which the database is actually inspected). Even if the time of the snapshot happens to be some time other than "now," it makes no material difference to the way the data are managed and used. As we will see, however, how the data are managed and used in a temporal database differs in a variety of important ways from how it is managed and used in a snapshot database; hence the present chapter.

The distinguishing feature of a temporal database is, of course, time itself. Temporal database research has therefore involved much investigation into the nature of time itself. Here are some of the issues that have been explored:

- Whether time has a beginning and/or end;
- Whether time is a continuum or occurs in discrete quanta;
- How best to characterize the important concept *now* (often referred to as "the *moving point* now");

and so on. But these issues, interesting though they might be in themselves, are not especially database issues, and we therefore do not delve into them in this chapter; instead, we simply make what we hope are reasonable assumptions at appropriate places. This approach allows us to concentrate on matters that are more directly relevant to our overall aim. However, we do note that portions of the temporal research have led to some interesting generalizations, suggesting strongly that ideas developed to support temporal data could have application in other areas as well. *Note:* This last point notwithstanding, we follow convention in referring throughout this chapter to "temporal" keys, "temporal" operators, "temporal" relations, and so forth, even though the concepts in question are often not limited to temporal data as such.

Caveat lector! We concentrate in what follows on what seem to us the most interesting and important of the various research ideas (in other words, the chapter is our attempt to distill out and explain "the good parts" of that research, though we do depart from the literature here and there over questions of nomenclature and other small matters). Be aware, however, that little if any of the proposed new technology has yet shown up in any commercial DBMS. Possible reasons for this state of affairs include the following:

- It is only recently that disk storage has become cheap enough to make the storage of large volumes of historical data a practical proposition. However, "data warehouses" are now becoming a widespread reality; as a result, users will increasingly find themselves faced with temporal database problems and will start wanting solutions to those problems.
- Although most if not all of the features we describe have been implemented in prototype form, their incorporation into existing products—especially SQL products, where SQL's departures from the

relational model will have to be catered for—could be a daunting prospect. Besides, most vendors currently have their hands full with attempts to provide *object/relational* support.

- The research community is still somewhat divided over the best way to approach the problem, and, for that matter, even what problem to approach. (This lack of consensus might have carried over to the vendors.) Some researchers favor a very specialized approach—one involving some departure from relational principles—that caters to temporal databases specifically and leaves certain other problems unsolved (see, for example, [1]). Others favor the provision of more general-purpose operators that could provide a basis for developing a specialized approach if desired, while not departing from the relational framework (see, for example, [2]). For purposes of exposition we follow the latter approach, which we also favor.

We defer an explanation of the structure of the chapter to the section immediately following.

5.2 Temporal Data

If data are an encoded representation of facts, then temporal data are an encoded representation of **timestamped** facts. In a temporal database, according to the extreme interpretation of that term, *all* the data are temporal, meaning every recorded fact is timestamped. It follows that a *temporal relation* is one in which each tuple includes at least one timestamp (that is, the heading includes at least one attribute of some timestamp type). It further follows that a *temporal relvar*[2] is one whose heading is that of a temporal relation, and a (relational) *temporal database* is one in which all of the relvars are temporal ones. *Note:* We are being deliberately vague here as to what data "of some timestamp type" might look like. We will take up this issue in Sections 5.3–5.5.

Having just offered a reasonably precise definition of the concept "temporal database" (in its extreme form), we now dismiss that concept as not very useful. We dismiss it because even if the original relvars in the database were all temporal, many relations that could be derived from that database

---

2. This term, proposed and defined precisely in [3], is short for "relation variable." It replaces the former term "base relation."

(for example, query results) would *not* be temporal. For example, the answer to the query "Get the names of all persons we have ever employed" might be obtained from some temporal database, but is not itself a temporal relation. And it would be a strange DBMS indeed—certainly not a relational one—that would let us obtain results that could not themselves be kept in the database.

In this chapter, therefore, we take a temporal database to be a database that does include some temporal data but is not limited to temporal data only. The rest of the chapter discusses such databases in detail. The plan for this chapter, then, is as follows:

- The remainder of the present section and Section 5.3 set the scene for subsequent sections; in particular, Section 5.3 shows why temporal data seem to require special treatment.

- Sections 5.4 and 5.5 introduce *intervals* as a convenient way of timestamping data. Sections 5.6 and 5.7 then discuss a variety of scalar and aggregate operators for dealing with such intervals.

- Section 5.8 introduces some important new relational operators for operating on temporal relations.

- Section 5.9 examines the question of integrity constraints for temporal data.

- Section 5.10 discusses the special problems of updating such data.

- Section 5.11 proposes some relevant (and possibly novel) database design ideas.

- Section 5.12 discusses a few miscellaneous issues that could not conveniently be handled elsewhere.

- Finally, Section 5.13 presents a summary.

Note: It is important to understand that—with just one exception, the *interval type generator* introduced in Section 5.5—all of the new operators and other constructs to be discussed in what follows are only shorthand. That is, they can all be expressed (albeit only very long-windedly, sometimes) in terms of features already available in a complete relational language such as **Tutorial D**.[3] We will justify this claim as we proceed (in some cases but not all).

---

3. **Tutorial D** is a hypothetical language used as a basis for many examples in this chapter, especially in Section 5.8. It might be characterized loosely as a Pascal-like language. It is defined in detail in [3], but we think the examples used in this chapter are so self-explanatory as to avoid any need to refer to that definition.

5.2.1 Some Basic Concepts and Questions

We begin by appealing to the way people express what might be called "timestamped statements" in natural language. Here are three examples:

1. Supplier S1 was appointed (that is, placed under contract) **on** July 1, 1999.

2. Supplier S1 has been a contracted supplier **since** July 1, 1999.

3. Supplier S1 was a contracted supplier **during** the period from July 1, 1999 to the present day.

Each of these statements is a possible interpretation of a 2-tuple containing the supplier number "S1" and the timestamp "July 1, 1999," and each of them might be appropriate of that 2-tuple if it appears in a snapshot database representing the current state of affairs in some enterprise. The **boldface** prepositions **on**, **since**, and **during** characterize the different interpretations. *Note:* Throughout this chapter we use "since" and "during" in the strong senses of "**ever** since" and "**throughout** (the period in question)," respectively, barring explicit statements to the contrary.

Now, although we have just referred to *three* possible interpretations, it might be argued that Statements 1, 2, and 3 are really all saying the same thing in slightly different ways. In fact, we do take Statements 2 and 3 to be equivalent, but not Statements 1 and 2 (or 1 and 3), for consider:

- Statement 1 clearly asserts that S1 was not a contracted supplier on the date (June 30, 1999) immediately preceding the specified appointment date; Statement 2 neither states that fact nor implies it.

- Suppose today ("the present day") is September 25, 2000. Then Statement 2 clearly states that S1 was a contracted supplier on every day from July 1, 1999 to September 25, 2000, inclusive; Statement 1 neither states *that* fact, nor implies it.

Thus, Statements 1 and 2 are not equivalent, and neither one implies the other.

That said, tuples in snapshot databases often do include things like "date of appointment," and statements like Statement 2 (or 3) often are the intended interpretation. If such is the case here, then Statement 1 in its present form is *not* a fully accurate interpretation of the tuple in question.

We can make it more accurate by rephrasing it thus: "Supplier S1 was *most recently* appointed on July 1, 1999." What is more, if this version of Statement 1 really is what our hypothetical 2-tuple is supposed to mean, then Statement 2 in its present form is not a fully accurate interpretation either—it needs to be rephrased thus: "Supplier S1 was not a contracted supplier on June 30, 1999, but has been one since July 1, 1999."

Observe now that Statement 1 expresses a time **at** which a certain **event** took place, while Statements 2 and 3 express an interval in time **during** which a certain **state** persisted. We have deliberately chosen an example in which a certain *state* might be inferred from information regarding a certain *event:* Since S1 was most recently appointed on July 1, 1999, that supplier has been in the state of being under contract from that date to the present day. Classical database technology can handle *time instants* (times at which events occur) reasonably well; however, it does not handle *time intervals* (periods of time during which states persist) very well at all, as we will see in Section 5.3.

Observe next that although Statements 2 and 3 are logically equivalent, their forms are significantly different. To be specific, the form of Statement 2 cannot be used for historical records (because "since" implies currency), while that of Statement 3 can—provided we replace the phrase "the present day" in that statement by some explicit date, say, September 25, 2000. (Of course, the statement would then correspond to a 3-tuple, not a 2-tuple.) We conclude that the concept of "during" is very important for historical records, at least for state data if not for event data.

Terminology: The time(s) at which a certain event occurred or the interval(s) during which a certain state persisted are sometimes referred to as *valid time.* More precisely, the **valid time** of a proposition p is the set of times at which p is believed to be *true.* It is distinguished from **transaction time**, which is the set of times at which p was actually represented in the database as being true. Valid times can be updated to reflect changing beliefs, but transaction times cannot; that is, transaction times are maintained entirely by the system, and no user is allowed to change them in any way (typically, of course, they are recorded, explicitly or implicitly, in the transaction log).

Note: The references in the foregoing paragraph to *intervals* and *sets of times* tacitly introduce a simple but fundamental idea—namely, that an interval with start time s and end time e actually denotes the set of all times t such that $s \leq t \leq e$ (where "<" means "earlier than," of course). Though "obvious," this simple notion has far-reaching consequences, as we will see in the sections to come.

Now, much of the foregoing discussion was deliberately meant to raise certain questions in your mind. Regardless of whether we succeeded in that aim, we now raise those questions explicitly and try to answer them.

1. Does not the expression "all times t such that $s \le t \le e$" raise the specter of infinite sets and the conceptual and computational difficulties such sets suffer from?

   Answer: Well, yes, it does appear to, but we dismiss the specter and circumvent the difficulties by adopting the assumption that the "timeline" consists of a finite sequence of discrete, indivisible *time quanta.* The interval with start time s and end time e thus involves a finite number of such quanta, *a fortiori.*

   Note: Much of the literature refers to a time quantum as a *chronon.* However, it then typically goes on to define a chronon as an interval (see, for example, the glossary in [4]), implying that it has a start point and an end point, and perhaps further points in between, and so is not indivisible after all. (What exactly are those points? What else can they be but chronons?) We find some confusion here and prefer to avoid the term.

2. Statements 1, 2, and 3 seem to assume that time quanta are *days,* but surely the system supports time precisions down to tiny fractions of a second. If S1 was a supplier on July 1, 1999, but not on June 30, 1999, what is to be done about the presumed period of time from the start of July 1 up to the very instant of appointment, during which S1 was still not officially under contract?

   Answer: We need to distinguish carefully between time quanta as such, which are the smallest time units the system can possibly represent, and the time units that are useful for some particular purpose, which might be years or months or days or weeks, and so forth. We call such units **timepoints** (*points* for short) in order to stress the fact that *for the purpose at hand* they too are considered to be indivisible. Now, we might say, *informally,* that a timepoint is "a section of the timeline"—that is, the set of time quanta—that stretches from one "boundary" quantum to the next (for example, from midnight on one day to midnight on the next). We might therefore say, again informally, that timepoints have a duration—one day, in our example. *Formally,* however, timepoints are (to repeat) indivisible, and the concept of duration strictly does not apply.

Note: Much of the literature uses the term *granule* to refer to something like a timepoint as just defined. As with the term *chronon*, however, it typically then goes on (unfortunately) to say that a granule is an interval. We therefore choose to avoid the term *granule* also.[4] We do, however, make use of the (informal) term **granularity**, which we define (again informally) as the duration of the applicable timepoint. Thus, we might say in our example that the granularity is one day, meaning that we are casting aside—in this context—our usual notion of a day being made up of hours, which are made up of minutes, and so forth (such notions can be expressed only by recourse to finer levels of granularity).

3.   Given, then, that the timeline is basically a sequence of timepoints, we can refer unambiguously to "the time immediately succeeding" (or preceding) any given point. Is that right?

   Answer: Yes, up to a point—the point in question being, of course, the end of time. And down to a point, too—the beginning of time. As far as we are concerned, the beginning of time is a timepoint that has no predecessor (it might perhaps correspond to cosmologists' best estimate of the very moment of the putative Big Bang); the end of time is a timepoint that has no successor.

4.   If some relation includes a 3-tuple representing the fact that supplier S1 was under contract from July 1, 1999 to September 25, 2000, does not the *Closed World Assumption*[5] demand that the same relation also include, for example, a 3-tuple representing the fact that S1 was under contract from July 2, 1999 until September 24, 2000, and a host of other 3-tuples representing other trivial consequences of the original 3-tuple?

   Answer: Good point! Clearly, we need a more constraining predicate as our general interpretation of such 3-tuples: "Supplier Sx

---

4.   It seems to us that the confusion over whether chronons and granules are intervals stems from a confusion over intuition *vs.* formalism. An intuitive belief about the way the world works is one thing; a formal model is something else entirely. In particular, we might *believe* the timeline is continuous and infinite, but we *model* it—for the purposes of computing in particular—as discrete and finite. *Note:* While we are on this subject, we should say too that while the concept "time quantum" (or "chronon") is useful as a basis for explaining the formal model at an intuitive level, it is not in itself part of that model at all and has no part to play in it.

5.   The assumption that a tuple with the heading of relation *r* appears in *r* *if and only if* the fact represented by that tuple is believed to be true. See Chapter 5 of [5].

was under contract on every day from date *s* to date *e*, but not on the day immediately preceding *s*, nor on the day immediately following *e*."[6] This more constraining interpretation, in its general form, provides the motivation and basis for many of the operators we describe in this chapter, in Sections 5.8 and 5.10 in particular.

5.3   What's the Problem?

We use a simplified "suppliers and parts" database as the basis for our examples in the rest of this chapter. Table 5.1 shows a set of sample data values for this database. Note carefully that the database is a snapshot database—it does not include any temporal features.

We interpret S as "Supplier S#, named SNAME, has status STATUS and is located in city CITY." We interpret SP as "Supplier S# is currently able to supply part P#."

We now proceed to discuss some simple constraints and queries for this database. Later we will consider what happens to those constraints and queries when the database is extended to include various temporal features.

Constraints (current snapshot database): The only constraints we want to consider here are the key constraints. The use of underlined and bold attribute names in Table 5.1 indicates that {S#} and {S#,P#} are the primary keys of S and SP, respectively. {S#} is a foreign key in SP referencing the primary key of S. {P#} in SP possibly constitutes a foreign key referencing the primary key of a "parts" relvar, P, but we do not use that relvar in this simplified example.

Queries (current snapshot): We consider just two queries, both of them deliberately very simple:

- *Query 1.1:* Get supplier numbers of suppliers who are currently able to supply some part.

    SP { S# }

---

6. Throughout this chapter we use the unqualified term "predicate" to refer to what in Chapter 8 of [2] is called the *external* or user-understood predicate, not the *internal* or system-understood predicate (this latter is what we call the *relvar predicate*). Moreover, we ignore aspects of such external predicates that are either "obvious" or not germane to the subject under discussion.

- *Query 1.2:* Get supplier numbers of suppliers who are currently unable to supply any part at all.

```
S { S# } MINUS SP { S# }
```

Observe that *Query 1.1* involves a simple **projection** and *Query 1.2* involves the **difference** between two such projections. Later, when we consider temporal analogs of these two queries, we will find that they involve temporal analogs of these two operators (see Section 5.8). Temporal analogs of other relational operators can be defined as well.

5.3.1 "Semitemporalizing" Suppliers and Parts

In order to proceed gently, our next step is to "semitemporalize" (so to speak) relvars S and SP by adding a timestamp attribute, SINCE, to each and renaming them accordingly. See Table 5.2.

For simplicity, we do not show real timestamps in Table 5.2; instead, we use symbols of the form *d01, d02,* and so on, where the "*d*" can conveniently be pronounced "day," a convention to which we adhere throughout this chapter. (Our examples thus all make use of timepoints that are, specifically, *days.*) We assume that day 1 immediately precedes day 2, day 2 immediately precedes day 3, and so on; also, we do not propagate the insignificant leading zeros when we write expressions such as "day 1" (as you can see).

The predicate for S_SINCE is "Since day SINCE it has been the case that supplier S# has been named SNAME, has had status STATUS, has been located in city CITY, and has been under contract." The predicate for SP_SINCE is "Since day SINCE it has been the case that supplier S# has been able to supply part P#."

5.3.1.1 Constraints (Semitemporal Database)

The primary and foreign keys for this "semitemporalized" database are the same as before. However, we need an additional constraint—one that might be thought of as *augmenting* the foreign key constraint from SP_SINCE to S_SINCE—to express the fact that no supplier can supply any part before that supplier is placed under contract. In other words, if tuple *sp* in SP_SINCE references tuple *s* in S_SINCE, the SINCE value in *sp* must not be less than that in *s*:

Table 5.2
The Suppliers and Parts Database (Sample Values)—Semitemporal Version

S_SINCE	S#	SNAME	STATUS	CITY	SINCE
	S1	Smith	20	London	*d04*
	S2	Jones	10	Paris	*d07*
	S3	Blake	30	Paris	*d03*
	S4	Clark	20	London	*d04*
	S5	Adams	30	Athens	*d02*

SP_SINCE	S#	P#	SINCE
	S1	P1	*d04*
	S1	P2	*d05*
	S1	P3	*d09*
	S1	P4	*d05*
	S1	P5	*d04*
	S1	P6	*d06*
	S2	P1	*d08*
	S2	P2	*d09*
	S3	P2	*d08*
	S4	P2	*d06*
	S4	P4	*d04*
	S4	P5	*d05*

```
CONSTRAINT AUG_SP_TO_S_FK
   IS_EMPTY (((S_SINCE RENAME SINCE AS SS) JOIN
   (SP_SINCE RENAME SINCE AS SPS)) WHERE SPS < SS);
```

With this example we begin to see the problem. Given a "semitemporal" database like that of Table 5.2, we will probably have to state many "augmented foreign key" constraints like this one, and we will soon begin to wish we had some convenient shorthand for the purpose.

5.3.1.2 Queries (Semitemporal Database)

We now consider "semitemporal" versions of Queries 1.1 and 1.2.

- *Query 2.1:* Get supplier numbers of suppliers who are currently able to supply some part, showing in each case the date since when they have been able to do so.

    If supplier Sx is currently able to supply several parts, then Sx has been able to supply some part since the earliest SINCE date shown for Sx in SP_SINCE (for example, if Sx is S1, that earliest SINCE date is *d04*). Hence:

```
SUMMARIZE SP PER SP {S#} ADD MIN (SINCE) AS SINCE
```

Result:

S#	SINCE
S1	*d04*
S2	*d08*
S3	*d08*
S4	*d04*

- *Query 2.2:* Get supplier numbers of suppliers who are currently unable to supply any part at all, showing in each case the date since when they have been unable to do so.

    In our sample data there is just one supplier who is currently unable to supply any parts at all, supplier S5. However, we cannot deduce the date since when S5 has been under contract but unable to supply any parts, because there is insufficient information in the database—the database is still only "*semi*temporalized." For example, suppose *d10* is the current day. Then it might be that S5 was able to supply at least one part from as early as *d02*, when S5 was first appointed, up to as late as *d09*; or, going to the other extreme, it might be that S5 has never been able to supply anything at all.

    To have any hope of answering *Query 2.2*, we must complete the "temporalizing" of our database, or at least the SP portion of it. To be more precise, we must keep historical records in the database showing which suppliers were able to supply which parts when, as in the section immediately following.

5.3.2   Fully Temporalizing Suppliers and Parts

Table 5.3 shows a fully temporalized version of our suppliers and parts database. Observe that the SINCE attributes have become FROM attributes, and

Table 5.3
The Suppliers and Parts Database (Sample Values)—First Fully Temporal Version,
Using Timestamps

S_FROM_TO	S#	SNAME	STATUS	CITY	FROM	TO
	S1	Smith	20	London	d04	d10
	S2	Jones	10	Paris	d07	d10
	S2	Jones	10	Paris	d02	d04
	S3	Blake	30	Paris	d03	d10
	S4	Clark	20	London	d04	d10
	S5	Adams	30	Athens	d02	d10

SP_FROM_TO	S#	P#	FROM	TO
	S1	P1	d04	d10
	S1	P2	d05	d10
	S1	P3	d09	d10
	S1	P4	d05	d10
	S1	P5	d04	d10
	S1	P6	d06	d10
	S2	P1	d02	d04
	S2	P2	d03	d03
	S2	P1	d08	d10
	S2	P2	d09	d10
	S3	P2	d08	d10
	S4	P2	d06	d09
	S4	P4	d04	d08
	S4	P5	d05	d10

each relvar has acquired an additional timestamp attribute called TO. The FROM and TO attributes together express the notion of an interval in time during which something is true; for that reason, we replace SINCE by FROM_TO in the relvar names. Because we are now keeping historical records, there are more tuples in this database than there were in either of its predecessors, as you can see. We assume for definiteness that the current date is *d10*, and so *d10* shows as the TO value for each tuple that pertains to the current state of affairs. *Note:* You might be wondering what mechanism could cause all of those *d10*'s to be replaced by *d11*'s on the stroke of midnight. Unfortunately, we have to set this issue aside for the moment; we will return to it in Section 5.11.

Note that the temporal database of Table 5.3 includes all of the information from the semitemporal one of Table 5.2, together with historical information concerning a previous period (from *d02* to *d04*) during which supplier S2 was under contract. The predicate for S_FROM_TO is "Supplier S# was named SNAME, had status STATUS, was located in city CITY, and was under contract, from day FROM (and not on the day immediately before FROM) to day TO (and not on the day immediately after TO)." The predicate for SP_FROM_TO is analogous.

5.3.2.1 Constraints (First Temporal Database)

First of all, we need to guard against the absurdity of a FROM-TO pair appearing in which the TO timepoint precedes the FROM timepoint:

```
CONSTRAINT S_FROM_TO_OK IS_EMPTY (S_FROM_TO WHERE TO
< FROM);
CONSTRAINT SP_FROM_TO_OK IS_EMPTY (SP_FROM_TO WHERE TO
< FROM);
```

Next, observe from the underlining in Table 5.3 that we have included the FROM attribute in the primary key for both S_FROM_TO and SP_FROM_TO; for example, the primary key of S_FROM_TO obviously cannot be just {S#}, for then we could not have the same supplier under contract for more than one continuous period. A similar observation applies to SP_FROM_TO. *Note:* We could have used the TO attributes instead of the FROM attributes; in fact, S_FROM_TO and SP_FROM_TO both have two candidate keys and are good examples of relvars for which there is no obvious reason to choose one of those keys as "primary." We make the choices we do purely for definiteness.

However, these primary keys do not of themselves capture all of the constraints we would like them to. Consider relvar S_FROM_TO, for example. It should be clear that if there is a tuple for supplier Sx in that relvar with FROM value *f* and TO value *t*, then we want there not to be a tuple for supplier Sx in relvar indicating that Sx was under contract on the day immediately before *f* or the day immediately after *t*. For example, consider supplier S1, for whom we have just one S_FROM_TO tuple, with FROM = *d04* and

TO = $d10$. The mere fact that {S#, FROM} is the primary key for this relvar is clearly insufficient to prevent the appearance of an additional "overlapping" S1 tuple with, say, FROM = $d02$ and TO = $d06$, indicating among other things that S1 was under contract on the day immediately before $d04$. Clearly, what we would like is for these two S1 tuples to be *coalesced* into a single tuple with FROM = $d02$ and TO = $d10$.[7]

The fact that {S#, FROM} is the primary key for S_FROM_TO is also insufficient to prevent the appearance of an "abutting" S1 tuple with, say, FROM = $d02$ and TO = $d03$, indicating again that S1 was under contract on the day immediately before $d04$. As before, what we would like is for the tuples to be coalesced into a single tuple.

Here then is a constraint that does prohibit such overlapping and abutting:

```
CONSTRAINT AUG_S_FROM_TO_PK
    IS_EMPTY (((S_FROM_TO RENAME FROM AS F1, TO
    AS T1) JOIN
            (S_FROM_TO RENAME FROM AS F2, TO AS T2))
        WHERE (T1 ≥ F2 AND T2 ≥ F1)) OR
            (F2 = T1+1 OR F1 = T2+1));
```

This expression is quite complicated, not to mention that we have taken the gross liberty of writing, for example, "T1 + 1" to designate the immediate successor of the day denoted by T1, a point we will come back to in Section 5.5. *Note:* Assuming this constraint is indeed stated (and enforced, of course), some writers would refer to the attribute combination {S#, FROM,TO} as a *temporal candidate key* (in fact, a temporal *primary* key). The term is not very good, however, because the "temporal" candidate key is not in fact a *candidate* key in the first place. (In Section 5.9, by contrast, we will encounter "temporal candidate keys" that genuinely are candidate keys in the classical sense.)

Next, note carefully that the attribute combination {S#, FROM} in relvar SP_FROM_TO is *not* a foreign key from SP_FROM_TO to S_FROM_TO (even though it does involve the same attributes, S# and FROM, as the primary key of S_FROM_TO). However, we certainly do

---

7. Observe that *not* coalescing such tuples would be almost as bad as permitting duplicates. Duplicates amount to "saying the same thing twice." And those two tuples for S1 with overlapping time intervals do indeed "say the same thing twice"; to be specific, they both say that S1 was under contract on days 4, 5, and 6.

need to ensure that if a certain supplier appears in SP_FROM_TO, then that same supplier appears in S_FROM_TO as well:

```
CONSTRAINT AUG_SP_TO_S_FK_AGAIN1
    SP_FROM_TO {S#} ⊆ S_FROM_TO {S#};
```

But constraint AUG_SP_TO_S_FK_AGAIN1 is not enough by itself; we also need to ensure that (even if all desired coalescing of tuples has been done) if SP_FROM_TO shows some supplier as being able to supply some part during some interval of time, then S_FROM_TO shows that same supplier as being under contract during that same interval of time. We might try the following:

```
CONSTRAINT AUG_SP_TO_S_FK_AGAIN2 /* Warning — incorrect! */
    IS_EMPTY ((S_FROM_TO RENAME FROM AS SF, TO
    AS ST) JOIN
        (SP_FROM_TO RENAME FROM AS SPF, TO AS
        SPT))
        WHERE SPF < SF OR SPT > ST);
```

As the comment indicates, however, this specification is in fact incorrect. To see why, let S_FROM_TO be as shown in Table 5.3, and let SP_FROM_TO include a tuple for supplier S2 with, say, FROM = *d03* and TO = *d04*. Such an arrangement is clearly consistent, yet constraint AUG_SP_ TO_S_FK_AGAIN2 as stated actually prohibits it.

We will not try to fix this problem here, deferring it instead to a later section (Section 5.9). However, we remark as a matter of terminology that if (as noted earlier) attribute combination {S#, FROM, TO} in relvar S_FROM_TO is regarded as a "temporal candidate key," then attribute combination {S#, FROM, TO} in relvar SP_FROM_TO might be regarded as a "temporal *foreign* key" (though it is not in fact a foreign key as such). Again, see Section 5.9 for further discussion.

5.3.2.2 Queries (First Temporal Database)

Here now are fully temporal versions of Queries 1.1 and 1.2:

- *Query 3.1:* Get S#-FROM-TO triples for suppliers who have been able to supply some part at some time, where FROM and TO together designate a maximal continuous period during which supplier S# was in fact able to supply some part. *Note:* We use the term "maximal" here as a convenient shorthand to mean (in the case at hand) that supplier S# was unable to supply any part on the day immediately before FROM or after TO.

- *Query 3.2:* Get S#-FROM-TO triples for suppliers who have been unable to supply any parts at all at some time, where FROM and TO together designate a maximal continuous period during which supplier S# was in fact unable to supply any part.

Well, you might like to take a little time to convince yourself that, like us, you would really prefer not even to attempt these queries. If you do make the attempt, however, the fact that they *can* be expressed, albeit exceedingly laboriously, will eventually emerge, but it will surely be obvious that some kind of shorthand is very desirable.

In a nutshell, therefore, the problem of temporal data is that it quickly leads to constraints and queries that are unreasonably complex to state—unless the system provides some well-designed shorthands, of course, which (as we know) today's commercial products do not.

5.4 Intervals

We now embark on our development of an appropriate set of shorthands. The first and most fundamental step is to recognize the need to deal with intervals as such in their own right, instead of having to treat them as pairs of separate values as we have been doing up to this point.

What exactly is an interval? According to Table 5.3, supplier S1 was able to supply part P1 during the interval from day 4 to day 10. But what does "from day 4 to day 10" mean? It is clear that days 5, 6, 7, 8, and 9 are included—but what about the start and end points, days 4 and 10? It turns out that, given some specific interval, we sometimes want to regard the specified start and end points as included in the interval and sometimes not. If the interval from day 4 to day 10 does include day 4, we say it is **closed** with respect to its start point; otherwise we say it is **open** with respect to that point. Likewise, if it includes day 10, we say it is closed with respect to its end point; otherwise we say it is open with respect to that point.

Conventionally, therefore, we denote an interval by its start point and its end point (in that order), preceded by either an opening bracket or an opening parenthesis and followed by either a closing bracket or a closing parenthesis. Brackets are used where the interval is closed, parentheses where it is open. Thus, for example, there are four distinct ways to denote the specific interval that runs from day 4 to day 10 inclusive:

[*d04, d10*]

[*d04, d11*)

(*d03, d10*]

(*d03, d11*)

Note: You might think it odd to use, for example, an opening bracket but a closing parenthesis; the fact is, however, there are good reasons to allow all four styles. Indeed, the so-called "closed-open" style (opening bracket, closing parenthesis) is the one most used in practice.[8] However, the "closed-closed" style (opening bracket, closing bracket) is surely the most intuitive, and we will favor it in what follows.

Given that intervals such as [*d04,d10*] are values in their own right, it makes sense to combine the FROM and TO attributes of, say, SP_FROM_TO (see Table 5.3) into a single attribute, DURING, whose values are drawn from some **interval type** (see the next section). One immediate advantage of this idea is that it avoids the need to make the arbitrary choice as to which of the two candidate keys {S#, FROM} and {S#, TO} should be primary. Another advantage is that it also avoids the need to decide whether the FROM-TO intervals of Table 5.3 are to be interpreted as closed or open with respect to each of FROM and TO; in fact, [*d04,d10*], [*d04,d11*), (*d03,d10*], and (*d03,d11*) now become four distinct possible representations of the same interval, and we have no need to know which (if any) is the actual representation. Yet another advantage is that relvar constraints "to guard against the absurdity of a FROM ≤ TO pair appearing in which the TO timepoint precedes the FROM timepoint" (as we put it in Section 5.3) are no longer necessary, because the constraint "FROM TO" is implicit in the very notion of an interval type (loosely speaking). Other constraints might also be simplified, as we will see in Section 5.9.

Table 5.4 shows what happens to our example database if we adopt this approach.

---

8. To see why the closed-open style might be advantageous, consider the operation of splitting the interval [*d04,d10*] immediately before, say, *d07*. The result is the immediately adjacent intervals [*d04,d07*) and [*d07,d10*].

Table 5.4
The Suppliers and Parts Database (Sample Values)—Final Fully Temporal Version, Using Intervals

S_DURING	S#	SNAME	STATUS	CITY	DURING
	S1	Smith	20	London	[*d04, d10*]
	S2	Jones	10	Paris	[*d07, d10*]
	S2	Jones	10	Paris	[*d02, d04*]
	S3	Blake	30	Paris	[*d03, d10*]
	S4	Clark	20	London	[*d04, d10*]
	S5	Adams	30	Athens	[*d02, d10*]

SP_DURING	S#	P#	DURING
	S1	P1	[*d04, d10*]
	S1	P2	[*d05, d10*]
	S1	P3	[*d09, d10*]
	S1	P4	[*d05, d10*]
	S1	P5	[*d04, d10*]
	S1	P6	[*d06, d10*]
	S2	P1	[*d02, d04*]
	S2	P2	[*d03, d03*]
	S2	P1	[*d08, d10*]
	S2	P2	[*d09, d10*]
	S3	P2	[*d08, d10*]
	S4	P2	[*d06, d09*]
	S4	P4	[*d04, d08*]
	S4	P5	[*d05, d10*]

5.5   Interval Types

Our discussion of intervals in the previous section was mostly intuitive in nature; now we need to approach the issue more formally. First of all, observe that the granularity of the interval [*d04,d10*] is "days." More precisely, we could say it is *type DATE*, by which term we mean that member of the usual family of "datetime" data types whose precision is "day" (as opposed to, say, "hour" or "millisecond" or "month"). This observation allows us to pin down the exact type of the interval in question, as follows:

- First and foremost, of course, it is some **interval** type; this fact by itself is sufficient to determine the *operators* that are applicable to the interval value in question (just as to say that, for example, a value *r* is of some *relation* type is sufficient to determine the operators—JOIN, etc.—that are applicable to that value *r*).

- Second, the interval in question is, very specifically, an interval from one **date** to another, and *this* fact is sufficient to determine the set of *interval values* that constitute the interval type in question.

The specific type of [*d04,d10*] is thus INTERVAL(DATE), where:

a. INTERVAL is a **type generator** (like RELATION in **Tutorial D**, or "array" in conventional programming languages) that allows us to define a variety of specific interval types (see further discussion below);

b. DATE is the **point type** of this specific interval type.

It is important to note that, in general, point type *PT* determines both the type *and the precision* of the start and end points—and all points in between—of values of type INTERVAL(*PT*). (In the case of type DATE, of course, the precision is implicit.)

Note: Normally, we do not regard precision as part of the applicable type but, rather, as an integrity constraint. Given the declarations DECLARE X TIMESTAMP(3) and DECLARE Y TIMESTAMP(6), for example, X and Y are of the same type but are subject to different constraints (X is constrained to hold millisecond values and Y is constrained to hold microsecond values). Strictly speaking, therefore, to say that, for example, TIMESTAMP(3)—or DATE—is a legal point type is to bundle together two concepts that should really be kept separate. Instead, it would be better to define two types T1 and T2, both with a TIMESTAMP possible representation but with different "precision constraints," and then say that T1 and T2 (not, for example, TIMESTAMP(3) and TIMESTAMP(6)) are legal point types. For simplicity, however, we follow conventional usage in this chapter and pretend that precision is part of the type.

What properties must a type possess if it is to be legal as a point type? Well, we have seen that an interval is denoted by its start and end points; we have also seen that (at least informally) an interval consists of a set of points. If we are to be able to determine the complete set of points, given just the start point s and the end point e, we must first be able to determine the point that immediately follows (in some agreed ordering) the point s. We call that immediately following point the **successor** of s; for simplicity, let us agree to refer to it as $s + 1$. Then the function by which $s + 1$ is determined from s is the **successor function** for the point type (and precision) in question. That successor function must be defined for every value of the point type, except the one designated as "last." (There will also be one point designated as "first," which is not the successor of anything.)

Having determined that $s + 1$ is the successor of s, we must next determine whether or not $s + 1$ comes after e, according to the same agreed ordering for the point type in question. If it does not, then $s + 1$ is indeed a point in $[s,e]$, and we must now consider the next point, $s + 2$. Continuing this process until we come to the first point $s + n$ that comes after e (that is, the successor of e), we will discover every point of $[s,e]$.

Noting that $s + n$ is in fact the successor of e (that is, it actually comes immediately after e), we can now safely say that the only property a type PT must have to be legal as a point type is that a successor function must be defined for it. The existence of such a function implies that there must be a **total ordering** for the values in PT (and we can therefore assume the usual comparison operators—"$<$," "$\geq$," etc.—are available and defined for all pairs of PT values).

By the way, you will surely have noticed by now that we are no longer talking about temporal data specifically. Indeed, most of the rest of this chapter is about intervals in general rather than time intervals in particular, though we will consider certain specifically temporal issues in Section 5.11.

Here then (at last) is a precise definition: Let PT be a point type. Then an **interval** (or **interval value**) i of type INTERVAL(PT) is a scalar value for which two monadic scalar operators (START and END) and one dyadic operator (IN) are defined, such that:

    a.   START(i) and END(i) each return a value of type PT.

    b.   START(i) $\leq$ END(i).

    c.   Let p be a value of type PT. Then p IN i is true if and only if START(i) $\leq p$ and $p \leq$ END(i) are both true.

Note the appeals in this definition to the defined successor function for type PT. Note also that, by definition, intervals are always nonempty (that is, there is always at least one point "IN" any given interval).

Observe very carefully that a value of type INTERVAL(*PT*) is a **scalar** value—that is, it has no user-visible components. It is true that it does have a possible representation—in fact, several possible representations, as we saw in the previous section—and those possible representations in turn do have user-visible components, but the interval value *per se* does not. Another way of saying the same thing is to say that intervals are *encapsulated.*

5.6 Scalar Operators on Intervals

In this section we define some useful scalar operators (most of them more or less self-explanatory) that apply to interval values. Consider the interval type INTERVAL(*PT*). Let *p* be a value of type *PT*. We will continue to use the notation $p + 1$, $p + 2$, and so on, to denote the successor of *p*, the successor of $p + 1$, and so on (a real language might provide some kind of NEXT operator). Similarly, we will use the notation $p - 1$, $p - 2$, and so on, to denote the value whose successor is *p*, the value whose successor is $p - 1$, and so on (a real language might provide some kind of PRIOR operator).

Let *p1* and *p2* be values in *PT*. Then we define MAX(*p1,p2*) to return *p2* if $p1 < p2$ is true and *p1* otherwise, and MIN(*p1,p2*) to return *p1* if $p1 < p2$ is true and *p2* otherwise.

The notation we have already been using will do for interval selectors (at least in informal contexts). For example, the selector invocations [3,5] and [3,6] both yield that value of type INTERVAL(INTEGER) whose contained points are 3, 4, and 5. (A real language would probably require some more explicit syntax, as in, for example, INTERVAL([3,5]).)

Let *i1* be the interval [*s1,e1*] of type INTERVAL(*PT*). As we have already seen, START(*i1*) returns *s1* and END(*i1*) returns *e1*; we additionally define STOP(*i1*), which returns $e1 + 1$. Also, let *i2* be the interval [*s2,e2*], also of type INTERVAL(*PT*). Then we define the following more or less self-explanatory interval **comparison** operators. *Note:* These operators are often known as *Allen's operators*, having first been proposed by Allen in [6].

- *i1* = *i2* is true if and only if $s1 = s2$ and $e1 = e2$ are both true.

- *i1* BEFORE *i2* is true if and only if $e1 < s2$ is true.

- *i1* MEETS *i2* is true if and only if $s2 = e1 + 1$ is true or $s1 = e2 + 1$ is true.

- *i1* OVERLAPS *i2* is true if and only if $s1 \leq e2$ and $s2 \leq e1$ are both true.

- *i1* DURING *i2* is true if and only if $s2 \leq s1$ and $e2 \geq e1$ are both true.[9]
- *i1* STARTS *i2* is true if and only if $s1 = s2$ and $e1 \leq e2$ are both true.
- *i1* FINISHES *i2* is true if and only if $e1 = e2$ and $s1 \geq s2$ are both true.

Following [2], we can also define the following useful additions to Allen's operators:

- *i1* MERGES *i2* is true if and only if *i1* MEETS *i2* is true or *i1* OVERLAPS *i2* is true.
- *i1* CONTAINS *i2* is true if and only if *i2* DURING *i1* is true.[10]
- To obtain the length, so to speak, of an interval, we have DURATION(*i*), which returns the number of points in *i*. For example, DURATION([*d03,d07*]) = 5.

Finally, we define some useful dyadic operators on intervals that return intervals:

- *i1* UNION *i2* yields [MIN(*s1,s2*),MAX(*e1,e2*)] if *i1* MERGES *i2* is true and is otherwise undefined.
- *i1* INTERSECT *i2* yields [MAX(*s1,s2*),MIN(*e1,e2*)] if *i1* OVER-LAPS *i2* is true and is otherwise undefined.

Note: UNION and INTERSECT here are the general set operators, not their special relational counterparts. Reference [2] calls them MERGE and INTERVSECT, respectively.

5.7 Aggregate Operators on Intervals

In this section we introduce two extremely important operators, *UNFOLD* and *COALESCE*. Each of these operators takes a set of intervals all of the same type as its single operand and returns another such set. The result in both cases can be regarded as a particular *canonical form* for the original set.

---

9. Observe that here (for once) DURING does *not* mean "throughout the interval in question."
10. INCLUDES might be a better keyword than CONTAINS here; then we could use CONTAINS as the inverse of IN, defining *i* CONTAINS *p* to be equivalent to *p* IN *i.*

T2 looks like this:

S#	X
S1	DURING [d04, d10] [d05, d10] [d09, d10] [d06, d10]
S2	DURING [d02, d04] [d03, d03] [d08, d10] [d09, d10]
S3	DURING [d08, d10]
S4	DURING [d06, d10] [d04, d08] [d05, d10]

Now we apply the new version of COALESCE to the relations that are values of the relation-valued attribute X:

```
WITH (EXTEND T2 ADD COALESCE (X) AS Y) {ALL BUT X} AS
T3 :
```

T3 looks like this:

S#	X
S1	DURING [d04, d10]
S2	DURING [d02, d04] [d08, d10]
S3	DURING [d08, d10]
S4	DURING [d04, d10]

Finally, we ungroup:

```
T3 UNGROUP Y
```

This expression yields the relation we earlier called RESULT. In other words, now showing all the steps together (and simplifying slightly), RESULT is the result of evaluating the following overall expression:

```
WITH SP_DURING {S#, DURING} AS T1,
    (T1 GROUP (DURING) AS X) AS T2,
    (EXTEND T2 ADD COALESCE (X) AS Y) {ALL BUT
    X} AS T3 :
T3 UNGROUP Y
```

Obviously it would be desirable to be able to get from T1 to RESULT in a single operation. To that end, we invent a new "relation coalesce" operator, with syntax as follows:

```
R COALESCE A
```

(where R is a relational expression and A is an attribute—of some interval type—of the relation denoted by that expression).[11] The semantics of this operator are defined by obvious generalization of the grouping, extension, projection, and ungrouping operations by which we obtained RESULT from T1. *Note:* It might help to observe that coalescing R on A involves grouping R by all of the attributes of R other than A (similarly, the expression "T1 GROUP (DURING) ...," for example, can be read as "group T1 *by* S#," S# being the sole attribute of T1 *not* mentioned in the GROUP clause).

Putting all of the foregoing together, we can now offer the following as a reasonably straightforward formulation of *Query 4.1*:

```
SP_DURING { S#, DURING } COALESCE DURING
```

Note: The overall operation denoted by this expression is an example of what some writers call *temporal projection*. To be more specific, it is a "temporal projection" of SP_DURING over S# and DURING. (Recall that the original version of this query, *Query 1.1*, involved the ordinary projection of SP over S#.) Observe that temporal projection is not exactly a projection as such but is, rather, a "temporal analog" of an ordinary projection.

We now move on to *Query 3.2*. *Query 4.2* is a restatement of that query in terms of the database of Table 5.4:

---

11. The A operand could be extended to permit a comma list of attribute names, if desired. Analogous remarks apply to the "relation unfold" and "temporal difference" operators also.

- *Query 4.2:* Get S#-DURING pairs for suppliers who have been unable to supply any parts at all at some time, where DURING designates a maximal continuous period during which supplier S# was in fact unable to supply any part.

Recall that the original version of this query, *Query 1.2*, involved a relational difference operation. Thus, if you are expecting to see something that might be called *temporal difference*, then of course you are right. As you might also be expecting, while "temporal projection" requires "relation coalesce," "temporal difference" requires "relation unfold."

"Temporal difference" (like the ordinary difference operation) involves two relation operands. We concentrate on the left operand first. If we unfold the result of the (regular) projection S_DURING {S#,DURING} over DURING, we obtain a relation—let us call it T1—that looks something like this:

S#	DURING
S1	[*d04, d04*]
S1	[*d05, d05*]
S1	[*d06, d06*]
S1	[*d07, d07*]
S1	[*d08, d08*]
S1	[*d09, d09*]
S1	[*d10, d10*]
S2	[*d07, d07*]
S2	[*d08, d08*]
S2	[*d09, d09*]
S2	[*d10, d10*]
S2	[*d02, d02*]
S2	[*d03, d03*]
S2	[*d04, d04*]
S3	[*d03, d03*]
...	....

Given the sample data of Table 5.4, T1 actually contains a total of 23 tuples. (*Exercise:* Check this claim.)

If we define a "unary relation" version of UNFOLD (analogous to the "unary relation" version of COALESCE), then we can obtain T1 as follows:

```
( EXTEND ( S_DURING { S#, DURING } GROUP ( DURING ) AS X )
      ADD UNFOLD ( X ) AS Y ) { ALL BUT X } UNGROUP Y
```

As already suggested, however, we can simplify matters by inventing a "relation unfold" operator with syntax as follows (and straightforward semantics):

```
R UNFOLD A
```

Now we can write

```
WITH ( S_DURING { S#, DURING } UNFOLD DURING ) AS T1 :
```

We treat the right "temporal difference" operand in like fashion:

```
WITH ( SP_DURING { S#, DURING } UNFOLD DURING ) AS T2 :
```

Now we can apply (regular) relation difference:

```
WITH ( T1 MINUS T2 ) AS T3 :
```

T3 looks like this:

S#	DURING
S2	[d07, d07]
S3	[d03, d03]
S3	[d04, d04]
S3	[d05, d05]
S3	[d06, d06]
S3	[d07, d07]
S5	[d02, d02]
S5	[d03, d03]
S5	[d04, d04]
S5	[d05, d05]
S5	[d06, d06]
S5	[d07, d07]
S5	[d08, d08]
S5	[d09, d09]
S5	[d10, d10]

Finally, we coalesce T3 on DURING to obtain the desired result:

```
T3 COALESCE DURING
```

The result looks like this:

S#	DURING
S2	[*d07, d07*]
S3	[*d03, d07*]
S5	[*d02, d10*]

Here then is a formulation of *Query 4.2* as a single nested expression:

```
((S_DURING {S#, DURING} UNFOLD DURING)
    MINUS
    (SP_DURING UNFOLD DURING))
COALESCE DURING
```

As already indicated, the overall operation denoted by this expression is an example of what some writers call **temporal difference**. More precisely, it is a "temporal difference" between the projections of S_DURING and SP_DURING (in that order) over S# and DURING. Note that, like temporal projection, temporal difference is not exactly a difference as such but is, rather, a "temporal analog" of an ordinary difference.

We are not quite done here, however. "Temporal difference" expressions like the one shown in the example are required so frequently in practice that it seems worthwhile defining a still further shorthand for them.[12] To be specific, it seems worth capturing as a single operation the sequence (a) unfold both operands, (b) take the difference, and then (c) coalesce. Here is our proposed further shorthand:

```
R1 I_MINUS R2 ON A
```

R1 and *R2* are relational expressions denoting relations *r1* and *r2* of the same type and *A* is an attribute of some interval type that is common to those two relations (and the prefix "I_" stands for "interval," of course). As we have

---

12. Note that (by contrast) we did not define a special shorthand for temporal projection.

more or less seen already, this expression is defined to be semantically equivalent to the following:

```
( ( R1 UNFOLD A ) MINUS ( R2 UNFOLD A ) ) COALESCE A
```

The definitions of possible further "I_" operators, such as I_UNION and
I_INTERSECT, are left as an exercise for the reader.

There is an important *performance* point to be made in connection with
operators such as I_MINUS. Going through the actual motions of unfolding
both operands, taking the difference and then coalescing could be inordi-
nately time and space consuming. Much more efficient methods than that
are available. In fact, it is to be hoped that the optimizer would use the
efficient method for I_MINUS even when the longhand expression is given
in its place. An area for further research presents itself here, for consider a
slightly more complex expression such as

```
( ( ( R1 UNFOLD A ) WHERE C ) MINUS ( R2 UNFOLD A ) )
COALESCE A
```

where *C* is some arbitrary condition. If it can be proved that this is logically
equivalent to

```
( R1 WHERE C ) I_MINUS R2 ON A
```

then the optimizer might do well to realize that and take advantage of it.

5.9 Constraints Involving Intervals

It is clear that the attribute combination {S#,DURING} is a candidate key
for relvar S_DURING; in Table 5.4, in fact, we used our underlining convention to show that key as the *primary key* specifically. (Observe that {S#} by
itself is not a candidate key, because it is possible for a supplier's contract to
be terminated and then reinstated at a later date—see, for example, supplier
S2 in Table 5.4.) Relvar S_DURING might thus be defined as follows:

```
VAR S_DURING RELATION
    {S# S#, SNAME NAME, STATUS INTEGER, CITY
     CHAR, DURING INTERVAL (DATE)}
    KEY {S#, DURING};      /* Warning—inadequate! */
```

However, the KEY specification as shown here (though it *is* logically correct) is also inadequate, in a sense, for it fails to prevent relvar S_DURING from containing, for example, both of the following tuples:

S2	Jones	10	Paris	[*d07, d10*]
S2	Jones	10	Paris	[*d02, d08*]

As you can see, these two tuples display a certain *redundancy,* inasmuch as the information pertaining to supplier S2 on days 7 and 8 is recorded twice.

The KEY specification is inadequate in another way also. To be specific, it fails to prevent relvar S_DURING from containing, for example, both of the following tuples:

S2	Jones	10	Paris	[*d02, d06*]
S2	Jones	10	Paris	[*d07, d10*]

Here there is no redundancy, but there is a certain *circumlocution,* inasmuch as we are taking two tuples to say what could be better said with one:

S2	Jones	10	Paris	[*d02, d10*]

It should be clear that, in order to prevent such redundancies and circumlocutions, we need to enforce a relvar constraint—let us call it *constraint C1*—along the following lines:

> "If two distinct S_DURING tuples are identical except for their DURING values *i1* and *i2*, then *i1* MERGES *i2* must be false."

(Recall that MERGES is the OR of OVERLAPS and MEETS, loosely speaking; replacing MERGES by OVERLAPS in constraint C1 gives the constraint we need to enforce to prevent redundancy, replacing it by MEETS gives the constraint we need to enforce to prevent circumlocution.) It should also be clear that there is a very simple way to enforce constraint C1: namely, by keeping relvar S_DURING coalesced at all times on attribute DURING. Let us therefore define a new COALESCED clause that can optionally appear in a relvar definition, as here:

```
VAR S_DURING BASE   RELATION
    {S# S#, SNAME NAME, STATUS INTEGER, CITY
     CHAR, DURING INTERVAL ( DATE ) }
    KEY {S#, DURING}
    COALESCED DURING; /* Warning—still inadequate! */
```

The specification COALESCED DURING here means that relvar S_DURING must at all times be identical to the result of the expression S_DURING COALESCE DURING (implying that coalescing S_DURING on DURING will thus have no effect). This special syntax thus suffices to solve the redundancy and circumlocution problems.[13] *Note:* We assume for the time being that any attempt to update S_DURING in such a way as to leave it less than fully coalesced on DURING will simply be rejected. However, see Section 5.10 for further discussion of this point.

Unfortunately, the KEY and COALESCED specifications together are still not quite adequate, for they fail to prevent relvar S_DURING from containing, for example, both of the following tuples:

S2	Jones	10	Paris	[d02, d08]
S2	Jones	20	Paris	[d07, d10]

Here supplier S2 is shown as having a status of both 10 and 20 on days 7 and 8—clearly an impossible state of affairs. In other words, we have a *contradiction* on our hands.

It should be clear that, in order to prevent such contradictions, we need to enforce a relvar constraint—let us call it *constraint C2*—along the following lines:

> "If two distinct S_DURING tuples have DURING values *i1* and *i2* such that *i1* OVERLAPS *i2* is true, then those two tuples must be identical except for their DURING values."

Note very carefully that constraint C2 is *not* enforced by keeping S_DURING coalesced on DURING (and it is obviously not enforced by the fact that {S#, DURING} is a candidate key). But suppose relvar S_DURING was kept **unfolded** at all times on attribute DURING. Then:

---

13. We note that an argument might be made for providing similar special-case syntax to avoid just the redundancy problem and not the circumlocution problem.

- The sole candidate key for that unfolded form S_DURING UNFOLD DURING would again be the attribute combination {S#, DURING} (because, at any given time, any given supplier currently under contract has just one name, one status, and one city).

- Hence, no two distinct tuples could possibly have the same S# value and "overlapping" DURING values (because all DURING values are unit intervals in S_DURING UNFOLD DURING, and two tuples with the same S# value and "overlapping" DURING values would thus be duplicates of each other—in fact, they would be the same tuple).

It follows that if we enforce the constraint that {S#, DURING} is a candidate key for S_DURING UNFOLD DURING, we enforce constraint C2 "automatically." Let us therefore define a new I_KEY clause ("I_" for interval) that can optionally appear in place of the usual KEY clause in a relvar definition, as here:

```
VAR S_DURING BASE  RELATION
    {S# S#, SNAME NAME, STATUS INTEGER, CITY
     CHAR, DURING INTERVAL (DATE)}
    I_KEY {S#, DURING UNFOLDED}
    COALESCED DURING;
```

(meaning, precisely, that {S#, DURING} is a candidate key for S_DURING UNFOLD DURING).[14] This I_KEY specification suffices to solve the contradiction problem.

Note carefully that if {S#, DURING} is a candidate key for S_DURING UNFOLD DURING, it is certainly a candidate key for S_DURING; it is this fact that allows us to drop the original KEY specification for S_DURING in favor of the I_KEY specification. Note further that {S#, DURING} can be regarded as a **temporal candidate** key in the sense of Section 5.3. As we have just seen, moreover, this temporal candidate key is indeed a true candidate key for its containing relvar (unlike the "temporal candidate keys" discussed in Section 5.3).

---

14. Some writers (see, for example, [2]) define the semantics of I_KEY in such a way as to take care of the redundancy problem also. We prefer to separate the issues (in any case combining them is unnecessary, since COALESCED is clearly sufficient to deal with the redundancy problem).

Of course, if such "I_KEY" syntax is supported for candidate keys, we can expect it to be supported for foreign keys as well. Thus, the definition of SP_DURING might include the following:

```
FOREIGN I_KEY { S#, DURING UNFOLDED } REFERENCES
S_DURING ...
```

The intent here is that if SP_DURING shows supplier Sx was able to supply some part during interval i, then S_DURING must show that Sx was under contract throughout interval i. If this constraint is satisfied, then attribute combination {S#, DURING} in relvar SP_DURING can be regarded as a **temporal foreign key** in the sense of Section 5.3. (It is still not a true foreign key in the classical sense, however.)

There is one more point to be made regarding relvar S_DURING. Suppose we do indeed keep that relvar coalesced on DURING at all times. Suppose too that from time to time we run a procedure that recomputes the status of suppliers currently under contract. Of course, the procedure is careful to record previous status values in S_DURING. Now, sometimes the recomputation results in no change of status. In such a case, if the procedure blindly tries to insert a record of the previous status in S_DURING, it will violate the COALESCED specification. In order to avoid such violations, the procedure will have to make a special test for "no change in status" and perform an appropriate UPDATE instead of the INSERT that does the job when the status *does* change. Alternatively, of course, we could decide not to keep S_DURING coalesced on DURING after all—a solution that is probably not appropriate in this particular case, but might be so in other cases.

5.10 Update Operators Involving Intervals

In this section we consider some problems that arise with the use of the usual update operators INSERT, UPDATE, and DELETE on a temporal relvar. Consider S_DURING once again; assume the definition of that relvar includes the "temporal candidate key" and COALESCED specifications as suggested in the previous section. Assume too (as usual) that the current value of S_DURING is as shown in Table 5.4. Now consider the following scenarios:

- *INSERT:* Suppose we discover that supplier S2 was additionally under contract during the period from day 5 to day 6 (but still was named Jones, had status 10, and was located in Paris, throughout that time). We cannot simply insert a tuple to that effect, for if we did so the result would violate the COALESCED requirement twice. In fact, what we have to do is delete one of the existing S2 tuples and update the DURING value in the other to [*d02,d10*].

- *UPDATE:* Suppose we discover that S2's status was temporarily increased on day 9 to 20. It is quite difficult to make the required change, even though it sounds like a simple UPDATE. Basically, we have to split S2's [*d07,d10*] tuple into three, with DURING values [*d07,d08*], [*d09,d09*], and [*d10,d10*], respectively, and with other values unchanged, and then replace the STATUS value in the [*d09,d09*] tuple by the value 20.

- *DELETE:* Suppose we discover that supplier S3's contract was terminated on day 6 but reinstated on day 9. Again, the required update is nontrivial, requiring the single tuple for S3 to be split into two, with DURING values of [*d03,d05*] and [*d09,d10*], respectively.

Observe now that the solutions we have just outlined to these three problems are *specific to the current value* of relvar S_DURING (as well as to the particular updates desired). Consider the insert problem, for example; in general, a tuple considered for insertion might just be insertable "as is," or it might need to be coalesced with a "preceding" tuple, a "following" tuple, or (as in our example) both. Analogously, updates and deletions in general might or might not require the "splitting" of existing tuples.

It is clear that life will be unbearably complicated for users if they are limited to the conventional INSERT, UPDATE, and DELETE operations; some extensions are clearly desirable. Here then are some possibilities:

- *INSERT:* Actually, the INSERT problem can be solved by simply extending the semantics of the COALESCED specification on the relvar definition appropriately. To be specific, we can permit the INSERT to be done in the normal way and then require the system to do any needed (re)coalescing following that INSERT. In other words, the COALESCED specification no longer merely defines a constraint, it also includes certain implicit *compensating actions* (analogous, somewhat, to referential actions on foreign key specifications).

  Unfortunately, however, extending the semantics of COALESCED in this way is not sufficient in itself to solve the UPDATE and DELETE problems.

- *UPDATE:* The UPDATE problem can be addressed by extending the UPDATE operator as suggested by the following example:[15]

```
UPDATE S_DURING
WHERE S# = S# ( S2 )
DURING INTERVAL ( [d09,d09] )
STATUS := 20 ;
```

The third line here specifies the interval attribute to which the COALESCED specification applies—DURING in the example—and the relevant interval value—[*d09,d09*] in the example (the syntax of that third line is basically name <attribute name> and <interval expression>). The overall UPDATE can be understood as follows:

   a. First, identify tuples for supplier S2.

   b. Next, out of those tuples, identify those where the DURING value includes the interval [*d09,d09*] (of course, there should be at most one such tuple).

   c. If no tuple is identified, no updating is done; otherwise, the system splits the tuple as necessary and performs the required update.

- *DELETE:* The DELETE problem can be addressed by extending the DELETE operator analogously. Our example becomes:

```
DELETE S_DURING WHERE S# = S# ( S3 ) DURING INTERVAL
( [d06,d08] ) ;
```

5.11 Database Design Considerations

Our example relvars, S_DURING and SP_DURING, have so far served us well, clearly illustrating the need for interval types and the desirability of defining special operators to deal with interval data. Now, those two relvars were originally "designed" by simply adding interval attributes to their snapshot counterparts. In this section, we question whether such an approach to design is really a good one. More specifically, we suggest some *further*

---

15. Our syntax is similar but not identical to the syntax proposed in [2].

decomposition of certain temporal relvars (where by "further decomposition" we mean decomposition beyond what classical normalization would require). In fact, we suggest both *horizontal* decomposition and *vertical* decomposition, in appropriate circumstances.

5.11.1 "Horizontal" Decomposition

Our running example assumes, reasonably enough, that the database contains historical information up to and including the present time; however, it also assumes that the present time is recorded as some specific date (namely, day 10), and that assumption is not reasonable at all. In particular, such an approach suggests that whenever time marches on, so to speak, the database is somehow updated accordingly (in our example, it suggests that every such appearance of *d10* is somehow replaced by *d11* at midnight on day 10). A different example, involving intervals of finer granularity, might require such updates to occur as often as, say, every millisecond.

Some authorities (see, for example, [1]) advocate the use of a special marker—we will call it *now*—to be permitted wherever a point value is permitted. Under this proposal, the interval [*d04, d10*], shown in Table 5.4 as the DURING value for supplier S1 in S_DURING, would become [*d04, now*]. The actual value of such an interval depends, of course, on the time at which you look at it, so to speak; on day 14 it would be [*d04, d14*].

Other writers, including this chapter's authors, regard the introduction of *now* as an incautious departure from the concepts on which relational systems are based. Note that *now* is really a *variable*. The proposal therefore leads to the notion of *values* containing *variables*, an apparent contradiction. In any case, the only variables in a truly relational database are the relation variables constituting that database. Here are some examples of questions arising from the notion of *now* that you might care to ponder over:

- What happens to the interval [*now, d14*] at midnight on day 14?
- What is the value of END([*d04, now*]) on day 14? Is it *d14* or is it *now*?

We believe it is hard to give coherent answers to questions of this nature. Thus, we prefer to look for an approach that stays with widely understood concepts.

Now, sometimes a "DURING attribute" will be used to record information regarding the future as well as (or instead of) the past. For example, we might want to record the date in the future at which a supplier's contract is to be terminated or considered for renewal. If such is the case, then the S_DURING design of Table 5.4 could be used. However, this approach will obviously not always be acceptable. In particular, it will not be acceptable if DURING is to carry the *transaction time* interpretation (see Section 5.2)—by definition, transaction times do not refer to the future.

The general problem is that there is an important difference between historical information and information regarding the current state of affairs. The difference is this: For historical information, the start and end times are both known; for current information, by contrast, the start time is known, but the end time is not (usually). This difference strongly suggests that there should be two different relvars, one for the current state of affairs and one for the history (after all, there are certainly two different *predicates*). In the case of suppliers, the "current" relvar is S_SINCE as shown in Table 5.2, while the "history" relvar is S_DURING as shown in Table 5.4 (except that tuples whose DURING values have end times of *d10* are omitted, the relevant information being recorded in S_SINCE instead).

This example thus illustrates the suggested horizontal decomposition: a relvar with a point-valued "since" attribute for the current state of affairs, and a relvar with an interval-valued "during" attribute for the history. We remark in passing that *triggered procedures* could be used to populate the history relvar; for example, deleting a tuple from S_SINCE could "automatically" trigger the insertion of a tuple into S_DURING.

The relational UNION operator can be used to combine history and current data into a single relation, for example:

```
S_DURING
UNION
( EXTEND S_SINCE ADD INTERVAL [ SINCE, TODAY() ] AS
DURING )
{ ALL BUT SINCE }
```

A possible disadvantage with horizontal decomposition arises if DURING has the *valid time* interpretation rather than the transaction time one. In that case, history is updatable. The update operators would be helpful here, but there will be some occasions when a desired revision has to affect both relvars. Suppose, for example, that the most recent change in some supplier's status is discovered to have been a mistake. Then we must not only delete a tuple from S_DURING but also update one in S_SINCE. As another example, if that most recent change in status was correct but made on the wrong day, then again the necessary revision will involve updates to both relvars.

If SP_DURING is similarly decomposed into SP_SINCE and SP_DURING, we need to take another look at the foreign key constraints. In the case of SP_DURING, we have already seen (in Section 5.9) that the relvar definition might include the following:

```
FOREIGN I_KEY { S#, DURING UNFOLDED } REFERENCES
S_DURING ...
```

As we said in Section 5.9, the intent of this specification is that if supplier Sx is shown as able to supply some part during interval *i*, then S_DURING must show that Sx was under contract throughout interval *i*. We went on to say that {S#,DURING} in relvar SP_DURING might now be regarded as a "temporal foreign key."

In the case of SP_SINCE, however, the corresponding foreign key is only "semitemporal;" thus, we are still faced with the problem of having to deal with the cumbersome constraint we showed in Section 5.3:

```
CONSTRAINT AUG_SP_TO_S_FK
    IS_EMPTY (((S_SINCE RENAME SINCE AS SS) JOIN
             (SP_SINCE RENAME SINCE AS SPS))
         WHERE SPS SS);
```

Thus, horizontal decomposition does arguably lead to certain problems—the problem of cumbersome constraints, and the problem of updating current and history relvars "simultaneously" (as it were). At the time of this writing, we have not seen any specific proposals for shorthands to help with either of these problems. Perhaps further research is needed. Of course, these problems do not arise in the case where the "DURING relvar" is used for information about the future as well as the past and present. While including the future allows us to drop the "SINCE relvar," it also requires us to predict the future ending times. We note also that the problems in question do not arise in the approach proposed in [1].

5.11.2 "Vertical" Decomposition

Even before temporal data was studied—and before SQL was invented, for that matter—some writers argued in favor of decomposing relvars as far as possible, instead of just as far as classical normalization would require. Some of those writers unfortunately damaged their cause by proposing database designs consisting entirely of *binary* relvars. One criticism of this idea was that sometimes unary relations are needed. Another was that some relvars of degree 3 or more really are nondecomposable. For example, the relation corresponding to the following triadic natural language predicate is non-decomposable:

Person *a* owes person *b* *x* dollars.

Our usual (nontemporal) relvar S, on the other hand, certainly can be further decomposed. Given the truth of the sentences "S1's name is Smith," "S1's status is 20," and "S1 is located in London," we can safely conclude the truth of the statement implied by the first tuple shown for S in Table 5.1. We can therefore decompose S into three binary relvars, each with S# as primary key.

The idea of decomposing all the way (as it were) is motivated by a desire for reduction to the simplest possible terms. Now, the case for such decomposition is perhaps not very strong in the case of relvar S; however, it is significantly stronger in the case of relvars like S_DURING. A supplier's name, status, and city vary independently over time. Moreover, they probably vary with different frequency, too. For example, it might be that a supplier's name hardly ever changes, while that same supplier's location changes occasionally and the corresponding status changes quite often—and it might well be a nuisance to have to repeat the name and location every time the status changes. Besides, the name history, status history, and city history of a supplier are probably each more interesting and more digestible concepts than the concept of a combined name-status-city history. We therefore propose decomposing S_DURING into three historical relvars that look like this (in outline):

```
S_NAME_DURING     {S#, SNAME, DURING}
S_STATUS_DURING   {S#, STATUS, DURING}
S_CITY_DURING     {S#, CITY, DURING}
```

The specifications I_KEY {S#, DURING UNFOLDED} and COALESCED DURING would apply to each of these three relvars. *Note:* We would probably want to include the following "master" suppliers relvar as well:

```
S#_ DURING { S#, DURING }
```

This relvar would indicate which suppliers were under contract when. Again the specifications I_KEY {S#, DURING UNFOLDED} and COALESCED DURING would apply. In addition, the combination {S#, DURING} would serve as a temporal foreign key in each of S_NAME_DURING, S_STATUS_DURING, and S_CITY_DURING (and SP_DURING), corresponding to the temporal candidate key {S#, DURING} in relvar S#_DURING. If it is an additional requirement that a supplier under contract at any time must have a name at that time, then {S#, DURING} in relvar S#_DURING would constitute a temporal foreign key referencing S_NAME_DURING.[16]

There is another point to be made here, too. With S_DURING as originally defined, we have to use a fairly nontrivial expression in order to obtain the status history:

```
S_DURING { S#, STATUS, DURING } COALESCE DURING
```

At the same time, the expression to give the much less interesting combined history is just a simple relvar reference. In a sense, therefore, the suggested decomposition "levels the playing field" for queries—or, rather, it makes it easier to express the more interesting ones and harder to express the less interesting ones.

The need to decompose S_SINCE is not so compelling. Note in particular that while (again) triggered procedures could be used to populate the three historical relvars—for example, deleting a tuple from S_SINCE could "automatically" trigger the insertion of tuples into S_NAME_DURING, S_STATUS_DURING, and S_CITY_DURING—there is no need to decompose S_SINCE in order to achieve such effects.

5.12   Further Points

In this section we briefly mention three additional points that do not conveniently fit into any of the main sections. We present them as questions for the reader to consider, followed by some suggested answers.

---

16. Problems arising from such requirements are discussed by C. J. Date, "A Note on 1-to-1 Relationships" in *Relational Database Writings, 1985–1989,* Reading, MA: Addison-Wesley, 1990.

Question 1: In this chapter we have shown how certain operators that apply to intervals in general can be especially useful for time intervals in particular. Are there other possible applications of these operators, involving intervals that are not intervals in time?

Here are some suggestions. Animals vary according to the range of *frequencies* of light and sound waves to which their eyes and ears are receptive. Various natural phenomena occur and can be measured in ranges in *depth* of soil or sea, or *height* above sea level. That tea is taken between the hours of 4 P.M. and 5 P.M. is a temporal observation, but one that is significantly different in kind from the examples discussed previously (how, exactly?). No doubt you can think of many similar examples on which interesting database applications might be based.

Question 2: Are there any realistic examples of relations with more than one interval attribute, temporal or otherwise?

Animals vary according to the range of frequencies of light *and* sound waves to which their eyes and ears are receptive. Besides, as soon as we wish to join two temporal relations $R1\{A,B\}$ and $R2\{A,C\}$, where B and C are interval attributes, we obtain a result, even if just an intermediate one, that has more than one interval attribute.

Question 3: Can you think of an example of a relvar with an interval attribute that you would *not* want to keep in coalesced form?

Actually, we have not been able to think of any compelling examples, but perhaps the reader can do better.

5.13 Summary

We began this chapter with reference to the growing requirement for databases to contain **historical** as well as current data. We showed that representing historical data using only **timestamps** leads to severe difficulties—in particular, it makes certain constraints and certain queries very hard to deal with—and we proposed the use of scalar ("encapsulated") **intervals** as a better approach. To be specific, we proposed an INTERVAL **type generator**, together with several new **operators** for dealing with interval data (though we remind you that almost all of those operators are really just shorthand). Intervals and their related operators are useful for more than just temporal data *per se*—despite the fact that our running example was based specifically on the type INTERVAL(DATE). We showed examples of **temporal** relations (and discussed **temporal relvars**) with attributes of this particular type.

An interval type must be defined over an underlying **point type**, and an associated **precision** must be specified (somehow) for that point type. A **successor function** must be defined for that point type and that precision.

The operators we described include operators on intervals *per se*, operators on sets of intervals, and operators on temporal relations. Operators on intervals *per se* include START, END, and **Allen's operators**. Operators on sets of intervals include **UNFOLD** and **COALESCE**. Operators on temporal relations include **relational versions** of UNFOLD and COALESCE. We also discussed certain specialized **update** operators and certain specialized **constraints** for temporal relvars. We showed that most of those new operators and constraints could effectively be regarded as temporal counterparts of familiar constructs.

We discussed two important *canonical forms* for sets of intervals of the same type, the **unfolded** form and the **coalesced** form. A set of intervals of type INTERVAL(PT) is in unfolded form if every interval in the set is a *unit interval*—that is, an interval containing just one *point*, where a point is a value of the underlying point type *PT*. A set of intervals of type INTERVAL(PT) is in coalesced form if no two distinct intervals in the set *overlap* or *meet*. Both canonical forms have the advantage of avoiding certain kinds of redundancy; the coalesced form maximizes conciseness and has very pressing psychological advantages, while the unfolded form is the easiest to operate on (obviating the need for the special constraints and update operators discussed in Sections 5.9 and 5.10). We showed how the concept of these canonical forms is extended to relations with interval attributes, leading to the important new relational operators, **UNFOLD** and **COALESCE**.

We drew attention in Section 5.11 to certain **database design** issues, having to do with **horizontal** and **vertical** decomposition of certain temporal relvars. Finally, we posed three questions concerning points that had not conveniently arisen in any of the earlier sections. We suggested answers for two of those questions and left the third for the reader to ponder.

Acknowledgement

The authors of this chapter are grateful to Nikos A. Lorentzos of the Agricultural University of Athens for his careful review and useful comments.

References

[1]   Snodgrass, R. T. (ed.), *The TSQL2 Temporal Query Language*, Boston, MA: Kluwer Academic Publishers, 1995.

[2]   Lorentzos, N. A., and Y. G. Mitsopoulos, "SQL Extension for Interval Data," *IEEE Trans. on Knowledge and Data Engineering*, Vol. 9, No. 3, May/June 1997.

[3]   Darwen, H., and C. J. Date, *Foundation for Object/Relational Databases: The Third Manifesto*, Reading, MA: Addison-Wesley, 1998.

[4]   Etzion, O., S. Jajodia, and S. Sripada (eds.), *Temporal Databases: Research and Practice*, New York: Springer, 1998.

[5]   Date, C. J., *An Introduction to Database Systems*, 7th ed., Reading, MA: Addison-Wesley, 2000.

[6]   Allen, J. F., "Maintaining Knowledge About Temporal Intervals," *CACM*, Vol. 16, No. 11, Nov. 1983.

Selected Bibliography

Etzion, O., S. Jajodia, and S. Sripada (eds.), *Temporal Databases: Research and Practice,* New York: Springer, 1998.

This is an anthology giving the state of the art as of 1997, and an excellent primary reference for further study. Part 4: General Reference includes a comprehensive bibliography and the February 1998 version of "The Consensus Glossary of Temporal Database Concepts." Part 2: Temporal Query Languages includes a paper entitled "Valid Time and Transaction Time Proposals: Language Design Aspects," in which Hugh Darwen argues against the approach taken in TSQL2 and claims to find significant flaws in the TSQL2 specification [1]. It also includes a paper by David Toman entitled "Point-Based Temporal Extensions of SQL and Their Efficient Implementation," which proposes an extension to SQL based on points instead of intervals. This idea raises some interesting questions concerning implementation. Answers to those questions might be relevant to interval-based languages too, because the unit intervals resulting from UNFOLD are "almost" points (indeed, they are points in IXSQL—see the annotation to the next entry in this section).

Lorentzos, N. A., and Y. G. Mitsopoulos, "SQL Extension for Interval Data," *IEEE Trans. on Knowledge and Data Engineering,* Vol. 9, No. 3, May/June 1997.

Many of the operators discussed in Chapter 5 (especially unfold and coalesce) are based on the work reported in this paper. The paper also includes many useful further references.

Before presenting their proposed SQL extension, the authors define an Interval-Extended Relational Algebra. The proposed SQL extension is called IXSQL (sometimes pronounced "nine SQL") and is not specifically for time intervals. Because the keywords INTERVAL and COALESCE are already used in SQL for purposes other than those at hand, the authors propose PERIOD (even for nontemporal intervals) and NORMALIZE in their place. Their UNFOLD differs from ours in that it yields points instead of unit intervals. As a consequence, they propose an inverse FOLD operator, which converts points to unit intervals, then coalesces. UNFOLD, FOLD, and NORMALIZE are proposed in the form of additional clauses on the familiar SELECT–FROM–WHERE construct. It is interesting to note that the proposed NORMALIZE ON clause is not only written last but—in what is a departure for SQL—is also executed last. That is, the output of the SELECT clause is input to the NORMALIZE ON clause (for good reasons).

Snodgrass, R. T. (ed.), *The TSQL2 Temporal Query Language,* Boston, MA: Kluwer Academic Publishers, 1995.

TSQL2 is a set of proposed temporal extensions to SQL. To a significant extent, the TSQL2 committee spurns the general approach of scalar and relational operators on intervals in favor of something that is more convenient in certain special cases. Instead of simply supporting an interval type generator and associated operators, therefore, they propose various special kinds of tables: snapshot tables, valid time state tables, valid time event tables, transaction time tables, bitemporal state tables, and bitemporal event tables.

- A snapshot table is an old-fashioned SQL table, possibly including columns of data type PERIOD (as in IXSQL [2], this keyword is used instead of INTERVAL because SQL already uses INTERVAL for another purpose).

- The other kinds of tables are said to have *temporal support*; temporal support implies the existence, alongside each row, of either one or two *temporal elements*. A temporal element is a set of *timestamps*, where a timestamp is either a PERIOD value or a value of some datetime data type. (Note, therefore, that the term "timestamp" is not being used in its conventional SQL:1992 sense.)

Temporal elements consisting of PERIOD values are specified to be coalesced.[17] Temporal elements do not appear as regular columns but instead are accessed by means of special-purpose operators.

Here is a quick survey of the various kinds of tables "with temporal support":

- In *valid time state tables* and *transaction time tables*, each timestamp is a PERIOD value.

- In *valid time event tables*, each timestamp is a value of some datetime data type.

- A *bitemporal* table is one that is both a transaction time table and either a valid time state table or a valid time event table. Each row in a bitemporal table has two temporal elements, one for the transaction time and one for the valid time. A bitemporal table can therefore be operated on either as a transaction time table or as a valid time table.

TSQL2 is strongly motivated by a notion it calls *temporal upward compatibility*. The idea is to be able to add "temporal support" to an existing base table, thus converting that base table from a snapshot table to a temporal table of some kind. From then on, all regular SQL operations on that base table are interpreted as operations on the current snapshot version of that table,[18] but now they might have new side effects. In particular, updates and deletes on the current snapshot version result in retention of the old versions of those rows as rows with temporal elements.

The big advantage of the TSQL2 approach accrues in connection with what are called *sequenced* operations. A sequenced operation is one that is expressed as an operation on a snapshot of the database, typically the current snapshot, but is executed, as it were, on *every* snapshot. The result of a sequenced query on valid time tables, for example, is a valid time table. The

---

17. The version of TSQL2 that was proposed to ISO (but not accepted) in 1996 for inclusion in the SQL standard differed from the version described in [1], in that tables with temporal support were always "unnested" (meaning each temporal element was a single timestamp, not a set of timestamps). Whether coalescing also took place was not specified.

18. Actually, there is another difference here between TSQL2 as defined in [1] and the version proposed to ISO. Reference [1] requires the keyword SNAPSHOT after SELECT to indicate that a query is against the current state of each of the tables it references; the version proposed to ISO does not.

This chapter contrasts and compares the relative strengths and weaknesses of the relational and object-oriented systems. We also discuss in detail the importance of "blended technologies" used to support the object-relational architecture. The discussion will include user-defined data types and set-based versus navigational access to data. Finally, we examine some simple modeling examples to illustrate the discussions.

6.2 A Quick Look at Relational and Object-Oriented Databases

There is no doubt that the strengths of the relational paradigm have revolutionized information technology. Relational DB technology was originally described by E. F. Codd. Not long afterward, companies like IBM and Oracle created spectacularly successful DB products. The relational DB standard is published by ANSI, with the current specification being X3H2 (SQL'92). The new specification dealing with object extensibility has been labeled X3H7. A relational DB stores data in one or more tables of rows and columns. The rows correspond to a record (tuple); the columns correspond to attributes (fields in the record), with each column having a data type like date, character, or number. Commercial implementations currently support very few data types. For example, character, string, time, date, numbers (fixed and floating point), and currency describe the various options. Any attribute (field) of a record can store only a single value.

Relational DBs enforce data integrity via relational operations, and the data themselves are structured to a simple model based on mathematical set theory. Relationships are not explicit but rather implied by values in specific fields, for example, foreign keys in one table that match those of records in a second table. Many-to-many relationships typically require an intermediate table that contains just the relationships. Relational DBs offer simplicity in modifying table structure. For example, adding data columns to existing tables or introducing entire tables remains an extremely simple operation. The beauty of relational DBs continues to be in its simplicity. The process of normalization establishes a succinct clarity to the management and organization of data in the DB. Redundancies are eliminated and information retrieval is governed by the associations created between primary and foreign keys. Why store the same piece of information in two or more places when a logical connection can be established to it in one place? Referential integrity (RI) has also made an important contribution because it enables business rules to be controlled through the use of constraints. The role of constraints is to prevent the violation of data integrity and, thereby, its normalization.

The origins of object-oriented DBs trace their beginnings to the emergence of object-oriented programming in the 1970s. Technically, there is no official standard for object DBs. The book *The Object Database Standard: ODMG-V2.0*, under the sponsorship of the Object Database Management Group (ODMG) (http://www.odmg.com), describes an industry-accepted de facto standard. Object DBMSs emphasize objects, their relationships, and the storage of those objects in the DB.

Designers of complex systems realized the limitations of the relational paradigm when trying to model complex systems. Characteristics of object DBs include a data model that has object-oriented aspects like class, with attributes, methods, and integrity constraints; they also have object identifiers (OIDs) for any persistent instantiation of classes; they support encapsulation (data and methods), multiple inheritance, and abstract data types.

Object-oriented data types can be extended to support complex data such as multimedia by defining new object classes that have operations to support the new kinds of information.

The object-oriented modeling paradigm also supports inheritance, which allows incremental development of solutions to complex problems by defining new objects in terms of previously defined objects. Polymorphism allows developers to define operations for one object and then share the specification of the operation with other objects. Objects incorporating polymorphism also have the capability of extending behaviors or operations to include specialized actions or behaviors unique to a particular object. Dynamic binding is used to determine at run time which operations are actually executed and which are not. Object DBs extend the functionality of object programming languages like C++ or Java to provide full-featured DB programming capability. The result is a high level of congruence between the data model for the application and the data model of the DB, resulting in less code, more natural data structures, and better maintainability and greater reusability of code. All of those capabilities deliver significant productivity advantages to DB application developers that differ significantly from what is possible in the relational model.

6.3 Contrasting the Major Features of Pure Relational and Object-Oriented Databases

In the relational DB, the query language is the means to create, access, and update objects. In an object DB, the primary interface for creating and modifying objects is directly via the object language (C++, Java, Smalltalk) using the native language syntax even though declarative queries are still possible. Additionally, every object in the system is automatically given an OID that is unique and immutable during the object's life. One object can contain an OID that logically references, or points to, another object. Those references prove valuable when in the association of objects with real-world entities, such as products, customers, or business processes; they also form the basis of features such as bidirectional relationships, versioning, composite objects, and distribution. In most ODBMSs, the OIDs become physical (the logical identifier is converted to pointers to specific memory addresses) once the data are loaded into memory (cached) for use by the object-oriented application. No such construct exists in the relational DB. In fact, the addition of navigational access violates the very principles of normalization because OIDs make no reliance on keys.

To further explore the divergent nature of relational and object-oriented DBs, let us look more closely at the drawbacks of each. Our discussion eventually leads us to the justification behind the object-relational paradigm.

6.4 Drawbacks of Pure Relational and Object-Oriented Databases

There is no doubt that the strengths of the relational paradigm have revolutionized information technology. If the relational paradigm is so wonderful, then what are the shortcomings that have precipitated an interest in object-relational? Let us address a simple question, namely, how does an asset like RI become a liability?

Traditional relational types demand decomposition of constituent objects to the most primitive level. That is necessary because of the declarative structure of SQL. The relational design model requires data objects to exist in a rudimentary state: numbers, characters, and dates. SQL simplified data access because cumbersome navigational mechanisms of the past (recall the use of linked lists and so on) were eliminated. The use of pointers, so commonly found in hierarchical and network DBs, was not needed to establish relationships between data tables. Data access is accomplished through the use of primary and foreign keys. The most outstanding benefit of the declarative structure is that the actual navigation path is hidden from the user. The work is performed by the SQL optimizer, which determines the navigation path. Unfortunately, the declarative approach begins to fall apart when working with complex data types, such as collection types, because such objects cannot be referenced by key. DB designers are increasingly challenged by today's modern systems.

The explosive popularity of object-oriented languages, namely Java, has precipitated a need to merge interfaces that exercise varying degrees of polymorphism, encapsulation, class/type structures, and behavior. Not only are developers faced with requirements for support of new data types such as multimedia, temporal, and video, but the nature of modern business systems is growing more complex. A real-world example of this phenomenon is the explosive popularity of e-commerce. Many of today's businesses live or die on their ability to respond to the marketplace via the World Wide Web. Complex technological systems require the implementation of user-defined data types. A common example of that is the requirement to store Geographical Information System (GIS) data like satellite imagery. How should a developer associate a set-based retrieval hook like a primary key to a satellite image? That is a concept for which object orientation is well suited but relational is not, for two reasons. First, relational set theory does not deal well with abstraction in the physical implementation. Second, the employment of user-defined data types and collection types requires the violation of normalization rules to succeed in the relational model.

If the shortcomings of the relational paradigm make it unworthy as the uncontested successor to the competitive DB marketplace, then what about object-oriented DBs? Ironically, the very aspects of object orientation that have proved to be it greatest assets, namely, its ability to encapsulate data and behavior and its capability to exercise abstraction, make the employment of a robust data-retrieval mechanism like SQL somewhat out of reach. Indexing, for example, a powerful aid in data retrieval (at least in terms of performance) for relational DBs, is next to impossible in an object-oriented DB.

We can see that the fundamental differences of the relational and object-oriented paradigms clearly delineate the criteria for which a successful object-relational definition will be made. In a perfect world, the new paradigm would possess all the features and benefits of both worlds without any of the drawbacks. While we may be a long way from a perfect solution, the road in that direction has been engaged by increments.

So, to recap the important points of our comparison, we find that the individual paradigms must move to the middle to meet the criteria for object-relational DB systems. Considering relational DBMSs first, we find the following challenges in migrating toward object orientation.

- Creating user-transparent interfaces between DBs of different vendor origin.

- Adding object-oriented layers (typically middleware components) on top of the relational DB to facilitate the integration of the object-oriented client interface and the DB backend.

- Redesigning the relational DBMS architecture to support multimedia functions. Recall the example of storing satellite imagery.

- Architectural shift from set-based query access to a blend of set-based and navigational.

- Storage techniques to handle objects. The very nature of objects—self-contained instantiations—currently require gateways and/or wrappers, which perform poorly.

If we consider the perspective of moving object-oriented DBs closer to the middle, we discover the following points.

- Object-relational DBs require a generalized object-oriented programming language interface versus a specific, hard-coded one. Normally, object-oriented DBs are geared for a specific programming language.

- Object-oriented DB architectures have been known historically for their slow performance.

- Object-oriented DBs are, by design, limited in terms of scalability.

- Object-oriented DBs are not designed for high concurrency.

Now that we have a clearer understanding of the strengths and weaknesses of the relational and object-oriented DB systems, let us explore the specifics of what it takes to define the object-relational paradigm.

6.5 Technology Issues: Enabling Object Functionality in the Relational World

Two important aspects must be considered in any definition of the object-relational paradigm. The first is the logical design aspects of the architecture. What data types will be supported? How will data be accessed? The other aspect is how the logical architecture will arrive at a physical implementation. For example, will the object-relational DB conform to the ANSI standard for SQL3? If so, many decisions regarding SQL semantics, object support, and so on will be decided. In all likelihood, SQL3 would be adopted because it is derived from the international standard produced by the ISO. Most vendors find it in everyone's interest to find a level of consistency.

From a technological standpoint, certain capabilities must be included in the list of logical capabilities, or the DB will not measure up to the minimal requirements for being object-relational. Those capabilities are behavior, collection types, encapsulation, polymorphism, and inheritance.

6.5.1   Behavior

A method, in the purely object-oriented paradigm, is the incorporation of a specific behavior assigned to an object or element. A method is a function of a particular class.

6.5.2   Collection Types

An aggregate object is essentially a data-type definition that can be composed of many subtypes coupled with behavior. In Oracle8, for example, there are two collection types: VARRAYs and nested tables. VARRAYs are suitable when the subset of information is static and the subset is small. A suitable implementation of a VARRAY might be in the same context where a reference entity might be used. The contents of reference entities remain relatively static and serve to validate entries in the referencing table. For example, a reference entity called *MARKETS* might be created to store the valid set of areas where a company does business. In the same way, a VARRAY might be substituted to perform the same reference and validation.

VARRAY constructs are stored inline. That means the VARRAY structure and data are stored in the same data block as the rest of the row as a RAW data type. Although they bear some similarity to PL/SQL tables, VARRAYs are a fixed size. Altering a VARRAY requires a DDL statement. Accessing individual elements of a VARRAY is limited. This task can be done only via the index within the PL/SQL code.

A nested table is essentially a table embedded within another table and linked to a specific column. Nested tables are suitable in situations where a table has one or more columns to be used as parameters, variables, or user-defined data types. They are also ideal when the number of items is indeterminate and the storage must be directly managed. Nested tables are stored out-of-line and have a more robust access than VARRAYs. Keep in mind, too, that the nested table is a somewhat clumsy structure compared to a conventional table with attributes. That is because the nested table becomes an attribute for another table. The most recognizable benefit of these structures is that they are fast because of their use of pointers instead of relational keys. They also provide a cleaner design alternative to many-to-many relationships than the use of associative entities. To implement a nested table, a pointer is defined in the column that references it. If a column is designated to reference the nested table, then all column entries for that column must contain a pointer to a nested table of the exact same definition.

6.5.3   Encapsulation

Encapsulation is the defining of a class with data members and functions. In other words, it is the mechanism that binds code and data together while protecting or hiding the encapsulation from outside of the class. The actual implementation is hidden from the user, who only sees the interface.

As an illustrative example, think of a car engine. You can open the hood and see that it is there, and you can get in the car and start the ignition. The engine causes the car to move. Although you can see the motor, the inner workings are hidden from your view. You can appreciate the function that the motor performs without ever knowing all the details of what occurs inside or even how.

6.5.4   Polymorphism

Polymorphism is the ability of different objects in a class hierarchy to have different behaviors in response to the same message. Polymorphism derives its meaning from the Greek for "many forms." A single behavior can generate entirely different responses from objects in the same group. Within the framework of the program, the internal mechanism determines what specific action should take place. In C++ programming, the use of the same function name for different purposes is known as function overloading. To experienced PL/SQL programmers, that is not an alien concept. It is accepted as good practice to develop overloaded PL/SQL packages whenever possible. Overloaded PL/SQL packages are flexible and require little revision when they are thought out carefully.

6.5.5   Inheritance

Inheritance is the ability of one class to inherit the properties of its ancestor. This concept is also known as *subclassing*. Inheritance allows an object to inherit a certain set of attributes from another object while allowing the addition of specific features.

6.6 ORDBMS: A Closer Look at Characteristics in the Physical Implementation

A philosophical solution to a problem in the information technology community is worthless if it cannot generate some physical benefit. That also holds true for any ORDBMS. The following points illustrate important characteristics that must manifest themselves in the object-relational DB.

The constituent elements for supporting object-oriented structures are the following:

- User-defined types;
- Type constructors for *row types* and *reference types*;
- Type constructors for *collection types*;
- User-defined functions and procedures (methods);
- Support for large objects—binary large objects (BLOB) and character large objects (CLOB).

Object-relational DBs must support normal built-in types defined by SQL and user-defined types. The latter may be used in the same way as built-in types. For example, columns in relational tables may be defined as taking values of user-defined types, as well as built-in types. A user-defined abstract data type (ADT) definition encapsulates attributes and operations in a single entity. In SQL3, an ADT is defined by specifying a set of declarations of the stored attributes that represent its value, the operations that define the equality and ordering relationships, and finally the operations that define its behavior. Operations are implemented by procedures called routines. ADTs can also be defined as subtypes of other ADTs. A subtype inherits the structure and behavior of its supertype. Instances of ADTs can be persistently stored in the DB only by storing them in columns of tables.

A row type is a sequence of field name–data type pairs resembling a table definition. Two rows are type equivalent if both have the same number of fields, and every pair of fields in the same position has compatible types. The row type provides a data type that can represent the types of rows in tables, so that complete rows can be stored in variables, passed as arguments to routines, and returned as return values from function invocations. This facility also allows columns in tables to contain row values. A named row type is a row type with a name assigned to it. A named row type is effectively a user-defined data type with a nonencapsulated internal structure (consisting of its fields). A named row type can be used to specify the types of rows in table definitions. A named row type can also be used to define a reference type.

A value for a reference type defined for a specific row type is a unique value that identifies an instance of the row type in question within some base (top-level) DB table. A reference-type value can be stored in one table and used as a direct reference (pointer) to a specific row in another table. That translates directly to navigational access as represented in the object paradigm whereby links are initiated. The same reference-type value can be stored in multiple rows, thus allowing the referenced row to be shared by those rows. For example, an accounting table with *account_t* as a row type contains a *cust* column with the reference type *REF(customer_t)*. A value of this column identifies a specific row of type *customer_t*. The reference type has three important characteristics: (1) The value of a reference type is unique within the DB; (2) it never changes as long as the corresponding row exists in the DB; and (3) the reference type value is never reused.

Reference types are an important functionality in the object-relational system for the following reasons:

- *Set referencing.* The first normal form can be violated, and a tabular column cell can contain a pointer to repeating values. The true benefit of this approach is that prebuilt aggregations can be created, simplifying DB design in the long run.

- *Accessing nondatabase objects in a flat file.* The importance of multimedia objects in new application systems was discussed earlier in this chapter. Large object (LOB) data types can be stored in the DB or on the file server. Pointers supply the means to effectively access these constructs.

- *Data relationships without referential foreign keys.* Utilization of pointers obviates the need for conventional SQL JOIN operations because each column instance references the object table containing the necessary aggregate data.

The introduction of reference types allows us to employ collection types. Collection types are aggregations that appear as sets, lists, and multisets. Using these types, columns of tables can contain sets, lists, or multisets, in addition to individual values. Currently in SQL: 1999, a table can be defined as either a SET table, a MULTISET table, or a LIST table. By default, a table is a MULTISET table. SET tables and LIST tables share all the properties of MULTISET tables, but have the additional properties that a SET table can contain no duplicate rows, and a LIST table has an order defined for the rows. Each table has a data type, which consists of the specification of whether the table is a MULTISET, SET, or LIST table, and the row type of the table. The row type of a table is the sequence of (column name, data type) pairs specified in the table definition. These data types can include ADTs as well as built-in types. The only way that an ADT instance can be stored persistently in the DB is as the column value of a table.

Tables have also been enhanced in SQL: 1999 with a subtable facility. The purpose of this functionality is to provide a degree of inheritance to what has been a relational concept, namely, the table. A table can be declared as a subtable of one or more supertables (it is then a direct subtable of those supertables), using an UNDER clause associated with the table definition. When a subtable is defined, the subtable inherits every column from its supertables and may also define columns of its own. The concept of subtable is completely independent from that of the ADT. Any base table that has a subtable or a supertable has a row identifier implicitly defined. The row identifier type for a table with supertables is a subtype of the row identifier type defined for each supertable. An example follows.

```
CREATE TABLE person
    (name CHAR(20),
    sex  CHAR(1),
    age  INTEGER,
    spouse person IDENTITY);

CREATE TABLE employee UNDER person
    (salary FLOAT);

CREATE TABLE customer UNDER person
    (account INTEGER);
```

By including the row identifier as an argument, routines can be associated with tables to implement object-like operations on rows, and more specialized routines can be associated with subtables to support polymorphism for those operations.

6.7 Design Issues: Capturing the Essence of the Object-Relational Paradigm

To resolve the differences between the two paradigms, one must understand them first. One of the striking dissimilarities between them is the handling of abstraction and encapsulation. The dissimilarity of abstraction and encapsulation handling first manifests itself in detailed analysis of the data flow diagram. Because of the unique qualities of abstraction and encapsulation that object-oriented structures bring to the DB, the data flow and store definitions must reflect the aggregate character of complex data types. Data flow diagrams help in defining the function-to-entity and function-to-attribute associations.

At the most general level, data structure within the data flow diagram is completely described, but as substantive detail is added, the developer must determine what DB mechanisms will be utilized (e.g., reference entity versus collection type). Because today's DB vendors are supporting complex data types, the effort of translating the function-to-attribute association becomes more complex. Nested tables and aggregate objects require a violation of normalization rules to associate them with source tables.

Inheritance is also an important point of departure for the relational and object-oriented paradigms. Inheritance is a natural characteristic of object-oriented design because of its treatment of object types and classes. Recall the earlier discussion that classes can be defined to describe the general or detailed characteristics of an object type. Recall also that a class does not identify an instance of an object but only its properties. That ability to categorize types is extremely useful in modeling because a hierarchical progression of properties can be defined, thus emulating objects in the real world. The relational paradigm is incapable of employing true inheritance as just described here.

Complex data object implementation calls for a technique known as *persistent storage*. Persistent storage is the concept that an object will have a physical location on the storage media even when the object is not in use. For example, an object called *PERSONNEL_HISTORY* might be created to store attributes such as skill level, specialty, and department. In the object metamodel, such a construct would become an abstract type physically residing in storage. In the relational world, a column must contain a single value. Complex data typing of the variety proposed by persistent storage is not possible under the relational model. In the relational metamodel, the individual attributes might exist in different tables and would be retrieved via query to assemble the aggregate data. No physical storage of the aggregate would take place except for the atomic elements spread about in various tables. Ad hoc SQL proves to be counter to the concept of encapsulation because the inherent protection afforded an object can be violated through the use of a DML statement.

In the relational paradigm, such problems are handled by creating constraints on the tables. Constraints vary from encapsulation for two reasons. First, constraints are not restricted to maintaining the behavior of a single object, and, second, they are external to the property set for the aggregated data type. The object paradigm defines more types of relationships than the relational one. Object relationships are primarily unidirectional in nature.

That means any efforts to reconcile these disparate methodologies must address the impedance mismatch by mapping the object relationships to those of the relational paradigm. Such a reconciliation should address the following:

- Relationship name, type, and cardinality;
- Implied direction of the relationship;
- The simplest object type to store the data (single values utilize standard relational data types; aggregates and complex data use collection types).

This pointed treatment of relationships, particularly with respect to directionality, is required to properly map the logical expressions from the DB design to the physical implementation in the DB. Business object relationships from the DB object model can specify an implementation in only one direction or in both directions. For example, consider CUSTOMER and BANK ACCOUNT tables. You will find that a CUSTOMER can implement a BANK ACCOUNT as an attribute. Conversely, a BANK ACCOUNT might incorporate multiple CUSTOMERS. In each case, the individual relationships do not infer or negate the possibility of the other.

From an academic perspective, it is often a simple task to describe the proper means to implement a methodology or technique. In this case, is there a set of real-world steps that can assist the developer in executing the correct object type with the corresponding relationship? The answer is a simple yes, so long as the rules as not interpreted too inflexibly.

A typical effort in Oracle8 to decipher the implementation of object types to relationships uses the following questions to make the necessary assertions.

1. What is the specified direction asserted for the relationship?
2. What is the cardinality of the relationship?
3. Is the cardinality *many*?
4. What data type is favored based on the response to question 3?
5. What is the cardinality of the relationship in the other direction (if applicable)?
6. Is embedding or referencing used to satisfy the relationship?

If the response to question 1 is *unidirectional*, then DDL is used to execute the task. That also means that the answer to question 6 is "no." To clarify the intent behind question 6, we should define embedding and referencing. Referencing is used when an instance of an object can be used by one or more objects at the same time. For example, one company could be a client, a supplier, and a distributor. The company holds three responsibilities, but the fact remains that all three responsibilities are executed by one company. Embedded relationships are relationships in which the object is not visible to the rest of the system or in which the object has no relative significance outside its relationship. For example, a shipping manifest can contain numerous line items. Outside the context of shipping manifest, the line items lose meaning.

Continuing on with the questions, if the answer to question 1 is *bidirectional*, then the cardinality of the relationship type must be determined in question 2. If a "many" relationship is indicated, then the answers to questions 3 and 4 determine that an aggregation (collection type) is needed. The description of collection types given earlier in the chapter should be used to determine the most proper type for use in a given situation. Question 5 determines the bidirectional nature of the relationship. If the relationship is unidirectional, then there is no effect on whether embedding or referencing is used.

Let us next examine a situation that helps to reinforce the advantages of the object-relational paradigm.

6.8 An Object-Relational Example

To properly illustrate the nature of object-relational systems in a real-world context, we will examine a small hypothetical company. ABC Corporation will be revisited several times in this chapter so that different aspects of object-relational development can be described. This first installment describes the target system and explains why it is a good candidate for an ORDBMS.

ABC Corporation produces telephonic systems to the business community. All systems delivered to clients are complete and ready to run without further modification from the user. Each system comprises a hardware and a software component. The hardware component may contain an assortment of parts. Some systems, depending on their complexity, include additional complex devices. A typical configuration has a Pentium-based server, a device known as a multiplexer, and one or more networking devices. The exact functionality of each piece is not germane to the understanding of this example, only that certain parts are required. An additional fact to bear in mind is that the combinations of hardware parts that will work together properly are almost limitless.

The software component is provided as a single package, but it has three integral parts. The first part is the operating system. The second is the code or mechanisms that cause the telephonic system to function. The last part is a series of drivers that facilitate the subtle differences between the operating systems so the code mechanism can operate problem free.

The first DB requirement facing ABC Corporation is to create a DB schema that will properly maintain all aspects of the telephony systems produced while enforcing the business rules of what parts will go with which. Briefly, the general rules can be summarized as follows:

- Each full system comprises a hardware and a software component.

- Each hardware component has a list of required parts; the other parts are optional, depending on the system to be delivered.

- Each software component requires three parts, which must be correctly matched.

The illustration in Figure 6.1 shows the logical representation of this modeling problem.

This example introduces two crucial concepts to the DB design problem that are classic problem areas in the relational model: class hierarchies and inheritance/versioning (the concept of one or more distinct instantiations from a single abstract class). The two criteria may sound similar, but there are aspects that make them unique.

Hierarchical structures in DB design have often been referred to as "Is-a" or "Is-a-type-of" relationships. These relationships were so termed because they provided a means to express different variants of the same

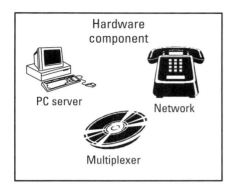
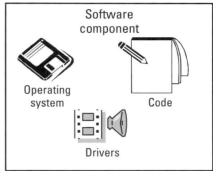

Figure 6.1 The logical relationship of the components of ABC Corporation's telephony system.

entity. That means each variant could have different attributes and methods. Hierarchical relationships infer a supertype or subtype association between two or more objects. In the case of ABC Corporation, the pattern is clear that we will be modeling systems, parts of systems, and parts of parts.

As a starting point for our modeling example (and a fundamental construct in object-oriented methodology), we will create a base class, which eventually leads us to a class structure. A base class equates to what is often termed a *generalization*. The base class contains the high-level properties and supporting functions common to all object classes. In object-oriented terms, the class is a logical abstraction that describes the characteristics that an object type will assume. Classes do not contain or represent actual instances of objects. Instead, objects take on the properties of classes under which they have been defined.

Inheritance is the essential ingredient that allows object-oriented programmers to create class hierarchies. The integration of true inheritance has never been possible before in the relational environment, because the physical representations of class objects in the relational structure lacked persistence.

To practice the concept of inheritance, we must establish one or more *derived* classes to our base class. The underlying concept behind the derived class is that of a specific base class implementation. The derived class retains all attributes and functions of the base class, but it can also specify additional properties and functions of its own. Derived class definitions can also override default properties stipulated in the default class so long as those properties are public. The relationship between the base class and the newly created derived class represents a generalization-specialization structure (gen-spec structure, for short). A gen-spec structure must pass a reasonableness test to be valid. If the generic statement "*specialization* is a kind of *generalization*" holds true, then the gen-spec structure is valid. To address the distinctive nature of specific objects under the base class, it is necessary to define specializations or derived classes. The process of creating derived classes can be compared to the activity that takes place in a functional decomposition. The creation of a class tree, or hierarchy, is the first step in establishing a pattern of inheritance. Inheritance is essentially the process of passing down general traits of a parent object to its children. DB developers will quickly recognize this relationship as being synonymous with the supertype-subtype construct used so often in data modeling. The most striking dissimilarity between class inheritance in object-oriented programming and supertype-subtype relationships in the relational world is that normalization eliminates duplicated data types while inheritance passes all elements down intact. That has to do with the fact that object-oriented class objects represent persistent elements whose behaviors are encapsulated into the class. In Oracle8, methods are now coupled with data elements, bringing the object-relational behavior in closer equivalence to that of object-oriented programming languages.

Referring back to Figure 6.1 and taking into consideration the discussion so far, we can see that these statements are true:

- The hardware component is a collection of parts.

- Each hardware part can be first classified by type/function, then by version (e.g., Pentium versus Pentium II).

- Versions of the software components (operating system, code, drivers) are variants of a base class.

- Each new combination of software components creates a new variant of a base software component.

It was easily demonstrated how simply this example was analyzed. We will reveal the difficulties in modeling that schema in the relational world. Before doing so, however, let us discuss a couple of important real-world aspects of DB design.

While the obvious purpose of this chapter is to give readers an essential understanding of the object-relational paradigm, no matter what methodology is chosen for implementation, simplicity is the key. Always strive to create the simplest, most straightforward, and easiest to maintain system. As an individual's knowledge increases (regardless of his or her technical discipline), there is a tendency to apply advanced techniques in places where they may not be needed. Remember to always seek out the simplest way.

Another point to keep in mind is that every DB design is a balance between maintainability and performance. Usually an increase in one yields a decline in the other. Always bear in mind what is most important to the client for whom you are designing a system.

6.9   The ABC Corporation Example

Now that we have examined the character of the object-relational paradigm, let us return to ABC Corporation. Understanding what we know about the functionality at our disposal, we can see that the telephony system can be logically depicted as shown in Figure 6.2.

The hardware component is an aggregation of three principal parts. Each part is abstractly represented as a class. For example, the server class is the generalized representation of all servers that can be configured in the telephony system. Figure 6.2 illustrates that there are multiple versions, or instances, of server. These simple facts also pertain to the other hardware components. Note that the multiple combinations for hardware parts create multiple versions of the hardware component. The association between different part combinations describing unique hardware component configurations is what creates the hierarchical nature of this DB example. SERVER, MX, and NETWK represent the base classes responsible for defining the

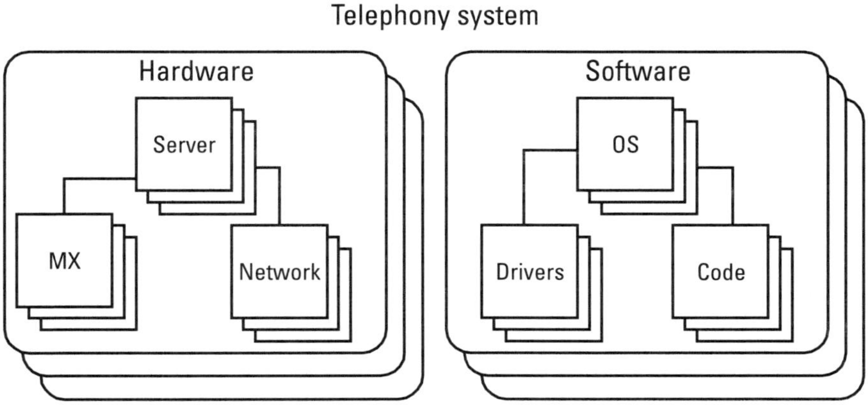

Figure 6.2 Logical representation of ABC Corporation's telephony system.

class hierarchy of distinct instances. All of this also applies to how the software component is modeled.

An interesting aspect of the software component is that multiple drivers are needed to support a single code-operating system combination. That leads us to understand that this is possibly a good collection-type candidate. A good analytical understanding of this design challenge is taking place. We have identified several opportunities for using object-relational techniques where conventional approaches (pure relational) would have been unmanageable. The one challenge that has not yet been addressed is how one goes about visualizing or modeling the object-relational model, an important fact that has not gone unnoticed in the DB design community.

6.10　Summary

The first step in developing the object-relational DB system is understanding the inherent strengths and weaknesses of its predecessors and combining the most noteworthy elements into one system. The object-relational paradigm faces a number of challenges because it must meld together characteristics of two diametrically opposed architectures.

The first object-relational DBs met most, if not all, relational criteria while addressing only 30–50% of the object-oriented spectrum. User-defined data typing, collection types, rudimentary support for behavior, and some encapsulation were addressed. The most anxiously awaited features, namely full support for inheritance, are needed to convince skeptical developers that object-oriented DBs have come into their own.

Some of the technological factors that will contribute to achieving total object-relational character are now entering the market. Oracle's release of 8i provides full support for Java. As a matter of fact, Java is on equal ground with PL/SQL in the DB kernel. The adoption of a true object-oriented language is the first step in achieving the last milestone in this new paradigm.

Selected Bibliography

Anyone interested in learning more about object-relational DBs and the techniques to model them is encouraged to read the following books:

The Unified Modeling Language User Guide, by G. Booch, J. Rumbaugh, and I. Jacobson (Reading, MA: Addison-Wesley, 1999).

An indispensable reference for anyone involved in modeling complex systems. Because UML is becoming the de facto standard for object-oriented and now object-relational systems, this is a good choice.

High Performance Oracle8 Object-Oriented Design, by D. A. Anstey (Scottsdale, AZ: Coriolis Group, 1998).

A good reference for understanding the technological direction that Oracle is taking with regard to the object-relational paradigm.

Oracle8 Design Using UML Object Modeling, by P. Dorsey and J. Hudicka (New York: McGraw-Hill, 1999).

This is the newest in object-relational references and offers good coverage of UML modeling in Oracle8. Good real-world examples are provided along with, as with the other titles in this list, solid information even for non-Oracle users.

Other worthwhile references include the following:

Barker, R., *CASE*METHOD Entity Relationship Modelling*, Workingham, England: Addison-Wesley, 1990.

Hunter, S. K., "Cutting to the Chase," *Object Magazine*, Aug. 1997, pp. 32–41.

McClure, S., "Object Databases Versus Object-Relational Databases," *IDC Bulletin #14821E*, International Data Corp., Aug. 1997.

McFarland, G., and A. Rudmik, "Object-Oriented Database Management Systems—A Critical Review/Technology Assessment," *Contract Number F30602-89-C-0082*, Rome, NY, Sept. 1993.

7

Object-Oriented Database Systems

Elisa Bertino and Esperanza Marcos

7.1 Introduction and Motivation

In spite of the fact that relational databases still hold first place in the market, object-oriented databases are becoming more widely accepted every day. Relational databases are suitable for traditional applications supporting management tasks such as payroll and library management. Recently, as a result of hardware improvements, more sophisticated applications have emerged. Engineering applications, such as computer-aided design/computer-aided manufacturing (CAD/CAM), computer-aided software engineering (CASE), and computer-integrating manufacturing (CIM); office automation systems; and multimedia systems, such as GIS and medical information systems, can be characterized as consisting of complex objects related to one another by complex interrelationships. Representing such objects and relationships in the relational model means that the objects must be decomposed into a large number of tuples. A considerable number of *joins* are necessary to retrieve an object when tables are too deeply nested; thus, performance is dramatically reduced. Object-oriented databases are quite suitable to store and retrieve complex data by allowing users to navigate through the data [1].

Another relevant problem of traditional database systems is that there is usually a complete mismatch between the modeling constructs typical of data models and the data structures provided by programming languages.

Whenever application objects need to be made persistent by storing them in a database, a mapping is required from the programming language data structures onto the data structures of the data model. Sometimes, such mapping wastes over 50% of the development time for applications and gives rise to several program bugs [2].

The first problem can be partially solved by object-relational technology, that is, relational systems extended with new capabilities, such as triggers (see Chapter 3) and object-oriented capabilities (see Chapter 6). Nonetheless, object-relational technology is not the best solution to the impedance mismatch problem. In addition, the difficulty in actually integrating the relational and the object-oriented models has made the market acceptance of a common object-relational model difficult.

Object-oriented databases solve those problems by supporting complex objects and integrating database technology with the object-oriented paradigm. Both object-oriented databases and programming languages support the same data model, removing the impedance mismatch of the relational model.

This chapter reviews the state of the art in object-oriented databases by presenting the main concepts of the object-oriented data model (Section 7.2) and a graphical representation of an object-oriented database schema (Section 7.3); the current standard for object-oriented database systems, the ODMG (Section 7.4); the current state of the object-oriented database technology, with some examples in different commercial products (Section 7.5); and finally some guidelines for object-oriented database design through an example (Section 7.6).

7.2   Basic Concepts of the Object-Oriented Data Model

Despite the fact that the object-oriented approach is widely used today and is characterized by large industrial efforts, there is no consolidated standard definition of an object model. Therefore, a large number of variations can be found when we compare the various object-oriented programming languages. Even though an object data model standard, known as the ODMG standard [3], has been recently developed, OODBMSs are not an exception; therefore, there is no consensus about the specific features of an object-oriented data model. It is possible, however, to identify some basic concepts, collectively referred to as core model. The core model is powerful enough to satisfy many of the requirements of advanced applications and moreover can be used as the basis for discussing the main differences with respect to objects. Note, however, that in some models and papers the term *complex object* is used with the meaning of *composite object.*

7.2.3   Methods

Objects in an object-oriented database are manipulated by the use of methods. In general, a method definition consists of two components. The first is the method *signature*, which specifies the method name, the names and classes of the arguments, and the class of the result, if there is one. Some systems, like Orion [4], do not require that the class of the arguments and of the results be declared. That happens when type checking is executed at run time; therefore, there is no need to know that information in advance. The second component is the method *implementation*, which consists of code written in some programming language. Different OODBMSs use different languages for method implementation. For example, both Vbase and O$_2$ use the C language, while Orion uses Lisp. GemStone uses OPAL, which is nearly identical to Smalltalk. ObjectStore uses C++. In addition to the method signature and implementation, other components may be present in a method definition. For example, in Vbase, a method definition may specify in addition to the base method some trigger methods and exceptions that can be raised by the method execution.

In object-oriented programming languages, an object attribute cannot be directly accessed. The only access to attributes is by invoking the methods available at the object interface (*strict encapsulation*). In databases, a lot of applications simply read or write attribute values. Queries are often expressed as a boolean combination of predicates on attribute values. Therefore, most OODBMSs provide direct access to attributes by means of system-defined methods. Examples of these methods are *get* and *set* of Vbase, which are used to read and write, respectively, a given attribute. These methods, being provided as part of the system, have an efficient implementation and save the users from writing a large amount of trivial code. Therefore, some systems (e.g., Vbase and the system described in [7]) allow users to redefine the implementation of these methods for a given attribute. Each time the attribute is accessed, the user-defined method implementation, instead of the system-defined implementation, is invoked.

In OODBMSs characterized by distributed or client/server architectures, an important architectural issue concerns the site where an invoked method is executed. In GemStone [8], for example, the application designer has the option of moving an object, on which a method has been invoked, to the workstation (and then execute the method locally) or executing the method remotely on the server. A similar option is provided in the O_2 system. In general, the choice concerning the method execution site may be complex, because different factors must be taken into account, such as the complexity of the manipulations executed on the object, the references made to other objects during method execution, the network bandwidth, and the competition for the network and the server.

7.2.4 Classes and Instantiation Mechanisms

The instantiation is the first reusability mechanism (the second is inheritance) in that it makes it possible to reuse the same definition to generate objects with the same behavior and structure. Object-oriented data models provide the concept of class as the instantiation basis. A class is an object that acts as a template. As such, a class specifies the intended use of its instances by defining

- A structure that is a set of instance attributes (or instance variables);
- A set of messages that define the external interface;
- A set of methods that are invoked by messages.

In this sense, the class can be viewed as a specification (*intention*) for its instances. Because the class factorizes the definitions of a set of objects, it is also an abstraction mechanism.

Given a class, it is possible to generate through the instantiation mechanism objects that "answer" all messages defined in the class.

So far, we have implicitly assumed that an object is an instance of only one class. However, in some models, the instances of a class *C* are also *members* of the superclasses of *C*. Note that, as in [9], we distinguish between the notions of "instance of a class" and "member of a class." An object is an instance of a class *C* if *C* is the most specialized class associated with the object in a given inheritance hierarchy. An object is a member of a class *C* if it is an instance of some subclass of *C*. Most object-oriented data models restrict each object to be an instance of only one class, even though they allow an object to be a member of several classes through inheritance. However, object-oriented data models [10] can be found allowing an object to be an instance of several classes.

In addition to acting as a template, in some systems the class denotes also the collection of all its instances, that is, its *extension*. That is important because the class becomes the base on which queries are formulated. The

7.5 Technology

This subsection briefly describes the models of three systems compliant with the ODMG standard: GemStone, ObjectStore, and POET. These systems have been chosen mainly because they differ in several aspects of the data model and the query and access languages. Note, however, that, to date, more than 20 OODBMSs are available as products. The Web sites of different products based on the ODMG standard are listed at the end of this chapter.

7.5.1 GemStone

The GemStone system [8] was one of the first OODBMSs to appear on the market. The data model and the access/manipulation language (initially called Opal and afterward SmalltalkDB [13]) were defined as an extension of the Smalltalk language. On closer analysis, Opal shows the features that must be added to a programming language to make it suitable as a database language. Applications can be written in a number of different languages, including Smalltalk, C++, C, and Pascal. Currently, GemStone provides a product based on Smalltalk language (called GemStone/S) and a product based on Java language (Smalltalk/J). Latest versions integrate the Java components with CORBA and an Object Transaction Monitor (www.gemstone. com/products/j/main.html). We present here GemStone/S as an example of Smalltalk-based OODBMS.

7.5.1.1   Basic Features

To illustrate the features of the GemStone/S data model, we show how the class Institute of the example database schema in Figure 7.2 is defined:

```
Object subclass  Institute
instVarNames: #( research-area , institute-name ,
     address , research-group )
classVars: #()
poolDictionary: #()
inDictionary: UserGlobals
constraints: #[#[#research-area, String],
    #[#institute-name, String],
    #[#address, Address],
    #[#research-group, Teams]]
instanceInvariant: false
isModifiable: false.
```

In GemStone/S, the definition of a class is always performed by sending to the proper superclass the message "subclass" for which there exists a system-defined method in each class in the database. In the above example, the class Institute is created as a subclass of the system-class Object. In addition to the name of the new class, a class definition message contains other arguments describing relevant characteristics of the new class. In particular,

- The clause *instVarNames* has a list of strings denoting the names of the instance variables (i.e., attributes) of the class. Domains are specified in the clause constraints.

- The clause *classVars* has as an argument a list of class instance variables (i.e., class-attributes).

- The clause *poolDictionary* has as an argument a list of *pool variables* that are shared by several classes and their instances. The pool variables enable several objects, instances of different class, to share common information.

- The clause *inDictionary* specifies the name of an already defined dictionary, where the name of class is inserted on its creation.

- The clause *constraints* specifies the domain's attributes.

- The clause *instanceInvariant* specifies whether the instances of the class can be modified.

- The clause *isModifiable* specifies whether the class itself can be modified.

7.5.1.2　Methods

Methods in GemStone/S are defined by means of the message "method." This message has as an argument the name of the class to which the method belongs and the method specification. The method specification consists of a message pattern and a body. The message pattern is, in essence, the specification of the method interface. Two example methods, defined for the class Institute, are the following. The first method, when invoked on an instance of class Institute, returns the value of attribute "research-area" of the instance, whereas the second method modifies the value of attribute "research-area."

```
method: Institute
 research-area    message pattern
 ^research-area   return statement
%


method: Institute
 research-area: anArea   message pattern
 research-area:= anArea
 ^self   return statement
%
```

Note that the two methods have different message patterns. Indeed, the first method has no input parameter, whereas the second method has one (i.e., the new value of attribute "research-area"). GemStone/S supports full encapsulation; therefore, a pair of methods like the preceding ones must be defined by the users for each attribute that must be directly accessed and modified.

7.5.1.3 Object Query Language

In addition to navigation capabilities commonly provided by all OODBMSs, GemStone/S provides a query language supporting set-oriented queries. Queries can be issued only against set objects, not against classes. For example, suppose that an instance of class Institute-Set has been defined having the name "an-Institute-Set" and that instances of class Institute have been added to this set. A query retrieving from the set "an-Institute-Set" all institutes doing research on databases is formulated in Opal as follows:

```
DB-Institutes := an-Institute-Set select: {aSet |
aSet.research-area =  Databases }
```

The result of the query is a set that is assigned to the variable "DB-Institute." Then the elements of the results can be extracted by using the usual operations on the sets. Queries may contain a boolean combination of predicates as well as path-expression.

7.5.2 ObjectStore

The ObjectStore system has been developed starting from the C++ language as a system to provide persistency to C++ objects according to the persistent programming language approach. In particular, ObjectStore exploits the C++ class definition language as data definition language extending it with specific constructs for data management. In addition to the C++ based definition language, ObjectStore currently provides interface for Java and ActiveX. It also supports CORBA, DCOM, and JavaBeans (www.odi.com/content/products/os/OstoreHome.html). We present here ObjectStore as an example of C++ based OODBMS.

7.5.2.1   Basic Features

The type system and the DDL in ObjectStore are based on the type system and the class definition mechanism of C++. In particular, C++ distinguishes between objects and values, as does ObjectStore.

To illustrate the features of the ObjectStore data model, we show how the class Institute of the example database schema in Figure 7.2 is defined:

```
class Institute {
  public:
  char* research-area;
  char* name;
  Address* address;
  os_set<Team*> research-group;
}
```

In the preceding example, the *public* clause introduces the list of declarations of public features (attributes and methods) of the class. Such features can be directly accessed from outside the objects. In the example, all features are public. The *private* clause, by contrast, introduces features that can be accessed only by methods of the class.

7.5.2.2   Relationships

A further important extension of ObjectStore with respect to C++ is related to the notion of relationship. This extension allows us to specify inverse attributes, representing binary relationships. This functionality is requested through the keyword *inverse_member* associated with an attribute and followed by the inverse attribute name. ObjectStore automatically ensures relationship consistency. On the deletion of a participating object, the relationship is also deleted. Thus, no dangling references can arise. It can also be specified that the object participating in the relationship with the deleted object must in turn be deleted. As an example, consider the schema in Figure 7.2 and suppose that a company can be a sponsor for at most a team and that an additional attribute, sponsor-of, having class Team as the domain, is included in the class Company. The relationship between a team a certain constructor, such as the list or the array? There are many factors that can determine the best design of a database schema. Nonetheless, it is possible to devise methodological guidelines that can help the database designer.

The rest of this section presents a methodological approach that supports the design of an object-oriented database schema. The approach that we present must be understood as only a set of guidelines, because there is no unique and exact method to design databases.

To a large extent, the object-oriented paradigm has changed the application design process, chiefly because the gap among the various design phases is reduced. In the same way, conceptual, logical, and implementation models in object-oriented databases (always object models) are closer than their corresponding models in relational databases (E/R and relational models). However, in spite of using the same paradigm in all design phases, object-oriented conceptual models generally are richer than object-oriented design and implementation models. Some of the concepts that are usually supported by conceptual models, and that are not provided by most of the design and implementation models, are: *n*-ary relationships, relationships with attributes, different kinds of generalizations (such as complete/incomplete or disjoint/overlapping generalizations), aggregations, constraints (such as the ordered constraint in a relationship), and so on. In addition, there are some decisions that must be taken at design level, such as, for example, the final representation of a multivalued attribute, because the conceptual schema must not specify when a multivalued attribute has to be defined as an array, as a list, or as a set.

The first step in a database design process is to define a *conceptual schema* in a language (usually called *model*) which has to be close to the user and independent of the final implementation (see Chapter 1). The model used in this step should be able to represent every user's requirements; therefore, it must be as expressive as possible. It would also be recommendable that the model should be supported by most of the CASE tools (see Chapter 13). We could use the Unified Modeling Language (UML) notation [17], which, apart from being the OMG standard notation, fulfills the previously mentioned characteristics.

Once the conceptual schema has been defined, it often can be directly translated into the final implementation in a specific OODBMS. Another possibility consists of getting, as an intermediate step, a schema described in ODL [3], which would represent the design details independently of the final product (improving portability, understandability, etc.) (see Figure 7.3). Even though we advise getting the implementation schema in three steps (from conceptual design to implementation design, going through the standard

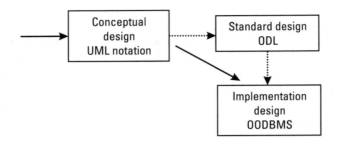

Figure 7.3 Design process of an object-oriented database schema.

design), in some cases, specially if the OODBMS does not support the ODMG data model, it could be more convenient to go directly from the conceptual schema to the implementation schema.

With regard to the final product, we could distinguish between the OODBMS based either on Smalltalk or on C++. However, the main difference lies in their ODL, because both kinds of OODBMSs are based on the ODMG data model. We are going to use POET as an example of OODBMS based on C++.

To illustrate the translation process, we will introduce an example that represents the organization of a Ph.D. course program. It is an academic example that tries to gather the main concepts of the object-oriented modeling.

7.6.1   Conceptual Design

The main activity of the first step is representation of the universe of discourse according to the UML notation. The universe of discourse of our running example is as follows.

Milano University (in Milan) and Rey Juan Carlos University (in Madrid) offer some Ph.D. programs jointly. The programs are taught in collaboration by the two universities, which require an object-oriented database that stores the information related to these programs. The system will have to store the following data:

- The data for each participant in the Ph.D. program, both lecturers and students: name, address (including number, street, city, country), and telephone number, as well as the program in which the participant is involved. Students are related with only one Ph.D. program (by the register number), but lecturers can be involved in

Supposing the class Topic has a self-association representing the relationship between different topics (e.g., object databases is a subtopic of the databases topic), that association can be defined in ODL just like any other association (see Figure 7.8).

Notice that self-relationships have to be defined twice to represent the two traversal paths.

If the association has attributes, there are two different possibilities:

- If the multiplicity is of the type *many-to-many*, we will have to convert the association into a new class. This class has to define the attributes of the association as well as two relationships.

- If the multiplicity is of the type *one-to-many*, we could define the attribute inside the associated classes that take part in the association with multiplicity one.

The ODMG data model supports only binary associations, so that *n*-ary relationships could be defined, as in the relational model, by creating a new class. This class will have a relationship for each class involved in the association.

If the association has an association class, the last one will be converted into another class. Therefore, there would be three classes (the two classes involved in the association and the association class itself) related to one another through a *n*-ary relationship. This relationship will be defined in ODL just as any other *n*-ary relationship.

The UML *or* the constraint between two associations has to be defined in ODL as an operation.

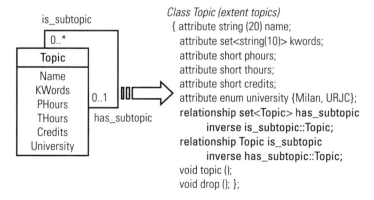

Figure 7.8 Self-association definition in ODL.

7.6.2.3   Generalizations and Realizations

UML supports disjoint/overlapping and complete/incomplete generalizations. Those two distinctions are orthogonal between them. The default generalization in UML is the disjoint and incomplete one, and it is also directly supported by the ODMG data model through the EXTEND relationship. Figure 7.9 shows an example.

The overlapping is not supported by the ODMG data model. It could be supported, as in other data models that do not support overlapping (e.g., the previous releases of the standard [12]), by adding a new class that inherits from the two overlapping classes. For example, to represent a lecturer who belongs to two different Ph.D. programs, as a lecturer and as a student, a class *Lecturer-Student*, which inherits from *Student* and *Lecturer*, should be defined. However, the latest version of the ODMG data model supports only multiple inheritance of behavior, but it does not provide multiple inheritance of state: "The EXTEND relationship is a single inheritance relationship between two classes" [3]. Thus, ODL does not allow the definition of an overlapping generalization that inherits the state and the behavior, and overlapping generalizations cannot be represented in the ODMG data model as a result.

With regard to complete generalization, the ODMG data model does not define any notation that explicitly supports it. A possibility would consist in defining the superclass as an abstract class. Because an abstract class cannot be directly instantiated, when the superclass is an abstract class, the generalization is complete [21]. Unfortunately, abstract classes are not directly supported by the ODL grammar. An abstract class could also be defined as a class with some deferred method, but ODL does not provide any syntax to

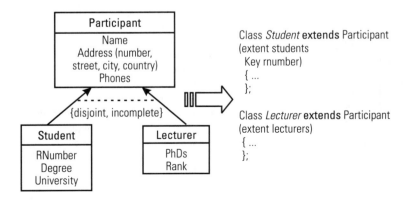

Figure 7.9 Disjoint and incomplete generalization in ODL.

define this kind of method either. Another possibility would consist in defining the superclass as an interface. In the ODMG data model, interfaces represent only the abstract behavior of the objects; that is why they cannot be directly instantiated: "Classes are types that are directly instantiable … Interfaces are types that cannot be directly instantiated" [3]. Therefore, an abstract class could be represented as an interface in ODMG. Thus, a complete generalization could be defined through an "is-a" relationship in ODL and the supertype being an interface. However, it is important to outline that an interface does not amount to an abstract class because an interface, in contrast to a class, does not represent the state [21]. That is the best way to represent the complete generalization in ODL.

The UML concept of realization corresponds to the "is-a" relationship in ODMG (inheritance of behavior).

7.6.2.4 Aggregation

UML supports two different ways of representing the aggregation concept: aggregation as a special kind of binary association and the aggregation tree notation. In spite of that, UML specifies that the difference is just one of notation. However, we find some semantic differences between aggregation (often called member-collection aggregation) and the aggregation tree (often called part-whole aggregation). Actually, there are other proposals concerning aggregation relationships in conceptual design [22, 23], richer than the UMLs. These proposals make a distinction between different kinds of aggregation, all of which support member-collection (aggregation in UML) and part-whole (aggregation tree in UML) aggregations.

Member-collection aggregation represents a collection of objects, all of which are of the same class and together give rise to another class. The most common example is a collection of *trees* that make up a *forest*. Part-whole aggregation represents a structured class that is composed of almost two different classes. For example, a window is composed of a menu and a tool bar. The main difference with respect to member collection aggregation is that component objects are of a different class. In addition, part objects have a structural relationship among them. For example, a car comprises four wheels, an engine, and a body, but those parts have to be placed in a specific position to complete the car. Nonetheless, in a member-collection aggregation, there is no structural relationship among members.

ODL does not provide any constructor that directly supports aggregation, so both kinds of aggregation could be represented through attributes. Member-collection aggregation could be translated as a collection type (see Figure 7.10). If the order is relevant, then the collection type will be a list.

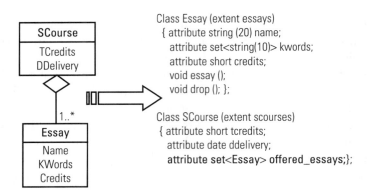

Figure 7.10 Member-collection aggregation in the ODMG data model.

The part-whole aggregation could also be represented in ODL defining each component class as an attribute in the composite class, just like different member-collection aggregations, missing the part-whole aggregation abstraction.

We can see that member-collection aggregation is supported as a collection attribute, in the same way as multivalued attributes are supported, and there are no differences between member-collection and part-whole aggregation. We could also consider other design alternatives, such as defining aggregation as a relationship. Object databases do not currently provide special constructors for the aggregation concept either. However, some theoretical proposals do extend the ODMG data model to support composite objects [24].

7.6.2.5 Collection and Structured Types

As we have seen, collection and structured types are key concepts in the object-oriented database design, and they also constitute one of the main differences with regard to the relational databases. They allow the definition of multivalued attributes, the cardinality of relationships, aggregations, and so on. The ODMG data model supports different kinds of collection types; now the question is how to choose the most appropriate type. As a rule, we should use the following:

- A *bag type*, if the collection type allows duplicates and has an unbounded number of elements, and the order is not relevant. For example, the drum for a lottery has an unbounded number of balls.

Two different balls can have the same number and the order is not relevant, so it can be designed as a bag type.

- A *set type*, if the collection type also has an unbounded number of elements and the order is not relevant, but, unlike the bag, duplicates are not allowed. For example, the drum for a bingo game has an unbounded number of balls. Each ball has a different number and the order is not relevant. Thus, it can be designed as a set type.

- A *list type* should be used if the collection type has an unbounded number of elements and the order is relevant, whether it has duplicated elements or not. A school register could be an example of a list type.

- A *dictionary type*, if the collection type has an unbounded number of pairs of elements (Key-value), with no duplicate keys. The most common example is a dictionary.

- An *array* or a *sequence type,* if the collection type has a bounded number of elements. For example, a week in the calendar could be represented as an array.

- A *structure type* is used when the element that we want to represent is a composite element and each component has a different data type. A structure has a bounded number of components. For example, the address is a structure with four components (number, street, city, and country). The main difference between a structure and a class lies in the fact that whereas the class represents an object type, the structure represents a value type (a literal in the ODMG terminology). The distinction between objects and values has been one of the most important discussions in the object-oriented paradigm. Smalltalk, for example, as well as ODL, does not distinguish between objects and values, so the address type has to be represented either as a literal (that is not exactly the same as a value) or as a class. On the contrary, C++, just like some OODBMSs such as ObjectStore (see Section 7.5.3), supports structures and classes, so the address would be represented as a structure.

Although their implementation could be similar, values and types are conceptually different. An object, in the database environment, is the computational representation of an object of the real world, which we want to represent in our database. However, values do not exist by themselves and they just allow the definition of objects. A real object can be seen as an object or as a value depending on the universe of discourse. Thus, for example, color is a value if we are talking about the characteristics of a person (the color of his or her eyes), but it can also be seen as an object if we are modeling a painting factory. When the difference between object and value types is not supported (which is the case of most pure object models), both of them are defined as classes (see the POET example in Section 7.6.3). In this example, both addresses and people are classes. For that reason, they have OIDs and we could query about addresses, as well as for people, as a result.

Before proposing an implementation schema, we will sum up the ODL schema (see Figure 7.11) that corresponds to the conceptual schema defined in Section 7.6.1 (see Figure 7.4). Although we have proposed different possibilities to translate it into the ODMG model, we will now take one of those proposals into consideration to implement it.

7.6.3   Implementation Schema Design

This section shows how the example of the Ph.D. programs can be translated into an implementation schema in POET 4.0 using the C++ binding. In addition to the definition language, which is C++ based, the translation from the ODL schema into a POET schema will carry out some changes.

Because we are defining a database schema, all classes must be persistent classes. Persistent classes are defined by the introduction of the key word persistent before the class declaration,

```
persistent class student {...};
```

To use the OQL provided by POET, an extent must be explicitly defined. For example, the following declaration,

```
define extent students for student;
```

defines an extent for the class *student*, called *students*. This extent is equivalent to the *StudentAllSet*, which is implicitly generated by POET when the class student is created.

In the POET definition, we have introduced the visibility levels, which could not be defined in ODL. Attributes and relationships have been defined as private members, and methods as public ones.

The type system of POET is based on the C++ type system. In addition to the C++ base types (int, float, char, double), POET provides the following data types: *PtString*, *PtDate*, *PtTime*, *PtBlob*, and *PtStorage*.

multimedia data, DBMSs designed to manage such data must have considerably more functionality and capability than conventional DBMSs. Our understanding about the requirements imposed by multimedia objects on the development of MM-DBMS is only partial and still evolving.

Hence, any architecture for an MM-DBMS ought to be extensible. One of the important goals in the design of an MM-DBMS is to provide extensibility, that is, the ability for the system developers and end users to extend the system by adding new types of media objects, devices, and protocols for storage, retrieval, and management of multimedia information. Extensibility can be classified into two types: logical extensibility and physical extensibility.

- *Logical extensibility* is the possibility of dynamically introducing new user-defined data types. Users should be able to define their own data types and use them seamlessly with the predefined data types. In other words, user data types and system data types should have the same status, although the system may support them differently. Logical extensibility is important in multimedia management, because adding a new type of media may introduce new operations.

- *Physical extensibility* is an architectural type of extensibility. Physical extensibility allows new system modules to be added to an operational system. This capability is useful in multimedia DB management because it allows modules to be introduced that are specialized in the management of new media or data types. Physical extensibility is necessary for two reasons. First, it is required to support logical extensibility, because introduction of new data types may require the introduction of new system modules. For example, image data types may be used differently for GIS. Second, data types used for different applications may require different types of system support for storage, indexing, and so on.

8.1.2.1 Storage

Extensibility in Access Methods

The multiple interpretation and application of different media data types preclude an international standard on indexing and search mechanism for multimedia objects. Therefore, various indexing techniques should be included in the system as they evolve. Searching in a multimedia DB can be computationally intensive or I/O intensive, depending on the media type.

For example, given that audio and video compression techniques are evolving, corresponding retrieval methods should be allowed to evolve in an MM-DBMS.

Extensibility in Storage Mechanisms

Methods for efficient data clustering and storage layout schemes for multimedia data are still evolving [2]. A multimedia storage manager component of MM-DBMS should store only raw data of multimedia objects. Storage details should be explicitly used by the object manager.

8.1.2.2   Retrieval: Query Languages

Content-based retrieval of multimedia data calls for content-based indexing techniques. Different from conventional DBs, in which data items are represented by a set of attributes of elementary data types, multimedia objects are represented by a collection of features; similarity of object contents depends on context and frame of reference; and features of objects are characterized by multimodal feature measures. These lead to great challenges for content-based indexing. On the other hand, there are special requirements on content-based indexing: To support visual browsing, similarity retrieval, and fuzzy retrieval, indexes should be enhanced with extra semantics [3].

This chapter emphasizes the structural complexity and mostly the spatiotemporal features of a multimedia document rather than the features of monomedia objects. Interested readers can find an extensive presentation of important aspects of IMDs such as modeling, integrity, authoring, and retrieval in [4].

The chapter is structured as follows. Section 8.2 provides an example application, an IMD, that motivates the requirements for MM-DBMS. An interactive multimedia application includes media objects modified accordingly and presented according to a predefined spatiotemporal sequence or to some interaction. The example application serves as a point of discussion throughout the rest of the chapter. Section 8.3 presents an integrated IMD model and discusses storage, retrieval, indexing, and other DBMS-related issues for the case of multimedia DBs. The chapter concludes with interesting issues and research prospects.

8.2   A Sample IMD

This section presents a sample IMD that motivates the requirements that will feed an MM-DBMS design. We emphasize the structural complexity and mostly the spatiotemporal features of a multimedia document rather than the features of monomedia objects.

As mentioned, the carriers of interactions in a multimedia document are the events (atomic or complex) that occur in the context of an IMD session. Hereafter, we refer to the events that the sample presentation will detect and consume. Some of them are the following: Double Click is raised when the user double-clicks the mouse; KeyEsc is raised when the user presses the Escape key; IntroStop is raised each time the audio clip "INTRO" ends its playback; ExitEvent is raised each time the user presses the "EXITBTN" button; TIMEINST is raised each time the timer "TIMER1" reaches the fiftieth second; AppTimerEvent is raised each time the Application timer reaches the time 2 minutes and 30 seconds.

Having the media objects available, we can build the application for the following scenario.

The application starts (event StartApp) with presentation of button LABELBTN immediately followed by the audio clip INTRO. After 3 seconds the image IMG2_1 is presented followed by IMG2_2 after 2 seconds. After 2 more seconds the image IMG1_2 is presented at position, while after 2 seconds IMG2_1, IMG2_2, and IMG1_2 stop their presentation, while after a second the video clip RUNS starts. This sequence of presentation actions may be interrupted whenever one of the following events occurs: _DoubleClick, _KeyEsc, or _IntroStop. Another set of presentations ("Stage2A") starts when the event _IntroStop is raised. The presentation actions that take place are presentation of image IMG1_3 in parallel with audio clip ACDDM (when the clip ends the image disappears). In parallel, two seconds after timer TIMER1 (which started when "Stage 2A" started) expires, the text INFOTXT is presented.

The next set of media presentations ("Stage 2B") is initiated when the sequence of events _IntroStop and _ACDSoundStop occurs. During "Stage2B" the video clip KAVALAR starts playback while the buttons NEXTBTN and EXITBTN are presented. The presentation actions are interrupted when any of the events _TIMEINST and _NextBtnClick occurs. The end of "Stage2B" raises the synchronization event _e1.

The following set of media presentations ("Stage3") starts when any two of the events _e1, _NextBtnClick, _TIMEINST occur. During "Stage3" the text INFOTXT disappears, just after the text YMNOS appears while the audio clip FLUTE starts while 2 seconds after images IMG1_1 and IMG3_1 appear. Three seconds after, the EXITBTN appears.

The last part of the scenario handles the presentation termination, which will occur when _ExitEvent occurs. An application timer limits the duration of the scenario through the _AppTimer event.

That rich example generates requirements for modeling and retrieval, central issues for an MM-DBMS capable of dealing with IMDs. As for modeling, we have to look into the specific features of an IMD, such as interaction modeling and spatiotemporal composition of the media objects to adhere to the author's specifications. Another important issue is assurance of the document integrity in temporal and spatial terms. Then having the IMD in an MM-DBMS, we need to retrieve and present it according to the scenario specifications. That means internal and external interaction has to be detected and the spatial and temporal relationships among objects rendered in the output device.

Another important requirement is the retrieval of IMDs from the MM-DBMS, according to several criteria, among which the spatial/temporal ones play a significant role.

8.3 Design of an MM-DBMS for IMDs

The design requirements in the context of an MM-DBMS can be classified into two groups: one related to the data model and the other related to retrieval issues. In an MM-DBMS, monomedia objects (i.e., single media objects) or IMDs are stored. The modeling requirements of the latter are unarguably richer and certainly are a superset of monomedia objects. This section presents the requirements for modeling IMDs as MM-DBMS objects.

8.3.1 Modeling IMDs

In regard to the *data model*, we will discuss the following features, which are specific to multimedia information: interaction, multidimensionality, space and time dependencies, complexity, and temporal integrity. An IMD involves a variety of individual multimedia objects presented according to a set of specifications called the IMD scenario. The multimedia objects that participate in the IMD are transformed, either spatially or temporally, to be presented according to the author's requirements. Moreover, the author has to define the spatial and temporal order of objects within the document context and the relationships among them. Finally, the way that the user will interact with the presentation session as well as the way that the application will treat application or system events has to be defined. The related application domains are challenging and demanding. These applications include, among others, interactive TV, digital movies, and virtual-reality applications. In the framework of IMDs, we consider events, spatiotemporal composition, and the scenario as cornerstone concepts in a modeling effort.

- Events are the fundamental means of interaction in the context of the IMD and are raised by user actions, by objects participating in the IMD, or by the system. They can be simple (i.e., not decomposable in the IMD context) or complex, and they have attached their spatiotemporal signature (i.e., the space and the time they occurred). For more details, refer to [5].

- Spatiotemporal composition is an essential part of an IMD and represents the spatial and temporal ordering of media objects in the corresponding domain. At this point, the issue of spatial and temporal relationships among the objects is critical [6].

- The scenario stands for the integrated behavioral contents of the IMD, that is, what kind of events the IMD will consume and what presentation actions will be triggered as a result. In our approach, a scenario consists of a set of self-standing functional units (scenario tuples) that include triggering events (for start and stop), presentation actions (in terms of spatiotemporal compositions) to be carried out in the context of the scenario tuple, and related synchronization events (i.e., events that get triggered when a scenario tuple starts or stops).

To support complex IMDs, a system that offers both a suitable high-level modeling of IMDs and interactive multimedia presentation capabilities is needed. The modeling should provide for the spatial and temporal composition of the participating media, the definition of interaction between the user and the IMD, and the specification of media synchronization.

We claim that modeling of IMDs should place more emphasis on the interactive parts of such an application. In principle, the modeling of interaction should cover all the procedures that somehow involve the machine and the user.

8.3.1.1 Modeling Interaction With Events

The concept of events is defined in several research areas. In the area of active DBs an event is defined as an instantaneous *happening of interest*. An event is caused by some action that happens at a specific point in time and may be atomic or composite. Multimedia information systems, however, widen the context of events, as defined in the domain of active DBs. In addition to the temporal aspect of an event, which is represented by a temporal instance, there are events in IMDs that convey spatial information. That is represented by a spatial instance. For example, an event captures the position of visual objects at a certain point in time. Another aspect that is also crucial in the IMDs context is that, although the number and multitude of events produced both by the user and by the system may be huge, we may be interested in only a small subset of them. We define an event in the context of IMDs as follows:

> An event is raised by the occurrence of an action and has attached a spatial and temporal instance. The event is recognized by some interested human or process.

As mentioned in the definition, all events have attached to them a temporal instance relative to some reference point, usually the beginning of the IMD. Apart from a temporal instance, we assign a spatial instance to an event in case it is related to a visual media object. This spatial instance is essentially the rectangle that bounds an event (e.g., the screen area where the presentation of an image takes place). In some trivial cases (e.g., a mouse click), the rectangle is reduced to a point. Thus, it is meaningful to integrate the two notions of temporal and spatial instances in the definition of events. Therefore, we introduce the term *spatiotemporal instance*, whose representation in tuple form is (sp_inst, temp_inst), where sp_inst is a spatial instance and temp_inst is a temporal instance as defined in previous sections. Events can be purely temporal, as is the case for the start event of an audio clip.

Classification

To assist the authors in the specification of IMDs, we have to provide them with a fundamental repertoire of events. In the framework of IMDs, we further classify the events into categories. The classification of the events is done on the basis of the entity that produces the event. The elaborated categories are presented in the following list.

- *User interaction.* The user interactions are the events that are generated explicitly by user interactions within the IMD context. They are mainly input events as the user interacts with the system via input devices such as mouse, keyboard, touch screen, and so on. Temporal access control events are the well-known actions *start, pause, resume, stop, fast forward, rewind,* and *random positioning in time* and concern the execution of one or a group of media objects.

- *Intra-object events.* This category includes events that are related to the internal functionality of an object presented in an IMD. This functionality is implemented in object-oriented approaches as method invocation.

- *Interobject events.* Interobject events occur when two or more objects are involved in the occurrence of an action of interest. These events are raised if spatial or temporal relationships between two or more objects hold. In the spatial case, an interobject event can occur if one object, moving spatially, meets another media object. A temporal interobject event can occur when the deviation between the synchronized presentation of two continuous media objects exceeds a threshold.

- *User-defined events.* Into this category we place the events that are defined by the IMD designer. They are related to the content of the IMD execution. A user-defined event can refer to the content of a media object, that is, to the occurrence of a specific pattern in a media object. For instance, an event is to be raised if the head of a news anchor occurs in a video frame to indicate that the boring advertisements are over and the interesting news is now on.

Now we present a model for simple and complex events in IMDs, based on the event concept and classification. A detailed presentation can be found in [5].

Modeling and Composition of Events

According to the definition of an event, we need the following attributes to represent a generic event: the subject and object attributes, which are of type objectList and which essentially represent the objects that caused or are affected by the event, respectively. The attribute spatio_temporal_signature takes the spatial and temporal instances attached to the event when it actually occurs.

Then the structure of the Event class in an object-oriented pseudolanguage is as follows:

```
class Event inherits from object
attributes // attribute name attribute's data type,
   subject     objectList;
   action      actionList;
   object      objectList;
   spatio_temporal_signature spatiotemp_instance;
end
```

As mentioned previously, it is important to provide the tools to the authors for the definition of composite events. The composition of events in the context of an IMD has two aspects:

- *Algebraic composition* is the composition of events according to algebraic operators, adapted to the needs and features of an IMD.

- *Spatiotemporal composition* reflects the spatial and temporal relationships between events.

This chapter elaborates on the first aspect. Readers can refer to [5] for the second one. First, however, we should define some fundamental concepts:

- The *spatiotemporal reference point* (θ) is the spatiotemporal start of the IMD scenario named as θ. This serves as the reference point for every spatiotemporal event and instance in the IMD.

- The *temporal interval* is the temporal distance between two events (e_1, e_2), namely, the start and the end of the interval $t\_int :== (e_1, e_2)$, where e_1, e_2 are events that may either be attached to predefined temporal instances relative to some reference or occur asynchronously.

Algebraic Composition of Events

In many cases, the author wants to define specific events that relate to other existing events. We distinguish among the following cases: disjunction, conjunction, inclusion, and negation.

Disjunction

$e :== OR(e_1, \ldots, e_n)$. This event occurs when at least one of the events $e_1, \ldots, e_n$ occurs. For instance, we may be interested in the event e occurring when button A (e_1) or button B (e_2) was pressed.

Conjunction

- $e :== \text{ANY}(k,e_1,\dots,e_n)$. This event occurs when at least any k of the events e_1, ..., e_n occur. The sequence of occurrence is irrelevant. For example, in an interactive game, a user proceeds to the next level when he or she is successful in two out of three tests that generate the corresponding events e_1, e_2, and e_3.

- $e :== \text{SEQ}(e_1, \dots,e_n)$. This event occurs when all events e_1, ..., e_n occur in the order appearing in the list. For example, in another interactive game, the user proceeds to the next level when he or she succeeds in three tests causing the events e_1, e_2, and e_3 one after the other.

- $e :== \text{TIMES}\ (n,e_1)$. This event occurs when there are n consecutive occurrences of event e_1. This implies that other events *may* occur between the occurrences of e_1.

In many cases, the authors want to apply constraints related to event occurrences in specific temporal intervals. To facilitate this requirement, we define a set of operators that are of interest in the context of multimedia applications:

Inclusion

$e :== \text{IN}(e_1,t\_int)$. Event e occurs when event e_1 occurs during the temporal interval t_int. For example, in an IMD we might want to detect three mouse clicks at intervals of 1 second, so that a help window appears. If $t\_int = (e_2,e_3)$, where e_2 corresponds to the starting point of a timer, while e_3 corresponds to the end of a timer whose duration is defined as 1 second. The desired event would then be defined as $e = \text{IN}\ (\text{TIMES}(3,\text{mouse.click}), t\_int)$.

Negation

$e :== \text{NOT}(e_1,t\_int)$. Event e occurs when e_1 does not occur during the temporal interval t_int.

The events of the sample application in Section 8.2 can then be represented using the primitives introduced in the current section.

8.3.1.2 Spatiotemporal Compositions of Actors

In an IMD there is a set of monomedia objects (referred to as *actors*) that participate, and in most of the cases their presentations are related temporally and/or spatially. A set of presentation actions may be applied to each actor (such as start, stop, show, hide). In the past, the term *synchronization* was widely used to describe the temporal ordering of actors in a multimedia application [7]. However, a multimedia application specification should describe both temporal and spatial ordering of actors in the context of the application. The spatial-ordering issues (i.e., absolute positioning and spatial relationships among actors) have not been adequately addressed. We claim that the term *synchronization* is a poor one for multimedia applications; instead, we propose the term *composition* to represent both the temporal and spatial ordering of actors. Many existing models for temporal composition of multimedia objects in the framework of an IMD are based on Allen's relations [8]. Nevertheless, those relations are not suitable for composition representation, because they are descriptive (they do not reflect causal dependency between intervals), they depend on interval duration, and they may lead to temporal inconsistency. Next, we refer briefly to a model for spatiotemporal compositions of actors [6] that we have exploited for the definition of the IMD scenarios.

Temporal and Spatial Relationships and Operators

In this section we briefly examine the temporal aspects of actor composition. We exploit the temporal composition scheme as defined in [9] and introduce a similar scheme that also captures the causality of the temporal relationships. In this scheme, the start and end points of a multimedia instance are used as events. Moreover, the well-known *pause* (temporarily stop execution) and *resume* procedures (start the execution from the point where the pause operator took place) are also taken into account.

Hereafter, we present a set of TAC operators that represent the temporal composition of actors, together with the causality of temporal relationships among presentation intervals. For more details, refer to [9]. These operators correspond to the well-known TAC actions: start (>), stop (!), pause (||), resume (|>), fast forward (>>), and rewind (<<). Therefore,

$$\text{TAC\_operator} :== \text{">"} \mid \text{"!"} \mid \text{"||"} \mid \text{"|>"} \mid \text{">>"} \mid \text{"<<"}$$

We have not defined an operator for the random positioning in time action because it would require an argument to denote the time point. We implement that action by defining an attribute for actors that specifies the point from which the actor should start playing.

We also have to illustrate the events arising from the temporal state changes of an actor, that is, when object A starts its presentation, then the "A>" temporal event is raised. Special attention should be paid to the event generated when the actor finishes its execution naturally when there are no more data to be presented ("<") and to distinguish this event from the TAC operator "!." Therefore,

$$\text{t\_event} := \text{">"} \mid \text{"<"} \mid \text{"|>"} \mid \text{"||"} \mid \text{">>"} \mid \text{"<<"}$$

We define now temporal composition representation. Let A, B be two actors. Then the expression A t_event t_interval TAC_operator B represents all the temporal relationships between the two actors, where t_interval corresponds to the length of a vacant temporal interval. Therefore,

$$\text{temporal\_composition} := (\Theta \mid \text{object } [\{\text{temp\_rel object}\}])$$
$$\text{temp\_rel} := \text{t\_event t\_interval TAC\_operator}$$

For instance, the expression: "Θ >0> A >4! B <0> C" conveys this message: "zero seconds after the start of the application, start A; 4 seconds after the start of A, stop B; 0 seconds after the end of B, start C."

Finally, we define the duration d_A of a multimedia object A as the temporal interval between the temporal events A> and A<. Another aspect of object composition in IMDs is related to the spatial layout of the application, that is, the spatial arrangement and relationships of the participating objects. The spatial composition aims at representing three aspects:

- The topological relationships between the objects (*disjoint*, *meet*, *overlap*, etc.);
- The directional relationships between the objects (*left*, *right*, *above*, *above-left*, etc.);
- The distance characteristics between the objects (*outside* 5 cm, *inside* 2 cm, etc.).

Spatiotemporal Composition Model

An IMD scenario presents media objects composed in spatial and temporal domains. A model that captures those requirements is presented here. For uniformity reasons, we exploit the spatiotemporal origin of the image, Θ, that corresponds to the spatial and temporal start of the application (i.e., upper left corner of the application window and the temporal start of the application). Another assumption we make is that the objects that participate in the composition include their spatiotemporal presentation characteristics (i.e., size, temporal duration). We define the spatiotemporal model as follows:

Assuming two spatial objects A, B, we define the generalized spatial relationship between those objects as $sp\_rel = (r_{ij}, v_i, v_j, x, y)$, where r_{ij} is the identifier of the topological-directional relationship between A and B; v_i, v_j are the closest vertices of A and B, respectively (as defined in [9]); and x, y are the horizontal and vertical distances between v_i, v_j.

We define now a generalized operator expression to cover the spatial and temporal relationships between objects in the context of a multimedia application. It is important to stress that, in some cases, we do not need to model a relationship between two objects, but to represent the spatial and/or temporal position of an object relative to the application spatiotemporal origin, Θ (i.e., object A to appear at the spatial coordinates (110, 200) on the tenth second of the application).

We define a composite spatiotemporal operator that represents absolute spatial/temporal coordinates or spatiotemporal relationships between objects in the application as $ST\_R(sp\_rel, temp\_rel)$, where sp_rel is the spatial relationship and $temp\_rel$ is the temporal relationship as already defined.

The spatiotemporal composition of a multimedia application consists of several independent fundamental compositions. In other words, a scenario consists of a set of acts that are independent of each other. The term *independent* implies that actors participating in them are not related explicitly (either spatially or temporally), though there is always an implicit relationship through the origin Θ. Thus, all compositions are explicitly related to Θ. We call these compositions, which include spatially and/or temporally related objects, *composition_tuples*.

We define the composition_tuple in the context of a multimedia application as *composition_tuple* :== *Ai* [{ *ST_R Aj*}], where *Ai*, *Aj* are objects participating in the application, and *ST_R* is a spatiotemporal relationship (as defined above).

We define the composition of multimedia objects in the context of multimedia applications as a set of composition_tuples: *composition = Ci*{, *Cj*}, where *Ci*, *Cj* are composition_tuples.

The EBNF definition of the spatiotemporal composition based on the above is as follows:

```
composition :== composition_tuple{[,composition_tuple]}
composition_tuple :==
    (Θ| object) [{spatio_temporal_relationship object}]
spatio_temporal_relationship :==      "[("[sp_rel")","("temp_rel")]"
sp_rel :== "(" rij "," vi "," vj "," x "," y ")"
x :== INTEGER
y :== INTEGER
temp_rel[1]:== t_event t_interval TAC_operator
```

where r_{ij} denotes a topological-directional relationship between two objects and vi, vj denotes the closest vertices of the two objects. The term *action* was defined previously.

8.3.1.3   The Scenario Model

The term *scenario* in the context of IMDs stands for the integrated behavioral contents of the IMD, that is, what kind of events the IMD will consume and what actions will be triggered as a result. The scenario, in the current approach, consists of a set of autonomous functional units (*scenario tuples*) that include the triggering events (for starting and stopping the scenario tuple), the presentation actions to be carried out in the context for the scenario tuple, related synchronization events, and possible constraints. More specifically, a scenario tuple has the following attributes:

- *Start_event* represents the event expression that triggers the execution of the actions described in *Action_List*.

- *Stop_event* represents the event expression that terminates the execution of this tuple (i.e., the execution of the actions described in *Action_List* before its expected termination).

- *Action_List* represents the list of synchronized media presentation actions that will take place when this scenario tuple becomes activated. The expressions included in this attribute are in terms of compositions as described in previous sections and in [9].

---

1. Specifically in the current implementation, we adopted the "∧" operator. Then the composition A∧B that corresponds to the expression (A>0>B);(A<0!B);(B<0!A) can be expressed in natural language: "Start A and B simultaneously and when the temporally shorter ends, the other object is stopped as well."

- *Synch_events* refers to the events (if any) generated at the beginning and the end of the current tuple execution. These events can be used for synchronization purposes.

The scenario tuple is defined as follows:

scenario:== scenario_tuple [{,scenario_tuple}]
scenario_tuple :== Start_event ',' Stop_event ',' Action_List ','
　　Synch_events
Start_event :== Event
Stop_event :== Event
Action_List :== composition
Synch_events :== '(' start, end ')'
start :== Event | " "
stop :== Event | " "

Section 8.2 presented a sample IMD scenario with rich interaction and composition features. One of the parts of the scenario adheres to the following verbal description.

The next set of media presentations ("Stage 2B") is initiated when the sequence of events _IntroStop and _ACDSoundStop occurs. During Stage2B the video clip KAVALAR starts playback while the buttons NEXTBTN and EXITBTN are presented. The presentation actions are interrupted when any of the events _TIMEINST and _NextBtnClick occurs. The end of Stage2B raises the synchronization event _e1.

The IMD scenario model can represent that functionality by the following scenario tuple definition:

TUPLE Stage2B
　　Start Event = SEQ(_IntroStop;_ACDSoundStop)
　　Stop Event = ANYNEW(1;_TIMEINST;_NextBtnClick)
　　Action List = KAVALAR 0 NEXTBTN 0 EXITBTN
　　Synch Events = (_, e1)

8.3.2　IMD Retrieval Issues

As regards retrieval issues, we will mainly discuss the issues related to retrieval and presentation of IMDs, which are broader than those of monomedia objects.

- *Synchronization and presentation:* The retrieval and presentation of multimedia objects from an MM-DBMS bear some specific features arising from the time-dependent features of most media types. For instance, for a video clip to be presented properly, we need to ensure adequate data throughput (i.e., 25 frames per second) so that the presentation is continuous and of acceptable quality. This is a multi-parameter issue involving several technological factors, such as communication networks, secondary storage technology, compression algorithms, and so on. Then, given that this issue (known as the intramedia synchronization problem) is tackled, we have to take into account the different synchronization relations among sets of objects. The well-known example of a "talking head" requires that the audio clip be in synchrony with the video clip so that lip synchronization is achieved.

- *Query languages, content-based retrieval, and indexing:* Another important issue related to retrieval is content-based retrieval, which has attracted important research efforts and industrial interest. Research has focused on content-based image indexing, that is, fast retrieval of objects using their content characteristics (color, texture, shape). For example, in [10] a system, called *QBIC*, that couples several features from machine vision with fast indexing methods from the DB area is proposed to support color-, shape-, and texture-matching queries. Nearest-neighbor queries (based on image content) are addressed in [11]. In general, indexing of objects' contents is an active research area, while indexing of objects extends in the spatiotemporal coordinate system sets a new direction. This chapter presents the research efforts we have completed in the area of indexing and retrieval of IMDs based on their spatiotemporal structures [6].

8.3.2.1 Retrieval of IMDs Based on the Spatiotemporal Structure

As mentioned previously, the retrieval of multimedia documents on the basis of their spatiotemporal structure is a challenging theme. This chapter presents the research effort we have completed in the area of indexing and retrieval of IMDs based on their spatiotemporal structures [6]. During the IMD development process, it can be expected (especially in the case of complex and large applications) that the authors would need information related to the spatiotemporal features of an IMD. The related queries, depending on the spatiotemporal relationships that are involved, can be classified in the following categories:

- *Pure spatial or temporal.* Only a temporal or a spatial relationship is involved. For instance, "Which objects temporally overlap the presentation of logo D?" "Which objects spatially lie above object D in the application window?"
- *Spatiotemporal.* Where such a relationship is involved. For instance, "Which objects spatially overlap with object D during its presentation?"
- *Layout, related to the spatial or temporal layout of the application.* For instance, "What is the screen layout on the 22nd second of the application?" "Which objects are presented between the 10th and 20th seconds of the application?" (temporal layout).

A simple serial storage scheme that includes objects' spatial and temporal coordinates is an inefficient solution because typical IMDs include thousands of objects. Hence, indexing techniques that could be able to efficiently handle spatial and temporal characteristics of objects need to be adopted. We propose such efficient indexing mechanisms to support queries, like the ones listed above, in a large IMD.

Indexing Techniques for Large IMDs

As discussed in preceding sections, IMDs usually involve a large amount of media objects, such as images, video, sound, and text. The quick retrieval of a qualifying set, among the huge amount of data, that satisfies a query based on spatiotemporal relationships is necessary for the efficient construction of an IMD. Spatial and temporal features of objects are identified by six coordinates: the projections on the x-axis (points x_1, x_2), y-axis (points y_1, y_2), and t-axis (points t_1, t_2).[2] A serial storage scheme, maintaining the object characteristics as a set of seven values (id, x_1, x_2, y_1, y_2, t_1, t_2) and organizing them into disk pages, is not an efficient solution. Lack of ordering leads to the access of all pages for answering any query, like the above example queries. However, this scheme is used as the baseline for the evaluation of our proposals later in this chapter. A more efficient but still simplified solution (as

---

2. We adopt a unified three-dimensional workspace for space (two dimensions) and time (one dimension) features.

presented next) is based on the maintenance of three disk arrays that keep low coordinates of objects (i.e., x_1, y_1, and t_1) separate in a sorted order.[3]

Several queries involving spatiotemporal operators require the retrieval of one array only, using divide-and-conquer techniques. Temporal layout queries belong to this group. However, the majority of queries involves information about more than one axis. Thus, the retrieval of more than one array and the subsequent combination of the answer sets are necessary for such cases. Efficient indexing mechanisms that could combine spatiotemporal characteristics of objects to efficiently support a wide range of spatiotemporal operators need to be present in an IMD authoring tool. The next subsections propose two indexing schemes and their retrieval procedures.

A Simple Spatial and Temporal Indexing Scheme

A simple indexing scheme that could handle spatial and temporal characteristics of media objects consists of two indexes:

- A *spatial (two-dimensional) index* for spatial characteristics (the id and the x_1, x_2, y_1, y_2 values) of the objects;

- A *temporal index* for temporal characteristics (the id and the t_1, t_2 values) of the objects.

As an example, Figure 8.1 shows such an index based on the well-known multidimensional indexing scheme of R-trees [12].

We argue that the adoption of this indexing scheme improves the retrieval of spatiotemporal operators compared to the sorted-arrays scheme. Even for complex operators where both tree indexes need to be accessed (e.g., for the *overlap_during* operator), the cost of the two indexes' response times is expected to be lower than the retrieval cost of the (three) arrays. A weak point of the scheme already has been mentioned. The retrieval of objects according to their spatiotemporal relationships (e.g., the *overlap_during* one) with others demands access to both indexes and, in a second phase, the computation of the intersection set between the two answer sets. Access to both indexes is usually costly, and, in many cases, most of the elements of the two answer sets are not found in the intersection set. In other words, most of the disk accesses to each index separately are useless. A more efficient solution is

---

3. Instead of using low coordinates, one can select high coordinates (or six arrays with low and high coordinates). The decision does not affect the discussion that follows and its conclusions.

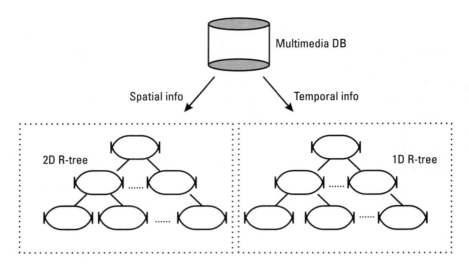

Figure 8.1 A simple (spatial and temporal) indexing scheme.

the merging of the two indexes (the spatial and the temporal one) in a unified mechanism. This scheme is proposed next.

A Unified Spatiotemporal Indexing Scheme

We propose a unified spatiotemporal indexing scheme that eliminates the inefficiencies of the previous scheme and further improves the performance of an IMD tool. The proposed indexing scheme consists of only one index: a *spatial (three-dimensional) index* for the complete spatiotemporal information (location in space and time coordinates) of the objects. If we assume that the R-tree is an efficient spatial indexing mechanism, then the unified scheme is illustrated in Figure 8.2. The main advantages of the proposed scheme, when compared to the previous one, are the following.

- The indexing mechanism is based on a unified framework. Only one spatial data structure (e.g., the R-tree) needs to be implemented and maintained.

- Spatiotemporal operators are more efficiently supported. Using the appropriate definitions, spatiotemporal operators are implemented as three-dimensional queries and retrieved using the three-dimensional index, so the need for (time-consuming) spatial joins is eliminated.

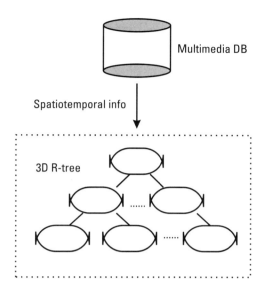

Figure 8.2 A unified (spatiotemporal) indexing scheme.

Retrieval of Spatiotemporal Operators Using R-Trees

The majority of multidimensional data structures has been designed as extensions of the classic alphanumeric index, B-tree. They usually divide the plane into appropriate subregions and store those subregions in hierarchical tree structures. Objects are represented in the tree structure by an approximation (the minimum bounding rectangle (MBR) approximation being the most common one) instead of their actual scheme, for simplicity and efficiency reasons. Unfortunately, the relative position of two MBRs does not convey the full information about the spatial (topological, direction, distance) relationship between the actual objects. For that reason, spatial queries involve the following two-step strategy [13]:

- *Filter step:* The tree structure is used to rapidly eliminate objects that could not possibly satisfy the query. The result of this step is a set of candidates that includes all the results and possibly some false hits.
- *Refinement step:* Each candidate is examined (by use of computational geometry techniques). False hits are detected and eliminated.

R-tree [12] is one of the most efficient hierarchical multidimensional data structures. A height-balanced tree, it consists of intermediate and leaf nodes

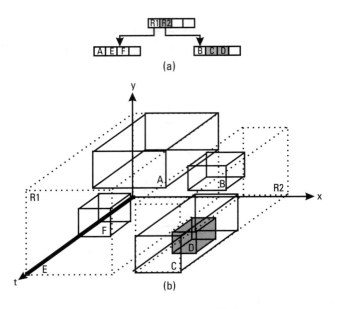

Figure 8.3 Retrieval of *overlap_during* operator using 3D R-trees.

(stored in secondary memory as disk pages). The MBRs of the actual data objects are assumed to be stored in the leaf nodes of the tree. Intermediate nodes are built by grouping rectangles (or hyperrectangles, in general) at the lower level. An intermediate node is associated with some rectangle that encloses all rectangles that correspond to lower level nodes. To retrieve objects that belong to the answer set of a spatiotemporal operator, with respect to a reference object, we have to specify the MBRs that could enclose such objects and then search the intermediate nodes that contain those MBRs. This technique was proposed and implemented in [14] to support spatial operators of high resolution (e.g., *meet, contains*) that are popular in GIS applications.

As an example, Figure 8.3(b) shows how the MBRs corresponding to the presentations of the objects are grouped and stored in the three-dimensional R-tree of our unified scheme. We assume a branching factor of 4, that is, each node contains, at most, four entries. At the lower level, MBRs of objects are grouped into two nodes, R1 and R2, which in turn compose the root of the index. We consider a spatiotemporal query, that is, the *overlap_during* operator, with D being the reference object *q*. To answer this query, only R2 is selected for propagation. Among the entries of R2, objects C and (obviously) D are the ones that constitute the qualified answer set. Note that only the right subtree of the R-tree index in Figure 8.3(a) was propagated to answer the query. The rate of the accessed nodes heavily depends on the size of the reference object q and, of course, the kind of the operator (more selective operators result in a smaller number of accessed nodes).

Let us now consider a spatial query, that is, the *overlap* operator with D being the reference object q. Because the query gives no temporal information on the reference object, the unified scheme transforms it to a large cube that covers the whole t-axis. In this case, the simple scheme, presented before, could be more efficient, since the two-dimensional R-tree that is dedicated to spatial information of objects is able to answer the query. Similarly, a temporal query (i.e., the *during* operator) could also be efficiently supported by the simple scheme.

A special type of query, which is popular in IMD authoring, consists of *spatial* or *temporal* layout retrieval. In other words, queries of the type "Find the objects and their position in screen at the T_0 second" (spatial layout) or "Find the objects that appear in the application during the (T_1, T_2) temporal segment and their temporal duration" (temporal layout) need to be supported by the underlying scheme. As we will present next, both types of queries are efficiently supported by the unified scheme, since they correspond to the *overlap_during* operator and an appropriate reference object q: a rectangle q_1 that intersects the t-axis at point T_0, or a cube q_2 that overlaps the t-axis at the (T_1, T_2) segment, respectively. The reference objects q_1 and q_2 are illustrated in Figure 8.4(a). In a second step, the objects that make up the answer set are filtered in main memory to design their positions on the screen (spatial layout) or the intersection of their t-projections to the given temporal segment (temporal layout).

In particular, spatial layout could be answered by exploiting the reference object q_1 at the specific time instance $T_0 = 22$ seconds. The result would be a list of objects (the identifiers of the objects and their spatial and temporal coordinates) that are displayed at that temporal instance on the screen. This result can be visualized as a screen snapshot with the objects that are included in the answer set drawn in, as shown in Figure 8.4(b). As for temporal layout query with constraints, it could be answered using as a reference object a cube q_2 having dimensions $(X_{max} - 0) \cdot (Y_{max} - 0) \cdot (T_2 - T_1)$ where $X_{max} \cdot Y_{max}$ is the dimension of the screen and $(T_2 - T_1)$ is the requested temporal interval; $T_1 = 10$ and $T_2 = 20$ in our example. The result would be a list of objects (the identifiers of the objects and their spatial and temporal coordinates) that are included or overlapped with cube q_2. This result can be visualized toward a temporal layout by drawing the temporal line segments of the retrieved objects that lie within the requested temporal interval $(T_2 - T_1)$, as shown in Figure 8.4(c).

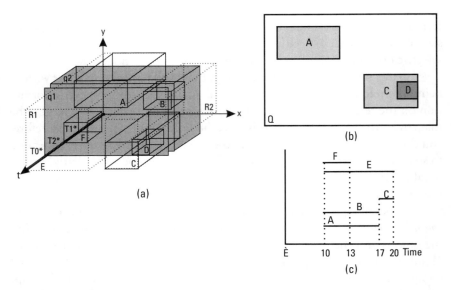

Figure 8.4 Spatial and temporal layout retrieval using 3D R-trees: (a) query windows for spatial and temporal layout; (b) spatial layout; (c) temporal layout.

On the other hand, the simple indexing scheme (consisting of two index structures) is not able to give straightforward answers to the above layout queries, because information stored in both indexes needs to be retrieved and combined.

8.4 Conclusions

8.4.1 Main Achievements of MM-DBMS Technology

So far, the MM-DBMS industry and research have invested significant efforts to the design and development of DB support for the special features of media objects and documents. The capabilities of the current MM-DBMS approaches in the research and industrial domains are summarized in [15]. A MM-DBMS may contain either single-media objects (i.e., images, video clips) or IMDs. Previous sections of this chapter elaborated on modeling and retrieval of IMDs; this section focuses on single-media DBs.

8.4.1.1 Modeling

There has been a substantial amount of work in recent years on multimedia. Zdonik [16] has specified various roles that DBs can play in complex multimedia systems. One role is the logical integration of data stored on multiple media. Kim et al. [17, 18] show how object-oriented DBs (with some enhancements) can be used to support multimedia applications. Their model is a natural extension of the object-oriented notions of instantiation and generalization. The general idea is that a multimedia DB is considered to be a set of objects that are interrelated to each other in various ways.

Little and Ghafoor [7] have developed methods for satisfying temporal constraints in multimedia systems. In a similar vein, Prabhakaran and Raghavan [19] show how multimedia presentations can be synchronized.

Other related works are the following: Gaines and Shaw [2] have developed an architecture to integrate multiple document representations. Eun et al. [20] show how Milner's calculus of communicating systems can be used to specify interactive multimedia, but they do not address the problem of querying the integration of multiple media.

8.4.1.2 Integrity

There have been research efforts on the issue of multimedia document verification and integrity. In [21], a synchronization model for the formal description of multimedia documents is presented, while [22] explores an approach for automatic generation of consistent presentation schedules. In [21], the user formalization is automatically translated into an RT-LOTOS formal specification, allowing verification of a multimedia document aiming to identify potential temporal inconsistencies. Multimedia documents are described through a hierarchical model, and incomplete timing is allowed. In [22], a temporal constraint satisfaction algorithm is presented. The algorithm generates consistent schedules, according to acceptable durations that the author defines. The system covers both preorchestrated specifications and interactive ones. The algorithm has two phases, and a compile time scheduler can smooth predictable temporal inconsistencies to produce duration of desired or necessary duration, contrary to our approach, in which durations are not smoothed.

In [23] an approach is presented that addresses the key issue of providing flexible multimedia presentation with user participation and suggests synchronization models that can specify the user participation during the presentation. A dynamic timed Petri net structure is proposed that can model preemptions and modifications to the temporal characteristics of the net. This structure can be adopted by the object composition petri nets (OCPN) to facilitate modeling of multimedia synchronization characteristics with dynamic user participation. In [24] a framework for checking the temporal consistency of a composition of media objects is provided. The temporal composition is defined in terms of directed acyclic graphs, in which the nodes are objects and the edges represent temporal relations. The concepts of qualitative and quantitative inconsistency are introduced. The first concept is related to the incompatibility of a set of temporal relations, and the second concept is related to the relations that arise from the errors that occur due to the specific durations of media objects.

8.4.1.3 Content-Based Retrieval

The retrieval of multimedia information from DBs is evolving as a challenging research and industrial area. There is already a substantial volume of results in both levels. This section reviews important efforts in this topic, specifically research for image and video retrieval based on content.

Image Retrieval

Image retrieval is concerned with retrieving images relevant to users' queries from a large image collection. The relevance is determined by the nature of the application. For instance, in a fabric-image DB, relevant images would be those matching a sample in terms of texture and color. In a news photography DB, date, time, and the occasion at which the photograph was taken may be just as important as the actual visual content. Many relational DB systems support fields for binary large objects (BLOBs) and facilitate access by user-defined attributes such as date, time, media type, image resolution, and source. On the other hand, content-based systems analyze the visual content of images and index extracted features.

Possible query categories involving one or more features are proposed in [25].

- *Simple visual feature query.* The user specifies certain values possibly with percentages for a feature. Example: "Retrieve images which contain 70 percent blue, 20 percent red, 30 percent yellow."

- *Feature combination query.* The user combines different features and specifies their values and weights. Example: "Retrieve images with green color and tree texture where color has weight 75 percent and texture has weight 25 percent."

- *Localized feature query.* The user specifies feature values and locations by placing regions on a canvas. Example: "Retrieve images with sky blue at the upper half and green at the bottom half."

- *Query by example.* The system generates a random set of images. The user selects one image and retrieves similar images. Similarity can be determined based on user-selected features. Example: "Retrieve images that contain textures similar to this example." A slightly different version of this type of query is one in which the user cuts a region from an example image and pastes it onto the query canvas.

- *Object versus image.* The user can describe the features of an object in an image as opposed to describing a complete image. Example: "Retrieve images containing a red car near the center."

- *User-defined attribute query.* The user specifies the values of the user-defined attributes. Example: "Retrieve images in which location is Washington, D.C., and the date is July 4, and the resolution is at least 300 dots per inch."

- *Object relationship query.* The user specifies objects, their attributes, and the relationships among them. Example: "Retrieve images in which an old man is holding a child in his arms."

- *Concept queries.* Some systems allow the user to define simple concepts based on the features extracted by the system. For instance, the user may define the concept of a beach as "Small yellow circle at top, large blue region in the middle, and sand color in the lower half."

Combination queries can involve any number of those query primitives as long as the retrieval system supports such queries. The visual content of an image is summarized as follows. Visual content can be modeled as a hierarchy of abstractions. At the first level are the raw pixels with color or brightness information. Further processing yields features such as edges, corners, lines, curves, and color regions. A higher abstraction layer may combine and interpret those features as objects and their attributes. At the highest level are the human-level concepts involving one or more objects and relationships among them. An example concept might be "a person giving a speech." Although automatic detection and recognition methods are available for certain objects and their attributes, their effectiveness is highly dependent on image complexity. Most objects, attribute values, and high-level concepts cannot be extracted accurately by automatic methods. In such cases, semiautomatic methods or user-supplied keywords and annotations are employed. Next, we describe the various levels of visual features and the techniques for handling them.

Some of the visual features of images are briefly presented next. Color plays a significant role in image retrieval. Different color representation schemes include red-green-blue (RGB), the chromaticity and luminance system of the International Commission on Illumination (CIE), hue-saturation-intensity (HSI), among others. The RGB scheme is most commonly used in display devices. *Texture* is a visual pattern in which a large number of visible elements are densely and evenly arranged. A texture element is a uniform-intensity region of simple shape that is repeated. *Shape-based* image retrieval is a hard problem in general image retrieval because of the difficulty of segmenting objects of interest in the images. Consequently, shape retrieval typically is limited to well-distinguished objects in the image.

For indexing visual features, a common approach is to obtain numeric values for *n* features and then representing the image or object as a point in the *n*-dimensional space. Multidimensional access methods, such as K-D-B-trees, quad-trees [26, 27], R-trees [28], or their variants (R*-trees, hB-trees, X-trees, TV-trees, SS-trees, SR-trees, etc.), are then used to index and retrieve relevant images. Problems arise in indexing in this context [25]. First, most multidimensional methods work on the assumption that different dimensions are independent; hence, the Euclidean distance is applicable. Second, unless specifically encoded, feature layout information is lost. In other words, the locations of the features can no longer be recovered from the index. The third problem is the number of dimensions. The index structures become very inefficient as the number of dimensions grows. To solve those problems, several approaches have been developed. We first look at the color-indexing problem. Texture and shape retrieval share some of these problems, and similar solutions are applicable.

An important constituent of the image content is the information on objects identified in the image. Object detection involves verifying the presence of an object in an image and possibly locating it precisely for recognition. In both feature-based and template-based recognition, standardization of global image features and registration (alignment) of reference points are important. The images may need to be transformed to another space for handling changes in illumination, size, and orientation. Both global and local features play important roles in object recognition. In local feature-based object recognition, one or more local features are extracted and the objects of interest are modeled in terms of those features. For instance, a human face can be modeled by the size of the eyes, the distance between the eye and the nose, and so on. Recognition then can be transformed into a graph-matching problem.

Cardenas et al. [29] have developed a query language called PICQUERY+ for querying certain kinds of federated multimedia systems. The spirit of their work is an attempt to devise query languages that access heterogeneous, federated multimedia DBs. However, many features in [29], such as temporal data and uncertain information, form a critical part of many domains (such as the medical domain).

Fagin in [30] presents work on atomic queries for a multimedia DB. Here we are often interested in "approximate matches." Therefore, an atomic query in a multimedia DB is typically much harder to evaluate than an atomic query in a relational DB. To make sense of that notion, it is convenient to introduce "graded" (or "fuzzy") sets, in which scores are assigned to objects, depending on how well they satisfy atomic queries. Then there are aggregation functions, which combine scores (under subqueries) for an object into an overall score (under the full query) for that object.

Video Retrieval

Video retrieval involves content analysis and feature extraction, content modeling, indexing, and querying. Video naturally has a hierarchy of units with individual frames at the base level and higher level segments such as shots, scenes, and episodes. An important task in analyzing video content is to detect segment boundaries.

A shot is a sequentially recorded set of frames representing a continuous action in time and space by a single camera. A sequence of shots focusing on the same point or location of interest is a scene. A series of related scenes form an episode [31]. An abrupt shot change is called a cut. There are several techniques for shot change detection.

An important issue here is the detection and tracking of objects. In video, two sources of information can be used to detect and track objects: visual features (such as color and texture) and motion information. A typical strategy is to initially segment regions based on color and texture information. After the initial segmentation, regions with similar motion vectors can be merged subject to certain constraints. Systems for detecting particular movements such as entering, exiting a scene, and placing or removing objects using motion vectors are being developed. It is possible to recognize certain facial expressions and gestures using models of face or hand movements.

Once features are detected, indexing and retrieval techniques have to be adopted to support queries. The temporal nature and comparatively huge size of video data require special browsing and querying functions. A common approach for quick browsing is to detect shot changes and associate a small icon of a key frame for each shot [32]. Retrieval using icons, text, and image (frame) features is possible. The hierarchical and compositional model of video [31] consists of a segment hierarchy such as shots, scenes, and episodes. This model facilitates querying and composition at different levels and thus enables a rich set of temporal and spatial operations. Example temporal operations include *follows*, *contains*, and *transition*. Example spatial operations are *parallel to* and *below*. Hierarchical Temporal Language (HTL) [33] also uses a hierarchical model of video consisting of units such as frames, shots, and subplots. The semantics of the language is designed for similarity-based retrieval.

8.4.2 Commercial Products and Research Prototypes

Several research and commercial systems provide indexing and querying based on visual features such as color and texture. Certain unique features of these systems are discussed here.

8.4.2.1 Research Systems

The Photobook system [34] enables users to plug in their own content analysis procedures and select among different content models based on user feedback via a learning agent. Sample applications include a face-recognition system, image retrieval by texture similarity, brain map, and semiautomatic annotation based on user-given labels and visual similarity. VisualSEEk [35] allows localized feature queries and histogram refinement for feedback using a Web-based tool. An important effort is VideoQ system [36]. The user interface that is provided is quite flexible and gives sufficient query abilities to the user.

8.4.2.2 Commercial Systems

IBM's DB2 system supports video retrieval via video extenders (http://www.software.ibm.com/data/db2/extenders). Video extenders allow for the import of video clips and the querying of those clips based on attributes such as the format, name/number, or description of the video, as well as last modification time.

Oracle (v.8) introduced integrated support for a variety of multimedia content (Oracle Integrated Multimedia Support [37]). The set of services includes text, image, audio, video, and spatial information as native data types, together with a suite of data cartridges that provides functionality to store, manage, search, and efficiently retrieve multimedia content from the server. Oracle8i has extended this support with significant innovations, including its ability to support cross-domain applications that combine searches of a number of kinds of multimedia forms and native support for data in a variety of standard Internet formats, including JPEG, MPEG, GIF, and the like.

Informix's multimedia asset management technology [38] offers a range of solutions for media and publishing organizations. In fact, Informix's

DB technology is already running at the core of innovative multimedia solutions in use. Informix Dynamic Server™ with Universal Data Option™ enables effective, efficient management of all types of multimedia content—images, sound, video, electronic documents, Web pages, and more. The Universal Data Option enables query, access, search, and archive digital assets based on the content itself. Informix's DB technology provides cataloging, retrieval, and reuse of rich and complex media types—video, audio, images, time series, text, and more—enabling viewer access to audio, video, and print news sources; high-performance connectivity between a DB and Web servers, providing on-line users with access to up-to-the-minute information; tight integration between DB and Web development environments, for rapid application development and deployment; and extensibility for adding features like custom news and information profiles for viewers.

QBIC (http://wwwqbic.almaden.ibm.com) [39] supports shape queries for semimanually segmented objects and local features as well as global features. The Virage system (http://www.virage.com) [40] supports feature layout queries, and users can give different emphasis to different features. Excalibur (http://www.excalib.com) Visual RetrievalWare systems enable queries on gray shape, color shape, texture, and color using adaptive pattern-recognition techniques. Excalibur also provides data blades for Informix DBs. An example data blade is a scene change detector for video. The data blade detects shots or scenes in video and produces a summary of the video by example frames from each shot.

8.4.2.3 Systems for the World Wide Web

WebSEEk [41] builds several indexes for images and videos based on visual features, such as color, and nonvisual features, such as key terms assigned subjects and image/video types. To classify images and videos into subject categories, a key term dictionary is built from selected terms appearing in a uniform resource locator (URL), the address of a page on the World Wide Web. The terms are selected based on their frequency of occurrence and whether they are meaningful subject terms. After the key term dictionary is built, directory portions of the image and video URLs are parsed and analyzed. The analysis produces an initial set of categories of the images and the videos, which are then verified manually. Videos are summarized by picking one frame for every second of video and then packaging them as an animated GIF image. The WebSeer project [42] aims at classifying images based on their visual characteristics. Novel features of WebSeer include image classification such as photographs, graphics, and so on; integration of face detector; and multiple key word search on associated text such as an HTTP reference, alternate text field of HTML reference, or page title. Yahoo Image Surfer (http://isurf.yahoo.com) employs Excalibur Visual RetrievalWare for searching images and video on the World Wide Web. Table 8.1 compares the features of the commercial systems and research prototypes.

8.4.3   Further Directions and Trends

There is now intense interest in multimedia systems. These interests span vast areas in computer science, including, but not limited to, computer networks, DBs, distributed computing, data compression, document processing, user interfaces, computer graphics, pattern recognition, and artificial intelligence. In the long run, we expect that intelligent problem-solving systems will access information stored in a variety of formats, on a wide variety of media. Next, we propose some direction on the research themes presented in this chapter.

8.4.3.1   Modeling—Integrity

In [43] the issue of uniform definition of the notion of an *update* in multimedia DB systems and efficiently accomplishing such updates is addressed. The authors claim that the update algorithms, especially the algorithm for deleting states, is less efficient than the others. In applications that require large-scale state deletions, it may be appropriate to consider alternative algorithms (and possibly alternative indexing structures as well).

The issue of authoring complex and consistent IMDs is still an open one. The integrity of a document is a multiparameter problem that has to be studied thoroughly, and formal verification techniques have to be developed. The issue of interaction especially should be studied in this perspective.

The spatiotemporal dependencies in the modeling and authoring level are an issue that requires special attention, because the spatial aspects have not been given the appropriate importance so far. Interaction is a key factor for successful document design and rendering. The interactions modeled so far in the DB models and document standards are primitive ones. There has to be a more thorough and elaborate study of complex interaction in the algebraic and spatiotemporal levels, because event carriers of interactions have many different facets.

8.4.3.2   Content-Based Retrieval

There are essential differences between multimedia DBs (which may contain complicated objects, such as images) and traditional DBs. These differences lead to interesting new issues and in particular cause us to consider new types

Table 8.1
Comparative Presentation of Content-Based Retrieval Systems

	QBIC	ORACLE	INFORMIX	DB2	VideoQ	Photobook	VisualSEEk	Virage
Color	Percentage, layout (histogram)	Global, local color	Excalibur (Image Dblade)	—	—	Histogram refinement	—	Color distribution (Image extender)
Texture	Similar	Visual Retrieval	Excalibur (Image Dblade)	—	—	—	—	Uses QBIC
Shape	—	Graininess, smoothness	Excalibur (Image Dblade)	—	—	—	—	—
Spatial relationships	Show position	—	—	—	Motion, spatiotemporal	—	—	—
Scene detection	—	—	MEDIAstra (Video Dblade)	—	—	—	—	Video Logger
Object detection	—	—	MEDIAstra (Video Dblade) MPEG-4 approach	—	—	Semiautomatic annotation	—	—

Table 8.1 (continued)

	QBIC	ORACLE	INFORMIX	DB2	VideoQ	Photobook	VisualSEEK	Virage
Captions and annotations	Manual annotation	—	DbFlix – metadata storage; time, frame, content-based approach	Description (img); format, frame rate, tracks (video) format, last update (audio)	—	Can be applied in video sequences	—	—
Extend functionality	—	—	Datablades	DB2 extenders	—	—	—	—
Sound	—	—	Muscle Fish Audio (content-based queries)	Limited	Global attributes weighting	Brain map	Localized feature queries	Audio Logger Snd2Txt
Other	Feature layout	Ideal for video on demand	Feature vector (Excalibur); video reproduction (media)	Feature layout; voice to text	—	—	—	—

of queries. Unlike the situation in relational DBs, where the semantics of a boolean combination are quite clear, in multimedia DBs it is not at all clear what the semantics are of even the conjunction of atomic queries. Multimedia DBs have interesting new issues beyond those of traditional DBs [30, 43, 44]:

- *Handling of uncertainty in queries toward underlying media and/or temporal changes in the data.* These changes need to be incorporated into the query language because they are relevant for various applications such as those listed by Cardenas et al. [29].

- *Handling boolean combinations of atomic queries.* In [30] a first step is made, by giving a reasonable semantics, involving aggregation functions, for evaluating boolean combinations, and by giving an efficient algorithm for taking conjunctions of atomic queries, that is optimal under certain natural assumptions.

- *The role of spatiotemporal structure and relationships.* Spatiotemporal structure is gaining more importance, which is reflected in the document standards evolution procedures (MPEG-4, MPEG-7 [45]). An interesting direction is the design of indexing schemes for the spatiotemporal structure of video objects or IMDs.

8.4.3.3 QoS Issues for Web Retrieval

The exponential growth of the World Wide Web content calls for enriched and complex multimedia content, which in turn imposes connection with an MM-DBMS. Then the following issues need to be searched.

- *Rendering of IMDs on the Web.* The presentation of a complex IMD imposes handling of complex internal and external interaction and also assurance of the spatiotemporal presentation specifications during IMD presentation. Initial work appears in [4].

- *Provision of quality of service(QoS).* Provisions could be made to ensure the QoS, and admission control could be the first step toward that goal. It is clear, though, that due to the massively distributed architecture of the system, there is no apparent way of applying a centralized QoS control. In its present state, the system operates on a best-effort basis.

Finally, we note that multimedia DBs form a natural generalization of heterogeneous DBs that have been studied extensively. How exactly the work on heterogeneous DBs is applicable to multimedia DBs remains to be seen, but clearly there is a fertile area to investigate here.

References

[1] Rakow, T., E. Neuhold, and M. Lohr, "Multimedia Database Systems—The Notions and the Issues," *BTW*, Springer Informatic Aktuell, Berlin, Germany, 1995.

[2] Gaines, B. R., and M. L. Shaw., "Open Architecture Multimedia Documents," *Proc. 1st ACM Intl. Conf. on Multimedia*, New York, 1993, pp. 137–146.

[3] Wu, J. -K., "Content-Based Indexing of Multimedia Databases," *IEEE Trans. on Knowledge and Data Engineering*, Vol. 9, No. 6, Nov./Dec. 1997.

[4] Vazirgiannis, M., *Interactive Multimedia Documents: Modeling, Authoring, and Implementation Experiences,* New York: Springer-Verlag, 1999.

[5] Vazirgiannis, M., and S. Boll, "Events in Interactive Multimedia Applications: Modeling and Implementation Design," *Proc. IEEE Intl. Conf. on Multimedia Computing and Systems (ICMCS'97)*, Ottawa, Canada, June 1997.

[6] Vazirgiannis, M., Y. Theodoridis, and T. Sellis, "Spatiotemporal Composition and Indexing for Large Multimedia Applications," *ACM/Springer-Verlag Multimedia Systems J.*, Vol. 6, No. 4, 1998, pp. 284–298.

[7] Little, T., and A. Ghafoor, "Interval-Based Conceptual Models for Time-Dependent Multimedia Data," *IEEE Trans. on Data and Knowledge Engineering*, Vol. 5, No. 4, Aug. 1993, pp. 551–563.

[8] Allen, J. F., "Maintaining Knowledge About Temporal Intervals," *Comm. ACM*, Vol. 26, No. 11, Nov. 1983, pp. 832–843.

[9] Vazirgiannis, M., Y. Theodoridis, and T. Sellis, "Spatio Temporal Composition in Multimedia Applications," *Proc. IEEE-ICSE '96 Intl. Workshop on Multimedia Software Development*, Berlin, Germany, 1996.

[10] Faloutsos, C., et al., "Efficient and Effective Querying by Image Content," *J. Intelligent Information Systems*, Vol. 3, July 1994, pp. 1–28.

[11] Chiueh, T., "Content-Based Image Indexing," *Proc. 20th Intl. Conf. on Very Large Databases (VLDB)*, 1994.

[12] Guttman, A., "R-Trees: A Dynamic Index Structure for Spatial Searching," *Proc. ACM SIGMOD Intl. Conf. on Management of Data*, 1984.

[13] Orenstein, J., "Spatial Query Processing in an Object-Oriented Database System," *Proc. ACM SIGMOD Intl. Conf. on Management of Data*, 1986.

[14] Papadias, D., and Y. Theodoridis, "Spatial Relations, Minimum Bounding Rectangles, and Spatial Data Structures," *Intl. J. Geographic Information Systems*, 1997.

[15] Pazandak, P., "Metrics for Evaluating ODBMSs Functionality To Support MMDBMS," *Proc. IEEE-MMDBMS '96,* Blue Mountain Lake, NY, 1996.

[16] Zdonik, S., "Incremental Database Systems: Databases From the Ground Up," *Proc. 1993 ACM SIGMOD Conf. on Management of Data*, 1993, pp. 408–412.

[17] Woelk, D., W. Kim, and W. Luther, "An Object-Oriented Approach to Multimedia Databases," *Proc. ACM SIGMOD*, 1986, pp. 311–325.

[18] Woelk, D., and W. Kim, "Multimedia Information Management in an Object-Oriented Database System," *Proc. 13th Intl. Conf. on Very Large Databases*, 1987, pp. 319–329.

[19] Prabhakaran, B., and S. V. Raghavan, "Synchronization Models for Multimedia Presentation With User Participation," *1st ACM Intl. Conf. on Multimedia*, 1993, pp. 157–166.

[20] Eun, S. B., et al., "Specification of Multimedia Composition and a Visual Programming Environment," *1st ACM Intl. Conf. on Multimedia*, 1993, pp. 167–174.

[21] Courtiat, J. P., and R. C. De Oliveira, "Proving Temporal Consistency in a New Multimedia Synchronization Model," *Proc. ACM Multimedia Conf.*, 1996.

[22] Buchanan, M. C., and P. T. Zellweger, "Automatically Generating Consistent Schedules for Multimedia Documents," *ACM-Multimedia Systems J.*, Vol. 1, No. 2, pp. 55–67.

[23] Prabhakaran, B., and S. V. Raghavan, "Synchronization Models for Multimedia Presentation With User Participation," *ACM/Springer-Verlag J. Multimedia Systems*, Vol. 2, No. 2, Aug. 1994, pp. 53–62.

[24] Layaida, N., and C. Keramane, "Maintaining Temporal Consistency of Multimedia Documents," *Proc. ACM Workshop on Effective Abstractions in Multimedia*, San Francisco, CA, Nov. 1995.

[25] Aslandogan, Y., and C. T. Yu, "Techniques and Systems for Image and Video Retrieval," *IEEE Trans. on Knowledge and Data Engineering*, Vol. 11, No. 1, Jan./Feb. 1999.

[26] Petrakis, E. G. M., and C. Faloutsos, "Similarity Searching in Large Image Databases," *Technical Report 3388*, Dept. of Computer Science, Univ. of Maryland, 1995.

[27] Samet, H., *The Design and Analysis of Spatial Data Structures*, Reading, MA: Addison-Wesley, 1989.

[28] Guttman, A., "R-Trees: A Dynamic Index Structure for Spatial Searching," *Proc. ACM SIGMOD Conf.*, June 1984, pp. 47–57.

[29]   Cardenas, A. F., et al., "The Knowledge-Based Object-Oriented PIQUERY and Language," *IEEE Trans. on Knowledge and Data Engineering* Vol. 5, No. 4, 1993, pp. 644–657.

[30]   Fagin, R., "Fuzzy Queries in Multimedia Database Systems," *Proc. ACM SIGACT-SIGMOD-SIGART Symp. on Principles of Database Systems*, 1998.

[31]   Markousis, T., et al., "WWW-Enabled Delivery of Interactive Multimedia Documents,"*Computer Communications J.*, Vol. 23, No. 3, 2000, pp. 242–252.

[32]   Nagasaka, A., and Y. Tanaka, "Automatic Video Indexing and Full Video Search for Object Appearances," *Proc. Conf. Visual Database Systems*, 1991, pp. 119–133.

[33]   Sistla, A. P., C. Yu, and R. Venkatasubrahmanian, "Similarity-Based Retrieval of Videos," *Proc. IEEE Data Engineering Conf.*, 1997.

[34]   Pentland, A., R. Picard, and S. Sclaroff, "Photobook: Tools for Content-Based Manipulation of Image Databases," *Storage and Retrieval of Image and Video Databases II*, Paper No. 2185-05, San Jose, CA, 1994, pp. 34–47.

[35]   Smith, J. R., and S. -F. Chang, "VisualSEEk: A Fully Automated Content-Based Image Query System," *Proc. ACM Multimedia Conf.*, 1996, pp. 87–98.

[36]   Chang, S. -F., et al., "An Automated Content-Based Video Search System Using Visual Cues," *Proc. ACM Multimedia*, 1997.

[37]   http://www.oracle.com/database/documents/idc/98232.html#anchor262366.

[38]   http://www.informix.com/informix/industries/media/medper.htm.

[39]   Jain, A., Y. Zhong, and S. Lakshmanan, "Object Matching Using Deformable Templates," *IEEE Trans. Pattern Analysis and Machine Intelligence*, 1996, pp. 408–439.

[40]   Gupta, A., "Visual Information Retrieval Technology: A VIRAGE Perspective," white paper, Virage, 1995.

[41]   Smith, J. R., and S. -F. Chang, "Searching for Images and Videos on the World Wide Web," *CTR Technical Report No. 459-96-25*, Columbia Univ., Aug. 1996.

[42]   Swain, M. J., C. Frankel, and V. Athitsos, "WebSeer: An Image Search Engine for the World Wide Web," *Technical Report No. TR-96-14*, Dept. of Computer Science, Univ. of Chicago, Chicago, IL, July 1996.

[43]   Marcus, S., and V. S. Subrahmanian, "Foundations of Multimedia Database Systems," *J. ACM*, Vol. 43, No. 3, May 1996, pp. 474–523.

[44]   Weiss, R., A. Duda, and D. K. Gifford, "Content-Based Access to Algebraic Video," *Proc. IEEE Intl. Conf. Multimedia Computing and Systems*, May 1994, pp. 140–151.

[45]   http://drogo.cselt.it/mpeg/, The MPEG Home Page.

Selected Bibliography

There is a rich bibliography related to MM-DBMSs. We recommend the following readings.

ACM Multimedia Systems Journal, Vol. 3, No. 5/6, 1995.

This special issue on multimedia database management systems (with guest editor Arif Ghafoor) contains a panoramic view spanning a variety of issues being researched in the multimedia DB community. It gives an idea of the scope and directions of future research in this important and promising field of study.

Narashimalu, D., "Multimedia Databases," *ACM Multimedia Systems Journal,* Vol. 4, 1996.

This tutorial on the topic contains an overview of MM-DBMS research issues, challenges, methods, models, and architectures.

Subrahmanian, V. S., *Principles of Multimedia Database Management Systems,* San Francisco, CA: Morgan Kaufmann, 1997.

This comprehensive presentation of tools and methodologies in the field covers the major issues of multimedia DB design, with a strong focus on distributed multimedia DBs. It also discusses important topics such as organization of the many data types, storage and retrieval, and creation and delivery of distributed multimedia presentations.

IEEE-MM-DBMS workshop proceedings series.
The IEEE MM-DBMS workshop has been organized since 1995 and provides the latest research results on the topic.

IEEE—Multimedia, Vol. 4, No. 3, July–Sept. 1997.

This special issue on MM-DBMSs looks into issues such as the nature of multimedia data, the need for MM-DBMSs, requirements and issues necessary for developing such systems, and an object database management system's suitability for developing multimedia applications.

IEEE Trans. on Knowledge and Data Engineering, Vol. 11, No. 1, Jan./Feb. 1999.

This special issue on multimedia contains very interesting articles on multimedia content-based retrieval.

9

Distributed Databases

Peter McBrien and Alexandra Poulovassilis

9.1 Introduction

The widespread use of computers for data processing in large distributed organizations means that such organizations often store their data at different sites of a computer network, possibly in a variety of forms, ranging from flat files, to hierarchical or relational DBs, through to object-oriented (see Chapter 7) or object-relational DBs (see Chapter 6). The rapid growth of the Internet is causing an even greater explosion in the availability of distributed information sources. Distributed DB (DDB) technology aims to provide uniform access to physically distributed but logically related information sources.

Before introducing the main concepts of DDBs, we first will review some necessary concepts and terminology from centralized DBs. A centralized DB system consists of a DBMS and a DB, which is held on disc. Users access the DB by submitting queries or transactions to the DBMS. Two major components of any DBMS are thus the query processor and the transaction manager.

The query processor translates queries into a sequence of retrieval requests on the stored data. There may be many alternative translations for a given query, which are known as *query plans*. The task of selecting a good query plan is known as *query optimization*. A "good" query plan is one that has a relatively low cost of execution compared with the alternative query plans.

A transaction is a sequence of queries and/or updates. The transaction manager coordinates concurrently executing transactions so as to guarantee the so-called ACID properties:

- *Atomicity.* Either all or none of a transaction is executed.

- *Consistency.* Transactions must leave the data in a consistent state, that is, satisfying all the stated integrity constraints.

- *Isolation.* It must appear to users that transactions are being executed one after the other, even though they may be interleaved.

- *Durability.* If a transaction has committed, its effects must not be lost.

The two mechanisms by which a transaction manager guarantees the ACID properties are concurrency control, which ensures consistency and isolation, and recovery, which ensures atomicity and durability.

A DDB system consists of several DBs stored at different sites of a computer network. The data at each site are managed by a DB server running some DBMS software. The servers can cooperate in executing global queries and global transactions, that is, queries and transactions whose processing may require access to DBs stored at different sites. There are a number of alternative architectures for DDB systems, which are reviewed in Section 9.2.

To improve the performance of global queries in DDBs, data items can be split into fragments that can be stored at sites requiring frequent access to them. Data items or fragments of data items can also be replicated across more than one site. Techniques are therefore needed for deciding the best way to fragment and replicate the data to optimize the performance of applications. This is part of the DDB design process, which is discussed in Section 9.3.

A key difference between processing global queries in a DDB system and processing queries in a centralized DB system is that DDB queries may require data to be transmitted over the network. Thus, new query-processing algorithms are needed that include data transmission as an explicit part of their processing. Also, the global query optimizer needs to take data transmission costs into account when generating and evaluating alternative query plans. Section 9.4 examines query processing and optimization in DDBs.

A key difference between global transactions in a DDB system and transactions in a centralized DB system is that global transactions are divided into a number of subtransactions. Each subtransaction is executed by a single DB server, which guarantees its ACID properties. However, an extra level of coordination of the subtransactions is needed to guarantee that the overall global transactions also exhibit the ACID properties. Section 9.5, which covers transaction management in DDBs, explores how such global coordination can be achieved.

The chapter concludes with a discussion of some current trends and challenges in DDBs.

9.2   Distributed Database Architecture

There are a number of alternative architectures for DDB systems. In the description of them in this chapter, we use an extended version of the taxonomy of [1], illustrated in Figure 9.1.

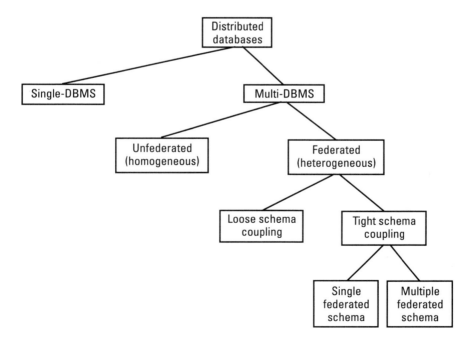

Figure 9.1 Taxonomy of DDB architectures.

A DDB system consists of several DBs distributed over several sites. Access to the DBs can be controlled by a single DBMS process; that is the single-DBMS architecture in Figure 9.1. Alternatively, there may be several independent DBMS processes, each controlling access to its own local DB; that is the multi-DBMS architecture in Figure 9.1.

There are two variants of the multi-DBMS architecture, depending on the amount of autonomy of each of the participating DBMS processes. In an unfederated multi-DBMS, a single DB administration authority decides what information is stored in each DB, how the information is stored and accessed, and who is able to access it. In contrast, a federated multi-DBMS separates the DB administration authority between the DB administrators (DBAs) of each local DB (the local DBAs) and the DBAs for the overall federation (the global DBAs). The local DBAs have complete authority over the information in their DBs, and what part of that information is made available to the federation, that is, to global queries and transactions. This information is represented in the form of one or more export schemas for each local DB. The global DBAs control global access to the system, but must accept the access restrictions imposed by the local DBAs.

A federated DDB is said to be tightly coupled if the global DBAs maintain one or more global schemas that provide an integrated view through which global queries and transactions can access the information stored in the local DBs. A federated DDB is loosely coupled if there is no global schema provided by a global DBA, and it is the users' responsibility to define the global schemas they require to support their applications. This chapter concentrates on tightly coupled DDBs, which present the extra difficulty of having to provide an integrated view of the information stored in the local DBs.

The presence of a single DB administration authority in an unfederated multi-DBMS makes it likely that the multi-DBMS will be a homogeneous one, both physically and semantically. Physical homogeneity means that the local DBs are all managed by the same type of DBMS, supporting the same data model, DDL/DML, query processing, transaction management, and so forth. Semantic homogeneity means that different local DBs store any information they have in common in a consistent manner, so that integration of the information does not require it to be transformed in any way.

In contrast, the presence of multiple DB administration authorities in a federated multi-DBMS makes it likely that it will be heterogeneous. The heterogeneity may be physical, semantic, or both. Physical heterogeneity means that different local DBs may be managed by different types of DBMSs for example, different products or different versions of one product. Thus, the local conceptual schemas may be defined in different data models (e.g., network, hierarchical, relational, object-oriented), the DDL/DML supported by local DBs may be different (e.g., network or hierarchical, different versions of SQL, OQL), the query processors may use different algorithms and cost models, the transaction managers may support different concurrency control and recovery mechanisms, and so forth. Semantic heterogeneity means that different local DBs may model the same information using different schema constructs or may use the same schema construct to model different information. For example, people's names may be stored using different string lengths, or a relation named *student* in one DB may contain only undergraduate students while a relation named *student* in another DB contains both undergraduate and postgraduate students. If there is semantic heterogeneity in a multi-DBMS, it is necessary to perform semantic integration of the export schemas. That requires the export schemas to be transformed so as to eliminate any inconsistencies between them. Section 9.3 examines this topic further in the discussion of DDB design.

We finally note that, in reference to multi-DBMSs, the terms *unfederated* and *homogeneous* are usually treated as almost synonymous, as are the terms *federated* and *heterogeneous.*

Of the various architectures in Figure 9.1, a heterogeneous multi-DBMS is the most challenging to implement. Thus, this section first considers a five-level model for a heterogeneous multi-DBMS architecture. We then simplify that model to a four-level model for homogeneous multi-DBMS and finally to a three-level model for single-DBMS. Section 9.2.4 continues with a discussion of physical DB connectivity, that is, mechanisms by which information can be exchanged by DBMSs in DDB systems.

Ideally, the manner in which data are physically stored in a DDB system should not alter the way that global queries and transactions are written. For example, it should be possible to change the location of a particular data item, perhaps to improve the performance of the DDB, without having to alter any application code that requires access to that data item. This property of DDBs, known as distributed data independence, is discussed further in Section 9.2.5.

We conclude the section on architectures with, in Section 9.2.6, a brief comparison of DDBs with two other decentralized DB architectures, client/server DBs and parallel DBs.

9.2.1   Five-Level Model for Heterogeneous Multi-DBMS

A heterogeneous multi-DBMS requires integration of the export schemas to be performed so the federation can be accessed as a single resource. This section examines how the three-level ANSI/SPARC architecture for centralized DBMSs [2] has been extended to a five-level architecture for heterogeneous DDBs. Several variations of the five-level model have been proposed [1, 3, 4], and the description here broadly follows that of [1], except that local DBs are termed *component databases* in [1] and global schemas are termed *federated schemas.*

A heterogeneous multi-DBMS must integrate the export schemas of the local DBs into one or more global schemas, which provide an integrated view through which global queries and transactions can access the federation. This view must be constructed while preserving the autonomy of the local DBs, that is, leaving control of them in the hands of the local DBAs. The five-level model illustrated in Figure 9.2 achieves that by requiring the following five types of schema to be present in a heterogeneous DDB system.

- *A local schema for each local DB.* The local schema is the conceptual schema of the local DB. Each local DB continues to operate as an autonomous entity, and the content of its local schema is under the control of its local DBAs. Each local DB will also have a physical schema and possibly a number of external schemas that are views of its local schema. However, those schemas are not considered to be part of the heterogeneous multi-DBMS architecture.

- *A component schema corresponding to each local schema.* The local DBs may support different data models and different DDL/DMLs. Thus, the local schemas have to be translated into some common data model (CDM) before they can be integrated. This may be some variant of the E/R model or an object-oriented data model. Each component schema is the translation of its corresponding local schema into this CDM.

- *One or more export schemas corresponding to each component schema.* Each export schema is a view over the component schema that the local DBAs want to make available to the federation. The export schemas define what part of the locally held information can be accessed by global queries and transactions.

- *One or more global schemas.* Each global schema is obtained by integrating one or more of the export schemas into a single schema. A

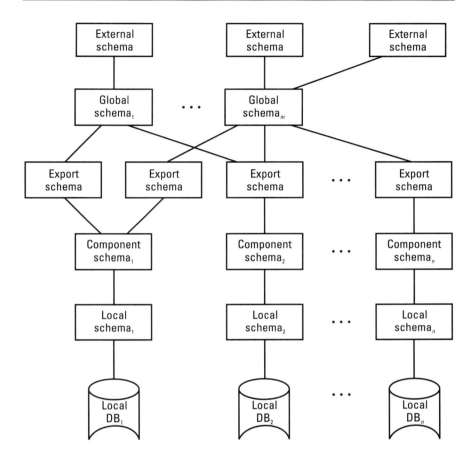

Figure 9.2 Five-level model for heterogeneous multi-DBMS.

global schema can be regarded as a conceptual schema for the heterogeneous DDB. However, in contrast to a centralized DB, it may not be possible—or desirable—to create a single global schema that encompasses all the export schemas. For example, it may not be possible to resolve some of the semantic heterogeneities between some of the export schemas, or different application domains may require access to different parts of the federation.

- *A number of external schemas.* Each external schema is a view over one global schema and contains information that a user needs for a specific application. The external schemas correspond to the external schemas of the three-level ANSI/SPARC model in that they provide views over the conceptual schema(s) of the federation.

9.2.2 Four-Level Model for Homogeneous Multi-DBMS

In a homogeneous multi-DBMS, all the local DBs are managed by the same type of DBMS. Thus, all the local schemas are expressed in the same data model. There is, therefore, no need for any component schemas, since this platform-specific data model can be used as the CDM. Thus, for a homogeneous multi-DBMS, the five-level model in Figure 9.2 simplifies to a four-level model that has no component schemas.

9.2.3 Three-Level Model for Single-DBMS

In a single-DBMS DDB, there is no role to be played by either the component schemas or the export schemas, and a single global schema is formed as the union of all the local schemas. Thus, a three-level model for single-DBMS DDBs can be obtained by omitting the component schema and the export schema from the five-level model in Figure 9.2.

9.2.4 Physical Database Connectivity

A large number of software tools support DDB architectures by allowing DBMSs to exchange information. We can summarize their functionality by placing them in two main categories: DBMS-independent approaches and DBMS-dependent approaches.

DBMS-independent approaches abstract the common capabilities of DBMSs, and in particular relational DBMSs, into a uniform API with associated communication protocols. Examples of this approach are Microsoft's Open Database Connectivity (ODBC) and SUN's Java Database Connectivity (JDBC) APIs. This approach allows the construction of open systems, because applications can be built using a uniform API and then physically connect to any DB that supports that API. However, variations in different DBMSs' capabilities, for example, with respect to query processing, transaction management, and access control, mean that some features of DBMSs will not be available through the uniform API.

DBMS-dependent approaches present the capabilities of specific DBMSs as a direct inter-DB communication protocol. The major DB vendors have provided this functionality for their products for some time, allowing different DBMSs running the same DBMS software to cooperate in executing distributed queries and transactions. The concept of gateways extends this approach by allowing a DBMS to exchange information with another type of DBMS, using the native DML and DDL of the first. A different gateway is required for each different type of DBMS; thus, this approach does not scale well in highly heterogeneous systems. However, it does give better performance and functionality than the DBMS-independent approach, because each gateway is tailored specifically to the two DBMSs it serves to connect. Examples of the gateway approach are Oracle's SQLNet and Sybase's Open Server. It can be seen that DBMS-independent approaches are best suited to building loosely coupled DDB systems, while tightly coupled DDB systems will require the use of a DBMS-dependent approach. We note that in DBMS-dependent approaches, as well as in DBMS-independent ones, it is normal to present the inter-DB communication protocol as an API that can be used by applications. Thus, one can write programs that integrate data from several types of DBMS by using the DBMS-specific API for each one. However, unless some DBMS-specific feature is required, it is simpler to use a DBMS-independent API where possible.

9.2.5   Distributed Data Independence

Recall that distributed data independence means that changing the physical location of data items in a DDB should not require application code to be altered. One way of achieving distributed data independence is to maintain a global catalog that describes all the data items stored at every site, associating both a logical name and a physical name with each one. The disadvantage of this approach is that the site where the catalog resides becomes a bottleneck for network traffic as well as a single point of failure for the DDB. The problem can be overcome by replicating the global catalog at multiple sites. But that makes updating the catalog complex because all its distributed replicas have to be updated to reflect the change before any of them can be used again. The commonly adopted solution to those problems is for the distributed DBMS to maintain a distributed catalog.

With that approach, each site maintains its own local catalog of all the data items stored at that site. Each data item recorded in the local catalog has both a local name and a global name. The global name identifies the site or sites whose catalogs contain full information regarding that data item, for example, its definition, its physical location(s), the integrity constraints it must satisfy, and user access rights to it. Applications running at each site use their own local names for data items. The DBMS handles the translation of the local names to global names. A change in the physical location of some data item does not require applications to be altered, and they can continue to use just their local name for the data item.

9.2.6   Other Decentralized Database Architectures

We conclude this section on architectures by briefly comparing and contrasting DDB systems with two other decentralized DB architectures, namely client/server DBs and parallel DBs.

A client/server DB system consists of multiple client processes and multiple server processes. Client processes are responsible for user interaction and data presentation, while server processes are responsible for query processing, transaction management, and storage management. Client processes can submit queries or transactions to any server process. However, coordinating queries and transactions that need access to multiple servers is the responsibility of the client, unlike in DDB systems, where servers can cooperate in the execution of global queries and transactions.

A parallel DB system utilizes multiple processors and multiple disks to provide parallel, and thus faster, execution of queries and transactions. An effective way to utilize multiple processors and disks is to split each relation into groups of rows according to some selection criterion and store each group on one disk. A query referencing that relation can then be translated into multiple subqueries, each requiring access to one fragment of the relation; the subqueries can be processed in parallel in a shorter time than the original sequential query. This is known as *intra-query parallelism*, that is, paralleling the execution of one query. Inter-query parallelism is also possible, that is, executing several queries concurrently.

The processors in a parallel DB system are linked by very high-speed connections; thus, interprocessor communication costs are negligible in comparison to I/O costs. That is in contrast to the typically slower communication links in DDB systems. Thus, although query processing algorithms and cost models in parallel and DDB systems share some commonalties, in that both architectures support inter- and intra-query parallelism, they also have this major difference. Moreover, parallel DBs differ from DDBs in that they do not support two levels of access to the DB (local and global) but only one integrated view of the data.

9.3   Distributed Database Design

The two main approaches to designing DDBs are bottom up and top down.

With bottom-up DDB design, the local DBs already exist and their export schemas need to be integrated into one or more global schemas. Section 9.3.3 considers bottom-up design for the case of heterogeneous multi-DBMS because they present the greatest integration difficulties and subsume the cases of homogeneous multi-DBMS and single-DBMS architectures.

With top-down design, there are no preexisting local DBs. The global schema is first designed, taking as input the requirements that all potential users will have of the new DDB system. The design of the local DBs then follows. The main challenge with top-down design is how to derive the local conceptual schemas from the global schema, that is, how to allocate the information in the global schema across the local DBs. Top-down design is most likely to occur in homogeneous multi-DBMS or single-DBMS architectures. Section 9.3.2 examines top-down design, assuming that this is indeed the case and that the DBMS is a relational one. Because the top-down design of a relational DDB is concerned with how relations should be fragmented and replicated across the local DBs, we begin with a general discussion of data fragmentation and replication in relational DDBs.

9.3.1   Data Fragmentation and Replication in Relational DDBs

In a relational DDB, relations can be fragmented horizontally or vertically. Horizontal fragmentation partitions a relation R into a number of disjoint subsets. For example, in Figure 9.3(b), the *account* relation has been partitioned into two subsets: $\sigma_{accno < 400}$ *account*, which is stored at S_1, and $\sigma_{accno \geq 400}$ *account*, which is stored at S_2.

Derived horizontal fragmentation of relations is also possible. It fragments a relation, R, according to the fragmentation of some other relation, S, with which R has attributes in common and hence is joinable. In particular, if the fragments of S are $S_1, \ldots, S_m$, then the fragments of R are $R_1, \ldots, R_m$, where each R_i is defined by

$$Ri = R \ltimes S_i$$

Here, $\ltimes$ is the semijoin operator, which is defined as

accno	name	balance
100	Anne	2000
123	Bob	300
130	Carla	−200
400	David	0
563	Emily	−5670
888	Fred	30
987	George	S_c −90

(a)

accno	name	balance		accno	name	balance
100	Anne	2000		400	David	0
123	Bob	300		563	Emily	−5670
130	Carla	−200		888	Fred	30
S_1				987	George	−90
				S_2		

(b)

accno	name		accno	balance
100	Anne		100	2000
123	Bob		123	300
130	Carla		130	−200
400	David		400	0
563	Emily		563	−5670
888	Fred		888	30
987	George		987	−90
S_1			S_2	

(c)

accno	balance		accno	name
100	2000		100	Anne
123	300		123	Bob
130	−200		130	Carla
S_1			S_2	

accno	name		accno	balance
400	David		400	0
563	Emily		563	−5670
888	Fred		888	30
987	George		987	−90
S_1			S_2	

(d)

Figure 9.3 Distribution of the *account* relation: (a) single database; (b) horizontal fragmentation; (c) vertical fragmentation; (d) hybrid fragmentation.

$$R \bowtie S = R \bowtie \pi_{R \cap S}(S)$$

where $\pi_{R \cap S}$ denotes projection on the common attributes of R and S. For example, the fragmentation of a relation *customer*(*name,address,telno*), which would be derived from the fragmentation of *account* shown in Figure 9.3(b), would partition *customer* into the two fragments *customer* $\bowtie$ ($\sigma_{accno <}$ $_{400}$ *account*) and *customer* $\bowtie$ ($\sigma_{accno \geq 400}$ *account*).

Vertical fragmentation splits a relation R into n projections π_{attrs1} R, π_{attrs2} R, ..., $\pi_{attrsn}R$, such that $R = \pi_{attrs1}$ $R \bowtie \pi_{attrs2}$ $R \mid ... \bowtie \pi_{attrsn}$ R, that is, into a lossless join decomposition of R. For example, in Figure 9.3(c), the relation *account* has been split into two vertical fragments, $\pi_{accno,name}$ *account*, which is stored at S_1, and $\pi_{accno,balance}$ *account*, which is stored at S_2. The original relation in Figure 9.3(a) can be reconstructed by forming the natural join of the two fragments over their common attribute, *accno*.

Hybrid fragmentation of a relation is also possible in that a relation can be fragmented both vertically and horizontally. Hybrid fragmentation is illustrated in Figure 9.3(d), where the *account* relation has been split into four fragments, $\pi_{accno,balance}(\sigma_{accno < 400}$ *account*), $\pi_{accno,name}(\sigma_{accno < 400}$ *account*), $\pi_{accno,name}(\sigma_{accno \geq 400}$ *account*) and $\pi_{accno,balance}(\sigma_{accno \geq 400}$ *account*), which are stored at, respectively, sites S_1, S_2, S_1, and S_2.

There are two main advantages in fragmenting relations in a DDB system:

- Applications running at different sites often require access to only part of a relation rather than to the entire relation. Thus, fragments can be stored at the sites where they are accessed most often rather than storing the entire relation at the sites. For example, it may be the case that accounts with numbers less than 400 are managed at one site of a DDB system, and the rest of the accounts at another site, in which case the *accounts* relation could be fragmented as shown in Figure 9.3(b). Or it may be that one site frequently requires information about customer names, while another frequently requires information about customer balances. In that case, the *accounts* relation could be fragmented as shown in Figure 9.3(c).

- Fragmentation of relations also makes intra-query parallelism possible, in that a single global query can be translated into multiple local subqueries that can be processed in parallel.

Two disadvantages of fragmentation are the increased query processing costs for those queries that need to access many distributed fragments of a relation and the increased cost and complexity of enforcing semantic integrity constraints on fragmented relations.

As already mentioned, fragments of relations or, indeed, entire relations can be replicated at multiple sites of a relational DDB. There are two general advantages to data replication.

- Processing of queries generally will be localized to fewer sites, thus reducing the amount of data being transmitted over the network and speeding up query processing.
- The reliability of the system is increased because if one site fails and its information is replicated at other sites, then those sites can be accessed instead of the failed site.

The disadvantage of replication is the added overhead of maintaining the consistency of all the replicas when updates are performed by transactions. Consistency can be maintained either synchronously or asynchronously [5]. With the synchronous approach, transactions must update all replicas of any relation that is being modified. That can have a significant effect on transaction throughput since write locks must be obtained for all replicas and held until the transaction commits.

With the asynchronous approach, one or more replicas are designated as primary copies and are updated synchronously. The rest of the replicas are designated secondary copies. They are not updated by transactions but have updates propagated to them by the primary copies. With this approach, users need to know which are the primary replicas and which are the secondary ones, and they have to access the desired replica explicitly. That violates the principle of distributed data independence, but it does give more flexibility and better performance than the synchronous approach.

9.3.2   Top-Down Design of Relational DDBs

Top-down design of relational DDBs addresses two main issues: What is the appropriate amount of fragmentation of each relation, and how fragments should be allocated across the sites of the DDB.

The central aim of fragmenting relations is to divide them among the local DBs in such a way that applications will place an equal load on each DB server. Thus, both horizontal and vertical fragmentation must be based on information about the expected accesses to relations.

To horizontally fragment a relation, we need to decide which rows of the relation should be placed in the same fragment. To do that, we need to examine the selection predicates that will be applied to the relation by applications, that is, by queries and transactions submitted to the DDB. The selection predicates will consist of one or more simple predicates of the form *attr op value*, where *op* can be $=$, $\neq$, $<$, $\leq$, $>$, or $\geq$, possibly connected by the boolean connective AND or OR.

Suppose that $P = \{p_1, \ldots, p_n\}$ is the set of simple predicates that will be applied to a relation R. Let $F(P)$ be the set of predicates of the form q_1 AND ... AND q_n, where each q_i is either the simple predicate p_i or its negation $\neg p_i$. Then, R is fragmented so that the rows in each fragment satisfy precisely one of the predicates in $F(P)$.

To illustrate, consider the *account* relation in Figure 9.3(a). Suppose that the simple predicates that will be applied to it are

accno < 400, *balance* < 0

Let P_0 denote this set of simple predicates. Then $F(P_0)$ consists of four predicates:

($accno$ < 400) AND ($balance$ < 0)
($accno$ < 400) AND ($balance \geq 0$)
($accno \geq 400$) AND ($balance$ < 0)
($accno \geq 400$) AND ($balance \geq 0$)

R will thus be fragmented into four fragments, F_1, ..., F_4, each one satisfying one of the above predicates.

The set of simple predicates, P, should be chosen so that it satisfies the properties of completeness and minimality. *Completeness* means that all the rows of any fragment generated by $F(P)$ should have the same probability of being accessed. For example, the set $P_0 = \{accno < 400, balance < 0\}$ is complete if all applications access the *account* relation using only combinations of those simple predicates or their negations. However, suppose a new application now includes the selection predicate *accno* > 600. Then some rows of the fragments F_3 and F_4 will have a greater probability of being accessed by this new application than others. To make P_0 complete, the predicate *accno* > 600 should be added to it. Let P_1 be this new set of simple predicates:

accno < 400, *balance* < 0, *accno* < 600

Then $F(P_1)$ consists of the eight predicates that result from combining those simple predicates or their negations. Some combinations of simple predicates may be simplifiable, for example, $(accno < 400)$ AND $(accno < 600)$ to *just accno* 400, and some combinations may not be satisfiable, for example, $(accno < 400)$ AND $(accno \geq 600)$. Thus, $F(P_1)$ reduces to the following six predicates:

> $(accno < 400)$ AND $(balance < 0)$
> $(accno < 400)$ AND $(balance \geq 0)$
> $(accno \geq 400)$ AND $(balance < 0)$ AND $(accno < 600)$
> $(accno \geq 600)$ AND $(balance < 0)$
> $(accno \geq 400)$ AND $(balance \geq 0)$ AND $(accno < 600)$
> $(accno \geq 600)$ AND $(balance \geq 0)$

Each of those predicates will generate one fragment of *account*, which has the desired effect of splitting each of the original fragments F_3 and F_4 of R into two. The completeness property is important because it means that all the rows of a fragment have the same statistical properties, so the fragment can be treated as one unit for the purposes of query optimization.

The minimality property of a set of simple predicates P means that if any one of the predicates in P is removed, the completeness property is violated. For example, it is easy to see that omitting any of the predicates from the preceding set, P_1, would violate its completeness property. However, if we were to add another predicate to P_1, say, *balance* < 2000, then it would introduce unnecessary fragmentation of the *account* relation in the sense that some of the fragments would have the same statistical properties (assuming there was no change in the applications accessing *account*). Thus, $P_1 \cup \{balance < 2000\}$ would not be minimal.

Turning now to vertical fragmentation, we need to decide which attributes of a relation should be placed in the same fragment. To guarantee the losslessness of the join of the vertical fragments, each vertical fragment should contain the primary key attributes of the relation. Alternatively, replication of the primary key attributes can be avoided by augmenting the relation with a system-maintained row identifier (ROWID) attribute, which is present in each vertical fragment. Fragmentation of the rest of the attributes depends on the frequency with which attributes are accessed together in the same query. For example, the vertical fragmentation of the *account* relation in Figure 9.3(c) favors applications in which the attributes *name* and *balance* will not often be accessed together in the same query, since such queries will require a join of the two fragments to be performed. Statistical clustering techniques can be used to cluster attributes into the same vertical fragment on the basis of information regarding the frequency with which pairs of attributes appear together in the same query.

Having discussed the first issue in the top-down design of relational DDBs, that is, what is the appropriate amount of fragmentation of each relation, we turn now briefly to the second issue, that is, how to allocate fragments across the sites of the DDB. Unlike fragmentation, which primarily uses semantic information about applications, allocation requires information about how applications are distributed over the network. The problem is how to allocate fragments to sites to minimize some performance metric. Possible metrics are the overall cost of running applications, the query response time, and the transaction throughput. Even very simple formulations of this problem are computationally intractable, so heuristic approaches must be used, such as those employed in operations research.

9.3.3 Bottom-Up Design of Heterogeneous DDBs

With bottom-up design of heterogeneous DDBs, the local DBs already exist and the main challenge is one of schema integration, that is, how to integrate a set of export schemas into a single global schema. Because the local DBs typically will have been designed by different people at different times, conflicts are likely to exist between the export schemas. For example, different export schemas may model the same real-world concept using different constructs, or they may model different real-world concepts using the same construct. Such conflicts must be removed by transforming the export schemas to produce equivalent schemas, which can then be integrated. The schema integration process thus consists of three main tasks [6]:

- *Schema conformance*, during which conflict detection and conflict resolution are performed, resulting in new versions of the export schemas that represent the same concepts in the same manner;

- *Schema merging*, during which related concepts in the export schemas are identified and a single global schema is produced;

- *Schema improvement*, during which the quality of the global schema is improved, in particular, removal of redundant information so that the resulting schema is the "minimum" union of the export schemas.

Those tasks are illustrated in Figure 9.4, which shows how two export schemas, ES_1 and ES_2, can be integrated. The export schemas are expressed using
an E/R model, which is often used as the CDM in heterogeneous DBs. Suppose that ES_1 and ES_2 have a conflict in that the *student* entity class of ES_1
represents all students, and the *student* entity class of ES_2 represents just postgraduate students. In the conformance step, we thus rename the latter entity
class *postgrad student* so distinct entity classes now have distinct names. In the
merging step, we identify that *postgrad student* is a subclass of *student* and
introduce an "is-a" relationship between them. Finally, in the improvement
step, we identify that *postgrad student* has a redundant attribute *id*, which it
can inherit from *student*. Thus, we remove *id* from *postgrad student*, resulting
in a final global schema *GS*.

Performing those tasks requires that a sequence of transformations be
applied to schemas in such as way that the resulting schema is equivalent to
the original one. The sequence of transformations gives a pathway for translating data expressed in the constructs of the export schemas ES_1 and ES_2
into data expressed in the constructs of the global schema *GS*. The transformations should be reversible in the sense that data and queries expressed
in the integrated schema *GS* must be translatable into data and queries
expressed in ES_1 and ES_2. With such reversible transforms, it is possible to
automatically translate queries and data between DBs [7].

In [8] we propose a new formal definition for equivalence of E/R schemas and give a set of primitive transformations that can be used to transform
E/R schemas into equivalent schemas. This set of primitive transformations
includes transformations for renaming entity classes, attributes, and relations
(*rename$_E$, rename$_A$, rename$_R$*) and transformations for adding and deleting
entity classes, attributes, and relations (*add$_E$, del$_E$, add$_A$, del$_A$, add$_R$, del$_R$*). For
example, the conformance step in Figure 9.4 is performed by the following
primitive transformation:

     rename$_E$ ‹student,postgrad student›

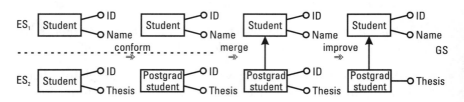

Figure 9.4 Example of semantic schema integration.

This transformation is successful provided there is not already an entity class with the name *postgrad student* in ES_2. The addition of the "is-a" link is performed by

$$add_I \langle postgrad\ student, student \rangle$$

This succeeds provided the actual extent of *postgrad student* is a subset of the extent of *student*. Finally, the improvement step is performed by

$$del_A \langle postgrad\ student, id \rangle$$

This succeeds provided the extent of the association between *postgrad student* and *id* can be derived from the remaining constructs in the schema, which is indeed the case, since *id* is also an attribute of *student*.

This example illustrates the distinction between schema-dependent transformations (such as the first and third transformations) and instance-dependent transformations (such as the addition of the "is-a" link). Schema-dependent transformations require only information about the schema, whereas instance-dependent transformations also require information about the DB contents.

One disadvantage with using a high-level CDM such as an E/R, relational, or object-oriented data model is that the conceptual schemas of local DBs will also be expressed in some high-level data model. Thus, to translate the local schema into the component schema, one high-level modeling language needs to be translated into another. This can cause problems, because there is rarely a simple correspondence between the modeling constructs of such languages. For example, if we want to translate an E/R local schema into a relational CDM, many-to-many relationships in the E/R model must be represented as relations in the relational model, whereas one-to-many relationships can be represented as a foreign key attribute [9]. Similarly, if we want to translate a relational local schema into an E/R CDM, an attribute that is part of a foreign key will be represented as a relationship in the E/R model, whereas other relation attributes will be mapped to E/R attributes [10].

An alternative approach is to use a more "elemental" modeling language as the CDM. We explore this approach in [11], where we introduce a low-level hypergraph data model (HDM). The HDM is based on a hypergraph data structure together with a set of associated constraints. A small set of primitive transformations can be used to transform schemas expressed in the HDM. Higher-level modeling languages are handled by defining their constructs and primitive transformations in terms of constructs and primitive transformations of the underlying HDM. That opens up the possibility of transforming between schemas expressed in different modeling languages, which we explore in [12]. It also makes it possible to create special-purpose CDMs that mix constructs from different modeling languages. This is particularly useful in integration situations in which there is not a single already existing CDM that can fully represent the constructs of the various data sources. For example, this approach can be used for integrating semistructured data (such as Web documents) with structured DBs.

9.4   Distributed Query Processing

The purpose of distributed query processing is to process global queries, that is, queries that are expressed with respect to the global or external schemas of a DDB system. The local query processor (LQP) at each site is still responsible for the processing of subqueries of global queries that are being executed at that site, as well as for the processing of local queries submitted directly to the local DB. However, a global query processor (GQP) is also needed to optimize each global query, distribute subqueries of the query to the appropriate LQPs, and collect the results of those subqueries. There are likely to be several GQPs in a DDB system, one at each site to which global queries can be submitted.

   This section first considers global query processing in homogeneous relational DDBs. We then briefly consider the additional challenges of global query processing in heterogeneous multi-DBMSs.

9.4.1   Query Processing in Relational DDBs

Processing global queries in a relational DDB consists of the following main steps:

1. Translation of the query into a query tree annotated with relations at its leaves and operations at its nonleaf nodes.

2. Replacement of fragmented relations in the query tree by their definition as unions and joins of their horizontal and vertical fragments.

3. Simplification of the resulting tree using several heuristics.

4. Global query optimization, resulting in the selection of a query plan for the query. This query plan will consist of subqueries, each

of which will be executed at one local site. It will also be annotated with the data transmission that will occur between sites.

5. Local processing of the local subqueries, which may include further local optimization of the local subqueries, based on local information about access paths and DB statistics.

To illustrate these steps, consider the relations

account(*accno*, *name*, *balance*)
customer(*name*, *address*, *city*, *telno*)

and the following global query, which finds the telephone numbers of customers with account numbers over 600:

```
SELECT telno
FROM customer, account
WHERE customer.name = account.name
AND accno > 600
```

Step 1 translates this query into the query tree shown in Figure 9.5(a). Assuming that *account* and *customer* are fragmented as discussed in Section 9.3.1, let $a_1 = \sigma_{accno < 400}$ *account*, $a_2 = \sigma_{accno \geq 400}$, $c_1 = customer \bowtie a_1$, and $c_2 = customer \bowtie a_2$. Then Step 2 results in the query tree shown in Figure 9.5(b). In Step 3, three main heuristics generally can be applied, the first two for horizontally fragmented relations and the third for vertically fragmented ones:

- Eliminating fragments from the argument to a selection operation that can contribute no tuples to the result;

- Distributing join operations over unions of fragments and eliminating joins that can yield no tuples;

- Eliminating fragments from the argument of a projection operation that have no nonkey attributes in common with the projection attributes.

In the case of the previous query, the subtree $\sigma_{accno > 600}(a_1 \cup a_2)$ can be simplified to $\sigma_{accno > 600} a_2$ by first distributing the selection operation over the union and then applying the first heuristic, because $\sigma_{accno > 600} a_1$ must always be empty. That results in the query tree shown in Figure 9.5(c). The second

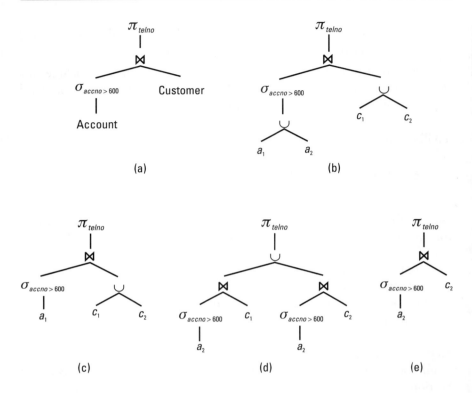

Figure 9.5 Query optimization.

heuristic can then be applied to first distribute the join operation over the union operation, obtaining the tree shown in Figure 9.5(d). The subtree $(\sigma_{accno > 600}\ a_2) \bowtie c_1$ can then be removed, because this must always be empty, giving the tree shown in Figure 9.5(e).

Step 4 consists of generating a set of alternative query plans, estimating the cost of each plan, and selecting the cheapest plan. It is carried out in much the same way as for centralized query optimization, but now communication costs also must be taken into account as well as I/O and CPU costs. Given the potential size of joined relations, efficient processing of the join operation is the major factor in DDBs, which we now consider. We base our discussion of this topic on that given in [13].

The simplest method for computing an operation $R \bowtie S$ at the site of S consists of shipping R to the side of S and processing the join operation there. This has a communications cost of $c_0 + c * size(R)$, where c_0 reflects the cost of initiating the communication between the two sites, c is the cost of transmitting one unit of data between them (e.g., one byte or one packet), and $size(R)$ is the size of the relation R expressed in those units. The cost of actually performing the join operation at the site of S needs to be added to the communications cost to obtain the overall cost of the operation. However, for simplicity, our discussion assumes that the communications cost is the dominant factor (this is a realistic assumption for slower wide area networks but not for higher-speed local area networks).

An alternative method for computing $R \bowtie S$ at the site of S is the semijoin method, which consists of the following steps:

1. Compute $\pi_{R \cap S}(S)$ at the site of S.
2. Ship the result to the site of R.
3. Compute $R \ltimes \Sigma$ at the site of R, using the fact that $R \ltimes S = R \bowtie \pi_{R \cap S}(S)$.
4. Ship the result to the site of S.
5. Compute $R \bowtie S$ at the site of S, using the fact that $R \bowtie S = (R \ltimes S) \bowtie S$.

This method has a communications cost of $c_0 + c * size(\pi_{R \cap S}(S))$ from Step 2 and $c_0 + c * size(R \ltimes S)$ from Step 4. Again, for simplicity, let us ignore the cost of the computation in Steps 1, 3, and 5. Thus, the semijoin method is cheaper than the simple join method if $c_0 + c * size(\pi_{R \cap S}(S)) + c * size(R \ltimes S) < c * size(R)$. If we ignore the constant c_0, on the assumption that the actual data transmission costs are much greater than this constant, the above inequality simplifies to $size(\pi_{R \cap S}(S)) + size(R \ltimes S) < size(R)$. The significant factor in comparing the two methods is how much smaller $size(R \ltimes S)$ is than $size(R)$. If few tuples of R join with S, then the semijoin method is likely to be cheaper. If most tuples of R join with S, then the full join method will be cheaper.

For example, consider the join operation in the previous query and let $R = \sigma_{accno > 600} \, a_2$ and $S = c_2$. Suppose those two relations are stored at different sites and the result of the query is needed at the site of S. The full join method will be cheaper than the semijoin method in this case, because *name* is a foreign key in the *account* relation and so every tuple of R joins with some tuple in S, that is, $size(R \ltimes S) = size(R)$.

However, suppose now that $S = \Sigma_{city = London} c_2$. Then, assuming a uniform distribution of customers across cities, $size(\pi_{R \cap S}(S))$ can be estimated as $size(c_2)/|dom(city)|$ and $size(R \ltimes S)$ as $size(R)/|dom(city)|$. Thus, the semijoin method will be cheaper if $size(c_2)/|dom(city)| + size(R)/|dom(city)| < size(R)$.

For example, suppose there are 100 cities; 10,000 customers, each with one account; and 5000 accounts with an account number greater than 600. Suppose also that all tuples are of size 1. Then the left side is equal to 10,000/100 + 5000/100 = 150, compared with the right side of 5000, and the semijoin method is cheaper.

9.4.2   Query Processing in Heterogeneous DDBs

Query processing in heterogeneous DDBs is considerably more complex than in homogeneous DDBs, for a number of reasons.

- In Steps 2 and 3 in Section 9.4.1, a global query expressed on a global schema now needs to be translated into the constructs of the export schemas from which the global schema was derived.

- In Step 4, the cost of processing local queries is likely to be different for different local DBs, which considerably complicates the task of defining a global cost model on which to base global query optimization of the global query. Moreover, the local cost models and local DB statistics may not be available to the global query optimizer. One way for the GQP to gather local cost information is to send sample test queries to the local DBs. Another way is for it to monitor the execution of actual local queries and maintain statistics about their behavior.

- Also in Step 4, different local DBs may support different data models. Thus, it may not be possible to translate the results of one local subquery into the data model of a different local DB. Global query plans need to take those limitations into account, and sites should be sent only data they can translate. Different local DBs may also support different query languages and hence may have different query processing capabilities. Thus, sites should be sent only subqueries that they can process.

- In Step 5, local subqueries expressed on the export schemas using the query language of the CDM have to be translated into queries expressed on the local schemas using the local query language.

- The points in the third entry in this list also mean that some postprocessing of local subqueries may have to be undertaken by the GQP to combine the results of the local subqueries. This is an extra sixth step, which will occur after the five steps described in Section 9.4.1.

9.5   Distributed Transaction Management

The purpose of distributed transaction management is to maintain the ACID properties of global transactions, that is, transactions expressed with respect to the global or external schemas of a DDB system. The local transaction manager (LTM) at each site is still responsible for maintaining the ACID properties of subtransactions of global transactions that are being executed at that site, as well as of local transactions that are submitted directly to the local DB. However, a global transaction manager (GTM) is also needed to distribute requests to and coordinate the execution of the various LTMs involved in the execution of each global transaction.

There are likely to be several GTMs in a DDB system, one at each site to which global transactions can be submitted. Each GTM is responsible for guaranteeing the ACID properties of transactions submitted to it for execution. To do that, a GTM must employ distributed versions of the concurrency control and recovery protocols used by centralized DBMSs for local transaction management. We discuss these distributed protocols in this section, but first we will briefly review the main aspects of concurrency control and recovery in centralized DBMSs.

In a centralized DBMS, the concurrency control mechanism ensures that transactions are interleaved in such a way that their net effect is equivalent to a sequential execution in some order, that is, that transactions can be serialized. This is the isolation part of the ACID properties listed in the introduction to this chapter. If each transaction is individually consistent, this also ensures the overall consistency of concurrently executing transactions, that is, the consistency property. The three main approaches to centralized concurrency control are locking, timestamping, and optimistic concurrency control. We will be focusing on locking, because it is the method most commonly used in commercial DBMSs, both centralized and distributed.

Concurrency control is concerned with preserving the semantic integrity of the DB in the face of concurrently executing transactions. In contrast, the recovery mechanism ensures the physical integrity of the DB in the event of a transaction aborting or a system failure occurring. It does that by logging the changes made by each transaction on stable storage, such as disk or tape, before the changes are applied to the actual data files. If a failure occurs, a redo phase applies all the changes recorded in the log to the data files. That brings the data files up to date and in particular ensures that the effects of committed transactions are not lost. This is the durability part of the ACID properties. An undo phase then reverses the changes performed by transactions that had not committed at the time of the failure, thus ensuring the atomicity property.

9.5.1   Distributed Concurrency Control

The most common approach to concurrency control in centralized DB systems is to use two-phase locking (2PL), in which transactions must first obtain the locks they require in a growing phase before releasing the locks in a shrinking phase. Often the shrinking phase is conducted only when the transaction commits, resulting in what is termed *strict 2PL*. However, this method presents the problem that two or more transactions may enter a deadlock state, in which each transaction holds locks required by the others and all the transactions are unable to proceed.

In a DDB, the locks obtained by 2PL must be distributed to the various sites that form the DDB, and some action must to taken to ensure that 2PL is obeyed globally over the DDB. There must also be some distributed deadlock-detection mechanism. To illustrate this discussion, we give several examples based on the two transactions shown in Figure 9.6, representing a fragment of a simple banking application operating on the relations in Figure 9.3(b). The transactions have been written so that it is clear which parts of each transaction need to operate on a particular fragment of the data. The read and write operations performed by the transactions are shown to the right of the SQL statement that performs the operations.

9.5.1.1   Distributed Two-Phase Locking

It might at first appear that it would be sufficient to run 2PL on each LTM involved in the distributed transaction. Indeed, that will ensure that the transactions executed at each server are locally serializable. However, the serialization order chosen may vary between LTMs, and thus the transaction may not be globally serializable. That is because one server may start its shrinking phase before the other starts its growing phase. To prevent that from occurring, 2PL must be applied to the global transaction sequence. In principle, that might be achieved by a protocol to ensure that GTM controls when the shrinking phase may begin on each LTM. In practice, the usual solution is to use strict 2PL and the atomic commitment protocols discussed in Section 9.5.2 to ensure that all locks are released at the same time.

9.5.1.2   Distributed Locks

One crude implementation of distributed locking would be to insist that each read and write lock must fully replicated, matching the replication of

BEGIN TRANSACTION T_1
   UPDATE account
   SET balance=balance+100 } $T_{1.1}$ $r_1(a_{987})$, $w_1(a_{987})$,
   WHERE accno=987

   UPDATE account
   SET balance=100−100 } $T_{1.2}$ $r_1(a_{123})$, $w_1(a_{123})$
   WHERE accno=123
   COMMIT TRANSACTION T_1

(a)

BEGIN TRANSACTION T_2
   DECLARE @X INT, @Y INT

   SELECT @X=SUM(balance)
   FROM account } $T_{2.1}$ $r_2(a_{100})$, $r_2(a_{123})$, $r_2(a_{130})$,
   WHERE accno<400

   SELECT @Y=SUM(Balance)
   FROM account } $T_{2.2}$ $r_2(a_{400})$, $r_2(a_{563})$, $r_2(a_{588})$, $r_2(a_{987})$
   WHERE accno>=400

   SELECT @X+@Y
   COMMIT TRANSACTION T_2

(b)

Figure 9.6 Sample SQL transactions: (a) T_1: transfer $100 to account 987 from account 123 and (b) T_2: find total credit/debit of all customers.

the data on which the locks operate. However, this clearly will lead to delays in transaction execution, because all locks need to be secured at all sites. To avoid this, conflicts should involve only write locks, and a conflict needs to be detected at only one site for the transaction to be prevented from executing incorrectly. Thus, in a DDB with n sites, assuming all sites are fault free, it is required only that one site detects either of the following conflicts:

- *A read-write conflict.* Suppose we have T_1 reading from o and T_2 writing to o, thus making T_1 and T_2 conflict. If we have placed read locks for object o in transaction T_1 at k sites, then the number j of write locks for o in transaction T_2 must exceed $n - k + 1$ (i.e., $j \geq n - k + 1$) to guarantee at least one site with both a read lock and a write lock for o and thus detect the conflict.

- *A write-write conflict.* Suppose we have T_1 writing to o and T_2 writing to o, thus making T_1 and T_2 conflict. If we have placed write locks in T_1 for object o at j_1 sites, then the number j_2 of write locks in transaction T_2 for o must be at least $n - j_1 + 1$. Because the situation is reflexive (the same argument could have been made swapping T_1 and T_2), we can determine that $j_1 = j_2$ and thus say that the number of write locks j placed by any transaction is given by $j \geq \lceil (n + 1)/2 \rceil$.

Often we can identify that in a particular system the number of read operations greatly outnumbers the number of write operations. Therefore, we want to minimize the cost of making a read operation, at the expense of greater cost in making a write operation. That can be achieved by using a write-locks-all scheme, where any write operation locks all sites (i.e., $j = n$). Therefore, from the above rules, we have $n \geq n - k + 1 \rightarrow k \geq 1$, that is, only one read lock is needed, because every site will already have the conflicting write lock present.

9.5.1.3 Deadlocks

For fragmented data, a deadlock may occur between transactions executing at separate sites, each running its own LTM. For example, consider the following concurrent execution of transactions T_1 and T_2 from Figure 9.6 that (when using strict 2PL) has reached a deadlocked state:

$$r_1(a_{987}), w_1(a_{987}), r_2(a_{100}), r_2(a_{123}), r_2(a_{130}), r_2(a_{400}), r_2(a_{563}), r_2(a_{888}), r_1(a_{123})$$

T_1 is unable to proceed because its next operation $w_1(a_{123})$ is blocked waiting for T_2 to release the lock obtained by $r_2(a_{123})$, and T_2 is unable to proceed because its next operation $r_2(a_{987})$ is blocked waiting for T_1 to release the lock obtained by $w_1(a_{987})$. In a single-server system, this results in a waits-for graph that contains a cycle, indicating the deadlock, and either T_1 or T_2 would be rolled back. In a DDB, if the *account* relation is fragmented as shown in Figure 9.3(b), then locks on a_{987} will be held at S_2, and locks on a_{123} at S_1, leading to a requirement that the waits-for graph is maintained on a global basis.

One simple way to achieve that is to use the GTM to hold the graph, but that leads to delays in transaction execution because a remote copy of the waits-for graph needs to be constantly updated during execution. An alternative mechanism is to store local waits-for graphs, with any transaction outside the local server being marked as an EXT node. Once a cycle is detected at the local server, the waits-for graph is fetched from any remote sites where other parts of the transactions involved in the cycle might be executing. In our example, the transaction fragments for $T_{1.2}$ and $T_{2.1}$ executing at S_1 would be involved in a cycle including an EXT node. This causes S_1 to contact S_2, from which the waits-for graph for $T_{1.1}$ and $T_{2.2}$ can be fetched.

9.5.2   Distributed Commit

Once a transaction has completed all its operations, the ACID properties require that it be made durable when it commits. In a centralized system, ensuring that the commit is atomic amounts to ensuring that all updates are written to log files and that the write operation to disk that marks the transaction as complete is atomic. In distributed transactions, there is the additional requirement for a protocol that ensures that all the servers involved in the transaction agree to either all commit or all abort. The basic framework for building such protocols will involve having a coordinator process in the GTM for each set of server processes in the LTMs that are executing the transaction. At some point, the coordinator will decide that the transaction should be concluded and will perform the following steps.

1. Ask all servers to vote if they are able to commit the transaction.
2. The servers may vote to commit or to abort.
3. The coordinator commits the transaction only if all servers vote to commit.

We next give two protocols that implement this voting procedure in a manner that is (to various extents) tolerant of failures of servers and the coordinator.

9.5.2.1   Two-Phase Commit

The most common protocol for ensuring atomic commitment is two-phase commit (2PC) [14–16], which has been implemented in commercial DBMSs such as Sybase [17] and Oracle [18]. It is such a common protocol that its messages make up the OSI application-layer commitment, concurrency, and recovery (CCR) protocol. We use these messages to describe the execution of 2PC, which involves the following two phases:

- Phase 1: The coordinator transmits the message *C-PREPARE* to all servers, informing them that the transaction should now commit. A server replies *C-READY* if it is ready to commit. After that point, it cannot abort the transaction unless instructed to do so by the coordinator. Alternatively, a server replies *C-REFUSE* if it is unable to commit.

- Phase 2: If the coordinator receives *C-READY* from all servers, it transmits *C-COMMIT* to all servers. Each server commits on receiving this message. If the coordinator receives *C-REFUSE* from any server, it transmits *C-ROLLBACK* to all servers. Each server aborts on receiving this message.

Provided none of the servers crashes and there are no network errors, 2PC will provide a reliable and robust distributed atomic commitment protocol. However, we must take into account failures occurring, which introduces the concept of having some termination protocol to deal with situations in which the atomic commitment protocol is not being obeyed. Some failures are easily handled by having timeouts associated with communication. For example, the coordinator may not receive a reply from one failed server and then might decide to abort the transaction using *C-ROLLBACK.* Alternatively, the coordinator may fail after asking for a vote, in which case all the servers will time out and then contact each other to elect a new coordinator and continue with the transaction.

For some errors, however, the protocol has a weakness in that a server may become blocked. That will occur after a server has sent a *C-READY* reply, which entails that it must commit if and when it receives *C-COMMIT.* In this circumstance, two failures can occur that require contradictory action by the server:

- Immediately after sending *C-PREPARE,* the coordinator might have crashed. One other server might have replied *C-REFUSE* and aborted its transaction. If this was the case, it would be correct for the server to abort its transaction, even after sending *C-READY.*

- The coordinator might have sent *C-COMMIT* to all other servers and then crashed. Those other servers might have committed their transactions and then also crashed. It would then be correct for the server to commit its transaction.

For the server that issued the *C-READY* and has received no reply, those two situations would be identical—the server is unable to get information from the coordinator. Thus the server is blocked, unable to either commit or abort the transaction; hence, it must maintain all the locks associated with the transaction indefinitely.

The factor that makes 2PC block is that once a server has voted to take part in a commit, it does not know what the result of the vote is until the command to commit arrives. By the time it has timed out, after not receiving the result of the vote, all other servers might have failed and so may not be able to be contacted. Eventually one of the failed servers will execute a recovery and be able to inform the blocked server of the result, but that may take a great deal of time. It can be argued that such scenarios are unlikely in practice; indeed, 2PC has been used successfully in commercial systems. However, in environments that require greater fault tolerance, we require protocols that do not block.

9.5.2.2 Three-Phase Commit

2PC can be made nonblocking by introducing an extra phase that obtains and distributes the result of the vote before sending out the command to commit. That requires that the OSI CCR protocol be extended with message types *C-PRECOMMIT* and *C-PRECOMMIT-ACK* to inform servers of the result of a vote separately from issuing the command to commit or roll back a transaction. The steps in such a three-phase commit (3PC) [14, 15, 19] protocol are the following:

- Phase 1: The same as for 2PC.

- Phase 2: If the coordinator receives *C-READY* from all servers, it transmits *C-PRECOMMIT* to all servers. Each server replies with a *C-PRECOMMIT-ACK*. If the coordinator receives *C-REFUSE* from any server, it transmits *C-ROLLBACK* to all servers. Each server aborts on receiving that message.

- Phase 3: If the coordinator receives a *C-PRECOMMIT-ACK* from all servers, it transmits *C-COMMIT* to all servers. If the coordinator is missing a *C-PRECOMMIT-ACK*, it transmits a *C-ROLLBACK* to all servers.

The fact that the vote is distributed to all servers and is confirmed to have arrived at those servers, before a command to commit is made by the coordinator, means that should any server be missing the *C-PRECOMMIT*, it will time out and contact some other server to find out the result of the vote and hence be in a position to commit. If all other servers have failed, the server can abort because none of the other servers could have committed before the timeout occurred. If a server has received a *C-COMMIT*, it can safely commit, knowing that all the other failed servers can later recover and determine the result of the vote.

3PC is a nonblocking protocol that ensures that all nonfailed sites can agree on a decision for transaction termination in the absence of communication failures. It achieves that by introducing an extra delay and set of messages to be exchanged; hence, it will have poorer performance than 2PC. Also, the number of different states that may arise in 3PC is greatly increased from that in 2PC. For that reason, implementations of 3PC are more difficult to produce and verify as correct.

9.5.3 Distributed Recovery

To a large extent, each LTM in the DDB will be able to use standard techniques based on redo/undo logs [15] to recover from system crashes by rolling back or committing transactions. As in a centralized system, the recovery process should be executed each time a server is restarted after a crash. In a DDB, extra complexity is introduced by the fact that a distributed commit decision has to be made, and failures might occur during the execution of the atomic commitment protocol. A full analysis of how 2PC and 3PC alter the recovery process is given in [20], but in overview the extra complexity is due to the fact the other sites might need to be contacted during the recovery process to determine what action should be taken. For example, in 2PC, a server might fail after having issued a *C-READY*. During recovery, it should contact the coordinator to determine what has been the result of the vote, so that it knows whether to use the undo log to roll back the transaction (if the decision had been *C-ROLLBACK*) or simply mark the transaction as complete in the local logs (if the decision has been *C-COMMIT*).

9.5.4 Transaction Management in Heterogeneous DDBs

We recall that a heterogeneous DDB consists of several autonomous local DB systems. There is thus a basic contradiction in executing global transactions over a heterogeneous DDB. This is because the GTM needs to exercise some degree of control over the LTMs to guarantee the ACID properties of global transactions, thereby violating the autonomy of the local DB systems.

For example, if one local DB server decides to roll back a subtransaction of a global transaction, it would require the other servers participating in the execution of the transaction to also roll back their subtransactions, thereby violating their autonomy. A further violation of local autonomy occurs if standard techniques such as 2PL are used to guarantee the serializability of global transactions, since this would require the LTMs of the various servers to export some of their transaction management capabilities in an external interface. In particular, the GTM needs access to the lock records, deadlock waits-for graph, and atomic commitment protocol of each LTM.

A further complication is that different servers may support different atomic commitment protocols (some may use 2PC, others 3PC) or different concurrency control methods (some may use 2PL, others timestamping), or that some servers may allow nonserializable execution of transactions. Coordinating such disparate functionality to achieve global ACID properties can be prohibitively complex.

These problems have led researchers to suggest that the serializability requirement be relaxed for heterogeneous DDBs by the adoption of different transaction models, such as workflow models. The next section briefly discusses alternative transaction models.

9.6 Current Trends and Challenges

9.6.1 Alternative Transaction Models

Conventional transaction models may be inadequate in distributed environments for two main reasons. First, there is the loss of autonomy of the local DBs. Second, there is the tying up of local resources, such as locks, at sites that are participating in the execution of long-running global transactions. One solution to those problems is relaxation of the serializability requirement, which has led to the development of several alternative transaction models.

One approach is the use of *sagas* [21] rather than serializable global transactions. Sagas consist of a sequence of local subtransactions $t_1; t_2; \ldots; t_n$, such that for each t_i it is possible to define a compensating transaction t_i^{-1} that undoes its effects. After a local subtransaction commits, it releases its locks. If the overall saga later needs to be aborted, then, for all subtransactions that have already committed, their compensating transactions can be executed. However, notice that sagas can see the changes of other concurrently executing sagas that may later abort, thereby violating the isolation property. This loss of isolation needs to be taken into account by applications, and any data dependencies between different sagas need to be explicitly tested for.

Another approach is workflow models [22]. Workflows relax the atomicity requirement of conventional transaction models in that it may be possible for one or more tasks of a workflow to fail without the entire workflow failing. The workflow designer is able to specify what the scheduling dependencies between the tasks making up a workflow are and what the permissible termination states of the workflow are. The workflow management system automatically guarantees that the workflow execution terminates in one of these states.

9.6.2 Mediator Architectures

The mediator approach [23] to DB integration is a development of the five-level model in Figure 9.2. With the mediator approach, the export schemas are replaced by wrappers, which include more functionality, such as locking for concurrency control. The semantic integration of export schemas into global schemas is replaced by mediators. Apart from sourcing information from wrappers, mediators can contact other mediators and provide some intelligence, which allows negotiation between mediators to occur.

In the mediator approach, the DDB is constructed in a top-down manner. A global schema is first created for a particular application. The application then requests one or more mediators to source the information in that global schema. The mediators use their knowledge to source data from the correct information wrappers. Note the use of the term *information* here rather than *data*. An advantage of the mediator approach is that semistructured data (such as Web documents) can be accessed by the mediators, as well as structured DBs. A second advantage is that changes to the structure of the information sources do not always require that the mediators be reconfigured.

There have been a number of research implementations of the mediator approach. In the *intelligent integration of information* (I3) architecture [24], the basic notion of a mediator as the middle layer between applications and information sources has three additional components: facilitators, which search for likely sources of information and detect how those sources might be accessed; query processors, which reformulate queries to enhance the chance of a query being successfully answered from the available sources of information; and data miners, which search the information sources for unexpected properties.

The *knowledge reuse and fusion/transformation* (KRAFT) architecture [25] extends the notion of wrappers so that information sources may initiate requests for information as well as service them. The middle layer between applications and wrappers is termed the KRAFT domain, where messages can be exchanged between applications and wrappers. Facilitators serve to route those messages, and mediators serve to process operations based on the messages.

9.6.3 Databases and the World Wide Web

The World Wide Web is based on the notion of browsers on client machines fetching from servers documents formatted in hypertext markup language (HTML), using a protocol called hypertext transfer protocol (HTTP). A DB can be statically connected to the World Wide Web by the use of an application on the server to read information from the DB and format the results in HTML. A DB can also be connected dynamically to the World Wide Web, by allowing requests from clients to cause the server to generate HTML documents from the DB. In both cases, the structure of the DB is lost, in that there is no standard method for describing the schema of HTML documents. They contain just the data with some formatting instructions; for that reason, HTML documents generally are referred to as semistructured data.

The focus of some more recent works has been on methods by which a schema can be extracted from the semistructured data (e.g., [19]) and data extracted from HTML (e.g., [26]). The introduction of the extended markup language (XML) allows a much richer range of types to be associated with values in World Wide Web documents, since the XML definition can be regarded as a kind of DB schema. An interesting area of future work will be methods to query and integrate XML documents from diverse sources.

References

[1]   Sheth, A., and J. Larson, "Federated Database Systems," *ACM Computing Surveys*, Vol. 22, No. 3, 1990, pp. 183–236.

[2]   Tsichritzis, D., and A. Klug, "The ANSI/X3/SPARC DBMS Framework," *Information Systems*, Vol. 3, No. 4, 1978.

[3]   Templeton, M., et al., "Mermaid: A Front-End to Distributed Heterogeneous Databases," *Proc. IEEE*, Vol. 75, No. 5, 1987, pp. 695–708.

[4]   Devor, C., et al., "Five-Schema Architecture Extends DBMS to Distributed Applications," *Electronic Design*, Mar. 1982, pp. 27–32.

[5]   Ramakrishnan, R., *Database Management Systems*, New York: McGraw-Hill, 1998.

[6]   Batini, C., M. Lenzerini, and S. Navathe, "A Comparative Analysis of Methodologies for Database Schema Integration," *ACM Computing Surveys*, Vol. 18, No. 4, 1986, pp. 323–364.

[7]   McBrien, P. J., and A. Poulovassilis, "Automatic Migration and Wrapping of Database Applications—A Schema Transformation Approach," *Proc. ER'99*, LNCS, Springer-Verlag, 1999.

[8]   McBrien, P. J., and A. Poulovassilis, "A Formalisation of Semantic Schema Integration," *Information Systems*, Vol. 23, No. 5, 1998, pp. 307–334.

[9]   Elmasri, R., and S. Navathe, *Fundamentals of Database Systems*, 2nd ed., Redwood City, CA: Benjamin/Cummings, 1994.

[10] Andersson, M., "Extracting an Entity Relationship Schema From a Relational Database Through Reverse Engineering," *Proc. ER'94*, LNCS, Springer-Verlag, 1994, pp. 403–419.

[11] Poulovassilis, A., and P. J. McBrien, "A General Formal Framework for Schema Transformation," *Data and Knowledge Engineering*, Vol. 28, No. 1, 1998, pp. 47–71.

[12] McBrien, P. J., and A. Poulovassilis, "A Uniform Approach to Inter-Model Transformations," *Proc. CAiSE'99*, LNCS, Springer-Verlag, 1999.

[13] Ullman, J. D., *Principles of Database and Knowledge-Base Systems*, Vol. 1, Rockville, MD: Computer Science Press, 1988.

[14] Bell, D., and J. Grimson, *Distributed Database Systems*, Reading, MA: Addison-Wesley, 1992.

[15] Bernstein, P. A., V. Hadzilacos, and N. Goodman, *Concurrency Control and Recovery in Database Systems*, Reading, MA: Addison-Wesley, 1987.

[16] Mullender, S. (ed.), *Distributed Systems*, Reading, MA: Addison-Wesley, 1993.

[17] McGoveran, D., and C. J. Date, *A Guide to SYBASE and SQL Server*, Reading, MA: Addison-Wesley, 1992.

[18] Leverenz, L., *Oracle8 Concepts*, Vol. 2, Oracle, 1997.

[19] Nestorov, S., S. Abiteboul, and R. Motwani, "Extracting Schema From Semistructured Data," *SIGMOD Record*, Vol. 27, No. 2, 1998, pp. 295–306.

[20] Özsu, M. T., and P. Valduriez, *Principles of Distributed Database Systems*, 2nd ed., Upper Saddle River, NJ: Prentice-Hall, 1999.

[21] Garcia-Molina, H., and K. Salem, "Sagas," *Proc. SIGMOD 1987*, 1987, pp. 249–259.

[22] Rusinkiewicz, M., and A. Sheth, "Specification and Execution of Transactional Workflows," in W. Kim (ed.), *Modern Database Systems: The Object Model, Interoperability, and Beyond*, Addison-Wesley/ACM Press, 1995.

[23] Wiederhold, G., "Mediators in the Architecture of Future Information Systems," *IEEE Computer*, Vol. 25, No. 3, 1992, pp. 38–49.

[24] Wiederhold, G., "Foreword to Special Issue on Intelligent Integration of Information," *J. Intelligent Information Systems,* Vol. 6, No. 2–3, 1996, pp. 93–97.

[25] Gray, P., et al., "KRAFT: Knowledge Fusion From Distributed Databases and Knowledge Bases," *Proc. 8th Intl. Workshop on Database and Expert System Applications, DEXA'97,* 1997.

[26] Adelberg, B., "NoDoSE—A Tool for Semi-Automatically Extracting Structured and Semi-Structured Data From Text Documents," *SIGMOD Record,* Vol. 27, No. 2, 1998, pp. 283–294.

Selected Bibliography

This chapter has given an overview of some of the many issues involved in the design and implementation of DDBs. An in-depth discussion of the whole area can be found in the book by Özsu and Valduriez [20]. This book also includes chapters on several topics that we have not covered here, including parallel DBs and distributed object-oriented DBs. Earlier books on DDBs include [14] and *Distributed Databases: Principles and Systems,* by S. Ceri and G. Pelagatti (McGraw-Hill, 1984). *Modern Database Systems: The Object Model, Interoperability, and Beyond,* edited by W. Kim (Addison-Wesley/ACM Press, 1995), contains several chapters on heterogeneous multi-DBMSs that collectively give a deeper treatment of the area than we have been able to do here. An extensive analysis of concurrency control and recovery, with some coverage of concurrency control and recovery in DDBs, is given in [15].

10

Mobile Computing: Data Management Issues

Alfredo Goñi and Arantza Illarramendi

10.1   Introduction

In the past few years, the use of portable computers and wireless networks has been widespread. The combination of both opens the door to a new technology: mobile computing. Although the wireless communication networks were designed for the transport of voice signals, their use for data transport is growing.

Mobile computing allows users to access from anywhere and at anytime the data stored in repositories of their organizations (i.e., the DBs of the company for which they work) and available data in a global information system through the Internet. Many professionals use mobile computers for their work (e.g., sales personnel and emergency services) to obtain and send information where and when they actually need it. Moreover, there are applications in this new framework in which the location is an important aspect, such as those applications that provide information about the nearest hotels, restaurants, and so on. Mobile computing adds a new dimension to distributed data computation, a dimension that enables a new class of applications.

So far, distributed data management has been considered mainly for fixed computers. DDBMSs, federated DBs, interoperable DBs, and GISs are areas in which a great research effort is being made (see Chapter 9). The new framework of mobile computing can profit from some new proposals on those topics. However, specific problems related to this new framework must be taken into consideration. Some problems are intrinsic to portable computers, which generally provide fewer resources than fixed computers because they must be small and light and consume little energy. Other problems are related to the wireless connection, which presents poor quality and is influenced by a multitude of factors that cause the wireless networks to have a high rate of errors and a limited bandwidth. There is also the problem of continuous disconnections. One could say that mobile computing is the worst case of distributed computation, because fundamental assumptions about connectivity, immobility, and scale have lost their validity.

With respect to related works, the different mobile software systems can be grouped in the following way:

- Systems that allow a disconnected or weakly connected access to file systems. Among the different issues that have to be dealt with are the possibility of prefetching files for later access, management of cached data, model of consistency used, how to propagate changes, transparency of support to client applications, and transparency of mechanisms to users. In the related literature, many works deal with some of those issues [1–6].

- Systems that allow a weakly connected access to DBs such as the Bayou system which proposes and implements an architecture for mobile-aware DBs. In the system architecture there are several Bayou servers containing the full replicated data and several client applications interacting (reading and writing) with those servers and that are aware that they may be working with inconsistent data. Disconnected operation with the system is not allowed [7].

- Systems that allow a disconnected and weakly connected access to the World Wide Web. These systems differ with respect to the systems that access file systems in the following aspects: a URL is not a file reference because it can contain embedded references, so some content filtering and transformation may need to be made. It is also possible to have dynamic URLs. In such systems, prefetching and caching techniques also can be applied and *proxies* added to the architecture. In some systems, namely, Caubweb [8], TeleWeb [9], and Weblicator [10], the proxy is added to the client part of the system. In other systems, like TranSend [11] and Digestor [12], the proxy is added to the Web server. Finally, in WebExpress [13], there are proxies in both parts, client and server.

- Systems that provide an environment for the development of mobile applications. For example, the Rover Toolkit is software that supports the construction of *mobile-transparent* and *mobile-aware* applications based on the idea of *relocatable dynamic objects* and *queued remote procedure call* [14]. Also interesting is the work developed by the DATAMAN group that has defined a set of classes, called *Mobjects*, that would form the basis of a toolkit to implement applications for mobile computing devices [15].

This chapter presents basic concepts and issues related to data management for mobile computing. First, we present a motivation and the widely accepted architecture. Then we explain briefly different wireless networks and introduce the problems inherent to the framework and, specifically, the impact of mobile computing in the area of data management. Finally, we explain the main features of the more frequently used communication models and those related to agent technology and describe some design characteristics.

10.2 Motivation

There is no doubt that mobile computing offers new computing opportunities to users. We present three scenarios in which the three main features of the new paradigm are reflected: (1) access to distributed information repositories anywhere, anytime, (2) information delivery by broadcasting, and (3) provision of user-tailored information.

The first scenario considers one day in the life of a salesperson equipped with a personal computer. Our salesperson plans her work days in advance, so before going to bed each night, she switches on her mobile computer and asks if there are any new assignments. After reading the messages, our salesperson adds the new tasks to her agenda and plans the following day's itinerary. The following morning, she leaves home to visit the first client of the day. Before leaving, however, she uses her mobile computer to find the best route to the client's office based on up-to-date traffic conditions. She also requests the client's file. Our salesperson stops in a café before arriving at the client's office, and while she has a coffee she reviews the most important data related to the client to prepare for the interview. Once the interview has been concluded, she enlarges the client's file, registering that day's visit and its results and sending the new data to her company's DB. During the rest of the day, our salesperson goes on in the same way, visiting clients and reading her e-mail and messages. When she is about to conclude her work day, she receives a broadcast message from her company's assistant director to all the salespersons. It is a report about the results of the previous month and the expectations for the current month.

The second scenario concerns an archaeologist, but in general it could be applied to any autonomous worker. Mobile computers allow our archaeologist to have a computer, albeit one with limited capacities, out in the field. Our archaeologist needs access to the Internet to be able to access the big data repositories of the universities and libraries that store the data he needs for his research. Let us imagine one day in this archaeologist's life. He gets up early; a day of fieldwork awaits him in the current excavation. In the excavation, the workers are examining the remains of prehistoric tools. While the archaeologist has breakfast, he switches on his mobile computer. He sends queries to obtain the information stored in a series of DBs about certain types of prehistoric tools: periods to which they correspond, areas in which they were located, information about the people who made and used them, and so on. He finishes his breakfast and, before driving to the excavation, examines the weather report provided by the computer. Later on, when he arrives at the excavation, he switches the mobile computer on again. The information in response to his earlier queries has arrived. The archaeologist begins his work with the found samples. He consults the stored data and formulates new queries to the DBs until he identifies the period to which the tools belong. He also obtains information about that period and the people, uses they gave to those tools, and similar discoveries at other digs.

Finally, the third scenario considers the case of a user equipped with a palmtop (equipment that has limited capabilities). Usually our palmtop user only registers data on her small mobile computer, but today, using specialized keys, she asks for information about movies playing tonight in the city. The information she receives is only textual; all the associated multimedia information has been eliminated, taking into account the limitations of the mobile computer.

In summary, we can conclude that mobile computing gives users all the advantages of fixed computers but in a mobile environment.

10.3 Architecture

In the widely accepted architecture for mobile computing (see Figure 10.1) [16], the following elements can be distinguished:

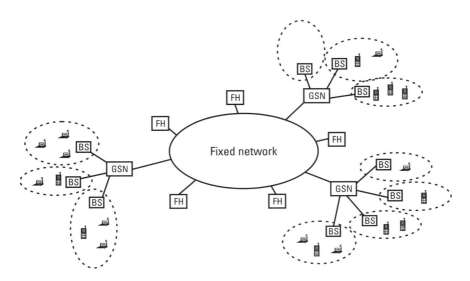

Figure 10.1 Mobile computing environment.

- *Mobile unit (MU)*. A portable computer equipped with a wireless interface.

- *Base station (BS)*. A fixed host augmented with wireless interface. It is also called a mobile support station (MSS). The geographical area covered by each BS is called a *cell*. MUs communicate with other units through those BSs of the cells in which they reside.

- *Fixed host (FH)*. A computer without a wireless interface.

Cell sizes vary widely, from 400 miles in diameter (covered by satellites), to a few miles (covered by cellular transceivers), to a building (covered by a wireless local area network). When MUs move, they may cross the boundary of a cell and enter an area covered by a distinct BS. This process is called *handoff*. Taking into account that MUs can be disconnected, an MU can abandon a cell and appear in another one far away. In other words, movement among cells is not necessarily among adjacent cells.

Previous architecture must support different kinds of MUs such as palmtops and laptops. Because palmtops provide fewer functionalities than laptops, the features of MUs must be taken into consideration in implementation of the architecture.

With respect to the wireless part of the architecture, there exist a lack of standards and limited performance features with today's second digital generation of mobile communications systems. However, a third generation of mobile communication systems is emerging. It is formed by systems like the European Universal Mobile Telecommunication Systems (UMTS) and the international Future Public Land Mobile Telecommunications in 2000 (FPLMTS/IMT 2000). These systems have the goal of providing services and capabilities on the same level as fixed networks, making those services globally available independent of the user's location, so there will be a strict distinction between network and service providers.

10.4   Technological Aspects: Wireless Networks

Nowadays, different wireless access technologies connect mobile users to wired networks: analog cellular networks, digital cellular networks, wireless wide-area networks (WANs), wireless local-area networks (LANs), and satellite systems. With those wireless access technologies, it can be possible to use circuit switch or packet switch communications with important implications in money spent and speed obtained.

10.4.1   Analog Cellular Networks

The first generation of analog cellular systems is called advanced mobile phone service (AMPS). It is still used for cellular telephone technology and utilizes analog frequency modulation (FM) for speech transmission. The technique of frequency division/multiple access (FDMA) is used to make individual calls. The bandwidth is divided into different channels, and neighboring cells use different channels controlled by MSSs.

10.4.2   Digital Cellular Networks

The second generation of cellular systems uses digital modulation instead of analog techniques and, apart from voice services, can offer integrated services digital network (ISDN) services. Although there are several advantages of using digital cellular communications such as error corrections, intelligence of the digital network, integration with wired digital networks, and encrypted communications, the effective data rate is low (ranging from 9 to 14 Kbps). There are two basic techniques for sharing the digital cellular network: time-division multiple access (TDMA) and code-division multiple access (CDMA). There are several basic standards deployed in Europe and the United States. In Europe, the Global System for Mobile Communications (GSM) is based on TDMA. In the United States, the IS-54 standard is based on TDMA, and the IS-95 standard is based on CDMA. There are also other cordless telephony technologies that are limited to short ranges, like the British second-generation cordless telephone (CT2), based on FDMA, and the digital European cordless telephone (DECT), based on TDMA.

10.4.3 Wireless Wide-Area Networks

Because the cellular products previously mentioned are relatively expensive and slow, some other technologies are being deployed that are based on packet switching instead of circuit switching. For example, the advanced radio data information system (ARDIS), which provides a data transmission rate from 8 to 19.2 Kbps; the RAM mobile data system, which provides a data rate of 8 Kbps; the cellular digital packet data (CDPD) system, which provides data services on top of the AMPS analog system with a maximum data transmission rate of 19.2 Kbps but with an effective rate of 9.6 Kbps; and the general packet radio service (GPRS), which is being developed by the GSM consortium to include packet switching with higher expected data rates than the previous ones. In general, with all these WAN technologies the transmission rates are not very high.

10.4.4 Wireless Local-Area Networks

Wireless LANs provide higher data rates (more than 1 Mbps) to mobile users who have less mobility (e.g., inside a building, on a campus). Some products try to provide wireless Ethernet connections and use different link technologies like radio frequencies, infrareds, and microwaves. Examples of products are FreePort, WaveLAN, and Altair, and standards, like the IEEE 802.11 and the HiperLAN, are being developed.

10.4.5 Satellite Networks

Mobile satellite networks allow global coverage for two-way voice communications but limited data capabilities. Data rates and propagation times depend on the type of satellites used. Geostationary satellites (GEOS) provide global coverage with few but expensive stations and with great delays when establishing communications that require a high power cost. Low earth orbit satellites (LEOS) are smaller and less expensive, and communications have low cost but also a low data rate. The cells are much smaller and allow for more frequency reuse but imply more handoffs. Medium earth orbit satellites (MEOS) represent a tradeoff between GEOS and LEOS.

10.4.6   The Future

Some trends known as personal communication service (PCS) in the United States and the UMTS in Europe may lead to a new generation of mobile communications. They try to define and develop communication systems with global coverage and integration with broadband public networks.

10.5   Special Issues for Consideration

Three main features of the new context require special consideration: mobility, wireless medium, and portability of mobile elements [17, 18].

10.5.1   Mobility

The location of MUs is an important parameter in the locating of a mobile station that may hold the required data and in the selection of information especially for location-dependent information services. But the search cost to locate MUs is added to the cost of each communication involving them. Two solutions have been discussed in the literature [16] for the first problem. In one solution, each MU has a home BS that keeps track of its location by receiving notification of its movements. The second solution is based on restricted broadcast within the area that the MU wants to access.

10.5.2   Wireless Medium

Some specific features of the wireless medium include the scarce bandwidth, asymmetry in the communications, and the high frequency of disconnections.

10.5.2.1   Scarce Bandwidth of Wireless Networks and Asymmetry in Communications

Wireless networks offer a smaller bandwidth than wired networks. Wireless networks offer a bandwidth that varies between 9 and 14 Kbps, while any Ethernet offers a bandwidth of 10 Mbps. The oscillation in the bandwidth is more noticeable than in traditional wired networks. There is, however, an asymmetry in the communication because the bandwidth for the downlink communication (from servers to clients) is much greater than the bandwidth for the uplink communication (from clients to servers). To resolve the previous constraints, one approach consists of the use of broadcasting to disseminate information of general interest. The use of broadcast saves bandwidth by reducing the need of point-to-point communications among the MUs and the BSs and saves MU battery power because it reduces uplink communications, which are more expensive in terms of energy than downlink communications.

10.5.2.2 Disconnections

Wireless communications are very susceptible to disconnections, an important aspect to keep in mind in the design of an architecture to support mobile computing. Disconnections can be classified into two types: *forced disconnections*, which are usually accidental and unavoidable (e.g., the disconnection that occurs when the user enters an out-of-coverage area), and *voluntary disconnections*, in which the user decides to disconnect the unit with the goal of saving energy. Voluntary disconnections can also occur when abrupt changes in the signal are detected or when the power level in the batteries is low. In those cases, the unit takes the necessary measures to change to disconnected mode in a stable way and without the risk of losing data. The undesirable effects of the disconnections can be mitigated using caching techniques [19, 20]. With caching techniques, the user can continue working even in a disconnection state, which will help avoid the unnecessary use of the wireless communication.

10.5.3 Portability of Mobile Elements

Although mobile computers exist that present different capabilities, in general their limitations are related mostly to their size and battery life.

10.5.3.1 Limitations on Size and Capabilities of Mobile Computers

The design of portable computers implies that they must be small and lightweight, and consume little energy. That means the computers generally have more limited functionalities than FHs, mainly in aspects such as computation power, storage capacity, screen size and graphic resolution, and autonomy. Among the solutions that try to overcome such limitations are those that adapt the images for their visualization by reducing their size, definition, or colors, or by using filters. Filters are programs used to process every message coming or going to the MUs. They can abolish the message, delay it, reorganize it into segments, or transform it [21].

10.5.3.2 Battery Power Limitation

Because of the limited autonomy of the batteries, optimizing the energy consumption is generally a critical aspect in mobile computing. Even with the new advances in battery technology, the typical lifetime of a battery is only a few hours. The problem is not likely to disappear in the near future. The use of asynchronous models allows the disconnection of the portable computer to the network while requests are processed in the server of the fixed network; the units are in "doze" mode, which saves energy.

10.6   Impact of Mobile Computing on Data Management

This section examines the impact that the issues of mobility, scarce bandwidth, disconnections, and limitations on size and battery power have on data management, particularly transactions, data dissemination, query processing, caching, and DB interfaces.

10.6.1 Transactions

As it is accepted in the DB community, all transactions must satisfy the ACID properties. They must be *atomic* (all actions performed or none of them), *consistent* (the DB must be left in a consistent state), *isolated* (a transaction does not read intermediate results made by other transactions), and *durable* (results must remain after the transactions commit). Moreover, the schedule in which different concurrent transactions are performed has to be *serializable.* This is enforced by the concurrency control methods, like 2PL or timestamping methods, implemented by the DBMS. However, the problem is more complicated in a distributed context, in which different protocols like 2PC and 3PC have been defined to ensure ACID properties for transactions performed in different computers (see [22]).

Mobile transactions are, in general, distributed transactions in which some actions are performed in mobile computers and others in FHs. The ACID properties are hard to enforce, especially when the mobile computers are disconnected, and techniques like 2PL and 2PC may seriously affect the availability of the DB system, for example, when a disconnected mobile computer owns a lock over DB items or if other computers are waiting for the mobile computer to know if it is ready to perform a commit. Therefore, it is necessary to provide transaction support for mobile environments or to define some notions of different kinds of transactions.

Some proposals work with the notion of *weak transactions*, transactions that read or write local and probably inconsistent data [23]. Other proposals present mechanisms so that applications have views of the DBs consistent with their own actions, mechanisms known as *session guarantees* (see [24]). Others present notions of transactions based on *escrow* methods, which are especially interesting in sales transactions. The total number of available items is distributed in the different sites, and local transactions can commit if the demand does not exceed the quantity in the local site (see [25]). In [26] *isolation-only transactions* are proposed, but the rest of the ACID properties are not. In [27] a technique is explained whereby the broadcast channel is used so that the mobile clients know if they have to abort the transactions that are running. To do that, certification reports sent through the broadcast channel contain items over which commits are going to be made. Another related idea, called *transaction proxies* and presented in [28], consists of defining dual transactions (one for each transaction performed in a mobile host) that will be executed in an FH that acts as the host support of the mobile one. The dual transactions contain only the updates made by the mobile transaction in case recovery is needed.

10.6.2 Data Dissemination by Broadcasting

The feature of asymmetry in mobile communications along with the power limitation of the mobile computing framework make the model of broadcasting data to clients an interesting alternative. Broadcasting is the delivery of data from a server to a large set of clients (sometimes it is also referred to as being *push-based*). By pushing data, the server avoids interruptions caused by requests of clients and thus optimizes the use of the bandwidth in the upstream direction.

The main aspects that a broadcasting system must take into consideration are the clients' needs and whether to send the data periodically or aperiodically. Periodic push has the advantage of allowing clients to disconnect for certain periods and still not miss items. In [29, 30] there appears the use of a periodic dissemination architecture in the context of mobile systems. Aperiodic dissemination, on the other hand, is a more effective way of using the bandwidth available. In [31, 32] those authors work with the concept of "indexing on air," that is, transmitting an index along with the data, so clients can tune in only during the times they need to. One issue that arises in the former approach is how the index is multiplexed with the data to make the latency and tuning time minimal.

Because no broadcast program can perfectly match the needs of individual clients, mechanisms have been defined to compensate the existing mismatches. One mechanism consists of intelligent caching and prefetching at the client side, which are examined in [29, 30]. The authors of [19] present a way of sending invalidation messages over a limited bandwidth network. With those messages, the server can notify clients about changes in the items they are caching. They also address the issue of relaxing consistency of the caches.

Alternatively, broadcasting can be achieved by the use of multicast addresses. The server sends data to a group of clients using the same address. *Hashing* can be efficiently used in combination with multicast addresses.

Moreover, there also exist works that integrate the pull-based and the push-based approaches. In a pull-based operation, clients explicitly request items by sending messages to the server, which in turn sends the information back to the clients. A system that includes both approaches uses two independent channels, a front channel and a back channel. The front channel is used for the push-based operations, while the back channel serves as the medium for the pull-based operations. The available bandwidth is shared between the two channels. Finally, some recent applications of data dissemination include information dissemination on the Internet [33] and private networks [34] and dissemination through satellite networks [35].

10.6.3 Query Processing

Query processing is affected when mobility is considered, and it is possible to formulate location-dependent queries. For example, "Where is the nearest gas station?" and "Which cinemas show a film at 8:00 P.M. in this city?" return different values depending on the location of the mobile computer.

In general, query optimization methods try to obtain execution plans that minimize CPU, I/O, and communication costs. In centralized environments, the cost that is the most prominent is that for I/O. In distributed environments, communication cost is the most important cost, but the other two may also be important if communication costs are not very high (e.g., in LANs) [36]. In a mobile distributed environment, the communication costs are much more difficult to estimate because the mobile host may be situated in different locations. The best site from which to access data depends on where the mobile computer is located. In general, it is not worth calculating plans and their associated costs statically; rather, dynamic optimization strategies are required in this mobile distributed context.

Among the works related to query processing in mobile computing we can mention [37–40]. In [37] those authors present how to deal with queries with location constraints, that is, queries that involve the individual locations of users. Because the location of a user is not exact, it is expensive, in terms of communication costs, to find out the missing information necessary to answer queries with location constraints. The rest of the mentioned works try to provide solutions to more specific problems. In [38, 39] the authors try to facilitate traveling by providing updated information on traffic conditions, weather, available parking, shortest distances, emergency services, and so forth. Needed data can be obtained by making specific requests (pull based) and by data dissemination or broadcasting (push based). In [40] a Web information system for a mobile wireless computing environment is described. The Web is extended to allow documents to refer and react to changing contextual information, like current location in a wireless network. It introduces the concept of *dynamic URLs* (which allow to return different documents or execute different commands depending on dynamic environ-ment variables) and the concept of *active documents*, which automatically update their contents in response to changes in the user's mobile context.

10.6.4 Caching

As mentioned previously, query optimization methods try to minimize CPU, I/O, and communication costs; in the mobile distributed context, the com-munication costs may be particularly important. It is accepted that applying caching techniques for query processing can reduce communication costs dramatically. However, it is more difficult to apply caching techniques in the mobile context because cache contents may change rapidly or become out-of-date due to mobility; in addition, because of disconnections of the MU, updates to the cache memory may not be sent. The authors of [18] present several techniques related to caching, such as prefetching, replacement strate-gies, and consistency of the cache memory, used in combination with broad-casting techniques. The idea is to send by broadcast channel some data that may be needed in the future (prefetching) or data that have become inconsistent.

10.6.5 Database Interfaces

The limited screen sizes of many mobile computers have motivated the development of new interfaces for them and, in particular, the design of new DB interfaces for mobile computers. In [41] there appears a query processing interface, called *query by icons*, that addresses the features of screen size along with the limitations in memory and battery power and the restricted communication bandwidth. In [42] the issue of how the pen and voice can be used as substitutes for the mouse and keyboard is addressed. Moreover, in [43] there appears an implementation of a pen-based graphical DB interface on a pen computer.

10.7   Communication Models and Agents

This section presents other issues that have to be considered in the building of systems that allow accessing services from mobile computers.

10.7.1   Communication Models

Two main types of models are being used in the mobile computing environment [18]: the client/server model (in its different versions) and the peer-to-peer model. An important difference between the two models is the role that each element of the environment plays. In the client/server, the MU—the client—requests a service from another computing system—the server—located at the fixed network. The peer-to-peer model makes no distinction between clients and servers. Each site (ideally) has the full functionality of both a client and a server. Although the peer-to-peer model is adequate for certain applications (e.g., two partners performing cooperative work on the same data using portable computers), the client/server model is more broadly used.

The traditional client/server model presents some shortcomings in wireless networks because wireless networks present a high rate of errors, limited and variable bandwidth, and continuous disconnections. For those reasons, the following client/server extensions have been proposed: the *client/agent/server* model and the *client/intercept/server* model (both can be grouped under what is called the *indirect model* [44]). The basic idea of the indirect model is that whenever the interaction between two computers takes place over two radically different media, like wire and wireless, their interaction is broken down into two phases, one for each kind of medium. An intermediary element is placed in one point between the two computers. That element manages the interaction between the computers, taking into account the different nature of the two media involved. It tries to relieve the more limited extreme of the communication of some tasks, but its existence can even remain unnoticed by the two computers. More particularly, the client/agent/server model alleviates the impact of the limited bandwidth and the poor reliability of the wireless link by continuously maintaining clients' presence on the fixed network via an agent. The agent splits the interaction between mobile clients and fixed servers into two parts, one between the client and the agent, and one between the agent and the server. This model moves responsibilities from the client to the agent. Moreover, agents are used in a variety of forms and roles. At one extreme, an agent acts as the complete surrogate of a mobile host on the fixed network. At the other extreme, the agent is attached to a specific service or application.

The client/intercept/server model [45] is used to address the shortcomings of the client/agent/server model. In the client/agent/server model, the mobile client cannot continue to operate uninterrupted when an event such as a disconnection happens. That model requires changes to the client code, and the agent can optimize only data transmission over the wireless link from the fixed network to the mobile client but not vice versa. The client/intercept/server model proposes the use of two agents, the client-side agent, which is co-resident with the client, and the server-side agent, which resides on the fixed networks. This model is transparent to both the client and the server, offers flexibility in handling disconnections, and optimizes data transmissions from the fixed network to the mobile client and vice versa.

10.7.2 Agents

Agent technology is not new in computer science [46]. It has been used in, for example, artificial intelligence. In general, an agent is a computer program that acts autonomously on behalf of a person or an organization. Each agent has its own thread of execution so it can perform tasks on its own initiative. An agent system is a platform that can create, interpret, execute, transfer, and terminate agents. When an agent moves, it travels between execution environments called *places*. A place is a context within an agent system where an agent can execute. The source place and the destination place can reside in the same agent system or in different agent systems that support the same agent profile [47].

The use of the agent technology in the implementation of mobile systems has the following advantages [48]:

- *Asynchronous communications.* The elements involved in the communication do not have to be connected all the time. That means MUs may decide to disconnect while the agents that represent them are working in other computers. This may be interesting, for example, in the accessing of DBs in which transactions can take a long time.

- *Autonomous communications.* The agents may make some decisions on behalf of the user when representing the MUs. This may be interesting, for example, when in the accessing of a DB some transactions fail; in such a case, the agent can make the decision of retrying the transaction or not, trying another one, and so on, considering the knowledge that it has about the MU.

- *Remote communications.* The agents can make use of remote facilities or resources such as memory, CPU, and so forth. This may be interesting when, for example, an MU does not have enough capacity to develop a task; in such a case, an agent can realize the task in a remote computer and, once the task is finished, return the results to the mobile computer.

Recently there has been a great research effort with respect to the mobility feature of agents. A mobile agent is not bound to the system where it begins execution; it has the unique ability to move from one system in a network to another. The ability to travel lets a mobile agent move to a system that contains an object with which the agent wants to interact and take advantage of being in the same host or network as the object. When an agent travels, it transports its state and the code with it. Mobile agent technology, apart from the previously mentioned advantages, allows us to migrate processes among different machines.

10.8 Mobile Computer Design Features for Accessing Data Services

The number of people who use or work with mobile computers is continuously increasing. Although the performance features of those kinds of computers in disconnected mode (e.g., laptops) are equivalent to those offered by fixed computers, when they are connected to a wireless network, the same performance does not hold. The intrinsic features of wireless communications—poor quality, limited bandwidth, continuous disconnections—make working connected to a wireless network more difficult. However, one important wish of mobile users is to have the possibility of working connected to a wireless network in the same way as working connected to a fixed network or at least with better QoS than that offered by existing networks.

Taking that wish into consideration, different research projects are trying to build mobile systems that overcome the existing limitations [49–54]. All the works cited so far in this chapter consider different aspects of mobile computing by using agent technology. In the same line, we present in [55] a system based on the use of the client/intercept/server model that incorporates some modules and agents in the mobile computer as well as in an intermediary element situated in the fixed network. That element, called a gateway support node (GSN) (see Figure 10.1), is the intermediary element in the communication between the mobile computers under its coverage and all other hosts of the network (mobile or fixed). Its aim is to relieve mobile computers from many tasks and increase their capabilities, while respecting their natural limitations and taking into consideration the problems of the mobile computing framework and trying to solve them. The pair formed by the GSN and the MU allows the MU to behave like a fixed computer for the rest of the network. The GSN lends its identity to the set of mobile computers it monitors, so that when the GSN receives messages and data sent to the mobile computers, it distributes them to the suitable MU.

Concerning the use of agents, in the works cited here, the process consists of creating an agent for each task to be carried out, giving it the data necessary to access a certain source of information and sending it from the mobile computer to the network. Once the results have been obtained, the agent returns to the mobile computer. In our proposal, the underlying philosophy is different. We advocate using a majordomo agent, *Alfred*, to avoid the continuous transferences of agents through the wireless link and, therefore, the high cost that it represents. Alfred is an efficient majordomo for mobile computers. Each mobile computer will have its own version of Alfred with the aim of giving adequate services to its owner. From the implementation point of view, Alfred is the union of two agents: static Alfred (SAlfred), a static agent situated in the mobile computer, and mobile Alfred (MAlfred), a mobile agent situated in the intermediary element. MAlfred is created in the mobile computer, but it travels to the intermediary element, where it works on behalf of the mobile user, representing the user in the network, becoming the common point to all the communications in which the MU is involved, even when the mobile computer is disconnected. When a task must be carried out, SAlfred sends a message to MAlfred with the necessary data. MAlfred then carries out the task or creates a new agent, a specialist (the specialist mobile agents are situated in the GSN), and orders it to carry out the task. Once the results have been obtained, MAlfred sends them with a message to SAlfred.

The system that we propose can be presented from two different points of view, depending on where the GSNs are situated and who owns them. On one hand, a GSN owned by the company that is offering the wireless communication infrastructure (e.g., a cellular phone company) can be considered. In that model, the GSN can offer some services for the general use of mobile users that contract them to the company. Those services include the following (see Figure 10.2):

- A *broadcast transmitter*, for disseminating general-interest information such as local traffic conditions and weather forecasts;

- *Yellow pages*, for providing access to different data repositories that contain general-interest information such as local restaurants;

- *Access to Internet à la carte*, for facilitating the use of the push technology to the mobile users;

- *Available software*, such as freeware software, that can be used on the mobile computer or on the GSN on behalf of the mobile user;

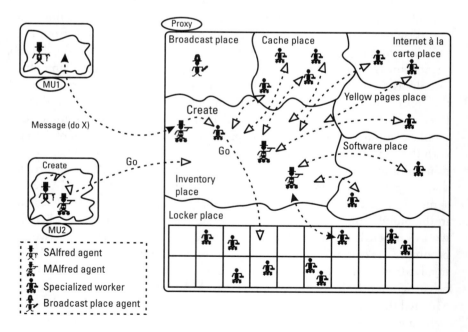

Figure 10.2 Mobile computing environment with GSN elements and mobile agents.

- *Rent of lockers*, which allows the mobile user to have services such as confidential access protected with a secret key to a "locker."

The GSN could also be situated in a computer that is in charge of monitoring the access to a private corporate network. That is, the GSN is part of the intranet of the company, and the offered services can be customized according to the needs and characteristics of the particular company and its mobile workers. For example, the GSN could offer the following services:

- *Access to data repositories*, to allow the users to perform queries and updates in any DB server of their organization;
- *Access to FHs*, for providing access to information stored in FHs and allowing a user to get and store files in any host of the fixed network where that user has the right access privileges;
- *Access to the World Wide Web*, to obtain Web pages, cache them in the GSN, and send them to the mobile users;
- *E-mail*, to allow mobile users to get and send e-mail to any e-mail server;
- A *blackboard*, which stores general-interest messages that the users can obtain in several ways.

10.9 Summary

This chapter briefly reviewed the main issues concerning data management in mobile computing. It illustrated the possibilities that this new paradigm offers and the widely accepted architecture, followed by the technologies that are being considered. It also introduced the main features that have a great influence on the performance of the mobile systems, focusing on the data management aspects. In summary, we can conclude that mobile computing opens new expectations for data applications. However, because mobile computing is not yet mature and many problems must be solved, it is expected that new proposals will appear in the future.

References

[1]   Kistler, J. J., and M. Satyanarayanan, "Disconnected Operation in the Coda File System," *ACM Trans. on Computer Systems*, Vol. 10, 1992, pp. 213–225.

[2]   Mazer, M. S., and J. J. Tardo, "A Client-Side-Only Approach to Disconnected File Access," *Proc. IEEE Workshop on Mobile Computing Systems and Applications,* Dec. 1994.

[3]   Heidemann, J., et al., "Primarily Disconnected Operation: Experience With Ficus," *2nd Workshop on Management of Replicated Data,* Nov. 1992.

[4]   AirAccess, http://www.airsoft.com/.

[5]   Howard, J. H., "Using Reconciliation To Share Files Between Occasionally Connected Computers," *4th Workshop on Workstation Operating Systems,* 1993.

[6]   Traveling-Software Laplink, http://www.travsoft.com/.

[7]   Demers, A., et al., "The Bayou Architecture: Support for Data Sharing Among Mobile Users," *Proc. IEEE Workshop on Mobile Computing Systems and Applications,* Dec. 1995.

[8]   LoVerso, J. R., and M. S. Mazer, "Caubweb: Detaching the Web With TCL," *Proc. 5th Annual USENIX TCL/TK Workshop,* July 1997.

[9]   Schilit, B. N., et al., "TeleWeb: Loosely Connected Access to the World Wide Web," *Proc. 5th Intl. World Wide Web Conf.,* May 1996.

[10] Lotus Weblicator, http://www2.lotus.com/weblicator.nsf.

[11] Fox, A., and E. A. Brewer, "Reducing WWW Latency and Bandwidth Requirements by Real-Time Distillation," *Proc. 5th Intl. World Wide Web Conf.,* May 1996.

[12] Bickmore, T. W., and B. N. Schilit, "Digestor: Device-Independent Access to the World Wide Web," *Proc. 6th Intl. World Wide Web Conf.,* Apr. 1997.

[13] Housel, B. C., and D. B. Lindquist, "WebExpress: A System for Optimizing Web Browsing in a Wireless Environment," *Proc. ACM/IEEE MOBICOM'96 Conf.,* Oct. 1996.

[14] Joseph, A. D., J. A. Tauber, and M. F. Kaashoek, "Mobile Computing With the Rover Toolkit," *IEEE Trans. on Computers,* Vol. 46, No. 3, Nov. 1997.

[15] Welling, G., and B. R. Badrinath, "Mobjects: Programming Support for Environment Directed Application Policies in Mobile Computing," *Proc. ECOOP'95 Workshop on Mobility and Replication,* 1995.

[16] Imielinski, T., and B. R. Badrinath, "Mobile Wireless Computing: Challenges in Data Management," *Comm. ACM,* Oct. 1994, pp. 19–27.

[17] Imielinski, T., and H. F. Korth (eds.), *Mobile Computing,* Boston, MA: Kluwer Academic Publishers, 1996.

[18] Pitoura, E., and G. Samaras, *Data Management for Mobile Computing,* Boston, MA: Kluwer Academic Publishers, 1998.

[19] Barbará, D., and T. Imielinski, "Sleepers and Workaholics: Caching Strategies in Mobile Environments (Extended Version)," *VLDB J.,* Vol. 4, No. 4, 1995.

[20] Si, A., and H. V. Leong, "Adaptive Caching and Refreshing in Mobile Databases," *Personal Technologies,* Sept. 1997.

[21] Zenel, B., and D. Duchamp, "A General Purpose Proxy Filtering Mechanism Applied to the Mobile Environment," *Proc. 3rd Annual ACM/IEEE Intl. Conf. on Mobile Computing and Networking,* Sept. 1997.

[22] Elmasri, R., and S. B. Navathe, *Fundamentals of Database Systems,* 3rd ed., Reading, MA: Addison-Wesley, 2000.

[23] Pitoura, E., and B. Barghava, "Building Information Systems for Mobile Environments," *Proc. 3rd Intl. Conf. on Information and Knowledge Management,* Washington, DC, Nov. 1994.

[24] Terry, D., et al., "Session Guarantees for Weakly Consistent Replicated Data," *Proc. Conf. Parallel and Distributed Computing,* Austin, TX, Oct. 1994.

[25] Barbará, D., and H. García-Molina, "The Demarcation Protocol: A Technique for Maintaining Constraints in Distributed Database Systems," *Proc. ACM SIGMOD Intl. Conf. on Management of Data,* San Jose, CA, May 1995.

[26] Lu, Q., and M. Satyanarayanan, "Improving Data Consistency in Mobile Computing Using Isolation-Only Transactions," *Proc. 5th IEEE HotOS Topics Workshop,* Orcas Island, WA, May 1995.

[27] Barbará, D., "Certification Reports: Supporting Transactions in Wireless Systems," *Proc. 17th Intl. Conf. on Distributed Computing Systems,* Baltimore, MD, May 1997.

[28] Pitoura, E., and B. Barghava, "Revising Transaction Concepts for Mobile Computing," *Proc. 1st IEEE Workshop on Mobile Computing Systems and Applications,* Dec. 1994, pp. 164–168.

[29] Acharya, S., et al., "Broadcast Disks: Data Management for Asymmetric Communications Environments," *Proc. ACM SIGMOD Intl. Conf. on Management of Data,* San Jose, CA, May 1995.

[30] Acharya, S., M. Franklin, and S. Zdonik, "Dissemination-Based Data Delivery Using Broadcast Disks," *Personal Communications,* Vol. 2, No. 6, Dec. 1995.

[31] Imielinski, T., S. Viswanathan, and B. R. Badrinath, "Data on Air: Organization and Access," *IEEE Trans. on Knowledge and Data Engineering,* Vol. 9, No. 3, 1997.

[32] Leong, H. V., and A. Si, "Database Caching Over the Air Storage," *Computer J.,* Vol. 40, No. 7, 1997, pp. 401–415.

[33] Hughes Network Systems DirecPC, http://www.direcpc.com.

[34] Glance, D., "Multicast Support for Data Dissemination in Orbix-Talk," *IEEE Data Engineering Bulletin,* Vol. 19, No. 3, Sept. 1996.

[35] Dao, S., and B. Perry, "Information Dissemination in Hybrid Satellite/Terrestrial Networks," *IEEE Data Engineering Bulletin,* Vol. 19, No. 3, Sept. 1996.

[36] Özsu, M. T., and P. Valduriez, *Principles of Distributed Database Systems,* 2nd ed., Upper Saddle River, NJ: Prentice-Hall, 1999.

[37] Imielinski, T., and B. R. Badrinath, "Querying in Highly Mobile and Distributed Environments," *Proc. 18th Intl. Conf. on Very Large Data Bases,* Vancouver, B.C., Canada, Aug. 1992.

[38] Shekhar, S., A. Fetterer, and D. Lui, "Genesis: An Approach to Data Dissemination in Advanced Traveler Information Systems," *IEEE Data Engineering Bulletin,* Vol. 19, No. 3, Sept. 1996.

[39] Shekhar, S., and D. Lui, "Genesis and Advanced Traveler Information Systems," in T. Imielinski and H. Korth (eds.), *Mobile Computing,* Boston, MA: Kluwer Academic Publishers, 1996, pp. 699–723.

[40] Voelker, G. M., and B. N. Bershad, "MOBISAIC: An Information System for a Mobile Wireless Computing Environment," in T. Imielinski and H. Korth (eds.), *Mobile Computing,* Boston, MA: Kluwer Academic Publishers, 1996, pp. 375–395.

[41] Massari, A., S. Weissman, and P. K. Chrysanthis, "Supporting Mobile Database Access Through Query by Icons," *Distributed and Parallel Databases,* Vol. 4, No. 3, July 1996, pp. 47–68.

[42] Le, M. T., et al., "Software Architecture of the InfoPad System," *Proc. MOBIDATA Conf.,* Rutgers Univ., NJ, Oct. 1994.

[43] Alonso, R., and V. S. Mani, "A Pen-Based Database Interface for Mobile Computers." *Proc. 1st IEEE Workshop on Mobile Computing Systems and Applications,* Vol. 4, No. 3, Santa Cruz, CA, Sept. 1994.

[44] Badrinath, B. R., et al., "Handling Mobile Clients: A Case for Indirect Interaction," *4th Workshop on Workstations Operating Systems,* 1993.

[45] Samaras, G., and A. Pitsillides, "Client/Intercept: A Computational Model for Wireless Environments," *Proc. 4th Intl. Conf. on Telecommunications, ICT'97,* Apr. 1997.

[46] Maes, P., "On Software Agents: Humanizing the Global Computer," *IEEE Internet Computing,* July–Aug. 1997.

[47] Object Management Group, *Mobile Agent System Interoperability Facilities Specification (MASIF),* Nov. 1997, http://www.camb.opengroup.org/RI/MAF/.

[48] Harrison, C., D. Chess, and A. Kershenbaum, "Mobile Agents: Are They a Good Idea?" *Mobile Object Systems: Towards the Programmable Internet,* 1997, pp. 46–48.

[49] Papastavrou, S., G. Samaras, and E. Pitoura, "Mobile Agents for WWW Distributed Database Access," *Proc. Intl. Conf. on Data Engineering,* 1999.

[50] Kovacs, E., K. Röhrle, and M. Reich, "Mobile Agents on the Move—Integrating an Agent System Into the Mobile Middleware," *ACTS Mobile Summit,* Rhodos, Greece, June 1998.

[51]   Hurst, L., and F. Somers, "Mobile Agents—Smart Messages," *Proc. 1st Intl. Workshop on Mobile Agents (MA 97),* 1997.

[52]   Sahai, A., and C. Morin, "Mobile Agents for Enabling Mobile User Aware Applications," *Proc. 2nd Intl. Conf. ACM Autonomous Agents (Agents 98),* 1998.

[53]   Gray, R., D. Rus, and D. Kotz, "Agent TCL: Targeting the Needs of Mobile Computers," *IEEE Internet Computing,* 1997.

[54]   Chess, D., and B. Grosof, "Itinerant Agents for Mobile Computing," *IBM Research Report RC 20010, IBM,* 1995.

[55]   Villate, Y., et al., "Mobile Agents for Providing Mobile Computers With Data Services," *Proc. 9th IFIP/IEEE Intl. Workshop on Distributed Systems: Operations and Management (DSOM 98),* 1998.

Selected Bibliography

The concepts presented in this chapter can be further explored in [17, 18] and in an article by Daniel Barbará, "Mobile Computing and Databases—A Survey" (*IEEE Trans. on Knowledge and Data Engineering,* Vol. 11, No. 1, Jan./Feb. 1999, pp. 108–117). Reference [17] starts with a good introduction to mobile computing and presents a set of projects and systems that studies the new problems related to mobile computing in different computing areas: networking, operating systems, and information systems. In relation to networking, it studies the mobility management, ad hoc networking protocol, and transport-layer issues. With respect to operating systems, it studies operating system support for mobile computing, energy-efficient CPU scheduling, storage alternatives, and disconnected operations in file systems. And in relation to information systems, it presents the problems of wireless access to information, application design, and so forth. Reference [18] concentrates more on the data management issues in mobile computing, although it also has a chapter about system-level support. As well as another good introduction to mobile computing, it presents different software architectures and techniques for information and location management (broadcasting, caching, replication, etc.). It finishes with some interesting case studies. The survey is focused on research in the area of data management in mobile computing and different techniques such as data dissemination over limited bandwidth channels, location-dependent querying of data, advanced interfaces for mobile computers, and techniques to maintain data consistency.

11

Secure Database Systems

Elena Ferrari and Bhavani Thuraisingham

11.1 Introduction

The number of computerized DBs has increased rapidly over the past three decades. The advent of the Internet as well as networking capabilities have made the access to data and information much easier. For example, users can now access large quantities of information in a short space of time. As more and more tools and technologies are developed to access and use the data, there is also an urgent need to protect the data. Many government and industrial organizations have sensitive and classified data that have to be protected. Various other organizations, such as academic institutions, also have sensitive data about their students and employees. As a result, techniques for protecting the data stored in DBMSs have become a top priority.

Over the past three decades, various developments have been made on securing DBs. Much of the early work was on statistical DB security. In the 1970s, as research in relational DBs began, attention was directed toward access control issues. In particular, work on discretionary access control models began. While some work on mandatory security started in the late 1970s, it was not until the Air Force study in 1982 that many of the efforts in multilevel secure DBMSs were initiated [1]. That resulted in the development of various secure DB system prototypes and products. In the new millennium, with the advent of new technologies such as digital libraries, the World Wide

Web, and collaborative computing systems, there is much interest in security, not only by government organizations but also by commercial industry.

This chapter provides an overview of the various developments in secure DB systems and addresses both discretionary and mandatory security issues. The organization of the chapter is as follows. Section 11.2 discusses access control and administration policies. Section 11.3 provides a detailed overview of discretionary security in DB systems. Section 11.4 examines mandatory security in detail, while Section 11.5 deals with secure DB design. Research directions in access control are discussed in Section 11.6.

11.2 Access Control: Concepts and Policies

This section introduces the basic concepts in access control, then discusses discretionary and mandatory access control policies. Finally, it explores administration policies.

11.2.1 Basic Concepts

Access control is usually performed against a set of authorization rules stated by security administrators or users according to some security policies. An authorization rule, in general, specifies that subject s is authorized to exercise privilege p on object o.

Authorization objects are the passive components of the system to which protection from unauthorized accesses should be given. Objects to be considered depend on the underlying data model. For instance, files and directories are objects of an operating system, whereas if we consider a relational DBMS, resources to be protected are relations, views, and attributes. With respect to the object dimension, we can classify access control mechanisms according to the granularity of access control, that is, according to whether it is possible to authorize a user to access only selected components within an object.

Access control models can be further classified according to whether the set of objects to be protected is a flat domain or is organized into a hierarchy. In the latter case, the semantics assigned to the hierarchy depends on the object nature. For instance, consider an object-oriented context. If objects to be protected are classes, the hierarchy represents the inheritance relations among classes. If objects represent class instances, the hierarchy reflects the way objects are organized in terms of other objects.

Authorization subjects are the entities in the system to which authorizations are granted. Subjects can be classified into the following categories: *users*, that is, single individuals connecting to the system; *groups*, that is, sets of users; *roles*, that is, named collections of privileges needed to perform specific activities within the system; and *processes*, which execute programs on behalf of users. These categories are not mutually exclusive. For instance, a model can support roles and groups, or users and processes.

Often, both roles and groups are hierarchically organized. The hierarchy imposed on groups usually reflects the membership of a group to another group. By contrast, the role hierarchy usually reflects the relative position of roles within an organization. The higher the level of a role is in the hierarchy, the higher its position is in the organization.

Processes need system resources to carry on their activities. Generally, processes refer to memory addresses, use the CPU, call other programs, and operate on data. All those resources must be protected from unauthorized accesses. Usually, a process is granted access only to essential resources, that is, resources necessary to the completion of the process's tasks. That limits possible damage deriving from faults of the protection mechanism.

As far as users are concerned, sometimes it would be useful to specify access policies based on user qualifications and characteristics, rather than user identity (e.g., a user is given access to an R-rated video only if he or she is older than 18). This is the case, for instance, in digital library environments. In access control models supporting those possibilities [2, 3], users must provide information, typically about themselves, that allows the access control mechanism to decide whether the access must be authorized or not.

Authorization privileges state the types of operations a subject can exercise on the objects in the system. The set of privileges depends on the resources to be protected. For instance, read, write, and execute privileges are typical of an operating system environment, whereas in a relational DBMS typical privileges are select, insert, update, and delete. Moreover, new environments, such as the digital library environment, are characterized by new access modes, such as usage or copying access rights.

Often, privileges are hierarchically organized, and the hierarchy represents a subsumption relation among privileges. Privileges toward the bottom of the hierarchy are subsumed by privileges toward the top (for instance, the write privilege is at a higher level in the hierarchy with respect to the read privilege, because write subsumes read operations).

11.2.2 Access Control Policies

Access control policies give the criteria to decide whether an access request can be authorized or should be denied. A basic distinction is between *discretionary* and *mandatory* access control policies.

11.2.2.1 Discretionary Access Control Policies

Discretionary access control (DAC) policies govern the access of subjects to objects on the basis of a subject's identity and the authorization rules. Authorization rules state for each subject the privileges it can exercise on each object in the system. When an access request is submitted to the system, the access control mechanism verifies whether there is an authorization rule authorizing the access. If there is such a rule, the access is authorized; otherwise, it is denied. Such mechanisms are discretionary in that they allow subjects to grant other subjects authorization to access the data at their discretion.

Discretionary policies are flexible in that they allow specification of a wide range of access control policies, by using different types of authorizations, from positive and negative authorizations to implicit and explicit authorizations to weak and strong authorizations.

Positive and Negative Authorizations

Most of the existing discretionary authorization models provide only *positive authorizations*, that is, authorizations stating permissions to exercise a given privilege on a particular object. Under such models, whenever a subject tries to access an object, the system checks whether a corresponding positive authorization exists and, only in that case, authorizes the subject to execute the access. The lack of an authorization is interpreted as no authorization. This approach has a major problem in that the lack of a given authorization for a given subject does not prevent the subject from receiving authorization later on. This drawback is overcome by models supporting *negative authorizations*, that is, authorizations expressing explicit denials.

Models that support both positive and negative authorizations can be further categorized according to the policy they adopt to deal with conflicts among authorizations. Conflicts arise when a subject has both a positive and a negative authorization for the same privilege on the same object. Different resolution policies can be adopted. The following are the most widely used:

- *No conflicts.* The presence of a conflict is considered an error. Therefore, whenever a user requires the insertion of a new authorization, the system checks whether the authorization conflicts with other authorizations already present in the system; if it does, the system rejects the insertion of the new authorization.

- *Denials take precedence.* The negative authorization prevails over the positive one.

- *Permissions take precedence.* The positive authorization prevails over the negative one.

- *Nothing takes precedence.* Neither the positive nor the negative authorization takes precedence. The final result is equivalent to the case in which no authorization has actually been specified. This approach differs from the no-conflicts approach in that it allows the presence of conflicting authorizations. However, the simultaneous presence of two conflicting authorizations invalidates both of them.

Strong and Weak Authorizations

Some of the models that support both positive and negative authorizations further distinguish between weak and strong authorizations. Strong authorizations (both positive and negative) cannot be overridden, whereas weak authorizations can be overridden, according to specified rules, by other strong or weak authorizations. In systems that support both strong and weak authorizations, conflicts among authorizations usually are solved according to the following rules:

- Strong authorizations have higher priority than weak authorizations.

- Conflicts among strong authorizations are solved according to the no-conflicts resolution policy.

- Conflicts among weak authorizations are solved according to one of the conflict-resolution polices illustrated above.

Explicit and Implicit Authorizations

A further distinction is among models that support only explicit authorizations and models that support both explicit and implicit authorizations. Implicit authorizations are automatically derived by the system from the set of explicit ones, according to a set of rules. Implicit authorizations can be derived according to two distinct mechanisms:

- A set of *propagation rules* that determine which authorizations are implied by an authorization of a certain type defined for a subject on a given object, based on the hierarchies supported by the model;

- A set of user-defined *derivation rules*, allowing the granting of an authorization to be conditioned to the presence or absence of other authorizations. For instance, a derivation rule can be used to express that a subject can access a given object only if another subject has an explicit denial to access it.

Moreover, different models use different *propagation policies*, that is, they make different choices with respect to whether or how the authorizations propagate along the hierarchies. For instance, consider a model in which roles are hierarchically organized and let *r* be a generic role. The propagation policy must determine which authorizations granted to *r* propagate to roles connected to *r* through the role hierarchy. The most common approaches are the following.

- A positive authorization given to a role *r* propagates to all the roles preceding *r* in the role hierarchy.

- A negative authorization given to a role *r* propagates to all the roles following *r* in the role hierarchy.

In some models privileges also are hierarchically organized, and that hierarchy is used to derive new authorizations, according to propagation rules similar to those illustrated for the role hierarchy. By contrast, for the group hierarchy, the most common approach is that an authorization given to a group propagates to all the members of the group. A similar approach is usually applied to the object hierarchy. In models that support both positive and negative authorizations and implicit and explicit authorizations, the propagation policy should also state what happens in case a subject holds an explicit authorization that conflicts with the propagated authorizations. The most common approaches are:

- *No overriding.* All the authorizations are propagated (regardless of the presence of other conflicting authorizations). Conflicts among authorizations are solved according to one of the conflict resolution policies previously explained.

- *Most specific overrides.* The most specific authorizations (with respect to the defined hierarchies) prevail.

Finally, when the model supports several hierarchies, the derivation policy should also take into account the interactions among the hierarchies. The most common approach is to establish a priority among the hierarchies.

Content-Based Authorizations

Discretionary models can be further categorized according to whether they support content-dependent access control. Content-dependent access control conditions the access to a given object to the content of one or more of its components. For example, in a relational DBMS that supports content-dependent access control, it is possible to authorize a subject to access information only about employees whose salaries are not greater than $30,000.

There are two common approaches according to which content-based access control is enforced. The first is association of a predicate (or a boolean combination of predicates) with the authorization. The predicate expresses the conditions on the object content that must be satisfied to authorize the access. The second approach is to define a view that selects the objects whose content satisfies a given condition and then grant the authorization on the view instead of on the basic objects.

11.2.2.2 Mandatory Access Control Policies

Mandatory access control (MAC) policies specify the access that subjects have to objects based on subject and object classification. This type of security is also referred to as *multilevel security*. DB systems that satisfy multilevel security properties are called multilevel secure DBMSs (MLS/DBMS) or trusted DBMSs (TDBMS). Many of the MLS/DBMSs have been designed based on the Bell and LaPadula policy [4] specified for operating systems. We will first state that policy and then discuss how it has been adopted for DBMSs.

In the Bell and LaPadula policy, subjects are assigned clearance levels, and they can operate at a level up to and including their clearance levels. Objects are assigned sensitivity levels. The clearance levels as well as the sensitivity levels are called *security levels*. The set of security levels forms a partially ordered lattice with Unclassified, Confidential, Secret, TopSecret. The following are the two rules in the policy:

- *Simple security property.* A subject has read access to an object if its security level dominates the level of the object.

- **-property* (read "star property"). A subject has write access to an object if the subject's security level is dominated by that of the object.

These properties also apply to DB systems. However, for DB systems, the *-property is modified to read as follows: A subject has write access to an object if the subject's level is that of the object. That means a subject can modify objects at its own level.

Figure 11.1 summarizes the differences between mandatory and discretionary policies. Under the discretionary policy, an access request is authorized if there exists an authorization rule authorizing the access. By contrast, under the mandatory policy, an access is authorized if a certain relation exists between the security level of the subject requiring the access and the security levels of the object to which access is required (the relation depends on the requested privilege).

Note that mandatory security is mainly about multilevel security. For that reason, from now on this chapter will focus on the multilevel security aspects of mandatory security.

11.2.3 Administration Policies

A further dimension along which access control models can be compared is the administration policies they support. *Administration* refers to the function of granting and revoking authorizations. We classify administration policies according to the following categories [5]:

- *DBA administration.* Under this policy, only the DBA can issue grant and revoke requests on a given object. The DBA administration policy is highly centralized (even though different DBAs can

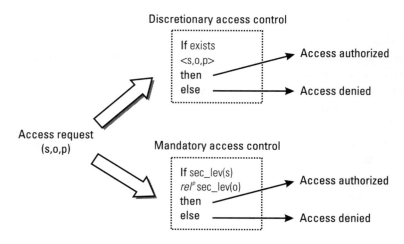

Figure 11.1 Discretionary and mandatory access control.

manage different parts of the DB), and it is seldom used in current DBMSs except in the simplest systems.

- *Object-owner administration.* Under this policy, which is commonly adopted by DBMSs and operating systems, the creator of the object is the owner of the object and is the only one authorized to administer the object.

- *Object "curator" administration.* Under this policy, a subject, not necessarily the creator of the object, is named administrator of the object. Under such policy, even the object creator must be explicitly authorized to access the object.

The second and third administration policies listed above can be further combined with *administration delegation* and *administration transfer.* Those two options are not mutually exclusive. Administration delegation means that the administrator of an object can delegate other subjects the administration function on the object. Delegation can be specified for selected privileges, for example, for only read operations. In most cases, delegation of administration to another subject implies also granting the subject the privilege of accessing the object according to the same privilege specified in the delegation. Most current DBMSs support the administration policy based on the owner administration with delegation. Note that, under the delegation approach, the initial administrator of the object does not lose his or her privilege to administer the object. Therefore, different administrators can grant authorizations on the same object.

Administration transfer, like delegation, has the effect of giving another subject the right to administer a certain object. However, the original administrator loses his or her administration privileges. When dealing with transfer, an important question concerns the authorizations granted by the former administrator. The following two approaches can be adopted:

- *Recursive revoke.* All authorizations granted by the former administrator are recursively revoked.

- *Grantor transfer.* All authorizations granted by the former administrator are kept; however, the new administrator replaces the old one as grantor of the authorizations (and is able to revoke them). The grantor transfer is not recursive. Therefore, if the older administrator has delegated other subjects for administration, those grants are left in place. Only the new administrator becomes their grantor.

Furthermore, transfer can be *with acceptance* or *without acceptance*. Acceptance means that the user to whom the administration (or ownership) is transferred must have explicitly accepted taking on the administration responsibility. Transfer without acceptance means that such explicit acceptance is not required.

A further possibility is the *joint administration* of data objects. Joint administration means that several subjects are jointly responsible for administering an object. Joint administration can be used in both the object "curator" administration and object owner administration policies. Joint administration is particularly useful in computer-supported cooperative work (CSCW) applications where subjects typically cooperate to produce a complex data object (a document, a book, a piece of software, a very large system integration (VLSI) circuit). In such applications, each subject in the working group is responsible for producing a component of the complex object; therefore, no single subject is the owner of the entire object. Authorization for a subject to access a data object, administered under the joint administration policy, requires that all the administrators of the object issue a grant request.

Figure 11.2 gives a taxonomy of the administration policies discussed in this section. Bold arrows denote mutually exclusive administration options for the same object, whereas nonbold arrows denote nonmutually exclusive administration policies.

11.3 Discretionary Access Control Models and Systems

This section describes DAC models and systems. Discretionary models can be categorized according to several criteria. This section classifies those models according to the DBMSs for which they are developed into three broad categories: authorization models for relational DBMSs, authorization models for object DBMSs, and authorization models for active DBMSs. We do not consider here other advanced DBMSs, like deductive DBMSs, because the research in security models is still in its early stages. Also, due to lack of space, we do not report here models such as the Harrison-Ruzzo-Ullman access matrix model or the Take-Grant model (we refer the interested reader to [6]

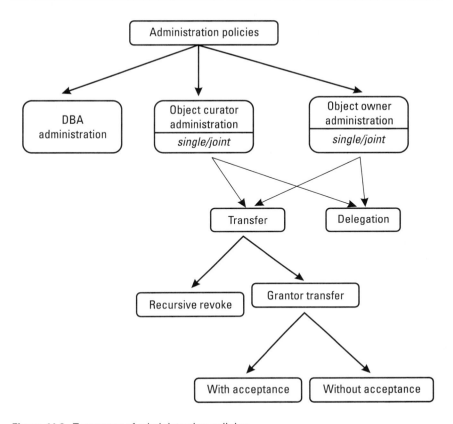

Figure 11.2 Taxonomy of administration policies.

for details). Those models, which were developed mainly for the protection of an operating system environment, greatly inspired most of the discretionary models developed for DBMSs.

11.3.1 Authorization Models for Relational DBMSs

This section reviews some of the authorization models developed for relational DBMSs. It starts by describing the System R authorization model, then surveys some of its extensions. The System R authorization model is an important milestone in the history of authorization models [7]. The importance of the System R authorization model is based on the fact that the model has served as a basis for the development of most of the authorization mechanisms provided as part of commercial DBMSs.

11.3.1.1 The System R Authorization Model

In the System R authorization model, objects to be protected are represented by tables and views on which subjects can exercise several privileges. Privileges supported by the model include *select*, to select tuples from a table, *update*, to modify tuples in a table, *insert* and *delete*, to add and delete tuples from a table, and *drop*, to delete an entire table. Groups and roles are not supported. The System R authorization model supports decentralized administration facilities. Whenever a subject creates a table, it receives the own privilege on it. The owner of a table can exercise all the privileges on the table as well as grant or revoke other subjects all the privileges (except drop) on the table. Moreover, the owner can grant authorizations with the *grant option*. If a subject owns an authorization for a privilege on a table with the grant option, it can grant the privilege, as well as the grant option, to other subjects.

The System R authorization model enforces recursive revocation: Whenever a subject revokes an authorization on a table from another user, all the authorizations that the revokee had granted because of the revoked authorization are removed. The revocation is iteratively applied to all the subjects that received the access authorization from the revokee.

11.3.1.2 Extensions to the System R Authorization Model

The System R authorization model has been extended in several directions, which is graphically illustrated in Figure 11.3. Wilms and Lindsay [8] have extended it to deal with group management capabilities. In the model of Wilms and Lindsay, authorizations can be granted to groups of users, as well as to single users. Authorizations granted to groups apply to all the members of the group. Moreover, in [8] the System R authorization model has been extended for the distributed DBMS System R∗. Bertino and Haas [9] further extended the System R∗ authorization model to deal with distributed views.

Additional extensions to the System R authorization model have been proposed by Bertino et al. in [10]. The first extension concerns a new type of revoke operation, called *noncascading revocation*: Whenever a subject revokes a privilege on a table to another subject, all the authorizations the subject may have granted by using the privilege received by the revoker are restated as if they had been granted by the revoker. Then the cascading revocation is applied to the resulting state. The second extension concerns negative authorizations. The authorization mechanism of System R, like those of most DBMSs, does not allow explicit denials to be expressed. The second extension proposed in [10] concerns the support for negative authorizations.

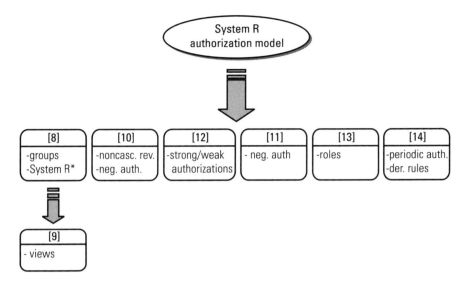

Figure 11.3 Extensions to the System R authorization model.

Conflicts between positive and negative authorizations are solved according to the denials-take-precedence policy. Thus, whenever a subject has both a positive and a negative authorization on the same object for the same privilege, it is prevented from accessing the object.

Negative authorizations are also supported by the SeaView model [11], by means of a special privilege denoted as *null*. A subject having the null privilege on a table cannot exercise any access on the table. Thus, it is not possible to selectively deny a subject accesses to a table. For instance, it is not possible to specify that a subject is authorized to read a table and, at the same time, it has the denial to write on that table.

In [12] a more flexible approach to deal with authorization conflicts is proposed in which negative authorizations do not always override positive ones. The model in [12] is based on the concept of strong and weak authorizations. Authorization subjects can be either single users or groups. Authorizations given to members of a group are considered as prevailing with respect to the authorizations given to the group. Conflicts among contrasting authorizations such that neither one of them overrides the other are solved in different ways according to the type (i.e., strong versus weak) of the authorizations. Conflicts between a weak and a strong authorization are always solved in favor of the strong authorization. Conflicts between strong authorizations are solved according to the no-conflicts policy. By contrast, conflicts between weak authorizations are solved according to the nothing-takes-precedence principle.

A further extension to the System R authorization model deals with the support for role-based authorizations [13]. Under role-based models, all authorizations needed to perform a certain activity are granted to the role associated with that activity rather than directly to users. In such models, user access to objects is mediated by roles; each user is authorized to play certain roles and, on the basis of that role, can perform accesses on the objects.

Finally, a recent extension is related to the temporal duration of authorizations. In many organizations, authorizations given to subjects must be tailored to the pattern of their activities within the organization. Therefore, subjects must be given access authorizations to data *only* for the time periods in which they are expected to need the data. An example of policy with temporal requirements is that "part-time employees can modify a given file every working day between 9 A.M. and 1 P.M." Authorization models of current DBMSs are not able to directly support such types of temporal constraints. The only way is to implement them as code in application programs. Such an approach makes it difficult to verify and modify the access control policies and to provide any assurance that the policies are actually enforced. An authorization model overcoming such drawbacks has been proposed [14]. Under such a model, each authorization has a temporal constraint that denotes the set of time periods in which the authorization holds. When such periods expire, the authorization is automatically revoked without requiring any explicit revoke operations. In addition, the model provides deductive temporal rules to derive new authorizations based on the presence or absence of other authorizations in specific periods of time.

11.3.2 Authorization Models for Object DBMSs

Object-oriented and recent object-relational DBMSs (in what follows, we refer to both kinds of systems as object DBMSs, ODBMSs for short) are today some of the most promising research directions in the DB area [15]. A reason for their success is that they are well suited for advanced applications, like CAD/CAM, multimedia, and cartography applications, because such applications require data models richer than the relational model. As far as authorization is concerned, an ODBMS is characterized by protection requirements different from those of traditional (i.e., relational) systems. This makes conventional authorization models for relational DBMSs not adequate for ODBMSs [16]. Despite the growing interest in ODBMSs, the research on authorization models for ODBMSs is still in its early stages. Indeed, although several proposals exist [17–23], of the existing ODBMSs, only Orion [23] and Iris [17] have an authorization model comparable to those of relational DBMSs.

11.3.2.1 The Orion Authorization Model

The Orion authorization model [17] supports positive and negative authorizations, as well as weak and strong authorizations. Strong authorizations always have higher priority than weak authorizations. Authorizations are granted to roles instead of to single users, and a user is authorized to exercise a privilege on an object, if there exists a role possessing the authorization and the user is authorized to play such role. Roles, objects, and privileges are organized into hierarchies to which a set of propagation rules applies. Propagation rules allow the derivation of implicit authorizations, according to the following criteria.

- If a role has an authorization to access an object, all the roles that precede it in the role hierarchy have the same authorization.

- If a role has a negative authorization to access an object, all the roles that follow it in the role hierarchy have the same negative authorization.

Similar propagation rules are defined for privileges. Finally, propagation rules on objects allow authorizations on an object to be derived from the authorizations on objects semantically related to it. For example, the authorization to read a class implies the authorization to read all its instances.

A consistency condition is defined on propagation rules, which requires that, given a weak or a strong authorization, the application of the propagation rules supported by the model to the authorization does not generate conflicting authorizations. Moreover, a further property is required: For any weak authorization (either positive or negative), there must not exist a strong conflicting authorization. The system ensures that this property is always satisfied. In particular, if the insertion of a weak authorization would not satisfy the above property, it is rejected. By contrast, if the insertion of a strong authorization would not satisfy the property, the strong authorization is inserted and all the weak authorizations causing the nonsatisfaction of the property are removed.

11.3.2.2 Extensions to the Orion Authorization Model

Bertino and Weigand [18] have proposed several extensions to the Orion authorization model. The model of Bertino and Weigand has several differences with respect to the model proposed in [17]. In the extended model new authorization types have been introduced and some propagation rules have been revised. However, the main extension concerns the introduction of content based access control. Another extension to the Orion model has been recently proposed by Bertino et al. in [19]. The main differences between the Orion model and the model in [19] can be summarized as follows. Reference [19] supports both roles and groups with a clear functional distinction between them. Moreover, [19] supports the possibility of granting authorizations to a single user, whereas in the Orion model authorizations can be specified only for roles. In the Orion model implicit authorizations can be derived only along the role, object, and privilege hierarchies, whereas in [19] authorizations can also be derived through user-defined derivation rules. Another difference is related to the concept of strong and weak authorizations. In the Orion model, strong authorizations cannot be overridden. This implies that the insertion of a strong authorization is rejected by the system if it conflicts with an existing strong authorization. This clearly prevents strong authorizations to be granted through derivation rules. To avoid these shortcomings, in [19] an approach is proposed that allows strong authorizations to be overridden by other positive or negative strong authorizations, under specific circumstances.

11.3.2.3 The Iris Authorization Model

Another relevant proposal is the authorization model developed for Iris [20]. In Iris, both attributes and methods are represented as functions. The only privilege supported by the model is the *call* privilege: A subject owning the call privilege on a function is authorized to call that function. The subject who creates a function is the owner of the function and automatically receives the call privilege on it. Moreover, the owner of a function can grant other subjects the call privilege on the function. Call privileges can be granted with the grant option, allowing the subject that receives the privilege to grant it to others. The Iris authorization model allows a privilege to be granted or revoked on both a per-group and per-user basis. A user can belong to several groups. Moreover, groups can be nested. Derived functions can be defined in terms of other functions. The Iris authorization model supports two approaches for the protection of derived functions. Under the approach called *static authorization,* the subject requesting the execution of a derived function must have the call privilege only on the derived function. In the other approach, called *dynamic authorization*, the caller must have the call privilege both on the derived function and on all the functions executed by the derived function. On creation of a derived function, the creator must specify which of the two approaches must be used to check the execution requests on the function. In both cases, the creator of the function must have the call privilege on all the functions that compose the function it creates.

The Iris authorization model also provides two novel constructs to enforce access control: *guard functions* and *proxy functions*. Guard functions are a means to express preconditions on the call of a function and are therefore used to restrict the access to a given function. The function to which a guard function refers is called the *target function*. A target function is executed only if the corresponding guard function is evaluated successfully. Conditions are imposed to guarantee that the evaluation of expressions involving guards will terminate. The main advantage of guard functions is that they restrict the access to a function without requiring changing the function code. Proxy functions provide different implementations of a specific function for different subjects (or groups of subjects). When a function is invoked, the appropriate proxy function is executed instead of the original one.

11.3.3 Authorization Models for Active DBMSs

Active DBs are characterized by a rule system that enables the DBMS to react to events by triggering rules. The rules describe the operations to be automatically executed on the DB on the occurrence of particular events or the satisfaction of given conditions. As an example of an authorization model for active DBMSs, the following subsections describe authorization facilities supported by the Starbust system [24].

11.3.3.1 The Starbust Authorization Model

Starbust is a prototype extensible relational DB system developed at the IBM Almaden Research Center. Starbust is characterized by a rule language fully integrated in the system. The authorization model of Starbust supports a hierarchy of privilege types that can be exercised on DB objects, where higher types subsume lower types. Examples of privilege types are *control*, which subsumes all the other privileges, *write*, *alter*, and *attach*. When a table is created, the owner receives the control privilege on the table, which implies the possibility of granting and revoking all the other privileges. Similarly, a hierarchy of privilege types for rules is defined, whose top element is *control* and whose bottom elements are *activate* and *deactivate*. As with tables, the rule creator receives the control privilege on the rules he or she creates. The creation and modification of rules are governed by the following constraints.

- The creator of a rule on a table T must have both the *attach* and the *read* privilege on T.

- The condition and action statements of the created rule are checked against the creator privileges. If the condition or action part of the rule contains statements that the creator is not allowed to execute, the create operation is not authorized.

- Subjects requesting the deletion of a rule r on a table T must have either the *control* privilege on r or the *attach* and the *control* privileges on T.

- Subjects requesting the modification of a rule must have the *alter* privilege on the rule.

- Subjects requesting the activation/deactivation of a rule must have the *activation/deactivation* privilege on the rule.

11.3.4 Comparative Analysis of Authorization Models

Table 11.1 is a comparative analysis of the authorization models considered in Section 11.3.3. The second column in the table lists, for each of the considered models, the granularity at which access control can be enforced. The third column specifies which subjects the model supports (e.g., roles, groups); the fourth column indicates which types of authorizations each model supports (e.g., positive, negative, weak, strong); and the fifth column deals with administration policies. The last column illustrates which is the semantic of the revoke operation for those models supporting delegation of administration.

11.3.5 Discretionary Access Control in Commercial DBMSs

In this section, we describe how DAC is enforced in the object-relational DBMSs Oracle and DB2, and in the object-oriented DBMS GemStone. Note that the products discussed here and in the following sections may be trademarks of various corporations. We do not mention trademarks in this chapter.

11.3.5.1 Oracle

In Oracle, privileges can be granted to either users or roles. Roles are hierarchically organized, and a role acquires the privileges of all the roles that are in

Table 11.1
Comparison of Discretionary Authorization Models

Approach	Objects	Subjects	Types	Administration Policies	Revoke
Bertino, Bettini, Ferrari, and Samarati	Not defined	Users, groups	Positive/negative, implicit	Owner administration, delegation	Recursive
Bertino, Buccafurri, Ferrari, and Rullo	Class instances	Users, groups, roles	Positive/negative, strong/weak, implicit	DBA administration	—
Bertino, Jajodia, and Samarati	Tables	Users, groups	Positive/negative, strong/weak, implicit	Owner administration, delegation	Recursive
Bertino and Weigand	Classes, class instances, sets of class instances, object components*	Roles	Positive/negative, strong/weak, implicit, content-based	DBA administration	—
Bertino, Samarati, and Jajodia	Tables, views[†]	Users, groups	Positive/negative, content-based	Owner administration, delegation	Recursive, noncascading
Bruggemann	Classes, class instances	Users, roles[‡]	Positive/negative, implicit	DBA administration	—
Fernandez	Classes, class instances, sets of attributes	Users, groups	Positive/negative, implicit, content-based	Delegation	Recursive
Iris	Functions	Users, groups	Positive, implicit	Owner administration[§], delegation	Not defined

Table 11.1 (continued)

Approach	Objects	Subjects	Types	Administration Policies	Revoke
Kelter	Class instances	Users, groups	Positive/negative, implicit	Owner administration	Not defined
Orion	DB, classes, class instances, sets of class instances, object components*	Roles	Positive/negative, strong/weak, implicit	DBA administration	—
SeaView	DB, tables	Users, groups	Positive/negative, implicit	Delegation	Noncascading
Starbust	Tables, rules	Users, groups	Positive, implicit	Owner administration	Not defined
System R	Tables, attributes, views[†]	Users	Positive, content-based	Owner administration, delegation	Recursive
Wilms	Tables, attributes, views[†]	Users, groups	Positive, content-based	Owner administration, delegation	Recursive

*Object components can be attributes, methods, or values.
[†]Views are used to support content-based access control.
[‡]More precisely, [21] provides the notion of subject class, to model subjects with the same authorization requirements.
[§]The model also supports a set of DBAs that hold privileges on each function in the system.

lower positions in the hierarchy. A user can be authorized to play several roles. Each role can be, at a given time, either enabled or disabled. The initialization parameter MAX_ENABLED_ROLES specifies the maximum number of roles a user can enable. With each role, a password can be associated to prevent unauthorized use of the privileges granted to the role. A set of predefined roles is provided, which can be modified as any other role in an Oracle DB. When a subject creates a role, the role is automatically granted to the creator with the *admin* option, which allows the subject to grant or revoke the role to or from any subject, with or without the admin option, and to alter or drop the role. Oracle also supports the special group PUBLIC, accessible to every subject. Privileges and roles can be assigned to PUBLIC to be accessible by everyone.

The privileges of an Oracle DB can be divided into two categories: *system privileges* and *object privileges*. System privileges allow subjects to perform a particular systemwide action or an action on a particular type of objects. More than 60 distinct system privileges are provided. Examples of system privileges are the privilege to delete the tuples of *any* table in a DB or to create a cluster. Because system privileges are powerful, they usually are available only to DBAs or application developers. Like roles, system privileges also can be granted with the admin option. If a subject has a system privilege with the admin option, it can grant or revoke system privileges to other subjects. Any subject with the admin option for a system privilege or a role can revoke the privilege or the role from any other subject. The subject does not have to be the one that originally granted the privilege or role. When a system privilege is revoked, there may be cascading effects, depending on the type of system privilege. If the revoked system privilege is related to a DDL operation, no cascading effects take place. By contrast, cascading effects are caused by the revocation of a system privilege related to a DML operation.

Object privileges allow subjects to perform a particular action on a particular object in the DB. The privilege to delete or insert tuples in a particular table is an example of object privilege. When a subject creates an object in its schema, it automatically receives all the object privileges on the created object as well as the right to grant those privileges to other subjects. If the grant includes the grant option, the subject receiving the privilege can further grant the privilege to other subjects. Privileges granted to a role cannot be granted with the grant option. Object privileges can be revoked only by the subjects that have granted them. Revocation of object privilege is recursive.

11.3.5.2 DB2

In DB2, subjects can be either single users or groups. The access control facilities provided by DB2 relies on two main concepts: *authorities* and *privileges*. The concept of authority is similar to that of Oracle system privileges in that an authority is a right to perform a particular administrative operation. Authorities usually are granted to particular groups rather than to single users. Several authorities are supported by DB2. The highest authority is the system administrator authority, usually held by a group, whose members have the ownership of all the DB2 resources and the ability to execute any DB2 command. Other authorities include the system maintenance authority, which conveys the right to perform maintenance operations, such as starting and stopping the DB2 server; the DB administration authority, which allows subjects to access and modify all the objects in a DB and to grant other users access authorizations and authorities; and the CREATETAB authority, which conveys the right to create tables in a DB.

Privileges are similar to the Oracle object privileges. They are rights to perform a certain action on a particular object in a DB. Privileges can be granted to both users and groups. When a subject creates an object, such as a table or a view, it receives the control privilege on it. The control privilege subsumes all the other privileges supported by DB2 and allows the possibility of granting any applicable privilege on the considered object to other users or groups. When a privilege on a table or view is revoked, all the privileges derived from the revoked privilege are recursively revoked.

11.3.5.3 GemStone

GemStone provides a simple authorization model. Authorizations can be granted both to single users and groups. The only type of authorization unit is the *segment*. A segment groups together a set of objects with the same level of protection. That implies, for instance, that if a subject has the authorization to read a segment, then it can read all the objects within the segment. Each segment has only one owner, which can grant and revoke authorizations on the segment. A default segment, whose identifier is stored in the subject profile, is associated with each subject. Normally, an object is stored into the default segment of its creator. A subject can transfer objects from one segment to another and can create new segments, given the appropriate authorizations. Transferring an object from one segment to another is a means to change the object accessibility.

Privileges that can be granted on a segment are of two distinct types: the *#read* privilege, which allows a subject to read all the objects in a segment, and the *#write* privilege, which allows a subject to modify all the objects in a segment. GemStone also supports the special privilege *#none*, which, when granted to a subject, deletes authorizations.

11.4 Multilevel Security in Database Systems

This section describes the multilevel security aspects of mandatory security for DB systems. The first part focuses mainly on relational systems. Then we provide an overview of secure object systems. Note that several other significant developments have been made in multilevel security for DB systems, including inference problems, secure concurrency control, and recovery algorithms, and multilevel security for distributed, heterogeneous, and federated DB systems. This chapter does not discuss all those developments. For details on inference problems, we refer the reader to [25]; for secure concurrency control, [26]; for secure distributed, heterogeneous, and federated DBs, [27].

11.4.1 Multilevel Relational Data Model

In a multilevel DB, not all the data are assigned the same security level. If such a DB is based on the relational model, the objects of classification may be the entire DB, relations, tuples, attributes, or data elements. Access to those objects is governed by the mandatory policy discussed in Section 11.2. A multilevel DBMS should protect the multilevel DB from unauthorized access or modification by subjects cleared at different security levels. A multilevel relational DB represents the multilevel DB as a set of relations. The corresponding model is called a multilevel relational data model.

A goal of a multilevel relational DB designer is to represent multiple versions of the same entity, action, or event at different security levels without violating the integrity or security rules. One of the mechanisms being proposed to represent multiple versions of an entity at different security levels is *polyinstantiation.* Polyinstantiation enables two tuples with the same primary key to exist in a relational DB at different security levels. However, having two tuples with the same primary key violates the entity-integrity property of the standard relational data model. If polyinstantiation is not supported, then it is possible for signaling channels to occur. Consider the following example. EMP is a relation with attributes SS#, NAME, SALARY, and DEPT#. Let SS# be its primary key. Suppose a subject enters the tuple (000, John, 60K, 120) first into EMP. Later suppose an Unclassified subject enters the tuple (000, John, 20K, 120) into EMP. If the tuple is accepted, then it is a polyinstantiated tuple. If the tuple is rejected due to entity-integrity violation, then the actions of a Secret subject have interfered with those of an Unclassified one.

Recently there has been much discussion on polyinstantiation. Some argue that polyinstantiation is necessary if we are to design multilevel DB systems with higher levels of assurance (see, e.g., [11]). Some argue that it is important to maintain the integrity of the DB and that polyinstantiation violates the integrity (see, e.g., [28]). Some have used partial polyinstantiation together with security constraint enforcement in their design (see, e.g., [29]). An interesting operational example that shows the disastrous effects of polyinstantiation is given in the paper by Wiseman [30]. Even among those who support polyinstantiation, there has been much discussion of the correct update semantics to use. A logic for formalizing concepts in multilevel relations that supports polyinstantiation is given in [31]. Various systems discussed here have proposed various types of multilevel data models. They all satisfy the security properties discussed in Section 11.2. The entities of classification are mostly the tuples. Polyinstantiation is supported in most of the models.

11.4.2 Architectures

This section describes various access control models that have been developed for MLS/DBMSs. While DBMSs must deal with many of the same security concerns as trusted operating systems (identification and authentication, access control, auditing), there are characteristics of DBMSs that introduce security difficulties over and above those that could be handled by traditional operating system security techniques. For example, objects in DBMSs tend to be of multiple sizes and can be of very fine granularity. That contrasts with operating systems in which the granularity tends to be coarse and uniform (e.g., files or segments). Because of the variety of granularity in TDBMSs, the objects on which MAC and DAC may be performed may differ. In trusted operating systems, MAC and DAC tend to be performed on the same objects.

There are also some obvious functional differences between operating systems and DBMSs, which affect how the two deal with security. Operating systems tend to deal with subjects attempting to access some objects. DBMSs are used to share data between users and to provide users with a means to relate different data objects. Also, DBMSs generally are dependent on operating systems to provide resources and isolation for the DBMS. Therefore,

TDBMS designs often must take into account how the operating system deals with security.

The differences between DBMSs and operating system functional and security requirements mean that the traditional approaches to developing secure systems that worked so well for operating systems need to be modified for TDBMSs. Currently, no single architectural approach has been agreed on or employed in the development of MLS/DBMSs. A variety of approaches to designing and building MLS/DBMSs have been proposed. Taxonomies for MAC have been proposed (see, e.g., [32, 33]). This chapter merges the various ideas proposed as well as uses the notes from tutorials the authors have given (see, e.g., [34]).

11.4.2.1 Single-Kernel Architecture

The single-kernel approach, also known as the Hinke-Schaefer approach, is characterized by having the underlying trusted operating system perform all the access control mediation. No access control mediation is performed by the DBMS. The DBMS objects (e.g., records) are aligned with the underlying operating system objects (e.g., files). Thus, Secret records are stored in Secret files, TopSecret records are stored in TopSecret files, and so on. Under this approach, no single DBMS has access to all the data in the DB; rather, there is an instantiation of the DBMS for each security level. The advantages of this approach are its simplicity and high degree of security. The disadvantage is that performance is likely to degrade significantly as the number of security levels increases (see, e.g., the work of Graubart in [32]).

11.4.2.2 Distributed Architecture

Under the distributed approach, there are multiple untrusted (in terms of MAC) back-end DBMS machines, and a single trusted front-end machine to which all the untrusted back ends communicate. There are two primary versions of this architecture. One version has only a single level of data per machine. Thus, one machine would have only Secret data, another would have TopSecret data, and so on. We refer to this version as the *partitioned approach*. Under the second version, lower level data are replicated on the various machines. Thus, the Secret machine will have the Secret data, the Confidential data, and the Unclassified data; the Confidential machine will have the Confidential data and the Unclassified data; and so forth. We refer to this second version as the *replicated approach*.

Under the partitioned approach, the trusted front end is responsible for ensuring that queries are directed to the correct machines and for performing joins on the data passed back by the various machines. Because the query itself could contain information classified higher than some of the target machines (and because the trusted front end would be unable to ascertain if that is the case), this partitioned approach suffers from a potentially high signaling channel, as queries are sent to machines that are operating at levels lower than the user. For the replicated approach, the trusted front end ensures that the query is directed to a single machine. Because only machines operating at the same level as the user are queried, replicated approach does not suffer from the signaling channel problem. Nor does the replicated approach require that the front end perform any of the join operations. However, because the data are replicated, the trusted front end must ensure consistency of the data maintained in the various machines.

The advantage of the distributed approaches is that they provide high-assurance separation between the data, and performance is likely to be independent of the number of security levels. The disadvantage is the high cost in hardware (one machine per security level) and the physical space requirements for the placement of the machines.

11.4.2.3 Trusted-Subject Architecture

The trusted-subject approach, also sometimes called a dual kernel–based architecture [32], does not rely on the underlying operating system to perform access control mediation. Under this approach, the DBMS performs its own access mediation for objects under its control. Thus, access to DBMS records is mediated by the TDBMS. The architecture is referred to as a trusted-subject approach because the access mediation provided by the TDBMS is not independent from the access mediation of the operating system and must act as a trusted subject to ensure that no violation of the overall security policy occurs. Under the trusted-subject approach, a single DBMS has access to all the data in the DB. The advantages of this architecture are that it can provide good security and that its performance is independent from the number of security levels involved. Its disadvantage is that the DBMS code that performs access mediation must be trusted, and often such code is both large and complex. Another disadvantage with this approach is that the evaluation of such architectures may require reevaluation of part or all of the underlying trusted operating systems on which the DBMS is built.

11.4.2.4 Integrity Lock Architecture

The integrity-lock approach employs an untrusted DBMS back end with access to all the data in the DB; an untrusted front end, which communicates with the user; and a trusted front end, which makes use of encryption technology (see, e.g., [35]). It is essential that the untrusted components are isolated from each other so there is no communication between the two without the intervention of the trusted filter. This isolation can be provided either by physical isolation (the front and back ends can be on two different machines) or by logical isolation via the MAC mechanism of the underlying operating system. Assuming the latter approach is employed, the back end should be maintained at system high. Multiple instantiations of the front end would be maintained, with one instantiation for each user level. The trusted filter exists at the same level as the back end.

Under this approach, every tuple that is inserted into the DB has associated with it a sensitivity label and a cryptographic checksum, employing a CBC algorithm (both supplied by the trusted front end). The sensitivity label should also be encrypted, but the data tuple itself remains unencrypted. For insertions, the untrusted DBMS back end takes the data tuple and associated label and checksum and places them in the DB, as it would with any other data tuple. On retrieval, the back end retrieves the data tuples and passes them to the trusted front end, which validates the label and the checksum. If the label and the checksum satisfy the validation check, the tuple is passed to the user or any waiting untrusted processes.

The advantage of this approach is that a minimal amount of additional trusted code is required for the TDBMS, and performance is independent of the number of security levels involved. The disadvantage is that this approach is subject to an inference threat, which occurs because the untrusted back end is able to view classified data, encode it as a series of unclassified data tuples, and pass the encoded data tuples to the trusted front end. Because the data tuples would all be unclassified, the trusted filter will allow the tuples to be passed on to a subject not cleared for classified data.

11.4.2.5 Extended-Kernel Architecture

The extended-kernel approach is an extension of the single-kernel approach. The underlying operating system is still employed to provide the basic MAC and DAC mediation. However, the TDBMS will supplement this access mediation by providing some additional access control mediation. Thus, if the operating system provides standard content-independent DAC on files, the TDBMS might provide context-dependent DAC on views. This approach differs from the trusted-subject approach because the policies enforced by the TDBMS are not dependent on those of the operating system and can only further restrict the access restrictions imposed by the operating system. This approach suffers from the same performance difficulties of the single-kernel approach. Also, it is likely to be somewhat complex. However, because it provides more sophisticated access control mechanisms, it is likely to be capable of addressing some additional real-world access control needs.

11.4.3 Prototypes

This section examines two prominent research prototypes that were designed in the late 1980s: SRI's SeaView and Honeywell's LOCK Data Views (LDV). Both are based on the extended-kernel approach. Many of the MLS/DBMS products discussed in this chapter have been heavily influenced by those two systems. Other MLS/DBMSs designed in the 1980s and the early 1990s include ASD-Views by TRW, integrity-lock prototypes by MITRE, Secure Distributed Database Systems by Unisys, SINTRA by Naval Research Laboratory, and SWORD by Defense Research Agency. Note that in describing SeaView and LDV, we discuss the design of the initial systems.

Table 11.2 classifies the various prototypes and products according to the design on which they are based. A discussion of some of these prototypes and products is given in the following sections. Since most multilevel object models also include policies for method execution, we have not considered them in this classification. There is no taxonomy yet for multilevel object systems.

11.4.3.1 SeaView

SeaView, which is an MLS relational DDBMS hosted on GEMSOS Trusted Computing Base (TCB), addresses the multilevel secure needs by enabling individuals possessing a range of clearances to create, share, and manipulate relational DBs that contain information spanning multiple sensitivity levels. Its designers' goal was to develop a high-assurance MLS/DBMS. The project

Table 11.2
Classification of Products and Prototypes Based on Their Architecture

Architecture	Prototypes and Products
Single kernel	Hinke-Schaefer, SeaView, Oracle (based on Hinke-Schaefer)
Distributed	Unisys's Secure Distributed Database, Naval Research Laboratory's SINTRA
Trusted subject	TRW's ASD-Views, Secure Sybase, Trusted Oracle (based on trusted subject), Trusted Informix
Integrity lock	MITRE prototypes, TRUDATA
Extended kernel	Honeywell's LDV

addressed some difficult issues such as polyinstantiation, inference, and aggregation. In addition, algorithms for decomposing multilevel relations into single-level relations as well as recombining the single-level relations to form a multilevel relation were developed. The relational query language SQL was extended to MSQL to include multilevel security constructs. Since the project began in 1985, it has attained much prominence, and SeaView is now being regarded by many as one of the key MLS/DBMS prototypes to be developed. We first provide an overview of SeaView and then discuss its security model, which is unique. This discussion of SeaView is obtained from [5].

To obtain high assurance, SeaView design is based on the *reference monitor* concept. Subjects have the view of multilevel relations, which are relations with data at different security levels. A subject at level L could have a view of a multilevel relation with data classified at or below level L. A multilevel relation is stored in one or more single-level relations. The single-level relations are transparent to the subject. A single-level relation is stored in a file (or segment) at the same level, and the reference monitor controls access to the single-level files. Implementing multilevel relations as virtual relations (or views) enables subjects to issue insert, delete, and update requests on those views. Appropriate algorithms are then used to translate the update on views to an update on the base relations, which are single level. An advantage of the SeaView approach is that the labels of the data elements need not be stored. That is because the level of the file in which a data element is stored is the level of the data element. However, if many security levels are to be supported, there will be considerable performance impact on query processing. That is because several files will have to be accessed to form a view of a multilevel relation.

Each DB operation is carried out by a single-level subject. When a subject at level L issues a request, a DB system subject operating at level L will process the subject's request. The designers believe that having single-level subjects carry out the DB operations will considerably reduce disclosure risks. However, with this approach there must be a DB server operating at each security level supported by the system, that is, multiple DB servers share the same logical DB.

The SeaView security model consists of two components: the MAC model and the TCB model. The MAC model defines the mandatory security policy. The basic constructs are subjects, objects, and access classes. Each subject is assigned a readclass and a writeclass. A subject can read an object if the subject's readclass dominates the access class of the object. A subject can write into an object if the object's access class dominates the writeclass of the subject. The TCB model defines discretionary security and supporting policies for multilevel relations, views, and integrity constraints, among others. The data model utilized by SeaView is a multilevel relational data model. It supports element-level classification. Polyinstantiation is the mechanism introduced by SeaView to handle cover stories as well as signaling channels. For example, in a multilevel world, it is possible to have multiple views of the same entity at different security levels. In the SeaView model, the two views may be represented by, say, two tuples with the same primary key but at different security levels. The primary key constraint is not violated because, in the multilevel relational data model proposed by SeaView, a modified entity integrity property is defined. Additional integrity properties such as referential integrity and polyinstantiation integrity are also defined in the SeaView model.

11.4.3.2 LOCK Data Views

The LOCK Data Views (LDV) system, which is an MLS relational DBMS hosted on LOCK TCB, addresses the multilevel secure needs by enabling individuals possessing a range of clearances to create, share, and manipulate relational DBs that contain information spanning multiple sensitivity levels. In LDV, the relational query language SQL is enhanced with constructs for formulating security assertions. Those security assertions serve to imply sensitivity labels for all atomic values, contexts, and aggregations in a DB. The labeled data are partitioned across security levels, assigned to containers with dominating security markings or levels, and may only flow upward in level unless authorized otherwise. The ability of LDV to perform in this manner is a function of its design and the operating system on which it is hosted. The design of LDV is unique because it is based on LOCK's type-enforcement mechanism. A detailed discussion of LDV is described in [25].

To understand the LDV security policy, it is essential to understand the LOCK security policy, which consists of a discretionary and a mandatory security policy. The discretionary policy allows subjects to specify and control the sharing of objects. The mandatory policy is based on controlling the potential interferences among subjects. It consists of a MAC policy and a type-enforcement policy. The MAC policy is based on the Bell and LaPadula policy. The type-enforcement policy deals with aspects of security policy that are inherently nonhierarchical in nature. It restricts accesses of subjects to objects based on the domain of the subject and the type of the object.

The additional concern for a DBMS in a multilevel secure environment beyond that of LOCK is the proper labeling of information. To provide for that concern, two extensions to the policy of the TCB are required.

One extension summarizes the actions that happen when a DB is updated and the other when a query is made to the DB. The update classification policy addresses the problem of proper classification of the DB data. That is, when the DB is updated, the classification level of the data is determined. The data are then inserted into an object whose level dominates the level of the data.

The response classification policy addresses the problem of proper classification of response to queries. This is a problem because the response may be built based on the data in many base relations. In the process of manipulating and combining the data, it is entirely possible that the data will be used in a manner that reveals higher level information. The problem becomes more acute when one realizes that the response will be released into an environment in which many responses may be visible. Thus, the problem becomes one of aggregation and inference over time as well as across relations. In light of that, it seems fairly clear that a response can be released only if it is placed in an object whose level dominates the derived level of the response. The derived level is the maximum level of any information that can be deduced from the response by a subject reading the response. LOCK's type-enforcement mechanism allows us to encapsulate applications such as DBMS in a protected subsystem, by declaring the DBMS objects to be of special types that are accessible only to subjects executing in the DBMS domain. The subjects who are allowed to execute in this domain are carefully restricted. It is this approach that makes LDV a unique design.

Some of the essential design concepts of LDV are the following.

- Subjects interact with LDV through a request importer and a request exporter.

- Access to data as well as to metadata is controlled by LOCK.

- Information in the DB as well as the meta-DB is stored in single-level files, that is, LOCK objects. LOCK ensures that the DB files may be opened for read/write operations only by subjects executing at the appropriate levels and in the appropriate DB domains.

- The LDV subsystems are the Data Dictionary Manager (DDM), which is responsible for maintaining all information about the multilevel DB; the User Request Manager (URM), which provides interface subjects; the Relational Access Manager (RAM), which is responsible for query optimization; and the Execution Manager (EM), which is responsible for file and transaction management.

11.4.4 Commercial Products

Since 1988, MLS/DBMS products have been developed. However, some of those products are not being marketed anymore. Furthermore, some corporations have merged with other corporations, so the ownership of the products also has changed. This section is an overview of the commercial products that emerged between 1988 and 1993. Note that in describing the product we do not mention the evaluation status. Our emphasis is on the technical aspects of the product for the initial release. We also briefly mention the platforms they were intended to run on initially. Because the MLS/DBMS commercial marketplace has been dominated by relational systems, we discuss only relational DBs.

11.4.4.1 TRUDATA

The initial version of the TRUDATA system designed in the late 1980s is an approach based on Integrity-Lock whose underlying security model is derived from the Naval Surveillance Model as well as from Integrity-Lock architecture. TRUDATA employs an untrusted Britton Lee DB machine as a back end and an AT&T 3B2 V/MLS system as a front end. The back-end DB machine is completely untrusted and has access to all the data in the DB. The back-end machine performs standard DBMS selection, joins, and projections, as well as being responsible for data storage and recovery. In TRUDATA physical, not logical, isolation is used to isolate the DB from non-DBMS code. Trusted code added to the MLS front end associates labels and a 64-bit CBC checksum to the data being stored in the DB. The trusted filter also performs all access mediation (MAC and DAC).

Objects in TRUDATA are view instances (pviews, mviews, and relations). Pviews are projections from a given relation. The pviews are defined a priori before data are inserted into the DB. Mviews are the join between two or more pviews. The intent of labeling only view instances is to limit the inference threat to which systems based on Integrity-Lock are vulnerable. TRUDATA provides two versions of its MAC policy: a "restricted" version, which allows only a write-equal policy, and an "unrestricted" version, which allows a write-up policy.

Objects in TRUDATA may be labeled with one of three types of labels: an actual security label (ASL), a default security label (DSL), or a container clearance requirement (CCR) label. An ASL may be associated with only a pview instance. A DSL is attached to every container. Pview instances, which do not have an ASL associated with them, inherit the DSL of their container. The inheritance mechanism allows subjects to avoid having to label all view instances explicitly. The CCR labels are associated with containers. The CCR labels are a pair of labels that constitute the ceiling and floor of the labels that may be associated with objects in the container. All labels may be changed (changed in place) through the use of the change command by an authorized subject.

In addition to providing MAC, TRUDATA also provides DAC. DAC is handled in TRUDATA via a combination of access control lists (ACLs): exclusionary access control lists (XACLs) and operator authorization lists (OALs). OALs are associated with subjects and specify which operators the associated subjects may apply to objects. The operators supported by TRUDATA are read, write, delete, create, change-level, and change-access. ACLs and XACLs are associated with objects. ACLs indicate which subjects may access the object (discretionary sense) and in what manner the objects may be accessed (e.g., read, write). XACLs explicitly exclude a specified subject from accessing the object in a specified manner. When an ACL is associated with a container, the access permission of the ACL applies to all the objects in the container unless excluded by an XACL. XACL permissions, like those of ACLs, are inherited by their containing objects. However, once an XACL excludes a subject from accessing an object, subsequent ACLs will not restore it. Access permission granted at the system level cannot be denied via lower level XACLs. That ensures that permissions granted to DBAs cannot be denied by lower level subjects.

11.4.4.2 Secure Sybase

Sybase's Secure SQL Server is a trusted-subject-based DBMS based on a client/server architecture. For the initial release, the client portion of the architecture ran on Ultrix, SE/VMS, and SUN MLS. The initial release of the server ran only on Ultrix. Because Ultrix is not a trusted product, it may not provide the trusted operating system support environment that a TDBMS requires. However, Sybase had discussed porting the server to DEC RISC CMW, SUN CMW, and SeVMS.

Secure Sybase provides security labels (16 hierarchical and 64 nonhierarchical) on each tuple of the system and performs MAC based on those labels. Because Sybase stores its metadata in relations, it is capable of labeling each row of the metadata relation, thus allowing for a very fine-grained and flexible labeling of the metadata. Secure Sybase provides DAC on relations but not views. Secure Sybase is unique in that identification and authentication functions are handled by the DBMS, not by the underlying operating system. The Secure Sybase server also provides for a trusted facility management capability by supporting separate security officer and system administrator roles. The current release of the server supports a trusted-path capability, but it is our understanding that Sybase is planning to do away with this capability in future releases of the system to allow for compatibility with the nonsecure versions of Sybase.

Secure Sybase supports polyinstantiation for insertion, updating, and deletion. Polyinstantiation can be turned off for deletions and updates, but it cannot be turned off for insertions. Secure Sybase allows for downgrading of the entire content of a relation. Subjects create empty relations at the desired lower level, and then the contents of the original relation are copied into the new relation. Downgrading selected tuples is more difficult. The selected tuples are copied into a new relation at the lower security level. The selected tuples in the original relation are then deleted. The selected tuples in the new relation are then copied into the old relation. Finally, the new relation (now empty) is deleted. Sybase intends to provide a less awkward means of reclassifying data in future releases. The new approach will entail copying tuples from one level to another and then deleting the original tuple, but unlike the current approach, only the tuples that are being reclassified need to be copied.

11.4.4.3 Trusted Oracle

Oracle's MLS/DBMS effort is unique in that Oracle had pursued both a Hinke-Schaefer approach and a trusted-subject approach. The Hinke-Schaefer approach draws heavily from the SeaView model. The early releases of trusted Oracle were targeted to run on the SE/VMS and the HP/UX operating systems. Also, Oracle has tried to maintain its trusted product to keep up with the nontrusted releases of Oracle.

The system enforces tuple-level MAC granularity. In the Hinke-Schaefer version, that is done by storing the tuples in the underlying trusted operating system storage object. Under both approaches, the number of security levels is the same as that enforced by the underlying operating system. Trusted Oracle provides polyinstantiation on insertions. The polyinstantiation is on a relation basis and can be turned on and off as desired. The system enforces a write-equal policy for updates and deletes. Subjects who have the appropriate privilege may change the sensitivity labels associated with tuples (label changes occur in place, as opposed to inserting new tuples at a different level and deleting the old tuple).

We discussed discretionary security for Oracle in Section 11.3.5.1. Here, we briefly discuss how DAC was handled in the early release of the trusted version. Trusted Oracle provides its own DAC mechanism (i.e., a

DAC mechanism independent from the underlying operating system). The DAC is enforced on views. Trusted Oracle is unique in that it does not employ locking to enforce concurrency control. Instead, it employs single-level multiversioning. Because there is no locking and no writing down under this approach, there is no chance of a covert signaling channel occurring.

The system metadata is handled as a normal relation. For the Hinke-Schaefer version of the product, that means the metadata is partitioned into operating system objects of the appropriate security level. For the trusted-subject version of the product, each tuple of the metadata relations is independently labeled.

11.4.4.4 Trusted Informix

Trusted Informix is intended to be a trusted-subject-based architecture and run on both the HP/UX operating system and the AT&T System V MLS. The product associates security labels on rows (tuples). However, rather than enforcing its own MAC mediation, the system makes calls to the underlying trusted operating system, which in turn makes calls to the operating system. Trusted Informix supports the ability of changing existing row labels; it does so by copying the data into a new row at a different level and then deleting the original row.

Content-independent DAC is enforced on DBs, tables, rows, and columns. The product supports polyinstantiation on insert, and the mechanism cannot be shut off once activated. The system metadata are all protected at system high. The product has a unique approach to handling MLS concurrency control. If a higher level subject locks an object, a lower level subject is still allowed to write the object. By permitting that writing, the product ensures that the higher level subject cannot signal the lower level subject via the locking mechanism. This approach opens up a potential data integrity problem, because even locked objects can be written by lower level subjects. Trusted Informix addresses the problem by alerting the higher level subjects when a "locked" object has been written and giving the subject the option of either backing out of the transaction or continuing.

11.4.5 Multilevel Object Data Models

This section describes some of the major multilevel object-oriented data models described in the literature.

11.4.5.1 SODA Model

Keefe, Tsai, and Thuraisingham were the first to incorporate multilevel security in object-oriented data models. The system they subsequently developed, called SODA [36], has a number of unique properties, both in its security model and in its data model.

The rules that govern operations within SODA are designed to enforce the Bell and LaPadula properties and conceptually are quite simple. First, any method activation can read a value within a labeled object or a labeled instance variable, provided the classification of the object is dominated by the clearance level of the method. However, if the classification of the object dominates the current classification of the method, the method's classification is raised to the level of the object being read. Second, a method activation may modify or create a new object of a particular classification if the method's current classification equals that of the object in question, the method's current classification is dominated by the upper bound of the classification range (as specified by the constraint), and the lower bound of the classification range specified by the constraint is dominated by the subject's clearance. If these rules are not satisfied, then a write/create operation fails. Because method activations in SODA can have their classifications dynamically upgraded, the TCB must be involved to perform the level change. If the nature of methods can be determined in advance, then a level change operation could be restricted to the message-passing mechanism. However, this situation is not generally the case, and the TCB must be invoked when a method activation attempts to read an object whose classification dominates the method's current classification. The TCB must then restart the method activation at the point where it invoked the TCB.

11.4.5.2 SORION Model

Thuraisingham investigated security issues for the ORION object-oriented data model [37]. The secure model was called SORION. It extends the Microelectronics & Computer Technology Corporation's ORION model with multilevel security properties. In SORION's security policy, subjects and objects are assigned security levels. The following rules constitute the policy:

1. A subject has read access to an object if the subject's security level dominates that of the object.

2. A subject has write access to an object if the subject's security level is equal to that of the object.

3. A subject can execute a method if the subject's security level dominates the security level of the method and that of the class with which the method is associated.

4. A method executes at the level of the subject who initiated the execution.

5. During the execution of a method, m_1, if another method, m_2, has to be executed, m_2 can execute only if the execution level of m_1 dominates the levels of m_2 and of the class with which m_2 is associated.

6. Reading and writing of objects during method execution are governed by rules 1 and 2.

Different architectures for implementing a system based on the SORION model have been examined, and an approach in which the TCB enforces all MAC has been proposed. Basically, the system runs as an untrusted application on a general-purpose TCB. The TCB controls all access to read, write, and method execution.

11.4.5.3 Millen-Lunt Model

Millen and Lunt have proposed a secure object model for knowledge-based applications, based on a layered architecture [38]. At the lowest layer is the security kernel, which provides MAC. At the next layer is the object system, which implements object-oriented services, providing the abstraction of objects, methods, and messages. The object system layer is assumed to be layered with respect to mandatory security. Here are the security properties of the model.

- The *hierarchy property* states that the level of an object dominates that of its class.

- The *subject-level property* states that the level of a subject created to handle a message dominates both the level of the subject that originated the message and the level of the object receiving the message.

- The *object locality property* states that a subject can execute methods or read variables only in the object where it is located or any superclass of that object. It can write variables only in that object.

- The **-property* states that a subject may write into an object where the subject is located only if its security level is equal to that of the object.

- The *return-value property* states that an invoking subject can receive a return value from a message only if the message handler subject is at the same security level as the invoking subject.

- The *object-creation property* states that the security level of a newly created object must dominate the level of the subject that requested its creation.

11.4.5.4 Jajodia-Kogan Model

Jajodia and Kogan present a secure object-oriented model that is conceptually simple and unique in that it relies almost wholly on its message-passing mechanism for the enforcement of its security policy [39]. The security model proposed by Jajodia and Kogan is based on a message-filtering algorithm that is used to determine if the execution of a method will cause an illegal flow of information within the system.

Two concepts are central to the Jajodia-Kogan security model. The first is that methods must always have one of two states: They are either restricted or unrestricted. If restricted, the method is prevented from modifying attributes or creating new objects. If unrestricted, the method can modify object attributes and create new objects. Under certain circumstances, method activation can attain a restricted status, and once attained, any further method invocations will also be restricted. The second concept is a simplifying assumption that is made in the model with respect to the nature of methods. All more complex methods are divided into a sequence of methods of the following four types:

- *Read:* a method that reads the value of an attribute;
- *Write:* a method that modifies the value of an attribute;
- *Invoke:* a method that invokes another method via the sending of a message;
- *Create:* a method that creates a new object.

The rules enforced by the message-filtering algorithm are separated into two sets. The first set restricts messages sent from one object to another. The second set restricts messages sent from an object to itself. Because the message-passing mechanism contains the filtering algorithm and all information flows are determined at the time that a message is sent, the TCB of this model could include the message passer and nothing more. It is conceivable that the

Jajodia-Kogan model could be implemented without relying on an underlying TCB for security policy enforcement, a situation that is not necessarily desirable but that is nevertheless one of the unique aspects of this model.

11.4.5.5 Morgenstern's Model

Morgenstern has proposed an object-oriented security model for multilevel objects with bidirectional relationships [40]. He argues that the use of multilevel attributes in the relational model suggests the need for multilevel objects in the object model. The model also distinguishes between the security levels of binary and *n*-ary relationships. Security constraints are used to specify the types of operations to be executed. Some of the constraints are listed here.

- The *method invocation constraint* states that the level of a method invocation is the least upper bound of (1) the minimum level among the range of levels associated with the method; (2) the level of the subject who requested the invocation; and (3) the levels of the arguments provided for that invocation.

- The *method output constraint* states that the level of any output or insertion produced by the method execution must dominate the level of the method invocation.

- The *property update constraint* states that the modification of a property instance must not change its level.

Morgenstern's model does not address issues on TCB enforcement. Because multilevel objects are decomposed by access classes, one could envision that the operating system provides the MAC to the decomposed objects. However, the module that enforces the security constraints must also be trusted.

11.4.5.6 UFOS Model

MITRE has developed a model called UFOS (uniform finegrained object security) [41]. After the various models proposed in the literature were examined, it was found that there is a need for a model that is consistent with industry trends, is flexible, provides element-level access control, and supports collections of data. Essentially the UFOS model classifies the associations between instance variables and their values. For example, consider an object called TANK-A. The association between its instance variable tankname and its value XXX could be Unclassified while the association between its instance variable mission and its value YYY could be Secret. The UFOS model also treats polyinstantiation in great depth. For example, the association between tank-name and its value at the Secret level could be ZZZ instead of XXX. The security policy of UFOS is essentially read-at-or-below-your-level and write-at-your-level. There does not appear to be any discussion of TCB with this effort.

11.5 Design Issues

DB security can no longer be considered a secondary requirement to be added to existing DB systems. Rather, it must be considered a primary need to be taken into account from the initial phases of the DB design. Various authors thus suggest the use of a methodological approach to the design of a secure DB system, along the lines of the methodologies used for DB design. Here, we briefly report some guidelines that can be used in designing a secure DB (some of the ideas presented here are taken from [6]). Secure DB design can be seen as an incremental process, consisting of the following steps: (1) preliminary analysis; (2) requirement analysis; (3) security policy specification; (4) design of the access control mechanism; and (5) implementation of the access control mechanism.

The aim of the preliminary analysis phase is to perform a feasibility study for the secure system to be developed, including an evaluation of the costs, risks, priorities, and human, hardware, and system resources to be employed. The protection requirements are fully specified during the requirement analysis phase. This second phase must start with a precise study of all the possible security threats to which the system could be exposed and an accurate analysis of the kind of protection you would like to ensure for the data stored in the system. The result of this phase is a specification of the type of accesses a subject can exercise on the DB objects. Such specification is usually expressed in an informal way, usually as a set of sentences expressed in natural language.

In the third phase, the security policies that best match the requirements specified in the preceding phase are selected. During the security policies specification phase, it must be defined in details which kinds of privileges the subjects can exercise on the objects in the system (e.g., update, read, execute). During this phase, it must also be defined which are the roles and/or groups (if any) in the systems and whether they are flat or hierarchically organized. It must also be defined at which granularity the access control should be enforced, that is, whether it is possible to require access to groups of objects, single objects, or portions of them.

Once the security policies have been specified, using some formal or informal notation, the next step is the design and implementation of an access control mechanism enforcing such policies (these activities are performed by steps 4 and 5, respectively). Basic components of an access control mechanism are a set of authorization rules by which the security policies can be enforced; an access control algorithm, which verifies whether an access request can be authorized according to the specified policies; and a set of tools for performing administrative operations. Such functions can be designed and implemented using the methodologies commonly used for software development.

Finally, it is important to mention that a very important research direction concerns the development of tools for the specification of security policies and for their automatic mapping into a set of authorization rules. Such tools are particularly crucial when dealing with sophisticated authorization models supporting a wide range of access authorizations (such as positive/negative, weak/strong, and implicit/explicit authorizations). This area, however, has not yet been widely investigated.

11.6 Some Research Trends

Many advanced application environments, such as distributed digital libraries, heterogeneous information systems, cooperative systems, workflow applications, and groupware, have articulated and rich access control requirements. These requirements cannot be adequately supported by current access control mechanisms, which are tailored to a few, specific policies. In most cases, either the organization is forced to adopt the specific policy built into the access control mechanism at hand, or access control policies must be implemented as application programs. Both situations are clearly unacceptable. A promising research direction is the development of access control mechanisms specifically tailored for these new environments. The following sections survey the access control requirements introduced by three of the most challenging environments, namely, digital libraries, workflow management systems, and the World Wide Web [42]. Issues discussed in what follows are summarized in Table 11.3. Note that many of the research trends are focusing on access control models for discretionary security and not on mandatory security. Therefore, mandatory security aspects are not addressed in this section.

Table 11.3
Some Open Research Directions

Environment	Issues
Digital libraries	Flexible subject specification; content-based access control to multimedia data; remote accesses; accesses to distributed digital libraries; copying and usage of information
Workflow management systems	Role-based access control; authorization constraints on role and user assignments; authorization models for the WfMC standard
World Wide Web	Efficient strategies for storing authorizations; caching and administrative operations; authorization models for XML

11.6.1 Digital Libraries

Digital libraries (DLs) introduce several challenging requirements with respect to the formulation, specification, and enforcement of adequate data protection policies.

Even though some of those requirements have been addressed by security research related to DBMSs, approaching them in the framework of DLs entails solving several new challenging problems. Other requirements, such as copyright and intellectual property protection are specific to DLs and have not been addressed by security research in DBMSs. We briefly discuss some of the main issues next.

11.6.1.1 Flexible Subject Specification Mechanism

In current authorization models, authorization subjects are stated in terms of user identifiers. In some systems, roles and groups can also be used as authorization subjects. In DLs, the user population is often very dynamic, with new users (also from remote sites) needing to get access to library objects. Moreover, the access policies that one expects to be stated in a DL may be based on specific user characteristics. Consider as an example the policy stating that "a video rated X can only be accessed by users who are 18 or older." Directly mapping such a policy, which requires knowledge of the age of the user submitting the access request, onto a traditional authorization model is not feasible, because such a model typically does not support the specification of authorizations based on subject characteristics. The need of such flexible user specification is even more evident when dealing with users belonging to organizations different from the organization owning the DL.

In such a case, the user characteristics may also include information such as the organization the user belongs to, whether the subject (or its organization) has paid the subscription (in case access is allowed upon payment), and so forth.

11.6.1.2 Content-Based Access Control to Multimedia, Unformatted Data

In many cases, granting access to objects is based on their content. In relational DBMSs, such access control policies are expressed in terms of views. In DLs, content-based access control is more difficult because of the presence of data such as text, image, and video, which makes it more difficult to automatically determine whether a certain object verifies a condition on its content. As an example, consider a policy stating that "all documents discussing how to operate guns must be available only to users who are 18 or older." The main issue is how to determine whether a certain text really deals with such a topic. The situation is even more complicated when dealing with images and videos, due to the inherent difficulty in content understanding for such data types.

11.6.1.3 Distributed DLs and Remote Accesses

Distribution entails two different aspects. The first concerns the fact that the DL itself may be distributed and may consist of several information providers, each maintained by possibly different organizations. Because different organizations may have different access control policies, several questions arise related to whether each organization should retain its own autonomy with respect to access control policies and how to solve conflicts that may arise, or whether the various policies should be integrated and global policies devised. Other questions are related to where to maintain authorization information and where to enforce access control. Some of these questions were addressed in the framework of distributed DBMSs. However, solutions proposed in such a framework may not be adequate to DLs.

The second aspect is related to the fact that subjects accessing a DL may be remote (i.e., they do not belong to the organization owning the DL). Remote accesses pose a number of problems, especially when remote subjects are required to provide information (such as age) for access control purposes. Access control information that is recorded at the subjects' organization may differ with respect to the information required by the access control system of the DL. Consider the case of a DL that requires the age of the subject for giving access to certain objects, whereas the subject's organization keeps the birth date. In such a case, the mapping between the two types of information is easy; however, more complicated situations may arise. Another related question is how a subject (or an organization) wishing to access a DL determines the information to supply for access control purposes. Finally, other important issues include the use of certification and other authentication mechanisms to ensure the authenticity of the information provided for access control as well as access anonymity.

11.6.1.4 Copying and Usage of Information

In some cases, accesses to objects from DLs can be allowed only upon payment; therefore, objects cannot be freely passed among users. In other cases, objects can be used only if copyright information is mentioned.

11.6.2 Data Protection for Workflow Management Systems

Another growing area characterized by peculiar security requirements is the area of workflow management systems (WFMSs). WFMSs have gained popularity in research as well as in commercial sectors. A workflow separates the various activities of a given organizational process into a set of well-defined tasks. The various tasks are usually carried out by several users according to the rules imposed by the organization. The stringent security requirements imposed by many workflow applications call for suitable access control mechanisms. The most important features an access control mechanism for WFMSs must provide are described here:

- *Role-based access control.* Quite often, security policies of a given organization are expressed in terms of the roles within the organization rather than individuals. To directly represent such organizational security policies, an access control mechanism must therefore be capable of supporting roles.

- *Authorization constraints on role and user assignments.* Although several role-based access control mechanisms already exist (see, e.g., [13]), a common drawback of such mechanisms is that they are not capable of modeling authorization constraints on roles and users. A typical authorization constraint, which is very relevant and well known in the security area, is *separation of duties.* It aims at reducing the risk of frauds by not allowing any individual to have sufficient authority within the system to perpetrate a fraud on his or her own. Separation of duties is a principle often applied in everyday life. For example, opening a bank safe requires two keys held by different individuals; taking a business trip requires the approval of the department manager as well as the accounting department. If no proper support is provided, constraints like separation of duties must be implemented as application code and embedded in the various tasks.

Bertino, Ferrari, and Atluri recently proposed a work in the modeling of authorization constraints in WFMSs [43]. Their model provides a logic language for defining constraints that support, among other functions, separation of duties. Another relevant research direction is the definition of access control models for the emerging workflow standard developed by the Workflow Management Coalition (WfMC).

11.6.3 Data Protection for the World Wide Web

The World Wide Web is enabling the deployment of a new generation of distributed information systems, whose communication platform is the Internet (or an intranet). Such an information system is characterized by a client/server architecture, in which the clients are potentially the entire population of Internet users and the servers are potentially the available set of Web servers. Clients are free to access data (like documents and multimedia data) and software independently of their physical location. Such an environment is characterized by a very large and dynamically changing user population, which is highly distributed. Data protection in such an environment entails addressing several issues, such as data access based on user credentials, secure data browsing software, access anonymity, distributed management of authorization and authentication information, and fault tolerance.

With respect to authorization management, an important issue is the development of access control protocols that reduce the communication overhead between the servers and the clients, since that affects the latency experienced by the users. When authorizations can be specified only on specific documents, the most efficient solution is storing the authorizations at the same place where the corresponding document resides. However, when authorizations on documents' groups are allowed, and such groups involve objects stored at different servers, that simple solution may affect performance. In that case, approaches based on a total or partial replication of the authorization must be considered. Several replication mechanisms can be adopted. For instance, authorizations can be stored at the hosts more frequently accessed or having the best response time.

Another relevant research direction deals with the management of administrative operations. In particular, the revoke operation is made more difficult by the caching mechanisms provided by most Web browsers that allow users to cache documents they frequently access. Therefore, the traditional revoke mechanisms, like the one provided by the System R authorization model, should be revised. A possible approach consists in associating a lifetime with the cached data. The main problem with that approach is the correct estimation of the lifetime interval: The interval should be small enough to guarantee that cached data are consistent with the authorizations and large enough to avoid the clients to have to reload the documents because of the lifetime expiration, even if no changes occurred to the authorizations. An alternative approach is to automatically propagate the revocation of authorizations to the cache, possibly invalidating its content. The main drawback of this approach is that it may not preserve security in that a failure in communicating authorization updates (e.g., because of a message or network partition) may lead to the inability to invalidate the cache.

Another topic is related to XML, the new standard format for data on Web. XML is a text-based format, providing a standard data model to encode the content, the semantics, and the schema of documents, structured records, and metacontent information about a Web site. The development of access control mechanisms for XML documents is an important research direction [44].

11.7 Summary

This chapter provided a fairly comprehensive overview of the developments in secure DB systems. Basic concepts in access control were introduced, as well as discretionary and mandatory policies. An overview of administration policies was presented, along with an examination of DAC models, commercial developments, and mandatory security. Data models, architectures, prototypes, and commercial products were discussed, and an overview of recent developments and trends presented.

Throughout the chapter, the concepts were illustrated with discussions of prototypes and commercial products. However, it should be noted that vendors are continuously updating their products. Therefore, to obtain the most up-to-date information, the reader is encouraged to keep up with the developments on products and prototypes from research papers as well as material published by vendors.

Directions in secure DB systems will be driven by the developments on the World Wide Web. Database systems are no longer standalone systems.

They are being integrated into various applications such as multimedia, electronic commerce, mobile computing systems, digital libraries, and collaboration systems. Security issues for all these new generation systems will be important. Furthermore, there are many developments on various object technologies such as distributed object systems and components and frameworks. Security for such systems is being investigated. Eventually the security policies of the various subsystems and components have to be integrated to form policies for the entire system. There will be many challenges in formulating policies for such systems. New technologies such as data mining will help solve security problems such as intrusion detection and auditing. However, these technologies can also violate the privacy of individuals. Finally, migrating legacy DBs and applications will continually be a challenge. Security issues for such operations cannot be overlooked.

References

[1]   Air Force Studies Board, Committee on Multilevel Data Management Security, *Multilevel Data Management Security*, National Academy Press, 1983.

[2]   Adam, N., et al., "A Content-Based Authorization Model for Digital Libraries," submitted for publication.

[3]   Winslett, M., et al., "Using Digital Credentials on the World Wide Web," *J. Computer Security*, Vol. 5, 1997.

[4]   Bell, D., and L. LaPadula, "Secure Computer Systems: Unified Exposition and Multics Interpretation," *ESD-TR-75-306*, Hanscom Air Force Base, Bedford, MA, 1975.

[5]   Bertino, E., and E. Ferrari, "Administration Policies in a Multipolicy Authorization System," *Proc. 10th IFIP Working Conf. on Database Security*, Lake Tahoe, CA, Aug. 1997.

[6]   Castano, S., et al., *Database Security*, Reading, MA: Addison-Wesley, 1995.

[7]   Griffiths, P. P., and B. W. Wade, "An Authorization Mechanism for a Relational Database System," *ACM Trans. on Database Systems*, Vol. 1, No. 3, Sept. 1976, pp. 242–255.

[8]   Wilms, P. F., and B. G. Linsday, "A Database Authorization Mechanism Supporting Individual and Group Authorization," *Distributed Data Sharing Systems*, 1982, pp. 273–292.

[9]   Bertino, E., and L. M. Haas, "Views and Security in Distributed Database Management Systems," *Proc. 1st Intl. Conf. on Extending Database Technology (EDBT'88)*, Venice, Italy, 1988.

[10] Bertino, E., P. Samarati, and S. Jajodia, "An Extended Authorization Model," *IEEE Trans. on Knowledge and Data Engineering*, Vol. 9, No. 1, Jan./Feb. 1997, pp. 85–101.

[11] Denning, D. E., and T. Lunt, "A Multilevel Relational Data Model," *Proc. IEEE Symp. on Security and Privacy*, Oakland, CA, Apr. 1987.

[12] Bertino, E., S. Jajodia, and P. Samarati, "Supporting Multiple Access Control Policies in Database Systems," *Proc IEEE Symp. on Security and Privacy*, Oakland, CA, 1996.

[13] Sandhu, R., et al., "Role-Based Access Control Models," *IEEE Computer*, Feb. 1996, pp. 38–47.

[14] Bertino, E., et al., "Reasoning With Temporal Authorizations and Periodicity Constraints in Database Access Control," *ACM Trans. on Database Systems*, Vol. 23, No. 3, Sept. 1998, pp. 231–285.

[15] Bertino, E., and L. Martino, *Object-Oriented Database Systems: Concepts and Architectures*, Reading, MA: Addison-Wesley, 1993.

[16] Bertino, E., and P. Samarati, "Research Issues in Discretionary Authorization for Object Bases," in B. Thuraisingham, R. Sandhu, and T. Y. Lin (eds.), *Security for Object-Oriented Systems*, New York: Springer-Verlag, 1994.

[17] Rabitti, F., et al., "A Model of Authorization for Next-Generation Database Systems," *ACM Trans. on Database Systems*, Vol. 16, No. 1, Mar. 1991, pp. 88–131.

[18] Bertino, E., and H. Weigand, "An Approach to Authorization Modelling in Object-Oriented Database Systems," *Data & Knowledge Engineering*, Vol. 12, No. 1, 1994.

[19] Bertino, E., et al., "A Flexible Authorization Model and Its Formal Semantics," *Proc. 5th European Symp. on Research in Computer Security (ESORICS'98)*, Louvain-La-Neuve, Belgium, Springer-Verlag, LNCS 1485, 1998.

[20] Ahad, R., et al., "Supporting Access Control in an Object-Oriented Database Language," *Proc. Intl. Conf. on Extending Database Technology (EDBT)*, Vienna, Austria, Springer-Verlag, LNCS 580, 1992.

[21] Bruggemann, H. H., "Rights in Object-Oriented Environments," *Proc. 7th Working Conf. on Database Security*, 1992, pp. 99–115.

[22] Fernandez, E., E. B. Gudes, and H. Song, "A Model for Evaluation and Administration of Security in Object-Oriented Databases," *IEEE Trans. on Knowledge and Data Engineering*, Vol. 6, Apr. 1994, pp. 275–292.

[23] Kelter, U., "Discretionary Access Controls in a High-Performance Object Management System," *Proc. IEEE Symp. on Research in Security and Privacy*, Oakland, CA, May 1991.

[24] Widom, J., R. J. Cochrane, and B. G. Lindsay, "Implementing Set-Oriented Production Rules as an Extension to Starbust," *Proc. VLDB Conf.*, 1991.

[25] Morgenstern, M., "Security and Inference in Multilevel Database and Knowledge Base Systems," *Proc. ACM SIGMOD Conf.*, San Francisco, CA, 1987.

[26] Bertino, E., B. Catania, and A. Vinai, "Transaction Modelling and Architectures," *Encyclopedia of Computer Science and Technology*, Vol. 38, No. 23, New York: Marcel Dekker, 1998, pp. 361–400.

[27] Thuraisingham, B., "Multilevel Security for Distributed Heterogeneous and Federated Databases," *Computers & Security*, Vol. 14, Dec. 1994.

[28] Burns, R., "Referential Secrecy," *Proc. IEEE Symp. on Security and Privacy*, Oakland, CA, May 1990.

[29] Stachour, P., and M. B. Thuraisingham, "Design of LDV—A Multilevel Secure Database Management System," *IEEE Trans. on Knowledge and Data Engineering*, Vol. 2, No. 2, 1990.

[30] Wiseman, S., "On the Problem of Security in Databases," *Proc. IFIP 11.3 Working Conf. in Database Security*, Monterey, CA, Sept. 1989.

[31] Thuraisingham, B., "NTML: A Nonmonotonic Types Multilevel Logic for Secure Databases," *Proc. Computer Security Foundations Workshop*, Franconia, NH, June 1991.

[32] Graubart, R. D., "A Comparison of Three DBMS Architectures," *Proc. IFIP 11.3 Working Conf. on Database Security*, Monterey, CA, Sept. 1989.

[33] TDI, "Trusted Database Interpretation," Department of Defense Document, 1991.

[34] Thuraisingham, B., "A Tutorial in Secure Database Systems," *MITRE Technical Report*, June 1992.

[35] Graubart, R. D., "The Integrity Lock Approach to Secure Database Management," *Proc. IEEE Symp. on Security and Privacy*, Oakland, CA, Apr. 1984.

[36] Keefe, T., T. W. Tsai, and B. Thuraisingham, "SODA—A Secure Object-Oriented Database System," *Computers & Security*, Vol. 8, No. 6, 1989.

[37] Thuraisingham, B., "Mandatory Security in Object-Oriented Database Management Systems," *Proc. ACM Conf. on Object-Oriented Programming Systems, Languages and Applications (OOPSLA)*, New Orleans, LA, 1989.

[38] Millen, J., and T. Lunt, "Security for Knowledge-Based Systems," *Proc. IEEE Symp. on Security and Privacy*, Oakland, CA, 1992.

[39] Jajodia, S., and B. Kogan, "Integrating an Object-Oriented Data Model With Multilevel Security," *Proc. IEEE Symp. on Security and Privacy*, Oakland, CA, 1990.

[40] Morgenstern, M., "A Security Model for Multilevel Objects With Bidirectional Relationships," *Proc. 4th IFIP 11.3 Working Conf. in Database Security*, Halifax, England, 1990.

[41] Rosenthal, A., et al., "Security for Object-Oriented Systems," *Proc. IFIP 11.3 Working Conf. on Database Security* (Hildesheim), 1994.

[42]   Bertino, E., "Data Security," *Data & Knowledge Engineering*, Vol. 25, No. 1–2, Mar. 1998, pp. 199–216.

[43]   Bertino, E., E. Ferrari, and V. Atluri, "The Specification and Enforcement of Authorization Constraints in Workflow Management Systems," *ACM Trans. on Information Systems and Security*, Vol. 2, No. 1, Feb. 1999, pp. 65–104.

[44]   Bertino, E., et al., "Controlled Access and Dissemination of XML Documents," *Proc. 2nd ACM Workshop on Web Information and Data Management (WIDM'99)*, Kansas City, MO, Nov. 1999.

Selected Bibliography

The book by Castano et al. [6] covers most of the aspects related to DB security, such as mandatory and DAC models, secure DB design, statistical DB security, and intrusion detection. An overview of DAC models can be found in the article by Bertino [42], which also provides a discussion of future research directions. Finally, more details on MAC can be found in the papers by Thuraisingham [27, 34, 37].

12

Component Database Systems

Andreas Geppert and Klaus R. Dittrich

12.1 Introduction

DBMSs support individual applications and comprehensive information systems with modeling and long-term reliable storage capabilities of data as well as with retrieval and manipulation facilities for persistent data by multiple, concurrent users or transactions. SQL [1], the transaction abstraction [2], and the concept of a data model—most notably the relational model [3] and, to a lesser extent, the object-oriented data models [4, 5]—are crucial ingredients of data management. DBMSs are well established and form the cornerstones of virtually every enterprise: IS.

Traditionally, data elements stored in DBs were simply structured, for example, employee records and product and stock information. Transactions typically were of short duration and often needed to access only a few data items. Queries were usually simple, and techniques to efficiently answer them well understood. Taking a broader view, DBMS-based information systems have usually been built in a rather DB-centric way, that is, environment decisions like the use of mainframe-based or client/server architectures are typically based on what the DBMS itself requires or supports in that respect.

Recently, however, more and more new and demanding application domains have emerged that also want to benefit from DB technology, and new requirements have been posed to DBMSs (see Chapter 1). First, many applications require the management of data types that are not handled well by conventional DBMSs. Examples of such new data types are multimedia data, documents, engineering artifacts, and temporal data, to name just a few.

Likewise, DBMSs are increasingly required to be integrated with other infrastructure parts of their environment. For instance, instead of letting the DBMSs manage existing data, it is often necessary to leave data where they are (possibly because there are applications that one would not want to migrate as well), but to enhance the external data management system with some sort of DB functionality [6]. It might also be necessary to integrate existing data stores with DB systems in a way that each of them is still independently operational, while users are provided with an integrated and uniform view of the entire system. In other words, often applications need support as offered by multidatabase systems or federated DB systems [7, 8], whereby the federation parties might be any kind of data store.

To meet all those new requirements, DBMSs (or whatever the resulting kinds of system will ultimately be called) apparently have to be extended by new functionality. However, enhancing a single system with modules implementing all the new functions is not a viable approach for several reasons.

- DBMSs would become so large and, in consequence, complex that they could no longer be maintained at reasonable costs.

- Users would have to pay a high price for the added functionality, even if they do not need every part of it.

- Users and applications also would have to pay a performance penalty for added functionality that they do not actually need.

- A DBMS vendor might not have the expertise to perform such extensions or the resources to undertake all extensions within a reasonable period of time.

Thus, beefing up a monolithic DBMS by adding ever more functionality does not work. Instead, it seems attractive to consider the alternative of extending DBMS in a piecemeal way, that is, supporting the addition or replacement of functionality in a modular manner as needed. Modular extensions to a DBMS require that a well-defined software architecture is imposed on the DBMS. Such an architecture would clearly define the places in the system where extensions are possible. In general, extensions will not be possible at any arbitrary place in the system, and implications of modifications on other parts should be avoided or at least minimized. To that end, (parts of) the DBMS needs to be "componentized" in such a way that new components can be added or existing components exchanged in a flexible yet well-defined way. Thus, a componentized architecture specifies and restricts the ways in which the DBMS can be customized. Ultimately, the architecture model also defines the notion of the component itself and hence the realm of valid extensions.

We refer to DBMSs that expose a componentized architecture and allow the adding of components as component DBMSs (CDBMSs). They allow the addition of new components (i.e., new or adapted functions) to the DBMS whenever needed. Due to the componentized architecture, the extensions are possible without requiring other system parts to be rewritten as well. Components can be provided by third parties and possibly even users, thus increasing the developer base of a DBMS. Ultimately, unnecessary components do not have to be added, and applications therefore do not pay (in terms of system cost and performance) for functionality they do not use.

The remainder of this chapter introduces principles and different forms of CDBMSs. The next section presents a more detailed motivation based on application scenarios. We then discuss the foundations of CDBMS (DBMS architecture and componentware) and classify CDBMSs into four groups. Each group is discussed in more detail, and examples for each are given. Section 12.5 addresses design issues, and Section 12.6 summarizes some past trends that are prerequisites for CDBMSs.

12.2 Motivation

This section further motivates the need for CDBMS (see also [6, 9]). We consider DB systems for advanced ISs and investigate the following issues: management of new data types, adapted and new DB functionality, and better integration with other IS parts and the IS environment.

Consider the following scenario. A meteorological institute wants DB technology for its data, of which it has tremendous amounts that need to be stored reliably and persistently. Among the kinds of data to be managed are images (such as satellite images), maps, climate data (temperatures, wind direction and velocity), and text documents (weather forecasts and climate analyses). To keep track of climatic trends, the application also needs time series, that is, pairs (point in time, data value). Ultimately, it must be possible to aggregate elements of these data types into complex objects. For instance, one might want to associate a time series of temperatures with geographic points or satellite images with regions on a map. By formulating typical queries, we might want to know the 30-year average temperature at a certain location, or we might ask for satellite images of hurricanes over Central America.

An important aspect of this scenario (and its commonality with other applications with which DBMSs are currently confronted) is that we no longer deal with the simply structured data for which relational DB systems were intended. Instead, multimedia data (such as images), temporal data (time series), textual data (documents), and geographic data are found in this scenario. Of course, each data type also comes with a characteristic set of operations and query modes.

Assume the perspective of a DBMS user (who can also be seen as a customer of the DBMS vendor), in this scenario, the meteorological institute. The traditional solution would be to develop applications over a DBMS and a set of file-based, dedicated data stores (see Figure 12.1). Applications receive support from a DBMS as far as it can handle the kinds of data they deal with. All other types of data remain in dedicated data stores, such as files, and applications are responsible for integrating the data from the various data stores, establishing an integrated, global view, and ensuring data consistency across multiple data stores.

In this solution, there is no DB support for the dedicated data stores such as image libraries. Thus, one might look for a DBMS that provides all the desired functionality, that is, a DBMS that in our scenario would also be able to handle nonstandard data so far kept in specialized data stores.

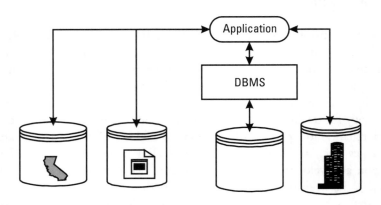

Figure 12.1 Nonstandard application using a DBMS and file-based data stores.

Unfortunately, in the current DBMS landscape, no single DBMS offers all the functionality applications that those described in our scenario require.

Assume now the perspective of a DBMS vendor. If such a system is really needed and customers ask for it, then why not build one (see Figure 12.2)? The prime reason for DBMS companies not to develop such a "one-size-fits-all" DBMS is that it would turn into an extremely complex system. Even if such a system could be built, it would be hardly maintainable and evolvable. Second, since a DBMS vendor introduced all the new functionality, the cost of a DBMS license would significantly increase, and users that need only part of the functionality would nonetheless have to pay for the entire, functionally rich system. Finally, because such a DBMS would be a fairly large system, it most likely would also exhibit much worse run-time performance. That would not, however, be acceptable for users not needing the new functionality.

We face the dilemma of users needing specific functionality and vendors not being able or willing to deliver systems meeting those requirements. The underlying problem lies in the monolithic character of current DBMSs: In such a system, any desired functionality is included in the system either right away or not at all, and all the parts of the DBMS are so tightly interconnected that extensions and modifications within the system are impossible. If, however, the monolithic architecture could be broken up in such a way that new components could be added to a common core on an as-needed basis, then in our scenario the institute could add one component each for images, geographic information, texts, and temporal information. Advanced

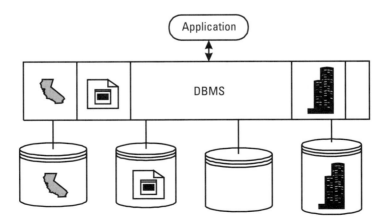

Figure 12.2 Information system on top of a monolithic DBMS.

functionality such as query processing techniques for those kinds of data also would be covered by those components.

In the first scenario, we expected the DBMS to model, store, and efficiently retrieve a fairly varied set of data. Consider now the following scenario. Large collections of satellite images, weather forecasts, and so forth already exist in files and are managed by specialized applications. It is not economic to move the data into a DBMS and rewrite all the applications. Nevertheless, the meteorological institute wants to ask queries against the integrated view of its data stores, ensure correct concurrent accesses to them, and so forth. The dilemma here is that integration (and providing the integrated system with DB functionality) is desired, but it is not possible under the roof of a single DBMS.

A practical remedy for the problem is to "hook" existing data stores into a common, integrating DBMS. If query processors and transaction managers were designed and implemented so that they could be easily combined with existing data stores, the data stores could be leveraged to recoverable and queriable systems (i.e., they would be enhanced with DB functionality). To that end, flexible mechanisms for connecting DBMSs and existing data stores are needed.

The general problem in the scenarios we have considered is the monolithic structure of traditional DBMSs. By monolithic structure or architecture, we mean that the DBMS is a single unit whose parts are connected with each other and dependent on each other to such a degree that modifications and extensions are not easily possible. In particular, each DBMS part might make assumptions about the requirements and operations of other parts, which leads to domino effects whenever changes are made in one place. Extensions can be made only if all the interconnections and dependencies are known. Evolution of and extensions to a DBMS are only possible by the vendor, who then, for each extension, also needs to make sure that other affected parts are adequately adapted. To prevent misinterpretations, it should be stressed that monolithic architectures, as they are prevalent, have not emerged simply because developers and vendors did not know better. In the past, they have been sufficient because applications posed restricted requirements to DBMSs. Moreover, a monolithic DBMS can be implemented in a way that optimizes run-time performance and throughput for all applications that need just the functionality offered by the DBMS. Nevertheless, whenever extensions and customizations are considered, problems with monolithic architectures occur with respect to system complexity, system performance, system cost (production and maintenance), and complexity of system evolution.

The general idea to overcome these problems and to still provide for the needed functionality as sketched in the above scenarios is to offer a core system and to extend it as needed. CDBMSs attempt to allow such extensions in a controlled and safe way. Although different forms of CDBMSs exist, their common basis is a componentized architecture and the support of components that can be added to or assembled into a DBMS. To effectively allow extensions, the DBMS architecture must be made explicit and well defined. While typically some parts of the CDBMS will need to be fixed without the possibility of altering them, others can be extended (we call this the *variable part*). "Explicit" means that the system structure is defined, preferably in a (formal) architecture model and that the system structure is visible to the actors modifying it. Second, the notion and the meaning of *component* need to be defined. Varieties range from abstract data types to implementations of internal tasks. However, the common characteristics of components are that they implement a coherent set of functions, make all restrictions concerning their use explicit in their interface, and are generally applicable across a variety of applications. Ultimately, a CDBMS architecture also defines places in the system (the variable part) where components can be added. These places can be thought of as hooks used to plug components into the enclosing system. Technically, the hooks are defined in terms of interfaces the component can use or should implement.

12.3 Principles of Component DBMSs

This section elaborates on the principles of CDBMSs. As mentioned, extensions to a DBMS affect its architecture and also require that certain prerequisites be met. We therefore first briefly address the issue of DBMS architecture. The subsequent section relates CDBMS to componentware, followed by a classification of CDBMS.

12.3.1 DBMS Architecture

Different kinds of "architecture" serve different purposes. For instance, the three-level schema architecture (which distinguishes external schemas that users work with, the internal, integrated schema of the entire DB, and the physical schema determining storage and organization of DBs on secondary storage) reflects the different levels of abstraction of data in a DB system. The layered architecture described below illustrates a hierarchy of mappings, where the topmost layer deals with data model entities and the one at the bottom deals with blocks and files. Finally, a task-oriented architecture identifies the relevant modules (i.e., their purpose and interface) and relationships to other modules, for example, in the form of exported and imported interfaces. Examples for such tasks include query optimization, concurrency control, and recovery. The latter two also are examples for tasks that are hard to assign to a specific layer in the layered architecture, or that might even be addressed by multiple layers. Although a task-oriented architecture is much more suitable for reasoning about extensibility and DBMS construction, reference architectures hardly exist (with the strawman architecture developed by the Computer Corporation of America (CCA) [10] as a notable exception), and concrete architectures are described at a granularity too coarse to be helpful for our purposes.

For educational purposes, it is convenient to consider a DBMS architecture as consisting of a number of layers [11, 12]. Each layer supports a set of data types and operations at its interface and typically consists of several components (modules or managers of some concrete or abstract resource). The data types and operations defined for the modules of one layer are implemented using the concepts (data types and operations) of the next lower level. Therefore, the layered architecture can also be considered as a "stack" of abstract machines. Concretely, the layered architecture model as introduced by Härder and Reuter [11] is composed of five layers (see Figure 12.3):

- The uppermost layer (L4) supports logical data structures such as relations, tuples, and views. Typical tasks of this layer include query processing and optimization, access control, and integrity enforcement.

- L3 implements a record-oriented interface. Typical entities are records and sets (e.g., as found in the Codasyl data model) as well as logical access paths. Typical components are the data dictionary, transaction management, and cursor management.

- The middle layer (L2) manages storage structures (internal records), physical access paths, locking, logging, and recovery. Relevant modules include the record manager, physical access path managers (e.g., a hash table manager), and modules for lock management, logging, and recovery.

- L1 implements (page) buffer management and the page replacement strategy. Typical entities are pages and segments.

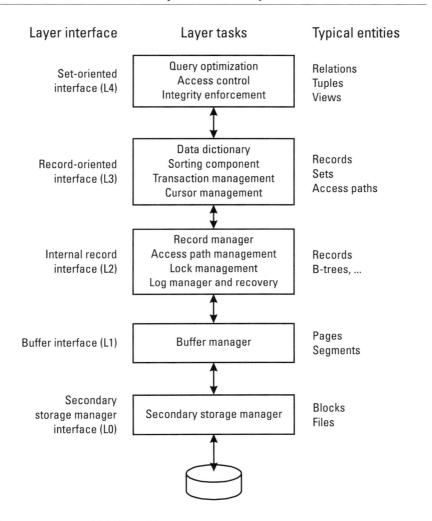

Figure 12.3 Layered DBMS architecture.

- The lowest layer (L0) implements management of secondary storage, that is, maps, segments, and pages to blocks and files.

In general, due to performance considerations, no concrete DBMS has fully followed the layered architecture proposal. Note further that different layered architectures and different numbers of layers are proposed, depending on the desired interfaces at the top layer. If, for instance, a solely set-oriented interface has to be offered, it is useful to "merge" the upper two layers.

From a more practical point of view, most DBMS architectures have been influenced by System R [13], which consists of two layers: the relational data system (RDS), providing for the relational data interface (RDI), and the relational storage system (RSS), supporting the relational storage interface (RSI). While RDS implements SQL (including query optimization, access control, triggers, and the like), RSS supports access to single tuples of base relations at its interface.

12.3.2 Components and DBMS Architecture

When we are striving for reusability, extensibility, openness, and interoperability in DB systems, looking at software engineering research and practice yields helpful insights. In particular, "componentware" [14–20] has recently been proposed as a paradigm to address those issues. This notion is meant to say that software systems are built in a disciplined manner out of building blocks with specific properties, called components. There is currently no widely agreed-upon definition of the term *component*; however, the following characteristics of components can be found in most definitions in the literature. A (software) component, then, is a software artifact modeling and implementing a coherent and well-defined set of functions. It consists of a component interface and a component implementation. Components are "black boxes," which means that clients can use them properly without knowing their implementation. Component interface and implementation should be separated such that multiple implementations can exist for one interface, and implementations can be exchanged. Components being black boxes also means that each component "sees" only the interfaces of other components, that is, access to internal operations and structures of other components is not permitted. A component should not have an overly high number of relationships to other components, because that might restrict its reuse potential.

Components usually possess a coarser granularity than objects in object-oriented systems and models. A well-designed component supports a coherent set of tasks (e.g., in one of our scenarios, storing and retrieving textual documents), while objects and classes typically address only a part thereof. Components and objects, however, are not mutually exclusive alternatives, but components rather leverage object-orientation to a higher level of abstraction and granularity. In fact, components are "under the hood," often assemblies of objects.

To put the right components together, that is, to obtain complete and adequate systems, a frame (into which components are plugged) and rules governing the composition process are needed. The frame is given by the software architecture [21, 22] of the system under construction. Similar software systems are then described by architecture skeletons or generic architectures [19] that are successively enhanced and completed by components. Thus, as a prerequisite, the underlying generic architecture needs to be defined in terms of components (acting as placeholders) and connections in such a way that later components can be added in a meaningful and consistent way.

We use the principles of componentware to better understand, abstract, and classify the various approaches to extend and customize DBMSs. Moreover, the characteristics of componentware (components, architecture) are crucial requirements for systematic and well-defined extensibility and integration. Extensions to a DBMS in that context are represented as components, that is, they should meet the aforementioned properties of components. Further, DBMSs should exhibit a componentized architecture, at least for those parts that are intended to be customizable.

12.3.3 Typology of Component DBMSs

This section presents the various types of CDBMSs. The following dimensions are considered.

- *Components.* What kinds of components are considered? Which kinds of DB functionalities or DBMS tasks can be represented as components? How are components defined?

- *Architecture.* What is the generic DBMS architecture that allows components to be plugged in? What are the fixed parts? The variable parts? How are components and plugs described?

12.3.3.1 Plug-In Style

The first category of CDBMSs comprises so-called universal servers. Their core system is formed by a fully functional DBMS that implements all the standard functionality expected from a DBMS. Nonstandard features or functionality not yet supported can be plugged into such a DBMS (see Figure 12.4). Such a system is functionally complete and meets basic requirements; extensions add further functionality for specialized needs.

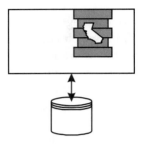

Figure 12.4 Principles of plug-in style CDBMS.

A typical case of component in this kind of CDBMS is families of base and abstract data types or implementations of some DBMS function, such as new access paths. The DBMS architecture, among others, defines a number of "plugs" components can use, for example, interfaces of functions the DBMS will invoke and which the component must thus implement. In other words, the architecture formulates expectations concerning interfaces that the component must meet to be integrated successfully.

12.3.3.2 Middleware DBMSs

The typical aim of systems falling into the category of middleware DBMSs is to integrate existing data stores, that is, to leave data items under the control of their original (external) management systems, while integrating them into a common DBMS-style framework. For instance, existing data stores should be integrated into query processing or transaction management of the entire system (the *integrating DBMS*). External systems will in many cases exhibit different capabilities, such as query languages with varying power or no querying facilities at all. The different data stores might also have different data models (i.e., different data definition and structuring means) or no explicit data model at all. Nevertheless, users and applications should be shielded from that kind of heterogeneity and be provided with a uniform and integrated view of the entire system. That is accomplished by a CDBMS acting as middleware [20] between the data stores and the applications of the integration. The overall aim of systems in this group is similar to that of multidatabase systems [7, 8], although the latter typically considers only integration of DB systems instead of any kind of data store.

That goal is achieved by componentizing a DBMS in the following way (see Figure 12.5). The architecture introduces a common (intermediate) format into which the local data formats can be translated. Components are introduced that are able to perform this kind of translation. Second,

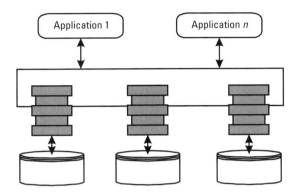

Figure 12.5 Middleware-style CDBMS.

common interfaces and protocols define how the DBMS and the components interact, for example, in order to retrieve data from a data store. The components (so-called wrappers) are able to transform requests issued via the interfaces (e.g., queries) into requests understandable by the external system. In other words, the components implement the functionality needed to access from within the DBMS data managed by the external data store.

12.3.3.3 Service-Oriented Architectures

The third type of componentized DBMS is characterized by a service-oriented view of DB functionality. All DBMS and related tasks are unbundled [23] into services: As a result, a monolithic DBMS is transformed into a set of standalone services. For instance, the unbundling process can result in persistence, query, and transaction services. Applications then no longer operate on a full-fledged DBMS, but use those services as needed (see Figure 12.6).

Each service is defined by one or more interfaces and implemented by some software systems. Services (i.e., their interfaces) are defined in a

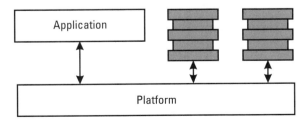

Figure 12.6 Principle of service-oriented architectures.

common model or language. Services are implemented using a common platform to render service implementations exchangeable and freely combinable.

12.3.3.4 Configurable DBMSs

In the previous form of componentized DBMS, the set of services has been standardized and fixed. One step further, *configurable DBMS,* allows the development of new DBMS parts and the integration of them into a DBMS (see Figure 12.7). Components are DBMS subsystems, which are defined in an underlying architecture model. In that approach, the architecture model is also used to model the DBMS architecture.

Like the previous type of CDBMS, configurable DBMSs also consider services as unbundled representations of DBMS tasks. However, the models underlying the various services and defining the semantics of the corresponding DBMS parts can now also be customized. As a consequence, components for the same DBMS task may vary not only in their implementations (for the same and standardized interface), but also in their interfaces for the same task. DBMS implementors select (or construct new) components implementing the desired functionality and obtain a DBMS by assembling the selected components (see Figure 12.7). The DBMS is thus the result of a configuration process.

12.4 Component Database Models

This section investigates the various types of component DB systems in more detail and describes example systems for each type.

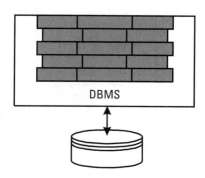

Figure 12.7 Principle of a configurable DBMS.

12.4.1 Plug-In Components

To date, all systems in the category of plug-in components are based on the relational data model and existing relational DBMSs, and all of them offer some object-oriented extensions. We thus discuss this type of CDBMS in an object-relational [24] context, although componentization is also possible for object-oriented DB systems. Example systems include Informix Universal Server [25], IBM's Universal Database [26], and Oracle8 [27]. Descriptions of sample component developments can be found in [28, 29].

These approaches aim at providing data management facilities for nonstandard, new data types and nonstandard or specialized DB functionality within the DBMS. Instances of these new data types are thus stored in the DB, and their manipulation and retrieval are implemented by the DBMS. We do not consider techniques that leave the data in files and just maintain links to those files.

Assume that an application needs support for data types not yet supported by the DBMS in use (e.g., spatial data, or a German character set including ä, ö, ü, etc.). The ultimate task is to "teach" the DBMS how to store, manipulate, and retrieve instances of those data types.

As a first step, the designer has to model the structure of the desired new data types as well as their type-specific behavior. From a user point of view, new data types are either complex or atomic. Complex data types possess structure, and their values can be represented as specialized records/tuples or collections, using the means of the data definition language. Atomic data types do not have an internal structure and consist of literal values (such as numbers or characters). For atomic types, the DBMS needs basic information, such as their length in bytes, to store their instances.

For spatial data, one would, for example, specify points as a complex data type modeling locations in three-dimensional space, that is, *3DPoint* could be specified as a tuple type with attributes x, y, and z, each of which is of type *decimal*. Another example would be *Region*, whose structure could be defined as a pair of points, *LowerLeft* and *UpperRight*. The German alphabet, in contrast, would be defined as an atomic type whose instances are, say, 2 bytes long. In addition to the structure of data types, the type-specific behavior of the new sorts of data needs to be specified. For each complex data type, its specific functions, operators, and predicates must be made known to the DBMS. In our example, a possible function would be the *move* function for points, and a typical predicate would be *overlaps*, which tests whether two regions intersect in some subregion.

While atomic types often most do not exhibit type-specific behavior, they do normally require special treatment with respect to ordering and representation. Indeed, one reason to introduce a new type for nonstandard alphabets is that existing DBMSs do not know how to sort them correctly. Thus, for new atomic types, it is necessary to define operators such as "<". Furthermore, functions that convert elements of atomic types from an internal (stored) representation to/from an external one are needed.

For each function, operator, and predicate, its signature (i.e., its name, arguments, and result) must be defined, and an implementation must be provided. The implementation language in turn depends on the DBMS, with possibilities ranging from DBMS-specific languages such as Oracle's PL/SQL to general-purpose programming languages like C/C++ or Java.

The collection of data types (their definition and implementation) forms a significant part of a component, which then needs to be plugged into the DBMS. To that end, DBMSs in this category offer a facility to "register" new components. Component registration introduces new definitions (for types, functions, and so forth), and also informs the DBMS where (in which files) implementations can be found.

After a data type has been registered, applications can in principle start to use them, that is, to create and retrieve instances of them. However, efficient retrieval and processing might require further enhancements to the DBMS, particularly to the access path manager and the query optimizer. Thus, we observe that extending a DBMS by plugging in new components often has some sort of domino effect, because other parts must be adapted accordingly.

Current DBMSs typically contain B-tree access paths and possibly also hash-based indexes. B-trees can handle one-dimensional keys very well, and they rely on the orderability of keys. New types such as spatial data types, however, can be multidimensional; thus, they would not be adequately served by B-trees, and consequently query processing might easily become inefficient. Therefore, in some situations it will be necessary to add new access methods to the DBMS, for example, one that supports multidimensional indexing [30]. To integrate well with other parts of the DBMS, such a new index has to implement exactly those functions that the DBMS calls for its indexes, that is, insertion and deletion of entries, index scanning, and so on.

The addition of new data types also affects query processing, in particular, query optimization. Cost-based optimization techniques, for instance, need information about the cost of each operator (in terms of CPU consumption and I/O operations) to find an optimal plan. To ensure efficient query processing in this case, it is necessary to provide the optimizer with adequate information, for example, some knowledge of how it can estimate the cost of evaluating newly defined predicates.

For a typical example of the aforementioned domino effect, consider concurrency control for access paths. Many DBMSs use specialized concurrency control protocols on indexes to prevent unnecessary locking conflicts [31, 32], which otherwise would increase lock contention and decrease transaction throughput. Therefore, whenever a new index is introduced, concurrency control (for this new index type) also should be adopted, which is not possible in current systems.

12.4.2 Middleware DBMS

This type of CDBMS aims at integrating external data stores into DB systems without requiring the data to be moved under control of the DBMS. Still, users should be provided with an integrated view, that is, queries and updates on the data source should be possible, and the disparate data formats should be resolved into a homogeneous form.

The underlying problem in that respect is that the DBMS needs to "understand" the data formats and the functions of each data source. Two extreme alternatives exist to tackle the problem. In one, information about the data sources' interfaces is hardwired into the (integrating) DBMS. The realm of integratable external data stores is thus restricted, and the DBMS needs to be extended for each specific type of data store. In the other extreme, a common data model, query language, or interface to external data stores is set as a prerequisite (e.g., SQL). Each data store that does not implement SQL right away would have to be extended to do so.

The solution that helps to overcome the intrinsic problems of both approaches lies in the introduction of additional components. In a nutshell, one component is pushed between the DBMS and each data source. The components serve to homogenize differences in formats and functionality from the DBMS's point of view. From the data sources' perspective, they level the different data source capabilities into a common basis. Thus, each component mediates between the data sources and the DBMS or—from the DBMS's point of view—wraps the data source.

The first prerequisite of this approach is a common data abstraction (e.g., objects). Second, the mediation components offer a common interface. This interface is used by the DBMS to request data from the data sources. Each component should at least support the "minimal" interface, such as scanning over a collection of data entities. Depending on the data source capabilities, its mediation component can contribute more or specialized functions, such as predicate evaluation. Whenever the DBMS executes a query and determines that it needs results from the data source, it sends a request to the corresponding component, which in turn translates the request into a form the data source can handle. Eventually, the component receives results from the data source and converts them into the common format expected by the DBMS.

For several reasons, this approach requires an appropriately defined notion of components for wrapping the external data stores, because it must match the requirements and characteristics of the DBMS while also taking as much benefit as possible of the capabilities of the data stores. Moreover, using the full potential of this approach means that a component is written once for each kind of data store (e.g., for a specific image management system) and used for all subsequent instances of the data store.

Ultimately, users should be allowed to introduce new components to integrate data stores not yet covered. To that end, the implementation of a component must be possible without knowing the internal structure and operations of the DBMS; the requirements to be met by a component must be entirely expressed in its interface.

An example for that approach is OLE DB [33–35]. The major abstraction in OLE DB is *rowsets*, which are sets of tuples. From a functional point of view, data and service providers can be distinguished. Data providers are components that are able to export rowsets. For instance, a sample data provider component might be able to convert data from a spreadsheet into rowsets. Service providers are components that offer operations on rowsets, for example, query processors. A service provider can also be a data provider.

Components in OLE DB are described using Microsoft's Component Object Model (COM). Each COM object implements a set of interfaces. The most general interface is called *IUnknown*, which defines a few generic functions (such as checking whether the object supports a given interface). *IRowset* is the most general interface for rowsets and includes functions for iterating over a rowset. Further interfaces for rowsets allow retrieval of information about the columns of a rowset. *IRowset* can be specialized to model further operations, such as inserting, updating, and deleting rows from a rowset. Commands (data definition, manipulation, queries) are represented in OLE DB as command objects, whose most general interface is *ICommand*. Queries (see Figure 12.8) are special command objects that consume and produce rowsets. Based on the common abstraction of rowsets, it is possible to build specialized query processors such as content-based search engines.

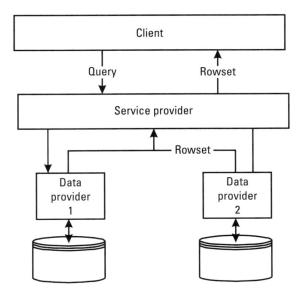

Figure 12.8 Query execution in OLE DB.

To integrate a new kind of data source, developers have to build a data provider for it. Its interfaces must conform to the existing interfaces (such as *IRowset*) or be specializations of those interfaces. To implement specialized behavior (such as a customized query processor), new command objects need to be built.

Another example for this category of CDBMS is Garlic [36]. In Garlic, data source-specific wrappers are used to mediate between the Garlic layer and the data sources. Garlic additionally allows components to exploit the query capabilities of data sources (via their wrappers) [37]. Minimally, each wrapper provides scans over collections. Depending on the data source capabilities, a wrapper can generate plans for more complex queries, such as predicates, joins, and aggregates. During query planning, the optimizer will request a plan for subqueries from the responsible wrapper, which then decides whether it can execute the entire subquery or only parts of it. In case the wrapper/data source can execute only parts of a query, the remaining operations are done by the Garlic query execution component.

A final representative for this group is the Sybase Adaptive Server Enterprise [38], which allows access to external data stores (called "specialty data stores" in Sybase) and other types of DB systems.

12.4.3 Service-Oriented DBMSs

In the service-oriented approach, DB tasks are unbundled from each other and represented as services. Each service is implemented on top of a common platform. Services should be as independent as possible from each other, that is, they should not rely on the availability of another service in the environment. Specifically, they should not assume that other services are implemented in a particular way. Thus, DB services and their implementations are viewed as components. Given that both the platform and the service interfaces are standardized, exchangeability and compatibility are guaranteed. Different implementations of a service can be exchanged, and implementations of different services—possibly from different vendors—can be plugged together.

An example of this approach is CORBAservices [39], which leverages several DBMS tasks to general object systems. These services are standardized by the Object Management Group (OMG). Service interfaces are defined using the IDL. Services related to DB functionality include persistency, concurrency, relationships, transactions, queries, and collections.

CORBAservices offers further non-DB services such as licensing and event notification. Whenever a system (e.g., an application server) to be implemented needs some DB functionality, it can receive the appropriate support by using the corresponding service. Such requests are handled in a location-transparent way by object request brokers (ORB) [40], which form the platform on top of which services are implemented.

In contrast to the other approaches discussed here, components (i.e., services) are not meant to extend or customize a DBMS. Rather, the systems constructable by using services are distributed applications located above the DBMS level. In fact, services like persistence could be implemented by a DBMS, and the transaction service is typically implemented by transaction processing monitors [41].

The underlying semantics and models (such as the transaction model and the query language) are fixed. Thus, for a transaction service, there will be different implementations all implementing transactions such as flat or nested ACID-transactions, but transactions such as cooperative or other forms of nonstandard transactions [42] would not be supported.

A second example for this approach is the so-called "strawman architecture" [10] developed at CCA. The aim of that study was to propose standard interfaces between users/applications and DBMSs as well as standards for internal interfaces (such that different DBMS subsystems can be combined more easily). The CCA study identified 79 subcomponents, which are grouped together into 38 components, some of which denote internal functions while others refer to external (i.e., visible at the DBMS interface) functions. The subcomponents are partitioned into six groups of related tasks. For each subcomponent, procedures and interfaces are proposed. Therefore, the view of a DBMS architecture is more service oriented, and concrete components are proposed to implement such services (to the best of our knowledge, however, a DBMS implementing this architecture has never been built).

12.4.4 Configurable DBMSs

Configurable DBMSs are similar to service-oriented DBMSs in that they also rely on unbundled DBMS tasks that can be mixed and matched to obtain DB support. The difference lies in the possibility of adapting service implementations to new requirements or even to define new services whenever needed.

For an example, configurable DBMSs have been investigated in the KIDS project [43, 44]. KIDS aims at constructing DBMSs by developing subsystems that implement various aspects of a DBMS (such as transaction management or constraint enforcement) and by finally configuring those subsystems together into a coherent and complete DBMS. The underlying architecture model provides for constructs that are adequate for defining the architecture of DBMSs. The tasks and functionality of a DBMS and its components are modeled by means of services. Services are provided by reactive components called *brokers*, which are responsible for services. In case of service requests, the responsible brokers react by providing the service. The functionality of each subsystem under construction is represented as a set of services, and one or more brokers are designated as components implementing the subsystem.

The construction process defines how to proceed to obtain a DBMS with the desired functionality. The process consists of several phases, including requirements analysis and design, implementation, and integration of multiple DBMS subsystems. Some phases of the process are common to all constructable DBMSs and independent of subsystems, for example, requirements analysis and architecture design. For each type of subsystem, a dedicated construction subprocess is defined and integrated into the enclosing DBMS construction process. For each subsystem, a dedicated specification language is used to define its functionality (such as ACTA in the case of transaction models [45] or SOS in the case of data models [46]). These specifications serve as input to subsystem-specific implementation phases, which in turn use techniques such as the generation of subsystems or the configuration of subsystems out of reusable, already existing components [43].

12.4.5 Categories of Component DBMS Models

We now summarize and examine component DBMS models. Table 12.1 summarizes the characteristics of the four categories.

The categories listed in Table 12.1 are not necessarily disjoint. For instance, it is conceivable that both plug-in components for nonstandard data as well as wrappers for accessing external data stores can be added to a single system. Such a system would therefore belong to the first two categories (e.g., as outlined in [47]). Likewise, OLE DB could also be classified as a configurable DBMS, because in principle it allows the exchange and addition of internal components, for example, to add specialized query processors.

12.5 Development of Component DBMSs and Their Applications

Given all the powerful new kinds of functionalities CDBMSs offer, the question is apparent of how users can effectively use them—we encounter the problem of design and development of component DBMSs and their applications. Because the type of systems considered here are only in the process of

Table 12.1
Classification of Component DBMS Models

Category	Purpose	Architecture, "Plugs"	Typical Components
Plug-in DBMSs	Extend existing DBMS with nonstandard functionality	Interfaces expected or provided by kernel	ADT definition and implementation, new indexes
Middleware DBMSs	Integrate existing data stores into DB system	Common format and interfaces between DBMS and wrappers	Wrappers for external data sources
Service-oriented architectures	Provide DB functionality in standardized, unbundled form	Service definitions	Service implementations
Configurable DBMSs	Compose nonstandard DBMS out of reusable components	Service definitions	DBMS subsystems

maturing, design methods for them are to a large extent still an open issue. This section thus aims mainly at identifying which development phases will be affected and how.

We concentrate on the development of components and of applications using components. A third kind of development is the design of CDBMSs themselves, that is, the definition of their architecture and component models (in cases where the component models are DBMS specific). Few people will ever be confronted with that task, so we do not address it here.

Requirements analysis is concerned with the specification of the functionality the application under development should have. The important results of this phase are

- Separation of DBMS tasks from application tasks;
- Identification of components meeting requirements;
- System selection.

With component DBMSs, tasks so far in the responsibility of applications could be "moved" into the DBMS. However, that might not always be useful, for several reasons. For instance, a DBMS is supposed to be responsible for general, application-independent functionality only. Likewise, computing-intensive yet not data-intensive operations are often better done by DBMS clients rather than DBMS servers. Thus, the increased number of options offered by component DBMSs also requires a more complex analysis of the separation of concerns between a DBMS and its potential applications.

Another important outcome of analysis is the identification of components that meet some of the requirements. For instance, analysis may yield the requirement to maintain an image library, and one might conclude that an image storage and retrieval component is needed.

In case a system (DBMS) selection is possible (i.e., the DBMS to be used is not already firmly determined by the current environment), this selection will also depend on the components most likely to be needed and the possibility of adding new components. Not all vendors will offer the same components, or different components will vary in adequacy or performance for a system under development. Thus, one criterion for DBMS selection would be the optimal match of required and offered components. In case some desired components are not available from DBMS vendors or third parties, an enterprise itself might want to develop the missing components. In that case, another criterion for DBMS selection is which of the vendors allows the addition of user-defined components.

With respect to DB design proper, it is useful to distinguish two types of users:

- Schema and application designers who develop applications by using the (enhanced) features of a CDBMS;
- DBMS implementors who extend a CDBMS by developing new components.

The distinction between the two kinds of developers leads to a distinction between two design tasks:

- Database design for a CDBMS;
- Component development in a CDBMS.

12.5.1 Database Design for CDBMSs

The first task is very much akin to common DB design [48, 49], that is, developing a conceptual schema, mapping the schema to a logical schema (expressible in the logical schema of the underlying DBMS), and finally defining a physical schema. The ability to extend the DBMS (e.g., by adding new types and treating them as co-equal to existing, built-in types) implies that more means to express a logical schema exist. Thus, instead of defining new types from scratch, designers could reuse already existing types. The challenge here is to enforce *design by reuse*, that is, to support designers in finding components that meet the requirements of the application in question.

Established design methods in the current state of the art are those that use the E/R model [50] to express conceptual schemas and map them into relational schemas; such mapping can even be automated. CDBMSs exploit object-oriented features such as type-specific behavior, complex objects, and inheritance. There is currently no commonly accepted DB design method exploiting these concepts or an object-oriented design method (e.g., one using the widely accepted UML notation [51]) that could be applied to CDBMSs. Moreover, given behavioral elements such as triggers [52] and user-defined functions [53], the sharp distinction between data-centric (done in DB design) and processing-oriented design (addressed by application development) is blurred.

Ultimately, the already complex problem of physical DB design is also aggravated. If in a CDBMS new access methods can be added, DB administrators can choose among more options. The rules of when to use which type of access path are no longer fixed, because newly added access paths can be equivalent to existing ones with respect to some properties, while outperforming them in other regards. While most of the work in CDBMSs has been devoted to extending the DBMS itself, effects on physical DB design and tuning practices have not been considered in depth so far.

Design problems are also aggravated for middleware CDBMSs. Designers "see" a common and uniform interface as far as data modeling and manipulation are concerned. However, the task of integrating existing data stores into a common system is far from trivial. Existing mediation components such as wrappers resolve disparities in terms of languages, interfaces, and data formats, but they do not consider the "meaning" of the various data stores. In consequence, semantic integration and resolution of semantic conflicts still have to be done during DB design (i.e., schema integration in the sense of federated DB systems [7, 54]). Although considerable research has been conducted in this area, consensual and practicable solutions are not yet in sight.

12.5.2 Development of CDBMS Components

Design issues are also of concern with regard to the development of components. Assume that a system has been selected and it has been decided that one or more new components are to be developed. The questions then arise about which functionality this component should expose and how it should be implemented.

Developing a component is meaningful only when it is defined in such a way that it is of effective use for future applications/schemas. In other words, the component interface should not necessarily be designed in such a way that it offers exactly the functionality the currently considered application needs. Instead, reuse payoff of all potential current and future applications should be optimized. That means that by abstracting from the concrete requirements of the current application under design, the component is designed for reuse.

From a more technical point of view, developing a component means that a piece of software is produced that is supposed to link with a DBMS, possibly on different platforms such as operating systems and network protocols. The software should be correct and adequate because it will be reused, and errors will multiply with applications using the software. Moreover, bugs introduced to internal subsystems of a DBMS, such as index structures, can easily corrupt not only the DBMS process but also the DB. Thus, methods and tools that guide and assist the design, implementation, and evaluation (or at least testing) of new components are of paramount importance. That is particularly true whenever users (not only vendors) are allowed to add components. An example for this type of tool support is the DataBlade Developers Kit by Informix [25].

12.6 Related Work: The Roots of CDBMSs

This section reviews the roots of component DB systems. In a nutshell, those roots are relational DB systems, object-orientation in general and object-oriented DBMSs in particular, and extensible DB systems.

In the mid-1970s, companies like IBM (with System R [13] and later DB2), Oracle, and Ingres started to build relational DBMSs. The success of those systems (i.e., the relational model and SQL, the transaction concept) for mission-critical applications in enterprises led to the desire for DB support in further areas, for which relational DBMSs were originally neither intended nor adequate.

Object-oriented DB systems [2, 3] were developed starting in the mid-1980s, with the objective of integrating into the data model object-oriented features such as object identity, specialization and inheritance, and classes, including class-specific behavior (methods). Thus, many enhancements like user-defined types and functions that recently have been made available in relational DBMSs have been supported in OODBMSs from the very beginning. Concepts like inheritance and complex objects are crucial for powerful extension mechanisms and component models; thus all component DBMSs surveyed in this chapter use object-oriented (DBMS) features to at least some degree.

Extensible DB systems [55–68] all attempted to ease the construction of DBMSs [69] by exploiting some kind of software reusability. They proposed a general core that could be customized or extended in some way by users or even to generate some DBMS parts. Hence, they shared the aims of component DBMSs. Several of the techniques proposed for extensible DBMSs (such as extensible query optimization [70] and user-definable types [66]) are now used in CDBMSs. However, many still open problems render the construction of entire, full-fledged DBMSs based on reuse impracticable.

- Most of the systems did not expose a real architecture model (except OpenOODB [58, 67] and KIDS [43, 44]). It thus remained unclear how to extend DBMSs to achieve the desired functionality.

- DBMS implementation (e.g., on top of object managers or by using toolkits) and customization have required way too much effort and have been too complex to be considered practical.

- Most of them addressed a single DBMS aspect such as transaction management or query optimization, and it remained unclear how the generated or customized subsystems could be integrated properly with other DBMS parts.

- Albeit extensible DBMSs have striven for reuse of existing artifacts in DBMS construction, they nonetheless failed to address problems known from software reuse research and practice [70], such as selection (support for finding the adequate reusable software artifact) or integration of reused parts into the entire system under construction. Libraries of reusable artifacts (specifications, designs, implementations) have been proposed but never built.

- Finally, building a full-fledged CDBMS is a voluminous piece of work and at the very limits of even larger academic research groups. On the other hand, the DBMS industry is preoccupied so far by maintaining and evolving their current product offers and thus is not yet interested enough to invest in entirely new approaches. Nevertheless, performance considerations and the domino effect of adding components are likely to push the plug-in approach further, so that DBMS parts that are currently fixed will be customizable in the future. In the end, plug-in approaches might well exhibit the power of configurable DBMSs.

By putting CDBMSs, in particular plug-in CDBMSs, into the context of recent research directions, they build on the well-established relational engines and make use of features found in object-oriented DBMSs, but they also have learned lessons from extensible DBMSs and try to avoid dead ends. Middleware DBMSs share their goals with multidatabase systems, and the systems in both groups overlap. The former, however, goes beyond multidatabase systems that had been proposed until recently in that their component-based approach allows integration of a broader set of external data stores, notably those without DB functionality.

12.7 Summary

This chapter introduced the notion of component DBMSs and surveyed the various types thereof. Component DBMSs attempt to meet nonstandard requirements for DBMSs by allowing extension and customization. Those objectives are achieved by componentizing DBMSs at least to some degree and by allowing insertion of components into such a componentized DBMS. The success and viability of component DBMSs thus rely on a properly expressed DBMS architecture that provides for the hooks to connect new components to the DBMS and a well-defined notion of "component."

Based on those two dimensions, we have identified four categories of CDBMSs:

- Universal servers with pluggable components;
- Middleware DBMSs able to integrate external data stores;
- Service-oriented architectures offering a set of unbundled DBMS tasks;
- Configurable DBMSs, full-custom DBMSs built out of specialized DBMS subsystems.

In the current state of the art, systems in the first two groups of CDBMSs are available on the market (with further ones to follow) and represent a practical technology. The third group is intended more for heterogeneous and distributed application systems that require some subset of DBMS tasks; they are not necessarily meant as a way to construct DBMSs. Configurable DBMSs are still in a research state and need a lot more work before they have practical relevance.

Despite initial success stories showing the benefits of CDBMSs, a number of questions remain. First, components are usually defined and implemented in a system-dependent manner. As a consequence, components developed for a system of one vendor cannot be added to the system of another one, that is, components are not portable across systems. Because component implementations depend on the (internal) interfaces of the DBMS they use, it is hard to imagine a standard that would make portability possible.

Furthermore, component implementations might be less efficient than code hardwired in the DBMS. One reason for performance penalties is that componentization can prevent optimizations that otherwise would be possible. Moreover, extensions to other parts of the system that would improve performance of new components might not be possible (e.g., specialized concurrency control for new index structures). As for the latter point, more research is needed to fully understand the implications and side effects of CDBMSs.

The work conducted in the area of CDBMSs has focused on extensions in the area of new data types (including indexes useful for those nonstandard types). Componentization of the DBMS kernel, including the transaction manager and the query processor in general and the optimizer in particular, has been considered less thoroughly so far. In those areas, a better understanding of the implications and limitations of componentization is necessary. It might turn out that subsystems also need to be componentized and that it might be possible to specialize them by adding or replacing new (sub)components.

Despite the problems that still need to be addressed, component DBMSs will certainly gain practical significance, and componentization of DBMSs will continue to be a major trend in DB technology.

References

[1]   Date, C. J., and H. Darwen, *A Guide to the SQL Standard*, 4th ed., Reading, MA: Addison-Wesley, 1997.

[2]   Bernstein, P. A., V. Hadzilacos, and N. Goodman, *Concurrency Control and Recovery in Database Systems*, Reading, MA: Addison-Wesley, 1987.

[3]   Codd, E., "A Relational Model for Large Shared Data Banks," *Comm. ACM*, Vol. 13, No. 6, 1970.

[4]   Atkinson, M. P., et al., "The Object-Oriented Database System Manifesto (A Political Pamphlet)," *Proc. 1st Intl. Conf. on Deductive and Object-Oriented Databases*, Kyoto, Japan, Dec. 1989.

[5]   Cattell, R. G. G., and D. Barry (eds.), *The Object Database Standard: ODMG 2.0*, San Francisco, CA: Morgan Kaufmann, 1997.

[6]   Vaskevitch, D., "Database in Crisis and Transition: A Technical Agenda for the Year 2001," *Proc. ACM-SIGMOD Intl. Conf. on Management of Data*, Minneapolis, MN, May 1994.

[7]   Sheth, A. P., and J. A. Larson, "Federated Database Systems for Managing Distributed, Heterogeneous, and Autonomous Databases," *ACM Computing Surveys*, Vol. 22, No. 3, Sept. 1990.

[8]   Elmagarmid, A., M. Rusinkiewicz, and A. Sheth (eds.), *Management of Heterogeneous and Autonomous Database Systems*, San Francisco, CA: Morgan Kaufmann, 1999.

[9]   Vaskevitch, D., "Very Large Databases: How Large? How Different?" *Proc. 21st Intl. Conf. on Very Large Data Bases (VLDB)*, Zurich, Switzerland, Sept. 1995.

[10] "An Architecture for Database Management Standards," *NBS Spec. Pub. 500-85*, Computer Corporation of America, 1982.

[11] Härder, T., and A. Reuter, "Concepts for Implementing a Centralized Database Management System," *Proc. Intl. Computing Symposium on Application Systems Development*, Nuernberg, Germany, Mar. 1983.

[12] Ramakrishnan, R., *Database Management Systems*, New York: McGraw-Hill, 1997.

[13] Astrahan, M. M., et al., "System R: Relational Approach to Database Management," *ACM Trans. on Database Systems*, Vol. 1, No. 2, 1976.

[14] Allen, P., and S. Frost, *Component-Based Development for Enterprise Systems*, New York: Cambridge University Press, 1998.

[15] Griffel, F., *Componentware*, Heidelberg, Germany: Dpunkt.Verlag, 1998.

[16] Hamilton, D. (ed.), *Java Beans*, Version 1.01, Sun Microsystems, 1997.

[17] Krieger, D., and R. M. Adler, "The Emergence of Distributed Component Platforms," *IEEE Computer*, Vol. 31, No. 3, Mar. 1998.

[18] Nierstrasz, O., and L. Dami, "Component-Oriented Software Technology," in O. Nierstrasz and D. Tsichritzis (eds.), *Object-Oriented Software Composition*, London, UK: Prentice-Hall, 1995.

[19] Nierstrasz, O., and T. D. Meijler, "Beyond Objects: Components," in M. P. Papazoglou and G. Schlageter (eds.), *Cooperative Information Systems: Trends and Directions*, San Diego, CA: Academic Press, 1998.

[20] Orfali, R., D. Harkey, and J. Edwards, *The Essential Client/Server Survival Guide*, 2nd ed., New York: Wiley, 1996.

[21] Perry, D. E., and A. L. Wolf, "Foundations for the Study of Software Architectures," *ACM SIGSOFT Software Engineering Notes*, Vol. 17, No. 4, 1992.

[22] Shaw, M., and D. Garlan, *Software Architecture: Perspectives on an Emerging Discipline*, Upper Saddle River, NJ: Prentice-Hall, 1996.

[23] Geppert, A., and K. R. Dittrich, "Bundling: Towards a New Construction Paradigm for Persistent Systems," *Networking and Information Systems J.*, Vol. 1, No. 1, June 1998.

[24] Stonebraker, M., and P. Brown, *Object-Relational DBMSs*, 2nd ed., San Francisco, CA: Morgan Kaufmann, 1999.

[25] "Developing DataBlade Modules for Informix Dynamic Server With Universal Data Option," White Paper, Informix Corp., Menlo Park, CA, 1998.

[26] "DB2 Relational Extenders," White Paper, IBM Corp., May 1995.

[27]   "Oracle8 Object-Relational Data Server: The Next Generation of Database Technology," Oracle Business White Paper, June 1997.

[28]   Bliujute, R., et al., "Developing a DataBlade for a New Index," *Proc. 15th Intl. Conf. on Data Engineering,* Sydney, Australia, Mar. 1999.

[29]   Dessloch, S., and N. M. Mattos, "Integrating SQL Databases With Content-Specific Search Engines," *Proc. 23rd Intl. Conf. on Very Large Data Bases (VLDB),* Athens, Greece, Aug. 1997.

[30]   Gaede, V., and O. Guenther, "Multidimensional Access Methods," *ACM Computing Surveys,* Vol. 30, No. 2, June 1998.

[31]   Bayer, R., and M. Schkolnick, "Concurrency of Operations on B-Trees," *Acta Informatica,* Vol. 9, 1977.

[32]   Kornacker, M., C. Mohan, and J. M. Hellerstein, "Concurrency and Recovery in Generalized Search Trees," *Proc. ACM SIGMOD Intl. Conf. on Management of Data,* Tucson, AZ, May 1997.

[33]   Blakeley, J. A., "OLE DB: A Component DBMS Architecture," *Proc. 12th Intl. Conf. on Data Engineering (ICDE),* New Orleans, LA, Feb./Mar. 1996.

[34]   Blakeley, J. A., "Data Access for the Masses Through OLE DB," *Proc. ACM-SIGMOD Intl. Conf. on Management of Data,* Montreal, Canada, June 1996.

[35]   "OLE DB Programmer's Reference: Version 1.0," Vol. 2, Microsoft Corp., July 1996.

[36]   Tork Roth, M., and P. Schwarz, "Don't Scrap It, Wrap It! A Wrapper Architecture for Legacy Data Sources," *Proc. 23rd Intl. Conf. on Very Large Data Bases (VLDB),* Athens, Greece, Aug. 1997.

[37]   Haas, L. M., et al., "Optimizing Queries Across Diverse Data Sources," *Proc. 23rd Intl. Conf. on Very Large Data Bases (VLDB),* Athens, Greece, Aug. 1997.

[38]   Olson, S., et al., "The Sybase Architecture for Extensible Data Management," *Bulletin of the Technical Committee on Data Engineering,* Vol. 21, No. 3, Sept. 1998.

[39]   "CORBAservices: Common Object Services Specification," The Object Management Group, Mar. 1995.

[40]   "The Common Object Request Broker: Architecture and Specification, Revision 2.1," The Object Management Group, Aug. 1997.

[41]   Bernstein, P. A., and E. Newcomer, *Principles of Transaction Processing for the Systems Professional,* San Francisco, CA: Morgan Kaufmann, 1996.

[42]   Elmagarmid, A. K. (ed.), *Database Transaction Models for Advanced Applications,* San Francisco, CA: Morgan Kaufmann, 1992.

[43]   Geppert, A., and K. R. Dittrich, "Strategies and Techniques: Reusable Artifacts for the Construction of Database Management Systems," *Proc. 7th Intl. Conf. on Advanced Information Systems Engineering (CAiSE),* Jyväskylä, Finland, June 1995.

[44] Geppert, A., S. Scherrer, and K. R. Dittrich, "KIDS: A Construction Approach for Database Management Systems Based on Reuse," *Tech. Report 97.01*, Dept. of Computer Science, University of Zurich, Zurich, Switzerland, Jan. 1997.

[45] Chrysanthis, P. K., and K. Ramamritham, "Synthesis of Extended Transaction Models Using ACTA," *ACM Trans. on Database Systems*, Vol. 19, No. 3, Sept. 1994.

[46] Gueting, R. H., "Second-Order Signature: A Tool for Specifying Data Models, Query Processing, and Optimization," *Proc. ACM-SIGMOD Intl. Conf. on Management of Data*, Washington, DC, May 1993.

[47] Stonebraker, M., P. Brown, and M. Herbach, "Interoperability, Distributed Applications and Distributed Databases: The Virtual Table Interface," *Bulletin of the Technical Committee on Data Engineering*, Vol. 21, No. 3, Sept. 1998.

[48] Batini, C., S. Ceri, and S. B. Navathe, *Conceptual Database Design: An Entity-Relationship Approach*, Redwood City, CA: Benjamin/Cummings, 1992.

[49] Elmasri, R., and S. B. Navathe, *Fundamentals of Database Systems*, 2nd ed., Redwood City, CA: Benjamin/Cummings, 1994.

[50] Chen, P. P., "The Entity-Relationship Model—Towards a Unified View of Data," *ACM Trans. on Database Systems*, Vol. 1, No. 1, 1976.

[51] Booch, G., I. Jacobson, and J. Rumbaugh, *The Unified Modeling Language User Guide*, Reading, MA: Addison-Wesley, 1999.

[52] ACT-NET Consortium, "The Active Database Management System Manifesto: A Rulebase of ADBMS Features," *ACM SIGMOD Record*, Vol. 25, No. 3, Sept. 1996.

[53] Lohman, G. M., et al., "Extensions to Starburst: Objects, Types, Functions, and Rules," *Comm. ACM*, Vol. 34, No. 10, 1991.

[54] Ram, S., and V. Ramesh, "Schema Integration: Past, Present, and Future," in A. Elmagarmid, M. Rusinkiewicz, and A. Sheth (eds.), *Management of Heterogeneous and Autonomous Database Systems*, San Francisco, CA: Morgan Kaufmann, 1999.

[55] Batory, D. S., T. Y. Leung, and T. E. Wise, "Implementation Concepts for an Extensible Data Model and Data Language," *ACM Trans. on Database Systems*, Vol. 13, No. 3, 1988.

[56] Biliris, A., and E. Panagos, "Transactions in the Client-Server EOS Object Store," *Proc. 11th Intl. Conf. on Data Engineering*, Taipei, Taiwan, Mar. 1995.

[57] Biliris, A., and E. Panagos, "A High Performance Configurable Storage Manager," *Proc. 11th Intl. Conf. on Data Engineering*, Taipei, Taiwan, Mar. 1995.

[58] Blakeley, J. A., "Open OODB: Architecture and Query Processing Overview," in A. Dogac, et al. (eds.), *Advances in Object-Oriented Database Systems*, New York: Springer-Verlag, 1994.

[59] Blott, A., L. Relly, and H. J. Schek, "An Open Abstract-Object Storage System," *Proc. ACM-SIGMOD Intl. Conf. on Management of Data*, Montreal, Canada, June 1996.

[60] Carey, M. J., et al., "Storage Management for Objects in EXODUS," in W. Kim and F. H. Lochovsky (eds.), *Object-Oriented Concepts, Databases, and Applications,* New York: ACM Press, 1989.

[61] Carey, M. J., et al., "The Architecture of the EXODUS Extensible DBMS," in K. R. Dittrich, U. Dayal, and A. P. Buchmann (eds.), *On Object-Oriented Database Systems,* New York: Springer-Verlag, 1991.

[62] Chou, H. T., et al., "Design and Implementation of the Wisconsin Storage System," *Software—Practice and Experience,* Vol. 15, No. 10, 1985.

[63] Graefe, G., and D. J. DeWitt, "The EXODUS Optimizer Generator," *Proc. ACM-SIGMOD Intl. Conf. on Management of Data,* San Francisco, CA, May 1987.

[64] Lindsay, B., J. McPherson, and H. Pirahesh, "A Data Management Extension Architecture," *Proc. ACM-SIGMOD Intl. Conf. on Management of Data,* San Francisco, CA, May 1987.

[65] Paul, H. B., et al., "Architecture and Implementation of the Darmstadt Database Kernel System," *Proc. ACM-SIGMOD Intl. Conf. on Management of Data,* San Francisco, CA, May 1987.

[66] Stonebraker, M., "Inclusion of New Types in Relational Database Systems," *Proc. Intl. Conf. on Database Systems,* Los Angeles, CA, Feb. 1986.

[67] Unland, R., and G. Schlageter, "A Transaction Manager Development Facility for Non-Standard Database Systems," in A. K. Elmagarmid (ed.), *Database Transaction Models for Advanced Applications,* San Mateo, CA: Morgan Kaufmann, 1992.

[68] Wells, D. L., J. A. Blakeley, and C. W. Thompson, "Architecture of an Open Object-Oriented Database Management System," *IEEE Computer,* Vol. 25, No. 10, 1992.

[69] Geppert, A., and K. R. Dittrich, "Constructing the Next 100 Database Management Systems: Like the Handyman or Like the Engineer?" *ACM SIGMOD Record,* Vol. 23, No. 1, Mar. 1994.

[70] Haas, L. M., et al., "Extensible Query Processing in Starburst," *Proc. ACM SIGMOD Intl. Conf. on Management of Data,* Portland, OR, May/June 1989.

Part III:
Advanced Design Issues

13

CASE Tools: Computer Support for Conceptual Modeling

Mokrane Bouzeghoub, Zoubida Kedad, and Elisabeth Métais

13.1 Introduction to CASE Tools

The acronym *CASE* (computer-aided software engineering) implies two aspects: software engineering and computer aid. Software engineering refers to the activities of analysis, design, implementation, and maintenance of information systems, to which we can add the complementary tasks of verification, assessment, and validation of all the decisions that have been taken and products that have been generated during the project's life cycle. Computer aid concerns all the possible supports that a computer can provide to facilitate the project management and documentation, to control the complexity of a design, and to reason on the specifications and models.

CASE technology emerged in the late 1970s and early 1980s with code generation and program testing. The success of relational DBs encouraged the development of data dictionaries and the maintenance of design traces. The explosion of computer graphics and workstations imposed CASE tools by providing attractive interfaces and by opening up a new era of cooperative distributed design and development. Evolution of traditional languages

439

from third generation to fourth generation and the success of reusable object libraries accompanying object-oriented languages like C++ and Java confirmed CASE tools as an advanced technology that cannot be bypassed in the development of modern information systems.

Current CASE tools have sparse functionalities, cover different phases in a project's life cycle, and are based on different formal specification models. This makes a comparison difficult. There is no standard architecture for a CASE tool, only products that address specific activities in software engineering. The project actors see CASE tools from their individual perspectives and from their own roles in the software project. Many classifications of CASE tools have been proposed; they are either based on the project's life cycle (analysis, design, implementation, validation, maintenance, administration, etc.), on the level of abstraction (upper CASEs, middle CASEs, and lower CASEs), or on the degree of automation (manual tools; semiautomated, or interactive, tools; fully automated tools). Programming experts focus on process modeling, formal verification of program behavior, and code generation. Database experts focus on conceptual data modeling, physical DB design, and integrity constraints validation. Project managers focus on data dictionaries, report generation, and assessment techniques.

The daisy in Figure 13.1 gives a flavor of an ideal integrated CASE toolset. The figure highlights a set of functionalities provided by CASE tools independently of any specific methodology and classification. One can imagine as many CASE environments as combinations of petals in the daisy.

Among CASE tools we can distinguish those related to project management and control, those related to DB modeling, those related to process modeling, and those related to IS administration and maintenance. The baseline of these tools is the knowledge repository that groups all the metadata concerning the application domain, the products and the processes of the project, and the generic reusable components. The cornerstone of the toolset is the fundamental inference and reasoning mechanisms that can be used by various tools. Graphical interfaces constitute a convenient way to synthesize specifications and to give a rapid understanding of the semantics of the system under construction.

13.1.1 Functional Classification of CASE Tools

The functional classification of tools given in Table 13.1 is not exhaustive, but it gives a good view of the diversity of CASE tools that support software engineering projects.

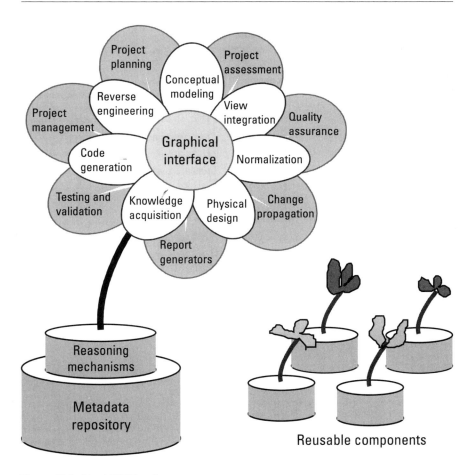

Figure 13.1 Ideal CASE toolset.

13.1.1.1 Project Management Tools

Among the project management and cost evaluation tools, we can distinguish planning and decision support tools such as PERT diagrams, spreadsheets, and workflows. Task assessment and product integration tools refer to the tools that help in evaluating deliverables and consolidating their integration into intermediate or final products. Report generation maintains progress reports, cost statements, and recovery actions in case of failure or delay. Current CASE tools for project management (e.g., Platinum Process Continuum by Platinum Technology, Autoplan by Digital Tools, and MS-Project by Microsoft) are not specific to software engineering but are taken among

Table 13.1
Functional Classification of CASE Tools

Project Management Tools	Database Design Tools	Process Modeling Tools	Administration and Maintenance Tools	Repository Management Tools
Project planning	Conceptual modeling	Functional decomposition	Code inspection	Knowledge representation
Cost evaluation	Logical design (normalization)	Formal specification	Database schema evolution	Graphical editors
Product integration	Physical design (optimization)	Formal verification	Report generation	Textual interfaces
Task assessment	Model transformation	Behavior validation	Tuning applications	Cross referencing
Report generation	DDL generation	Code generation	Tuning DB systems	History management
—	View integration	Code testing	Version management	—
—	Reverse engineering	Reverse engineering	Impact search	—

the tools provided for any other management activity. Integration of those tools within the software engineering environment is usually done through the knowledge repository.

13.1.1.2 Database Design Tools

Database design tools (e.g., Designer 2000 by Oracle Corp.) are formal or semiformal supports that help in the definition of the global DB schema and user views. Some tools support conceptual modeling; others support logical or physical design. Model transformation tools allow users to map schemas of different formalisms into one pivot design model. View integration tools reconcile different perceptions of the real world into one single consistent schema. Database reverse engineering tools allow the extraction of data structures from legacy systems and abstract them into a logical or conceptual schema. Database design tools are perhaps the most well-integrated tools provided in the marketplace.

13.1.1.3 Process Modeling Tools

Process modeling tools help in functional decomposition of a given system, in the formal specification and verification of each function, and in code generation (e.g., Developer 2000 by Oracle Corp, Pacbench by IBM). Code testing tools are also among the oldest tools in software engineering. Because of its complexity, reverse engineering of programs is less developed than that of data structures. Code generation and code testing tools are probably the most important tools whose productivity profit is the highest. Automatic coding produces, in principle, correct programs whose maintenance is easy, thanks to their standard way of generation and documentation. Important problems in code generation are the definition of the input specification language and the optimization of the generated code. Among the interesting subproducts of automatic code generation are prototyping tools that allow validation of user requirements and interfaces.

13.1.1.4 Maintenance and Administration Tools

Administration and maintenance tools refer to all the support that allows the information system administrator to evolve applications by changing specifications and propagating the change to the implementation, by changing technology and migrating data and code to the new one, and by improving performance with DB tuning or program tuning. Multiple-version management and code inspection for errors are also among administration tools. Administration and maintenance activities may result in inconsistencies and inefficiencies. Decision support tools, such as simulation tools and cost estimation tools, which are able to trace or evaluate the impact of a specific system change, are valuable tools that avoid system downgrading. These kinds of tools are called impact search tools. They are usually supplied by DB system providers and platform providers. An example of such a tool is Openview RPM (Hewlett-Packard), which helps in tuning the resources.

13.1.1.5 Repository and Metadata Tools

Repository management refers to a set of tools that support other CASE functionalities. The knowledge repository is the memory of the design and maintenance activities. It contains metadata describing DBs and processes, cross referencing between data and processes, inputs and outputs of each CASE tool, metamodels driving the tools, design decisions, history of changes, trace of simulations, and so on. The repository is a common shared memory between CASE tools and between designers and programmers. The cooperative realization of a software project is organized around the knowledge repository.

13.1.2 Communication Between CASE Tools

The proliferation of CASE tools has rapidly posed the problem of communication among the tools. Data dictionaries are now recognized as basements for the construction of a software engineering environment, and most of the provided CASE tools propose their own data dictionaries. A valuable effort was carried out in the late 1980s for normalizing structures with the ANSI standard, called IRDS [1]. Recent work done by OMG on unifying modeling concepts and representations, proposed in UML [2], may lead to the definition of a new generation of metadata repositories. Besides data dictionaries, the European projects PCTE [3] and ESF [4] proposed generic protocols and software bus, and CORBA [5] provided ORBs as a base technology to exchange objects between different heterogeneous systems. Figure 13.2 summarizes the different approaches to cooperating CASE tools.

The next section focuses on CASE tools that help in the analysis, design, and implementation of DBs. We highlight the fundamental knowledge and reasoning mechanisms used by these tools. The purpose is to show the internal aspects of CASE tools through their intelligent components, that is, how they contribute to acquire application knowledge, how they structure

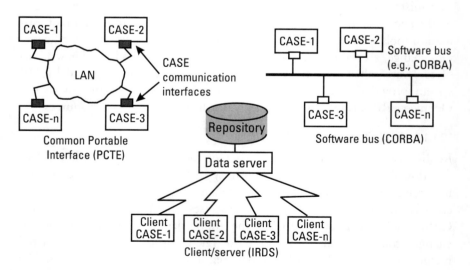

Figure 13.2 Different approaches to integrate CASE tools.

that knowledge and form conceptual and logical schemas, how these are schemas validated and transformed into low-level representations, and how they are verified and validated. Our aim is to provide the basic ideas that govern the design and implementation of a CASE tool and to show the balance between what a CASE tool can do and what remains the designers' creativity and decisions. We particularly insist in these sections on CASE functionalities that help in solving hard problems, such as knowledge acquisition, conceptual modeling, and design validation.

13.2   A CASE Framework for Database Design

Database design has been widely investigated and explored during the past three decades. Many design frameworks have been proposed, and there is a consensus to distinguish among four abstraction levels: external, conceptual, logical, and physical design. Based on these levels, different modeling notations, techniques, and approaches have been proposed. Early provided design tools support relational normalization, schema mapping between the entity-relationship model and the relational model, and DDL generation. The early 1980s saw the promotion of expert systems and knowledge-based tools that integrated heuristics, design alternatives, and high-level interaction with the human designer [6]. The late 1980s confirmed the industrial use of DB design tools; hundreds of CASE tools were proposed in the software engineering market. The 1990s saw the emergence of object-oriented languages and methodologies with their companion tools. Database design tools gained in maturity and in complexity.

To understand the role and the contribution of these tools, we use the framework in Figure 13.3. The framework serves as an ideal CASE environment, one that illustrates most of the possible tools related to DB design.

Knowledge acquisition concerns the collection of all the knowledge necessary for the conceptual modeling of the DB. Knowledge acquisition is done during user requirements analysis, either by interaction with potential DB users, extraction of data from forms and texts, or by the use of some appropriate graphical interface. Knowledge acquisition is driven by preexisting domain knowledge, a predefined enterprise model, or any procedure that helps in requirement analysis.

Data abstraction and structuring consist of organizing the knowledge acquired during the acquisition phase and defining the main entities and relationships that best capture the views of the users. That corresponds to the effective conceptual modeling phase. Depending on the complexity of

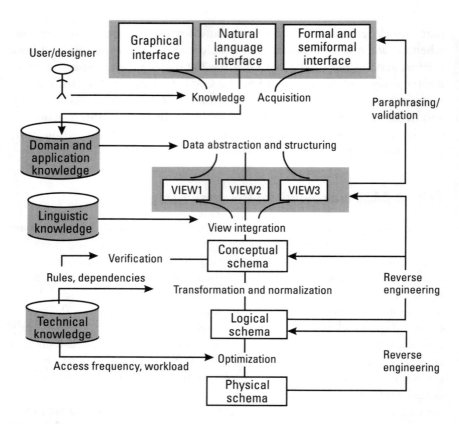

Figure 13.3 A framework for DB design environment.

the target information system, the conceptual schema may either be obtained in one shot or after the integration of several separate schemas that correspond to different user views. Reverse engineering is another way to abstract conceptual entities and relationships from existing files or DBs.

Verification checks the formal verification of the conceptual model, and validation checks its relevance to user requirements. Formal verification guarantees consistency, irredundancy, and completeness. Formal verification techniques depend on the conceptual model used. Conformance with user requirements is much harder. It is usually based on heuristics, expert rules, and prototyping. Validation is the most powerful aid that CASE tools can provide. Indeed, the minimum requirement expected from a CASE tool is at least to check that the design is correct.

View integration or schema integration is a design approach necessary when the complexity of the problem requires its decomposition and modular formalization. Integration is also required in modern ISs that are built from legacy systems or from multiple heterogeneous sources like distributed systems or Web sites. Schema integration is often completed by data integration, which deals with instances and their heterogeneous representations.

Transformation and normalization concern the multiple mappings a schema may undergo to achieve a canonical representation or another formalization. For example, mapping an entity-relationship schema into a relational schema is one of the important DB design steps. Relational normalization can also be considered as a mapping process from first normal form to third or fourth normal form.

Optimization covers all the implementation and tuning decisions that influence the performance of DB queries. Optimization cannot be done without knowledge of all the important queries that represent the main activity of the DB. Optimization may lead to changing physical DB schema, introducing indexes, replicating data, reducing redundancy, and so forth. Optimization requires a good understanding of DB system internals and more generally the software and hardware technologies used to realize the information system.

Our aim in the rest of this chapter is to describe, for the conceptual and logical levels, tools that support corresponding design activities. For each design task, we summarize the main problems to be solved and how far CASE tools go in the automation of that task. Besides the established techniques and algorithms, we will particularly examine the other design expertise that can enhance CASE tools capabilities and bring them up toward the human designer competence.

13.3 Conceptual Design Tools

Conceptual modeling covers several design activities, such as defining conceptual schemas from scratch or by integrating several predefined schemas, verifying the consistency of the schema, and validating the relevance of the schema with respect to user expectations. This section investigates the different CASE tools that can support those activities. Before defining the tools, we present a reference conceptual model that will be used to describe illustrative examples.

13.3.1 The Choice of the Conceptual Model

The purpose of a conceptual schema is to describe in a formal way the part of the real world to represent into a DB. The choice of the conceptual language influences the modeling tasks and determines the necessary knowledge to perform those tasks. There is a general agreement, although never standardized, to use an E/R model [7] or one of its extensions as a high-level formalism to describe conceptual DB schemas. The extended E/R model used in this chapter is summarized by the metamodel in Figure 13.4.

In this model, entities represent concrete or abstract objects relevant to the given real world. They are described by lists of attributes that may be simple or composite, monovalued or multivalued. Relationships are binary or *n*-ary associations between not necessarily distinct entities. Each link between an entity and a relationship materializes the role played by the entity in the relationship. Each role is characterized by cardinalities that specify, on one hand, the number of entity instances involved in a relationship instance, and on the other hand, the number of relationship instances in which the same entity instance participates. Each of these numbers is actually represented by a couple of values, minimal cardinality and maximal cardinality, which respectively specify the minimum and maximum instances involved in each role. Relationships may or may not have their own attributes. Entity instances are identified by one or several of their attributes. Relationship instances are identified by a combination of identifiers of the participating

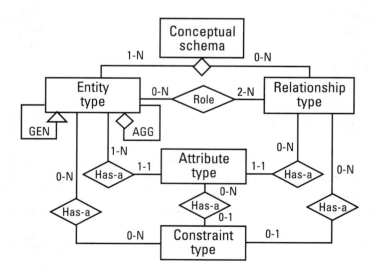

Figure 13.4 The E/R metamodel.

entity instances. Entities can form a hierarchy of generalizations or aggregations.

13.3.2 Conceptual Modeling Tools

Conceptual design tools are those which support concept discovery, the organization of concepts into a coherent schema, and the validation of the schema with respect to user requirements. This section addresses three kinds of tools: those that help in the creative design done by the user, those that help in abstracting the conceptual schema from existing files and DBs, and those that derive conceptual schemas from natural language sentences.

13.3.2.1 Creative Design

Creative design is a modeling activity that starts from scratch or, more precisely, from the informal knowledge a designer has in mind. Every conceptual entity and relationship is abstracted directly from the designer's perception of the real world. Actually, many DB schemas are designed that way. The designer translates users' needs into the conceptual language used to formalize those needs.

CASE tools required by creative design are simple, but they must also be attractive. They are limited to a graphical interface that supports the conceptual model and a data dictionary to store the resulting schemas.

The success of the interface is obviously related to its friendliness, ease of use, and semantic expressiveness. Friendliness is related to the graphical "widgets" used to represent the concepts of the conceptual model. It is recommended that the designer use either standard or well-accepted representations or metaphors that do not give rise to confusion and misunderstanding. Ease of use means providing an interface that can be manipulated by intuition and that conforms to the most popular actions used in Office Works and other successful products. Semantic expressiveness depends on the conceptual model used. A rich semantic model reduces the gap between a perception and its formal representation and allows easy capture of the meaning of the real world considered. A poor conceptual model requires many more skills in the design because it often leads to a reformulation of the perception into more basic facts that can be expressed in the conceptual model.

Although creative design is based on the use of some diagrammatic interface, it requires minimal support in terms of syntactic and semantic verifications. An attractive graphical interface should implement procedures that enforce the structuring rules of the model. For example, in the E/R model, relationships do not link other relationships but entities; there are no cycles in generalization hierarchies; entities must have identifiers; and so forth. Such rules should be hardwired into the graphical interface. Their existence liberates the designer from tedious checking and allows the designer to concentrate on the semantics of the problem.

In addition to that syntactic verification, the graphical interface should provide some semantic checking. For example, when there are different relationships between the same entities, there might be some inconsistencies between their cardinalities. An example of inconsistency between cardinalities is given in Figure 13.5. The cardinalities of the R1 relationship imply that $card(E1) \geq 2 * card(E2)$, and the cardinalities of the R2 relationship imply that $card(E2) \geq card(E1)$. Except for the trivial solution, $card(E1) = card = (E2) = 0$, that leads to a contradiction. In [8] and [9], an inequality system is built with all the cardinalities. If the system has no solution, a contradiction is detected.

The detection of inconsistencies can be completely automated. To make the CASE tool attractive, it has to check that kind of consistency and spot the contradiction. Consequently, a CASE tool that supports creative design is not a static graphical editor but rather an intelligent system, able to automatically enforce syntactic and semantic rules. These features contribute to increasing designer productivity because they save checking time, and they enhance the schema quality because the enforcement is more rigorously done by the tool than by a human designer. Figure 13.6 gives the general architecture of a creative design tool.

13.3.2.2 Reverse Engineering

Reverse engineering techniques have been proposed to reduce the increasing cost of maintaining and modifying existing software [10]. The goal of reverse engineering is to understand how software operates. This is done by

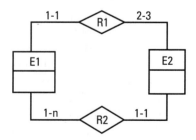

Figure 13.5 An inconsistency due to a cardinality conflict.

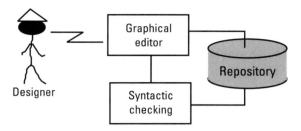

Figure 13.6 Creative design tool.

identifying the different modules of the software and the interactions between them in order to produce an abstract representation of the considered software. In the DB field, the reverse engineering process consists of extracting the DB semantics from its implementation and abstracting the semantics into the conceptual model. The process is based upon the analysis of physical data structures and data instances. The reverse engineering of DBs can be considered as conceptual modeling techniques to which CASE support can be associated.

Three classes of reverse engineering approaches have been proposed [11]: (a) reverse engineering of COBOL files, (b) reverse engineering of navigational DBs, which include hierarchical and Codasyl DBs [12], and (c) reverse engineering of relational and object DBs [11].

Compared to creative design, which starts from scratch, design by reverse engineering starts from concrete structured components. The design process is viewed as a transformation problem that maps a physical data structure into an abstract schema. However, this mapping process is not trivial, and it should be preceded by a discovering process of the entities and relationships between those entities. The discovering process is a kind of data mining process that exploits knowledge sources such as the following:

- File records, their internal structure with the embedded attributes, types of attributes (particularly when they are multivalued or complex attributes), the physical or logical pointers that relate different records, primary and secondary keys, and so forth. The description of file records is often embedded in data divisions of COBOL programs or in similar other languages.
- DDL statements in the case of legacy DBs. These statements may be Codasyl statements or SQL statements. In both cases, it is useful to

extract the logical structure underlying the definitions. From physical DB schemas, it is often possible to extract some integrity constraints such as unicity of values and functional dependencies.

- DML statements, that is, DB queries written in a standard language such as Codasyl or SQL. Database queries allow us to compute some abstract objects from materialized objects. As is generally known, the choice of objects to implement is done with respect to performance. At the conceptual level, both abstract and materialized objects are of the same importance with respect to their semantics. Then, the former as well as the latter can be considered to be potential elements of the conceptual schema.

- Data instances can also be exploited to abstract some structure, especially within legacy systems, either when source code is too large to investigate or unavailable. Data mining techniques used for this purpose are inspired by machine learning, knowledge discovering, and statistics [13].

From this list, we can see how useful a CASE tool is in reverse engineering, especially in conceptual modeling by reverse engineering. Indeed, there is no unified approach or common techniques or algorithms that exploit all the knowledge referred to here. The only possible approach is to combine several techniques into one common design environment and allow the designer to apply the technique that best fits each situation. A general architecture for a reverse engineering CASE tool is portrayed in Figure 13.7.

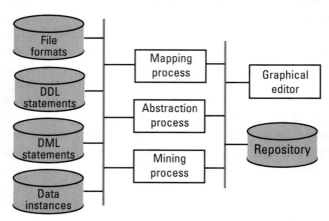

Figure 13.7 Reverse engineering CASE tool.

13.3.2.3 Natural Language Understanding

Extracting data structure from natural language sentences is a difficult problem that may differ from natural language understanding or natural language translation. Indeed, in a text written in natural language, only a part of the global semantics is captured by DB models. Other aspects that deal with processing and dynamics of the described information system are not captured in static data models. Extracting knowledge relevant to conceptual modeling mainly consists in solving two problems: sorting relevant and irrelevant assertions, and stating correspondences between natural language concepts and conceptual modeling concepts.

Within the semantic part that can be captured by a conceptual data model, one of the difficult problems is to decide whether a term in a given sentence should be considered an attribute, object, relationship, or integrity constraint. None of the classical techniques used in natural language processing can solve that problem; only expert rules can produce relevant results.

At first glance, a sentence is turned into conceptual schema by abstracting verbs into relationships, subjects and complements into participating entities, and adverbs and adjectives into attributes. Some verbs are recognized as well-known relationships; for example, the verb "to be" usually indicates a generalization link, whereas the verb "to have" indicates a relationship role or link between an entity (or a relationship) and its attribute.

Sentences can be interpreted as independent units, but they also appear in the context of a global text. The interpretation of a given sentence can be modified by the interpretation of other sentences. For example, from the sentence, "a product has a number, unit price, and supplier," we understand that there is an entity named "product" characterized by three attributes: "number," "unit price," and "supplier." If we add a new sentence, such as, "Each product supplier, described by name and address, supplies 1 to 10 parts," we modify the previous interpretation by transforming the attribute "supplier" into an entity described by two attributes ("name" and "address"), and a relationship ("supplies") that links it to "product." The second sentence introduces additional complexity related to the usage of synonyms ("product" and "parts") that have to be solved by the presence of a dictionary.

Redundancy is a frequent problem in the textual specification. Some new sentences, although true, do not augment the semantics of the application, because the newly described facts can be deduced from the previous ones. For example, in the following description, the third sentence is redundant to the first two: "A person has a name and age. An employee is a person.

An employee has a name and an age." Again, in the following example, there is a redundancy, but it is an underhanded one: "Employees and secretaries are persons. A secretary is an employee." Indeed, the second sentence makes a part of the first one redundant—because a secretary is an employee, it is not necessary to say that he or she is a person, as that fact can automatically be deduced.

Conceptual modeling from a natural language interface involves many aspects: natural language parsing, knowledge elicitation, and the sorting and recovering of pertinent information with respect to the conceptual modeling. Figure 13.8 shows a possible tool architecture for conceptual modeling from natural language.

To reduce the complexity of natural language parsing, often only restricted grammar is allowed, which leads to a technical jargon, easy to specify by the designer and easy to understand by the CASE tool. In the KASPER project [14], a very restricted language called "normalized language" is imposed, which uses standard grammar and standard terms. Both human partners of different languages can use it as a specification language, and the CASE tool can easily transform it into conceptual structures. However, some experts may argue [15] that this simplicity provides only the appearance of a natural language, and it is not the usual natural language dealing with the three essential aspects of polysemy (homonymy, homotaxy), paraphrases (synonymy, allotaxy, definition), and relation to the context (anaphora, implicit, trope, spot). Some research projects of CASE tools such as DMG [16] and NIBA [17] have extended their languages to quite complex sentences.

The interpretation of a natural language specification is not only a syntactic process, but a very high level semantic process based on expert knowledge from research in natural language processing and DB modeling.

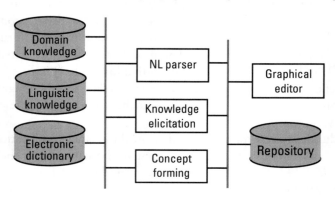

Figure 13.8 Conceptual modeling from natural language.

13.3.3 Verification and Validation Tools

This section deals with the properties of a good conceptual schema and shows how CASE tools support the verification of these properties. We can divide the desired properties into three categories: (a) formal properties, (b) quality factors, and (c) conformance with user needs. With respect to formal properties, a good conceptual schema has to be consistent, complete, and irredundant, if it is to give birth to a sound DB. With respect to quality, a conceptual schema has to be understandable and able to evolve wherever the analysis progresses. With respect to the user needs, a conceptual schema has to conform to the requirements, that is, represent exactly what the user wants to represent. The following subsections illustrate how CASE tools contribute to the assessment of those desired properties and how far one can go in the identification of those properties.

13.3.3.1 Formal Verification

As stated earlier, a good conceptual schema has to be intrinsically correct, that is, consistent, complete, and irredundant. Depending on the conceptual model used, these properties may vary from one model to another. Consequently, the following desired list of properties is not exhaustive and applies to the extended E/R model described in Figure 13.4.

Schema Consistency

Consistency is defined with respect to both the syntactic rules of the conceptual model and the semantic rules. A schema is syntactically consistent if it satisfies the construction rules of the model. With respect to our conceptual model, an instance of this model is syntactically consistent if it satisfies the following properties:

- The names of entities and relationships are distinct, that is, there is unicity of names.

- None of the attributes, entities, and relationships can exist independently in the schema without characterizing or being related to the others. This property is called nonisolation of concepts.

- A relationship is at least a binary relationship between not necessarily distinct entities.

- A given relationship does not participate in another relationship.

- Cardinalities are specified as intervals bounded by positive integers; for example, minimal cardinality is less than or equal to maximal cardinality.
- There are no cycles in generalization hierarchies.

This list is just an illustrative sample of syntactic rules; it can be extended with more refined rules if the conceptual model is defined in more detail. We have already seen how syntactic correctness can be hardwired into the graphical interface, which does not allow the user to get around these laws. It is also obvious that when a schema is automatically generated by reverse engineering or natural language processing, the obtained schema is correct because the corresponding CASE tool respects the construction rules of the model.

A conceptual schema is semantically consistent with respect to a conceptual model if the concepts are used according to their definition and if no contradiction can be found within the concepts of the schema (e.g., cardinality constraint, identifier). The first part of the definition is, in general, hard to verify. Given a concept in the real world, it is difficult to automatically decide whether it is an attribute, an entity, or a relationship. The second part of the definition concerns logical inconsistencies that may occur in a specification.

Consistency of the "functional dependencies" given in the specification has to be checked. There is a functional dependency from a set of attributes X to an attribute Y (noted as $X \rightarrow Y$) in an R relation if two tuples of R cannot have the same values for X and different values for Y. For example, the number of a book functionally determines its title (number $\rightarrow$ title), because one given number corresponds to only one title, but its author does not functionally determine its title (author $\nrightarrow$ title), because an author can be related to several titles.

Within a set of functional dependencies, there is a systematic approach, based on Armstrong's inference rules [18], that decides whether a given functional dependency can be derived from others.

- R1 (reflexivity): If $Y \supseteq X$, then $Y \rightarrow X$.
- R2 (augmentation): If $X \rightarrow Y$ and $W \supseteq Z$, then $X,W \rightarrow Y,Z$.
- R3 (transitivity): If $X \rightarrow Y$ and $Y \rightarrow Z$, then $X \rightarrow Z$.
- R4 (pseudo-transitivity): If $X \rightarrow Y$ and $Y,W \rightarrow Z$, then $X,W \rightarrow Z$.

- R5 (union): If X → Y and X ⊇ Z then X → Y,Z.
- R6 (decomposition): If X → Y and Y ⊇ Z, then X → Z.

These rules are used to detect inconsistencies between functional dependencies. Reference [19] introduces rules between independencies, and [6] defines a complementary set of rules that combines functional dependencies and cardinalities.

Section 13.3.2.1 presented an example of logical inconsistency between cardinalities. We can add another example that illustrates inconsistency between multivalued attributes and functional dependencies. In the example in Figure 13.9, it is stated that a library has several telephone numbers, but the name of the library determines its telephone number. That is obviously inconsistent and should be detected by the CASE tool that implements semantic rules.

The combination of all these rules constitutes a sample of reasonable expertise that can be used to build a sophisticated CASE tool able to detect most of the important inconsistencies in a conceptual schema. However, once a contradiction is detected, only the human designer can solve it. The only complementary service a CASE tool can provide is to suggest a list of solutions for the designer to choose from. Obviously, the process may be completely automated if default answers are allowed. Heuristics can also be used to make the CASE tool more intelligent. Choices can be based on statistical use of the rules as the tool gains in expertise.

Irredundancy of the Schema

A schema is irredundant if no element can be removed without loss of semantics. Redundancy can occur for any fact represented in the conceptual

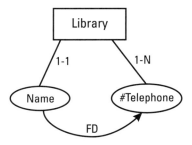

Figure 13.9 Inconsistency between multivalued attribute and functional dependency.

schema. However, checking redundancy of entities, that is, whether two different entity names represent the same universe of discourse, is difficult. The only redundancy that can be checked in a conceptual schema concerns integrity constraints and some relationships.

Checking whether a given integrity constraint is redundant is a logical inference problem. If the integrity constraint can be logically derived from other constraints, it is redundant; otherwise, it is not. If we restrict the set of constraints to those usually represented in a conceptual schema—cardinalities, unicity of keys, functional dependencies, inclusion dependencies, and so forth—we can use specific rules to check redundancy of each type of constraint. Most of the rules are the same as those used for checking consistency. Inference rules between functional dependencies can be used to check both their consistency and their redundancy.

For example, given the following known dependencies and independencies: $\{A \rightarrow B; (B,D) \rightarrow E; (C,F) \rightarrow G; (A,F) \not\rightarrow G\}$, we can use the same inference rules to check that $(A,D) \rightarrow E$ is redundant and to check that $A \not\rightarrow C$ is inconsistent. More precisely, in both cases we use pseudo-transitivity. The theorem proves for redundancy checks whether the goal can be derived from other constraints, while the theorem proves for consistency checks whether the negation of the goal can be derived from other constraints.

As for the consistency, an intelligent CASE tool should combine all the known inference rules for functional dependencies, inclusion dependencies, and cardinalities into the same theorem proof in order to check the redundancy or irredundancy of a conceptual schema.

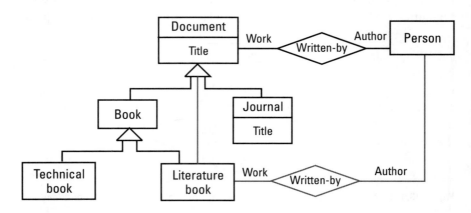

Figure 13.10 Redundancy.

As mentioned earlier, some other redundancies may be detected among relationships. For example, in Figure 13.10, the generalization link between Literature Book and Document is redundant because the link is transitive. The relationship between Literature Book and Person is redundant because it can be inherited from the relationship between Document and Person. Similarly, the attribute in Journal is redundant to that of Document.

After its detection, removing a redundancy implies making a choice between the redundant statements. Depending on the nature of the redundancy, the choice is automatically made if the redundant fact does not play a symmetric role as those from which it is derived. Otherwise, it is left to the user.

Completeness of the Schema

The completeness of a conceptual schema can be defined with respect to either the metamodel or the universe of discourse represented. The first part of the definition concerns the mandatory elements that constitute a conceptual schema. For example, the definition of a conceptual schema is not considered to be terminated until the following are verified:

- Each entity has at least one attribute.
- Each entity has at least one identifier.
- Each attribute has its domain.
- All relationship roles and cardinalities are specified.

The second part of the definition relates to the validation with respect to user requirements. Checking whether a conceptual schema represents all the necessary knowledge for a given information system is a difficult problem and is generally considered in the validation phase, which refers to conformance of the conceptual schema to the real world. We address that problem in Section 13.3.3.3. However, part of completeness checking can be automatically performed by cross-checking the conceptual schema with the information system processes. If all the data types needed by the processes are in the conceptual schema, it is considered to be complete.

Based on these simple rules, it is easy to build a tool that reminds the designer of all the knowledge that remains unknown in the conceptual model. An interactive acquisition process can be implemented to force the designer to complete the specification before starting consistency and redundancy checking.

13.3.3.2 Quality Assessment

Quality assessment of a conceptual schema deals with desired properties that cannot be proved by a logic-based approach. These properties define a subjective evaluation of a conceptual schema and assign a value that is placed against the user's expectations. Among those properties, we can mention readability and reusability of conceptual schemas (see Chapters 2 and 14).

Readability of a Conceptual Schema

The readability of a schema can be measured according to two criteria: the percentage of the schema that the reader may understand and the time needed for that understanding. To fulfill these criteria, a schema has to be as close as possible to the real world it is supposed to represent.

A schema is close to the real world if (a) the names of entities and relationships correspond to usual names and verbs in the application domain, (b) the construction rules reflect the real world, and (c) the objects are clustered in the graphical representation with respect to semantic criteria.

The starting point to evaluate readability of names may be a general electronic dictionary or a specialized business domain dictionary. Each name given to an entity in the conceptual schema must exist in the dictionary. If the entity name does not match any entry in the dictionary, that means that either the dictionary is not complete or the entity name is not a concept of the real world. In the first case, a new entry is added to the dictionary; in the second case, the name is rejected.

The choice of the conceptual model and its corresponding structuring rules may affect the readability of conceptual schemas. Indeed, generalization and aggregation hierarchies are the most natural relationships that users can understand and read easily. The distinction between an entity and a relationship is not so clear. Relationships can become entities when one wants to relate them to other entities or relationships. In that case, the conceptual model perpetuates the ambiguities and variations that exist in natural language. To push designers to intensively use generalization hierarchies, [16] has proposed a tool that checks the overlapping of two entity types; if they have common attributes, it is suggested that a generic entity type be introduced.

Graphical presentation of complex schemas also influences the readability of the schemas. Clustering techniques based on semantic classification are defined in [20]. They permit the division of large schemas into relatively small semantic units by grouping entities and relationships that deal with the same subject in the real world.

Testing and improving readability of a conceptual schema are two complementary services provided by the same CASE tool. The cornerstone of this tool is the linguistic dictionary and the structuring rules of the conceptual model. Semantic clustering and interactive restructuring are additional functionalities that improve readability as well. However, in spite of some sophisticated techniques, the readability remains user dependent.

Reusability of the Schema

A recent trend in conceptual modeling has been to integrate the reuse of conceptual schemas into the methodology, especially in the context of object-oriented models. In this context, reusability is a desired property for object types, and conceptual schemas are considered objects, too. A conceptual schema is reusable in a further DB application if we can expect that selecting, understanding, and customizing the schema will be faster than designing a new one.

To be reusable, a conceptual schema must satisfy the following properties: (a) the conceptual schema must be correct, that is, consistent, complete, and irredundant, and (b) the conceptual schema must be documented. Correctness has already been addressed. Documentation consists in the definition of a metadescription that defines the application domain to which the schema is relevant (e.g., library application), the activities for which it is designed (e.g., book borrowing), and a list of key words (e.g., on book topics) that summarizes its global semantics [21].

Improving reusability may consist in providing a high-level interface that allows documentation of a conceptual schema and provision of online guidelines for the documentation. Another useful support a CASE tool can provide for reusability is an appropriate query language that allows, through fuzzy queries, selection of schemas that are the most relevant to the subject concerned by the conceptual modeling of a given application. This language is particularly useful when object libraries have thousands of reusable components. Reference [22] has proposed an extended SQL language that permits object retrieval by the use of domain knowledge and semantic distance. (We will come back to this point in Section 13.3.5.)

13.3.3.3 Schema Validation

Conceptual schema validation deals with conformance of a given schema with respect to user requirements. It is one of the important issues that contribute to the decision of whether a conceptual schema is good or not. One of the techniques frequently proposed for validation is the conformance of the conceptual schema with applications processes. This is much more useful in checking for completeness than whether conceptual entities and relationships effectively represent the semantics in users' minds. A technique explored for several years by research tools consists of paraphrasing conceptual schemas in natural language. The validation process of the conceptual schema is transformed into a validation process of a text, which is much more adapted for final users than abstract data structures.

Paraphrasing can be split into two theoretical parts: deep generation and surface generation. The deep generation corresponds to the question "What do we say?" The surface generation corresponds to the question "How do we say it?"

In the deep generation, the paraphrasing algorithm strongly depends on the conceptual model. First, each model is associated with a set of rules that link the concepts of the model to linguistic component types. In the E/R model [7], a relationship corresponds to a verb, and its participating entities are its subject and complements. Patterns of sentences are also elaborated for the translation of cardinalities. However, paraphrasing an E/R-like model, without any other source knowledge, may produce only generic sentences like "Leasing is a relationship between an agency, a person, and a vehicle," instead of a more natural and pertinent one like "An agency leases a vehicle to a person." To reach that level of paraphrasing, three kinds of solutions have been explored:

- The first solution consists of enriching the model with linguistic considerations (e.g., CSOM [23]).

- The second one consists of adding a linguistic level between the specification level and the conceptual level. This new level is supplied by the parser (e.g., Kheops [24]).

- The third solution aims to deduce the lacking linguistic information lost during the conceptual modeling from external sources such as lexicons, linguistic dictionaries, or any other knowledge base (e.g., KISS [25], COLOR-X [23], Kheops [24]).

In the surface generation, other linguistic knowledge is needed for building the sentences. They include syntactic, morphologic, and pragmatic knowledge developed for natural language processing. For example, to generate French sentences, we have to know the gender of the nouns, which are dependent on their sense, while homonyms may have different genders. Some researchers have worked on the coherence and readability of the discourse. For example, [26] proposes a method to aggregate atomic sentences to present a synthetic discourse. The presentation of the discourse is important, because the purpose of paraphrasing is to make the conceptual schema closer to nonexpert users.

13.3.4 Conceptual Design by Schema Integration

Modeling large DB schemas having tens or hundreds of entities and relationships is a complex problem. The natural approach to the issue is to divide the application domain into subdomains, model each subdomain separately, and integrate the results to form the global conceptual schema. Integration of different schemas also happens when conceptual modeling recovers schemas of existing DBs or aims to define a global schema on top of distributed DBs. For both issues, we are faced with the same problem of integrating semantically heterogeneous schemas that may overlap and contradict on some of their elements.

Detection and resolution of conflicts between heterogeneous schemas are the core problem in schema integration. The remainder of this section recalls some of the conflicts that may arise between two schemas and presents the main integration techniques upon which a CASE tool can be based to support integration process.

13.3.4.1 Possible Conflicts Between Schemas

Given two conceptual schemas, several kinds of conflicts may occur.

- *Terminology problems.* A terminology problem occurs when the same real-world object is referred to using different names or when two different real-world objects are referred to using the same name.

- *Incompatible constraints.* A conflict occurs when two incompatible constraints are defined over two equivalent concepts belonging to distinct schemas. For example, the value of Salary may be declared as less than 2000 in schema 1 and greater than 3000 in schema 2.

- *Structural conflicts.* A structural conflict occurs when two objects representing the same real world are described with different sets of properties. For example, the two objects Worker and Employee in Figure 13.11 are semantically equivalent despite their disjoint sets of attributes.

- *Representation conflicts.* A representation conflict occurs when different concepts in two different schemas are used to represent the same real-world object. For example, in Figure 13.12, both schemas

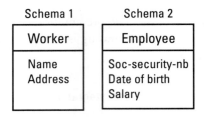

Figure 13.11 Example of a structural conflict.

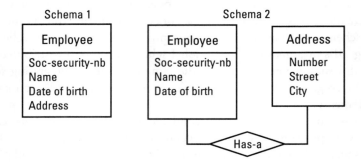

Figure 13.12 Example of a representation conflict.

contain the concept of Address. However, in the first schema, Address is represented as an attribute describing the entity Employee, while in the second schema it is represented as a separate entity.

Solving these conflicts necessitates different techniques organized into a specific methodology. Next we describe the techniques used at each step and the way they can be organized to form a CASE tool.

13.3.4.2 Schema Integration Steps

Many integration approaches have been proposed in the literature [27]. Apart from the data model, which varies from one approach to another, the difference among them is mainly the degree of their automation and the type of inputs they assume. The general integration process is based on four steps: (1) schema comparison, (2) schema conforming, (3) schema merging, and (4) schema restructuring. The following paragraphs detail each integration step by giving the essential knowledge on which it is based and the corresponding support a CASE tool can provide.

Schema Comparison

This step is critical during schema integration. It provides the essential knowledge used to merge two different schemas. The main task of this step is to compare two distinct schemas and decide for each pair of compared objects whether they represent the same real-world object or not. The result of this step is a set of correspondence assertions that state which pairs of concepts are semantically equivalent. Schema comparison is either done manually or supported by an automated tool. In the first case, equivalence assertions are elaborated by the designer [28]. In the second case, they are discovered by a structure-matching algorithm [29], although the validation of the assertions is done by a human designer, due to the high level semantics required to enforce the equivalence between concepts.

To illustrate some of the problems that can arise during the comparison step, let us consider the two E/R schemas in Figure 13.13. The comparison of entities must state that Worker and Employee, in schema 1 and schema 2, respectively, are semantically equivalent despite the fact that they have different names and different attributes, while Worker and Department are not semantically equivalent despite the fact that they have identical attributes.

If there are only a few small schemas, the comparison can be done manually. The correspondence assertions established by the human designer are generally of high semantic quality; they can be used profitably as inputs to the remaining integration steps. However, in large application domains, the comparison process becomes tedious and complex as a human activity. Different comparison tools have been proposed to aid in this combinatory task [29]. However, the produced equivalence assertions are of low-level semantics, and a human intervention is again necessary to elicit those that are pertinent. For example, syntactic comparison of the schemas given in

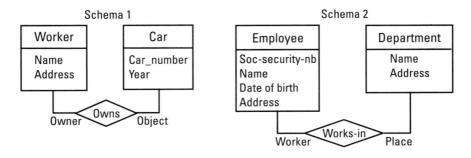

Figure 13.13 Two initial schemas.

Figure 13.13 is generally not able to provide the right correspondence assertions, that is, equivalence between Worker and Employee. Rather, it produces a potential equivalence between Worker and Department because of their identical lists of attributes.

A CASE tool that supports the comparison process has been proposed in [29]. A structure-matching algorithm produces a set of similarity vectors that comprises four comparative components: names, types (domain or structure), attached constraints, and instances. The value of each component varies between 0 and 1, depending on whether the corresponding objects are distinct, similar, or equivalent, according to the component. Two improvements to this algorithm have been proposed. The first one [30] introduces linguistic knowledge into the comparison algorithm by way of an electronic dictionary (e.g., WordNet [31]). Besides the lexicon entries and their definitions, the dictionary contains semantic knowledge that provides linguistic use of the terms, that is, the relationships between them, the context in which they can be used, their synonyms and homonyms, and so forth. The use of such a dictionary allows us to state, for example, that the entities Worker and Employee, in Figure 13.13, are semantically equivalent, while Worker and Department are not. The second improvement concerns the validation. To ease the analysis and validation of the similarity vectors, [20] proposes a classification algorithm that organizes the vectors into distinct classes, based on a semantic distance. Then the validation process considers only similarity vectors inside a class.

Other Integration Steps

- *Schema conforming.* When correspondence assertions are established in the comparison step, the initial schemas are conformed to make them mergeable.

- *Schema merging.* After schema comparison and schema conforming, the initial schemas are merged into a single global schema according to the correspondence assertions found during schema comparison.

- *Schema restructuring.* The resulting schema may be redundant and inconsistent. Then a verification and validation step is performed.

Other integration tasks can be added, such as transforming initial schemas if they are described in different data models, or ordering the initial schemas before integration, giving priorities to some schemas to be integrated first.

13.3.5 Conceptual Design Based Upon Reusable Components

Object-oriented methods recommend the reuse of existing components in the design of new systems. Translated in the context of DB design and in contrast to the classical design approach in which a conceptual schema is constructed directly from user requirements or from legacy systems, reuse implies that the designer must endeavor to construct a conceptual schema mainly from existing elements. There is a difference between design by reuse and design by integration. In design by integration, all the integrated schemas concern the same real-world application, while design by reuse means customization of elements that have been designed for different purposes.

A simple example that highlights this difference is illustrated by a conceptual schema devoted to flight booking that can be reused in train booking or hotel booking. Another example concerns a conceptual schema designed for the management of a specific conference (paper reception, participant registration, reviewer assignment, evaluation synthesis, and program scheduling) that can be reused for another conference that does not necessarily have the same organizational rules (different number of reviewers, different evaluation systems, different organization of the final program). Designing by reuse means searching for one or several schemas that have similar purposes but not necessarily in the same application domain as the one addressed in the given application, customizing those schemas to adapt them to the given application, and possibly integrating them when there are several to have one unique global schema. We can summarize the reuse process into three steps: (1) searching, (2) customizing, and (3) integrating. While the third step is the same as design by schema integration, the first two steps are specific to design by reuse.

The first task in design by reuse is to investigate and select those elements that best match the modeling purpose, according to the given application requirements. Then the selected building blocks are retouched and customized by changing the names of concepts, removing or adding some concepts, changing some relationship roles and cardinalities, changing some attribute domains, and so forth.

Retrieval mechanisms of reusable components usually follow one of two methods: browsing or querying. Although it is more interesting to browse a reasonably sized repository of objects, it quickly becomes a time-consuming and burdensome task with an increasing number of resulting schemas. Reference [22] has proposed a flexible language that combines querying and browsing. The proposed retrieval solution has two main characteristics: It permits imprecise querying, and it deals with the semantics (concept meaning), syntax (concept structure), and pragmatics (concept meaning related to a given context and to the users' expectations) contained within the components.

Customization of each component is also done manually before integration of the selected elements into a global conceptual schema. Customization is supported by the graphical tools for adding or removing small parts of the schemas or renaming objects. The tool may also provide an algebra to compose a new schema by union, difference, or intersection of schemas [21].

13.3.6 Conclusion on the Conceptual Level

Although the conceptual design activity is based upon informal user requirements and is strongly subject to variations of semantics, we have seen that it is possible to define a set of design aids that help solve many combinatorial problems, extract pertinent knowledge from text, reuse existing solutions, audit schemas and evaluate their correctness, and generate a customized conceptual schema.

Many CASE tools that assist in conceptual design are available. Oracle Designer/2000 (Oracle), Rational Rose (Rational Corporation), Platinum ERwin (Platinum), Objectering (Softeam), Pacbase (CGI), OPENTOOL (TNI), ORCA (Telelogic), and all those mentioned below provide graphical interfaces for creative design and verification tools for schema checking. Graphical models are rather object-oriented, mainly by extending the E/R model, and they tend to support the UML notation; for a list of UML-dedicated tools, see http://www.essaim.univ-mulhouse.fr/uml/outillage. html. Increasingly, CASE provides the capability to customize one's own model, and this leads to "metaCASEs" such as metaEdit+ (MetaCase Consulting), MEGA (MEGA International), and Pragmatica (Pragmatix Software). RIDL (from IntelliBase) also deals with natural language specifications. Validator (AONIX) helps the user in the validation process with respect to the requirements. Most tools—such as DB-Main (University of Namur), Software through Picture (AONIX), RoboCASE (Db Logic Inc.), Paradigm (Platinum technology), Pragmatica (Pragmatic Software) and INNOVATOR (MID GmbH)—offer reverse engineering and reuse functionalities, although they are sometimes quite restricted. Functionalities for schema integration are growing with the emergence of multisource information systems design. For example, PowerDesigner (Sybase) and VIS (Meta system) help integrate several schemas graphically.

13.4　Logical Design Tools

At the logical level, the purpose of the CASE tool is to derive a good logical schema from the conceptual schema, assuming the latter is consistent, complete, and irredundant. The model used at the logical level is the relational model in most DB applications. Given that model, this section presents the main tools that can be provided to support relational design.

As for the conceptual level, we first define the notion of a good relational schema, the way to build it and to validate it. Compared to the conceptual level, relational design is better understood and the theory well established. Consequently, design tools are easier to identify and implement. The following sections recall the fundamentals of relational normalization and focus on the complementary tools that help in the acquisition of functional dependencies, which is the most important problem after the theory is defined.

13.4.1　Fundamentals of Relational Design

The properties of a good relational schema have been formalized by the definition of normal forms and the corresponding algorithms that produce them [32]. Normalization is defined with respect to update anomalies. To permit any update without loss of information, relations have to be at least in third normal form (3NF) or fourth normal form (4NF), in which the only functional or multivalued dependencies are those implied by a key. Functional and multivalued dependencies are among the main semantic links relating attributes within a relation.

Well-known algorithms exist for producing a set of normalized relations starting from a universal relation (the set of all attributes composing a DB) and the set of dependencies over those attributes. Normalization algorithms are traditionally sorted into two categories: synthesis algorithms [33], which compute 3NF relations, and decomposition algorithms [34], which compute Boyce-Codd normal form (BCNF) and 4NF relations.

It is easy to implement these algorithms to provide a powerful CASE tool that automatically derives a good relational schema from a set of attributes and a set of dependencies. Obviously, these algorithms can be used to decompose any user-defined relation, without necessarily being a universal relation. Such CASE tools can be extended with another functionality that is often desired: checking whether a given relation with certain key and dependencies is normalized at a certain degree or not.

Although the normalization process is well defined and the correspond-ing algorithms easy to implement, few existing CASE tools provide normali-zation support for relational schemas. The common reason always given is that normalized schemas are not optimized schemas, and the necessary denormalization step that follows makes the process useless and time con-suming. Obviously this argument is not acceptable because it is clear that logical design has nothing to do with physical design. The purpose of logical design is to build a sound relational schema that will serve as a reference for the DB evolution, while the physical design intends to provide an implemen-tation that optimizes the set of actual queries. Physical design is subject to change more frequently than logical design, as the application queries and technology evolve.

The main problem of the normalization theory is the acquisition of dependencies. Functional dependencies are semantic assertions stated about attributes. Although inference rules between dependencies [18] allow us to derive some dependencies from others, elementary dependencies cannot be defined without the users' support. This is probably the most important obstacle to the use of normalization tools. The next section investigates dif-ferent techniques that can support functional dependencies acquisition and can be added to the normalization process to make it more pragmatic.

13.4.2 Functional Dependency Acquisition

Given that the number of possible functional dependencies between n attrib-utes is the function of $n!$, the acquisition of these dependencies is the bottle-neck of the normalization process. A question-answering system becomes useless without intelligent techniques to dramatically reduce the number of questions for the users or designers. To deal with the combinatory aspect of this problem, we present a panel of heuristics and techniques that reduce the search space of functional dependencies.

Removing the Universal Relation Assumption

The universal relation assumption allows the definition of functional dependencies in the absence of existing relations. In the case where the rela-tional schema is derived from the conceptual schema by mapping rules, as we will see in Section 13.4.3, there is no need to have this assumption. Indeed, functional dependencies can be defined on first normal form (1NF) relations that resulted from the transformation of the conceptual schema. Each of these 1NF relations can be considered a universal relation over which func-tional dependencies must be defined. The normalization algorithm will therefore be applied to each 1FN relation. All the design techniques used at the conceptual level can be considered to be a method to define concepts. Thanks to those conceptualization techniques, the search space of dependencies is drastically reduced to the set of attributes of each relation.

Avoiding the Combination of Several Attributes

Although each 1NF relation has few attributes—say, fewer than 10 or 15—it is not meaningful to consider dependencies where the left side is composed of more than five or six attributes. Indeed, searching for functional dependencies is equivalent to searching keys for the decomposed relations, and it is not practically manageable to have relation keys composed of more than five or six attributes. Based on this hypothesis, the question-answering system will not consider all the possible combinations of attributes but only those built with fewer than five or six attributes. The gain is important, although many combinations still remain as potential questions to ask. Obviously, five or six attributes is a heuristic that can be chosen differently, depending on each application. Inside a CASE tool, it should be a parameter the designer sets before activating the acquisition process.

Applying Deduction Rules

As already mentioned in the discussion of conceptual modeling, several techniques can be used to infer functional dependencies from other functional dependencies and constraints. The following three approaches, if appropriately used in the question-answering system, help avoid asking all the questions that concern functional dependencies that can be automatically derived, using the following sets of rules.

- Inference rules between dependencies stated by Armstrong [18] can be used by the question-answering system to avoid asking questions relative to all dependencies that could be deduced.

- Inference rules between independencies [19] are also a way to introduce new rules that avoid asking questions for which the answer can be automatically derived using the rules. For example, having the functional dependency $Y \rightarrow Z$ and the functional independency $X \nrightarrow Z$, we can easily infer that the functional independency $X \nrightarrow Y$ holds, too.

- Inference rules involving relation keys, attribute cardinalities, and functional dependencies [6] can derive functional dependencies from other knowledge such as attribute cardinalities (which specify whether a given attribute can take one or several values for the same entity occurrence) and entity identifiers. For example, knowing that Social Security numbers identify employees and knowing that each employee has a single address, we can derive that the Social Security number determines the employee's address. We can use the same key and cardinality constraints to infer independencies.

Combinations of all those inference rules reduce the number of potential questions to ask the user, because answers to the questions can be automatically derived.

Learning From Small Examples

Given a relation schema and a set of tuples for the relation, we can infer from this example whether some functional independencies hold between two different attributes. For example, from the extension of the relation in Figure 13.14, we can easily derive that the following functional independencies hold: {Author $\nrightarrow$ Title,Editor,Date; Title $\nrightarrow$ Author; Editor $\nrightarrow$ Title, Author,Date}.

This technique is based on the idea that domain expert users are not familiar with the concept of functional dependency, so example is one of the different ways to acquire this knowledge.

Mining Dependencies From Existing Files or DBs

Many current DBs are built from legacy files or DBs, in which there exist not only a small sample of tuples but most of the real-world images representing the application. Exploiting huge amounts of real tuples cannot be done by the simple techniques presented in the preceding paragraph. Advanced techniques based upon data mining algorithms have already been suggested in the literature [13]. While exploiting a few examples leads to discovering independencies, mining a large number of instances aims to find valid dependencies.

Author	Title	Editor	Date
A1	T1	E1	D1
A2	T1	E1	D1
A2	T2	E2	D2
A3	T3	E2	D3

Figure 13.14 Learning from examples.

Some mining algorithms search for approximate dependencies that are functional dependencies that almost hold. Such dependencies arise in many DBs when there is a natural dependency between attributes, but some rows contain errors and missing data or represent exceptions to the integrity constraints. Such cases occur frequently in legacy systems. Approximate dependencies in the legacy system can be confirmed by the user as valid dependencies for the ongoing application.

The combination of the previous techniques makes functional dependency acquisition possible and the relational theory applicable to real applications.

13.4.3 Mapping From Conceptual Schema to Logical Schema

Current design methodologies provide high-level conceptual models that are either extended E/R models or object-oriented models. These models are better suited to reducing the semantic distance between user perception and the formal representation of that perception. However, no current DB systems support all the concepts provided in conceptual models. Consequently, conceptual schemas are always transformed into logical models supported by a class of DB systems. Next we discuss the transformation rules between an extended E/R model and a relational model, and between an object-oriented model and a relational model.

13.4.3.1 Mapping an Entity-Relationship Schema Into a Relational Schema

As a general rule, given an extended E/R model such as the one summarized in Figure 13.4, one can say that any attribute of the conceptual level is an attribute of the relational model, and any entity or relationship in the conceptual level can be transformed as a relation in the relational model. However, conceptual attributes may be multivalued, while they are not in the relational model. Entities and relationships may have complex attributes, while relations have simple attributes. Conceptual schemas may contain aggregation and generalization hierarchies, while relational schemas cannot. Conceptual schemas have roles and cardinalities that are not supported by the relational model. Then mappings between an extended E/R model and a relational model are not direct mappings. There should first be some transformations within the E/R model before direct transformations are applied. We briefly summarize the two types of transformation and show how a CASE tool can apply them with respect to a certain methodology.

Intermediate Mapping Rules

Intermediate mappings constitute a set of rules that transform any E/R schema into a canonical form in which any entity or relationship is in 1NF, that is, any of their attributes is monovalued for each entity instance or relationship instance.

For example, an entity type having multivalued attributes should be transformed using one of the two following rules:

- R1: If an attribute may take only a very few values, say, two or three, the attribute is duplicated as many times as it has possible values.

- R2: If an attribute may take several values, it is represented as an independent entity, related to the mother-entity by a binary relationship, generically named "has-a." The cardinalities of this relationship are 1-N, where N is the maximum number of values that the attribute may take in the mother-entity.

Figure 13.15 illustrates an application of these two rules. In the Book entity, the attribute Author is multivalued but has a maximum of four authors, while the attribute Chapter may have more than 10 values. Author attribute is transformed using R1, while Chapter attribute is transformed using R2.

Other rules concern structured attributes. If the original E/R model allows specification of structured attributes, the attributes have to be transformed using one of the following two rules:

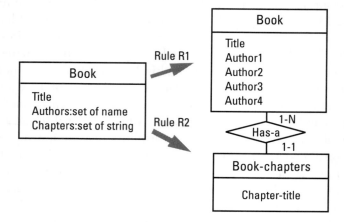

Figure 13.15 Eliminating multivalued attributes.

- R3: Each structured attribute in an entity (or a relationship) should be unnested in such a way that only primitive attributes are visible in the entity type. Intermediate names are missed.

- R4: Each structured attribute in an entity is transformed into an independent entity related to the mother-entity by a binary relationship, generically named "has-a." The cardinalities of this relationship are those of the complex attribute in the original mother-entity.

Figure 13.16 illustrates an application of these rules. The Address attribute has been unnested in the Editor entity. The Bookstore's attributes have been defined as an entity related to Editor.

Other intermediate mapping rules concern the homogenization of specialization hierarchies to make them complete and not overlapping.

Given that the conceptual schema is in a canonical form after these transformations, the remaining mappings are direct mappings to the relational model.

Direct Mappings

Each entity in the conceptual schema is a candidate to become a 1NF relation in the logical schema. However, relationships and generalization hierarchies also have to be transformed. Transforming relationships can be done by applying one of the following two rules:

- R5: If the conceptual relationship is a binary relationship and one of its roles has a 1-1 cardinality, it can be transformed into a reference

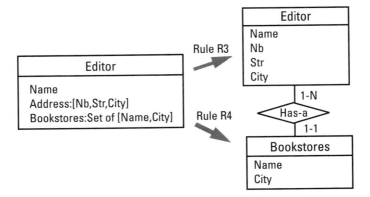

Figure 13.16 Eliminating complex attributes.

in the relational schema, that is, a link represented by a foreign key from the referencing entity (the one whose role cardinality is 1-1) to the other. Possible attributes of the relationship are transferred to the referencing entity.

- R6: Any conceptual relationship can be transformed into a relation in the logical schema. This relation references all the participating entities.

Generalization hierarchies are not supported by the relational model. There are different ways to represent them, specified in the following three rules:

- R7: Given a generalization hierarchy of conceptual entities, each entity of this hierarchy is a candidate to become a base relation in the logical level. Generalization links between these conceptual entities are represented by references from specialized entities to the generic entity.

- R8: Given a hierarchy of conceptual entities, only specialized entities are candidates to become base relations. The generic entity is defined as a view computed by the union of the previous relations. This rule assumes that the generalization hierarchy is complete, that is, each generic instance is also an instance of one of the specialized entities.

- R9: Given a hierarchy of conceptual entities, only the generic entity is a candidate to be a base relation. Specialized entities are represented as views, computed by a selection on the base relation. This selection assumes that a new attribute, generically named "role," is defined in the base relation such that its domain is composed of the names of the specialized entities.

Figure 13.17 illustrates a successive application of those three rules to the same generalization hierarchy.

13.4.3.2 Mapping a Conceptual Object-Oriented Schema Into a Relational Schema

The difference between an extended E/R model, such as the one defined in Figure 13.4, and an object-oriented model, as defined in OMT [35] and UML [2], is mainly the addition of operations on entities and relationships, and messages between objects. Consequently, the structural mapping

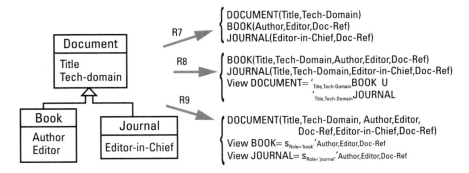

Figure 13.17 Transforming generalization hierarchies.

between an object-oriented model to a relational model is similar. We just add a few rules concerning the behavioral aspect.

In the relational model, the behavioral aspect of applications is represented through direct queries, embedded queries within a programming language, DB procedures, and triggers. They may also be simply integrated within application programs. A flexible approach is to gather the behavioral aspect within a front end between the DB system and user applications (see Figure 13.18). This solution permits a better isolation of shared behavior and allows for the evolution of the behavior without changing the DB schema and user applications. The front end also allows the application of some optimization techniques that cannot be used for sparse triggers.

13.4.3.3 CASE Support of the Mapping Process

We have seen some of the mapping rules that can transform a conceptual schema into a logical schema. For a given schema, there are often several candidate rules to apply. The choice among these rules is based upon heuristics, which are derived from the expertise acquired in conceptual modeling, and upon the needs of specific applications.

For example, R1 applies when the number of attribute values is small. This is general knowledge in logical modeling, but the number of values under which R1 instead of R2 is applied may vary from one application to

Figure 13.18 Behavioral front end to represent object behavior in the relational context.

another, although R1 suggests two or three values. Similarly, R3 and R4 apply concurrently to the same situation. The decision whether R3 should apply instead of R4 depends on the designer's perception. If the structured attribute has a meaning as a whole with respect to the application, then R4 applies. Otherwise, if nested attributes are of the same importance as non-nested attributes, R3 applies.

Regarding R5 and R6, R6 is more generic and applies to every situation. However, R5 is relevant when there is no need to multiply the number of relations and when the conditions in which it applies hold.

Similarly, R7 applies for any generalization hierarchy. However, applying this rule leads to a complex management of update propagation. Indeed, each time an instance is created for a generic entity, it must be created for one of its specializations and vice versa. If one wants to avoid the control of this update propagation, R8 and R9 are relevant. However, R9 cannot be applied without a loss of information in the case where specialized entities have their own attributes or relationships. Applying this rule must then be preceded by a kind of generalization of all the properties of the specialized entities. This assumes that for every generalized attribute or relationship, there is a corresponding rule that controls its instantiation in the generic entity. This is a quite complex specification. Consequently, R9 applies only when specialized entities have few specific properties. Rule R8 applies provided inheritance of the generic properties has been done before. Besides the arbitrary choice among these three rules, there is another strategy to define: scanning generalization hierarchies can be done by starting from the root or from the leaves.

In the case of an object-oriented schema, the behavioral aspect is also transformed using some know-how in DB modeling and heuristics, which capture user needs and DB administration needs. Figure 13.19 shows a possible architecture for a mapping tool.

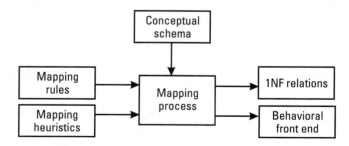

Figure 13.19 Mapping CASE tool.

This discussion has shown that the mapping process from the conceptual level to the logical level, although based on a few simple rules, is actually driven by some extra knowledge, which can be modeled as parameters or metarules, precisely instantiated for each class of applications. This knowledge can also be obtained through a dialogue between the designer and the CASE tool during each design session.

13.4.4 Concluding Remarks on the Logical Design

In spite of the high-level formalization of the relational model, the definition of normalization algorithms, and the specification of a good set of mapping rules, logical design remains complex and characterized by a high level of expertise. Acquisition of functional dependencies, as well as heuristics to choose mapping rules, necessitates advanced skills in DB modeling, a good understanding of the user requirements, and a good intuition of the administration problems.

As for the conceptual modeling, logical modeling does not produce a unique solution. Depending on the different technical choices and on the decisions taken by the designer, several logical schemas may represent the information system DB. CASE tools help in combining formal knowledge, domain knowledge, and heuristics in the same methodological environment.

13.5 Summary

This chapter gave a global overview of CASE tool functionalities and showed the main features of specific DB CASE tools. We focused this study on those functionalities that capture as much as possible the design expertise, in order to demonstrate that CASE tools do not concentrate solely on metadata management or graphical editing. All of the functionalities presented and many other techniques have been successively tested in the SECSI and Kheops projects [6, 36, 37]. The industrial use of SECSI has shown the contribution and the pertinence of such intelligent functionalities. But it has also shown that many designers use only the passive parts of this tool, because they continue to think that while CASE tools may provide nice graphical editors and code generators, the creative activity still remains on their hands.

The study in this chapter is not exhaustive; many other possible tools can be built. Physical design is a hard problem that needs computer support as well as DB maintenance and tuning. Physical design depends upon several parameters, some of which characterize the DB workload, others which characterize the DB system and the hardware environment. Denormalization, replication, partitioning, and index selection are some of the main techniques used to optimize a physical DB schema. But while there is a precise theory for normalization, denormalization and physical design in general use empirical approaches. Knowledge of DB systems, of software and hardware environments, and of the evolution of users' needs is the base knowledge used to select a good DB implementation.

Modern applications such as data warehousing, World Wide Web information systems, workflows, mobile DBs, and multimedia DBs introduce a high degree of complexity to the design and increase the need for powerful design aids. CASE tools that deal with view materialization, multidimensional data, semistructured data, and audio and video data are still far from being a reality in the marketplace, although strong research efforts have been invested in these areas. Active rules, design patterns, reusable libraries, and formal specification languages will certainly be the main ingredients that make up the next generation of CASE tools.

References

[1] ANSI-X3-138-1988, *Information Resource Dictionary System (IRDS)*, New York, 1988.

[2] Rumbaugh, J., I. Jacobson, and G. Booch, *The Unified Modeling Language Reference Manual*, Reading, MA: Addison-Wesley, 1999.

[3] ECMA, "A Reference Model for CASE Environments," *Tech. Report TR-55 European Computer Manufacturers Association*, 1990.

[4] ESF, Seminar proceedings, Berlin, Germany, Nov. 1990.

[5] OMG, *CORBA: Architecture and Specification*, Framingham, MA, Aug. 1995.

[6] Bouzeghoub, M., G. Gardarin, and E. Métais, "Database Design Tools: An Expert System Approach," *11th Intl. Conf. on Very Large Databases (VLDB)*, Stockholm, Sweden, Aug. 1985.

[7] Chen, P. P., "The Entity-Relationship Model: Toward a Unified View of Data," *ACM Trans. on Database Systems*, Vol. 1, No. 1, 1976.

[8] Lenzerini, M., "On the Satisfiability of Dependency Constraints in Entity-Relationship Schemata," *Info. Sys.*, Vol. 15, No. 4, 1990.

[9] Zamperoni, A., and P. Löhr-Richter, "Enhancing the Quality of Conceptual Database Specification Through Validation," *12th Intl. Conf. on Entity-Relationship Approach*, Arlington, VA, Dec. 1993.

[10] Hainaut, J. L., "Database Reverse Engineering: Models, Techniques and Strategies," *10th Intl. Conf. on Entity-Relationship Approach*, 1991.

[11] Comyn-Wattiau, I., and J. Akoka, "Reverse Engineering of Relational Database Physical Schema," *15th Intl. Conf. on Entity Relationship Approach*, 1996.

[12] Batini, C., S. Ceri, and S. B. Navathe, *Conceptual Database Design: An Entity-Relationship Approach*, Redwood City, CA: Benjamin/Cummings, 1992.

[13] Mannila, H., and K. J. Räihä, "Algorithms for Inferring Functional Dependencies From Relations," *Data and Knowledge Engineering*, Vol. 12, No. 1, 1994.

[14] Ortner, E., and B. Schienmann, "Normative Language Approach—A Framework for Understanding," *15th Intl. Conf. on Entity-Relationship Approach*, 1996.

[15] Sabah, G., *L'Intelligence Artificielle et le Langage*, Hermès, 1988.

[16] Tjoa, A. M., and L. Berger, "Transformation of Requirement Specifications Expressed in Natural Language Into EER Model," *12th Intl. Conf. on Entity-Relationship Approach*, 1993.

[17] Fliedl, G., et al., "NTS-BASED Derivation of KCPM Perspective Determiners," *3rd Intl. Workshop on Applications of Natural Language to Information Systems (NLDB'97)*, Vancouver, Canada, 1997.

[18] Armstrong, W. W., "Dependency Structures of Database Relationships," *Proc. IFIP*, North Holland, Netherlands, 1974.

[19] Wijesekera, D., et al., "Normal Forms and Syntactic Completeness Proofs for Functional Independencies," *Tech. Report 96-066*, University of Minnesota, Computer Science Department, Minneapolis, MN, 1996.

[20] Comyn-Wattiau, I., J. Akoka, and Z. Kedad, "Combining View Integration and Schema Clustering to Improve Database Design," *14èmes Journées Bases de Données Avancées*, Hammamet, Tunisia, Oct. 1998.

[21] Ruggia, R. J., 1996, "A Reuse-Based Approach to Conceptual Modelling," Ph.D. thesis, University of Paris.

[22] Ambrosio, A. P., "Introducing Semantics in Conceptual Schema Reuse," *Conf. on Information and Knowledge Management (CIKM'94)*, MD, Nov. 1994.

[23] Burg, J. F., *Linguistic Instruments in Requirements Engineering*, Burke, VA: IOS Press, 1996.

[24] Ambrosio, A. P., E. Métais, and J. N. Meunier, "The Linguistic Level: Contribution for Conceptual Design, View Integration, Reuse, and Documentation," *Data and Knowledge Engineering (DKE)*, Vol. 21, No. 2, Jan. 1997, pp. 111–130.

[25] Frölich, M. O., and R. P. Van de Riet, "Conceptual Models as Knowledge Resources for Text Generation," *3rd Intl. Workshop on Applications of Natural Language to Information Systems (NLDB'97)*, Vancouver, Canada, 1997.

[26]   Dalianis, H., "Aggregation, Formal Specification, and Natural Language Generation," *1st Intl. Workshop on Applications of Natural Language to Data Bases (NLDB'95)*, Versailles, France, 1995.

[27]   Spacapietra, S., and C. Parent, "View Integration: A Step Forward in Solving Structural Conflicts," *TKDE*, Vol. 6, No. 2, 1994.

[28]   Batini, C., and M. Lenzerini, "A Methodology for Data Schema Integration in the E-R Model," *IEEE Trans. on Software Engineering*, Nov. 1984.

[29]   Bouzeghoub, M., and I. Comyn-Wattiau, "View Integration by Semantic Unification of Data Structures," *9th Intl. Conf. on Entity-Relationship Approach*, Lausanne, Switzerland, Oct. 1990.

[30]   Métais, E., et al., "Implementation of a Third Generation Tool," *2nd Intl. Workshop on Application of Natural Language to Information Systems (NLDB'96)*, Amsterdam, Netherlands, June 1996.

[31]   Miller, G. A., "WordNet: A Lexical Database for English," *Comm. ACM*, Vol. 38, No. 11, Nov. 1995.

[32]   Ullman, J. D., *Principles of Database Systems*, Rockville, MD: Computer Science Press, 1982.

[33]   Bernstein, P. A., "Synthesizing Third Normal Form Relations From Functional Dependencies," *Trans. on Database Systems ACM*, Vol. 1, No. 4, 1976.

[34]   Delobel, C., and R. G. Casey, "Decomposition of Database and the Theory of Boolean Switching Functions," *IBM J. Research and Development*, Vol. 7, No. 5, 1973.

[35]   Rumbaugh, J., et al., *Object-Oriented Modeling and Design*, Englewood Cliffs, NJ: Prentice-Hall, 1991.

[36]   Bouzeghoub, M., "Using Expert Systems in Schema Design," in P. Loucopoulos (ed.), *Conceptual Modeling, Databases, and CASE: An Integrated View of Information System Development*, New York: Wiley, 1992.

[37]   Bouzeghoub, M., and E. Métais, "Contribution of Expert Systems in CASE Development: The Secsi Experience," in L. M. Delcambre and F. E. Petry (eds.), *Advances in Databases and Artificial Intelligence*, Greenwich, CT: JAI Press Inc., 1995.

Selected Bibliography

Batini, C., S. Ceri, and S. B. Navathe, *Conceptual Database Design: An Entity-Relationship Approach*, Redwood City, CA: Benjamin/Cummings, 1992.

This book examines conceptual design, functional analysis, and logical design. It presents a step-by-step design methodology and incorporates realistic case studies.

Loucopoulos, P., and R. Zicari, *Conceptual Modeling, Databases, and CASE,* New York: Wiley, 1992.

International experts join together in this book to present the state of the art and their works in conceptual modeling, DBs, and CASE.

Free Shareware CASE Tools

http://selab.postech.ac.kr/casetool.html

Demonstrations of CASE Tools

http://osiris.sunderland.ac.uk/sst/case2/tools.html

List of Available CASE Tools

http://www.qucis.queensu.ca/Software-Engineering/vendor.html

14

Database Quality

Mario Piattini, Marcela Genero, Coral Calero, Macario Polo, and Francisco Ruiz

14.1 Introduction

IS quality is one of the most pressing challenges facing organizations today. Global, national, even local enterprises are driven by information. Many companies have discovered how critical information is to the success of their businesses. Yet few companies have effective ways of managing the quality of that information, which is so important to their competitiveness.

DBs have become the essential core of ISs; therefore, their quality must be improved as much as possible to guarantee successful ISs.

Because of the growing complexity of ISs, continuous attention to and assessment of DB quality throughout the development process are necessary to produce quality systems [1]. Commitment to quality in software development is essential both to satisfy customers and to improve the productivity of the development process [2].

Consider what we mean by the term *quality*. There is a bewildering range of formal and informal definitions available [3]. Some of the most significant ones are shown in Table 14.1.

Quality is a relative concept in that the importance of different features varies among designers and over time. It is therefore important that any approach to the evaluation of data models recognizes these differences and

Table 14.1
Definitions of Quality

Author	Definition of Quality
Crosby [4]	"Conformance to requirements"
Juran [5]	"Fitness for purpose"
ISO [6]	"The totality of features and characteristics of a product or service that bear on its ability to satisfy specified or implied needs"
English [7]	"Consistently meeting customers' expectations"

allows different features to be weighted according to the context or situation under consideration.

We also have to take into account the distinction between product quality and process quality (see Figure 14.1):

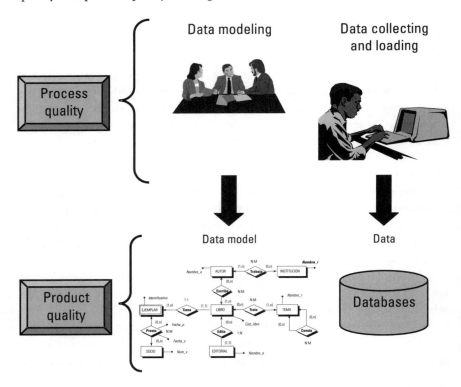

Figure 14.1 Process quality and product quality.

- Product quality focuses on the characteristics of the product itself. The approach is to carry out inspections of the finished product, look for defects, and correct them.

- Process quality focuses on the characteristics of the process used to build the product. The focus of process quality lies on defect prevention rather than detection and aims to reduce reliance on mass inspections as a way of achieving quality [8].

In the context of DBs, product quality relates to characteristics of the data model and the data itself (the product), while process quality relates to how data models are developed and how the data are collected and loaded (the process). This chapter focuses on product quality.

We refer to information quality in a wide sense as comprising DB system quality and data presentation quality (see Figure 14.2). In fact, it is important that data in the DB correctly reflect the real world, that is, the data are accurate. It is also important for the data to be easy to understand. In DB system quality, three different aspects could be considered: DBMS quality, data model quality (both conceptual and logical), and data quality.

This chapter deals with data model quality and data quality. To assess DBMS quality, we can use an international standard like IS 9126 [9], or some of the existing product comparative studies (e.g., [10] for ODBMS evaluation).

Unfortunately, until a few years ago, quality issues focused on software quality [3, 9, 11–14], disregarding DB quality [15]. Even in traditional DB

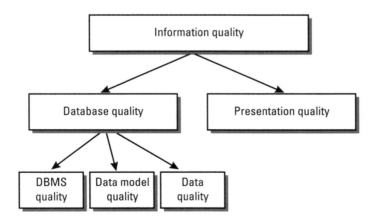

Figure 14.2 Information and DB quality.

design, quality-related aspects have not been explicitly incorporated [16]. Although DB research and practice have not been focused traditionally on quality-related subjects, many of the developed tools and techniques (integrity constraints, normalization theory, transaction management) have influenced data quality. It is time to consider information quality as a main goal to achieve, instead of a subproduct of DB creation and development processes.

Most of the works for the evaluation of both data quality and data model quality propose only lists of criteria or desirable properties without providing any quantitative measures. The development of the properties is usually based upon experience in practice, intuitive analysis, and reviews of relevant literature. Quality criteria are not enough on their own to ensure quality in practice, because different people will generally have different interpretations of the same concept. According to the total quality management (TQM) literature, measurable criteria for assessing quality are necessary to avoid "arguments of style" [17]. Measurement is also fundamental to the application of statistical process control, one of the key techniques of the TQM approach [8]. The objective should be to replace intuitive notions of design "quality" with formal, quantitative measures to reduce subjectivity and bias in the evaluation process. However, defining reliable and objective measures of quality in software development is a difficult task.

This chapter is an overview of the main issues relating to the assessment of DB quality. It addresses data model quality and also considers data (values) quality.

14.2   Data Model Quality

A data model is a collection of concepts that can be used to describe a set of data and operations to manipulate the data. There are two types of data models: conceptual data models (e.g., E/R model), which are used in DB design, and logical models (e.g., relational, hierarchy, and network models), which are supported by DBMSs. Using conceptual models, one can build a description of reality that would be easy to understand and interpret. Logical models support data descriptions that can be processed by a computer through a DBMS. In the design of DBs, we use conceptual models first to produce a high-level description of the reality, then we translate the conceptual model into a logical model.

Although the data modeling phase represents only a small portion of the overall development effort, its impact on the final result is probably greater than that of any other phase [18]. The data model forms the foundation for all later design work and is a major determinant of the quality of the overall system design [19, 20]. Improving the quality of the data model, therefore, is a major step toward improving the quality of the system being developed.

The process of building quality data models begins with an understanding of the big picture of model quality and the role that data models have in the development of ISs.

There are no generally accepted guidelines for evaluating the quality of data models, and little agreement even among experts as to what makes a "good" data model [21]. As a result, the quality of data models produced in practice is almost entirely dependent on the competence of the data modeler.

When systems analysts and users inspect different data models from the same universe of discourse, they often perceive that some models are, in some sense, better than others, but they may have difficulty in explaining why. Therefore an important concern is to clarify what is meant by a "good" data model, a data model of high quality.

Quality in data modeling is frequently defined as a list of desirable properties for a data model [22–27]. By understanding each property and planning your modeling approach to address each one, you can significantly increase the likelihood that your data models will exhibit characteristics that render them useful for IS design. The quality factors are usually based on practical experience, intuitive analysis, and reviews of relevant literature. Although such lists provide a useful starting point for understanding and improving quality in data modeling, they are mostly unstructured, use imprecise definitions, often overlap, often confuse properties of models with language and method properties, and often have goals that are unrealistic or even impossible to reach [28].

Expert data modelers intuitively know what makes a good data model, but such knowledge can generally be acquired only through experience. For data modeling to progress from a craft to an engineering discipline, the desirable qualities of data models need to be made explicit [22]. The conscious listing (or bringing to the surface) of those qualities helps to identify areas on which attention needs to be focused. This can act as a guide to improve the model and explore alternatives. Not only is the definition of quality factors important to evaluate data models, but we also have to consider other elements that allow any two data models, no matter how different they may be, to be compared precisely, objectively, and comprehensively [29]. So, in this chapter, we propose and describe the following elements: quality factors, stakeholders, quality concepts, improvement strategies, quality metrics, and weightings.

14.2.1 Quality Factors

In the literature related to quality in data modeling, there exist a lot of quality factors definitions. We list here the more relevant ones:

- *Completeness.* Completeness is the ability of the data model to meet all user information and functional requirements.

- *Correctness.* Correctness indicates whether the model conforms to the rules of the data modeling technique in use.

- *Minimality.* A data model is minimal when every aspect of the requirements appears once in the data model. In general, it is better to avoid redundancies.

- *Normality.* Normality comes from the theory of normalization associated with the relational data model; it aims at keeping the data in a clean, "purified" normal form.

- *Flexibility.* Flexibility is defined as the ease with which the data model can be adapted to changes in requirements.

- *Understandability.* Understandability is defined as the ease with which the concepts and structures in the data model can be understood by users of the model.

- *Simplicity.* Simplicity relates to the size and complexity of the data model. Simplicity depends not on whether the terms in which the model is expressed are well known or understandable but on the number of different constructs required.

While it is important to separate the various dimensions of value from the purposes of analysis, it is also important to bear in mind the interactions among qualities. In general, some objectives will interfere or conflict with each other; others will have common implications, or concur; and still others will not interact at all.

14.2.2 Stakeholders

Stakeholders are people involved in building or using the data model—therefore, they have an interest in its quality. Different stakeholders will generally be interested in different quality factors.

Different people will have different perspectives on the quality of a data model. An application developer may view quality as ease of implementation, whereas a user may view it as satisfaction of requirements. Both viewpoints are valid, but they need not coincide. Part of the confusion about which is the best model and how models should be evaluated is caused by differences between such perspectives.

The design of effective systems depends on the participation and satisfaction of all relevant stakeholders in the design process. An important consideration, therefore, in developing a framework for evaluating data models is to consider the needs of all stakeholders. This requires identification of the stakeholders and then incorporation of their perceptions of "value" for a data model into the framework.

The following people are the key stakeholders in the data modeling process.

- *Users.* Users are involved in the process of developing the data model and verifying that it meets their requirements. Users are interested in the data model to the extent that it will meet their current and future requirements and that it represents value for money.

- *DB designer.* The DB designer is responsible for developing the data model and is concerned with satisfying the needs of all stakeholders while ensuring that the model conforms to rules of good data modeling practice.

- *Application developer.* The application developer is responsible for implementing the data model once it is finished. Application developers will be primarily concerned with the fact that the model can be implemented given time, budget, resource, and technology constraints.

- *Data administrator.* The data administrator is responsible for ensuring that the data model is integrated with the rest of the organization data. The data administrator is primarily concerned with ensuring data shareability across the organization rather than the needs of specific applications.

All these perspectives are valid and must be taken into consideration during the design process. The set of qualities defined as part of the framework should be developed by coalescing the interests and requirements of the various stakeholders involved. It is only from a combination of perspectives that a true picture of data model quality can be established.

14.2.3 Quality Concepts

It is useful to classify quality according to Krogstie's framework [30] (see Figure 14.3).

Quality concepts are defined as follows:

- *Syntactic quality* is the adherence of a data model to the syntax rules of the modeling language.
- *Semantic quality* is the degree of correspondence between the data model and the universe of discourse.
- *Perceived semantic quality* is the correspondence between stakeholders' knowledge and the stakeholders' interpretation.
- *Pragmatic quality* is the correspondence between a part of a data model and the relevant stakeholders' interpretation of it.
- *Social quality* has the goal of feasible agreement among stakeholders, where inconsistencies among various stakeholders' interpretations of the data model are solved. Relative agreement (stakeholders' interpretations may differ but remain consistent) is more realistic

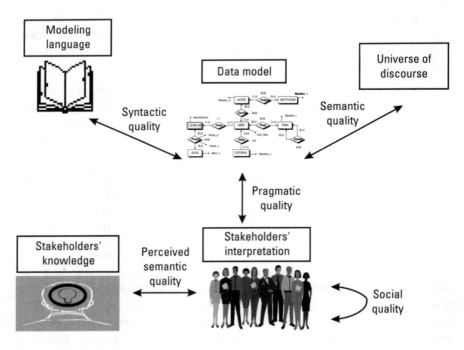

Figure 14.3 Quality concepts.

than absolute agreement (all stakeholders' interpretations are the same).

Each quality concept has different goals that must be satisfied. If some of those goals are not attained, we can think about an improvement strategy.

14.2.4 Improvement Strategies

An improvement strategy is a process or activity that can be used to increase the value of a data model with respect to one or more quality factors. Strategies may involve the use of automated techniques as well as human judgment and insight.

Rather than just simply identifying what is wrong with a model or where it could be improved, we need to identify methods for improving the model. Of course, it is not possible to reduce the task of improving data models to a mechanical process, because that requires invention and insight, but it is useful to identify general techniques that can help improve the quality of data models.

In general, an improvement strategy may improve a data model on more than one dimension. However, because of the interactions between qualities, increasing the value of a model on one dimension may *decrease* its value on other dimensions.

14.2.5 Quality Metrics

Quality metrics define ways of evaluating particular quality factors in numerical terms. Developing a set of qualities and metrics for data model evaluation is a difficult task. Subjective notions of design "quality" are not enough to ensure quality in practice, because different people will have different interpretations of the same concept (e.g., understandability).

A metric is a way of measuring a quality factor in a consistent and objective manner. It is necessary to establish metrics for assessing each quality factor. Software engineers have proposed a plethora of metrics for software products, processes, and resources [31, 32]. Unfortunately, almost all the metrics proposed since McCabe's cyclomatic number [33] until now have focused on program characteristics, without paying special attention to DBs.

Metrics could be used to build prediction systems for DB projects [34], to understand and improve software development and maintenance projects [35], to maintain the quality of the systems [36], to highlight problematic areas [37], and to determine the best ways to help practitioners and researchers in their work [38].

It is necessary that metrics applied to a product be justified by a clear theory [39]. Rigorous measurement of software attributes can provide substantial help in the evaluation and improvement of software products and processes [40, 41]. Empirical validation is necessary, not only to prove the metrics' validity but also to provide some limits that can be useful to DB designers. However, as DeChampeaux remarks, we must be conscious that "associating with numeric ranges the qualifications *good* and *bad* is the hard part" [37].

To illustrate the concept of quality metrics, this section shows some metrics that measure the quality factor of simplicity, as applied to E/R models. All the metrics shown here are based on the concept of closed-ended metrics [42], since they are bounded in the interval [0,1] which allows data modelers to compare different conceptual models on a numerical scale. These metrics are based on complexity theory, which defines the complexity of a system by the number of components in the system and the number of relationships among the components. Because the aim is to simplify the E/R model, the objective will be to minimize the value of these metrics.

- The *RvsE metric* measures the relation that exists between the number of relationships and the number of entities in an E/R model. It is based on M_{RPROP} metric proposed by Lethbridge [42]. We define this metric as follows:

$$RvsE = \left(\frac{N^R}{N^R + N^E} \right)^2$$

where N^R is the number of relationships in the E/R model, N^E is the number of entities in the E/R model, and $N^R + N^E > 0$.

When we calculate the number of relationships (N^R), we also consider the IS_A relationships. In this case, we take into account one relationship for each child-parent pair in the IS_A relationship.

- The *DA metric* is the number of derived attributes that exist in the E/R model, divided by the maximum number of derived attributes that may exist in an E/R model (all attributes in the E/R model except one). An attribute is derived when its value can be calculated or deduced from the values of other attributes. We define this metric as follows:

$$DA = \frac{N^{DA}}{N^A - 1}$$

where N^{DA} is the number of derived attributes in the E/R model, N^A is the number of attributes in the E/R model, and $N^A > 1$.

When we calculate the number of attributes in the E/R model (N^A), in the case of composite attributes we consider each of their simple attributes.

- The *CA metric* assesses the number of composite attributes compared with the number of attributes in an E/R model. A composite attribute is an attribute composed of a set of simple attributes. We define this metric as follows:

$$CA = \frac{N^{CA}}{N^A}$$

where N^{CA} is the number of composite attributes in the E/R model, N^A is the number of attributes in the E/R model, and $N^A > 0$.

When we calculate the number of attributes in the E/R model (N^A), in the case of composite attributes we regard each of their simple attributes.

- The *RR metric* is the number of relationships that are redundant in an E/R model, divided by the number of relationships in the E/R model minus 1. Redundancy exists when one relationship R_1 between two entities has the same information content as a path of relationships R_2, R_3, ..., R_n connecting exactly the same pairs of entity instances as R_1. Obviously, not all cycles of relationships are sources of redundancy. Redundancy in cycles of relationships depends on meaning [22]. We define this metric as follows:

$$RR = \frac{N^{RR}}{N^R = 1}$$

where N^{RR} is the number of redundant relationships in the E/R model, N^R is the number of relationships in the E/R model, and $N^R > 1$.

When we calculate the number of relationship (N^R), we also consider the IS_A relationships. In this case, we consider one relationship for each child-parent pair in the IS_A relationship.

- The *M:NRel metric* measures the number of *M:N* relationships compared with the number of relationships in an E/R model. We define this metric as follows:

$$M:N\ Rel = \frac{N^{M:NR}}{N^R}$$

where $N^{M:NR}$ is the number of *M:N* relationships in the E/R model, N^R is the number of relationships in the E/R model, and $N^R > 0$.

When we calculate the number of relationships (N^R), we also consider the IS_A relationships. In this case, we think over one relationship for each child-parent pair in the IS_A relationship.

- The *IS_ARel metric* assesses the complexity of generalization/specialization hierarchies (IS_A) in one E/R model. It is based on the M_{ISA} metric defined by Lethbridge [42]. The IS_ARel metric combines two factors to measure the complexity of the inheritance hierarchy. The first factor is the fraction of entities that are leaves of the inheritance hierarchy. That measure, called *Fleaf,* is calculated thus:

$$Fleaf = \frac{N^{Leaf}}{N^E}$$

where N^{Leaf} is the number of leaves in one generalization or specialization hierarchy, N^E is the number of entities in each generalization or specialization hierarchy, and $N^E > 0$.

Figure 14.4 shows several inheritance hierarchies along with their measures of *Fleaf. Fleaf* approaches 0,5 when the number of leaves is half the number of entities, as shown in Figure 14.4(c) and (d). It approaches 0 in the ridiculous case of a unary tree, as shown in Figure 14.4(c), and it approaches 1 if every entity is a subtype of the top entity, as shown in Figure 14.4(d). On its own, *Fleaf* has the undesirable property that, for a very shallow hierarchy (e.g., just two or three levels) with a high branching factor, it gives a measurement that is unreasonably high, from a subjective standpoint; see Figure 14.4(a). To correct that problem with *Fleaf,* an additional factor is used in the calculation of the IS_ARel metric: the average number of direct and indirect supertypes per

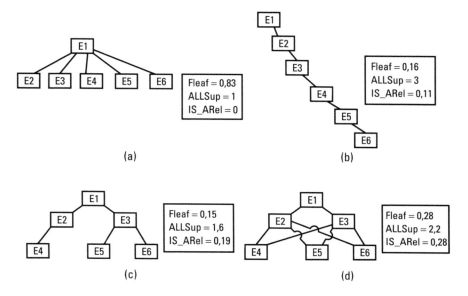

Figure 14.4 Examples of IS_A relationships.

nonroot entity, ALLSup (the root entity is not counted because it cannot have parents).

The IS_ARel metric is calculated using the following formula:

$$IS\_ARel = Fleaf - \frac{Fleaf}{ALLSup}$$

This metric assesses the complexity of each IS_A hierarchy. The overall IS_ARel complexity is the average of all the IS_ARel complexities in the E/R model.

Table 14.2 summarizes the meaning of the values of the proposed closed-ended metrics. Columns indicate the interpretation of measurements at the extremes of that range and in the middle.

Now we will apply the outlined metrics to the example shown in Figure 14.5, taken from [43].

Table 14.3 summarizes the values of the metrics calculated for the example in Figure 14.5.

Table 14.2

An Interpretation of Measurements

Metrics	tends to 0 when...	tends to 0,5 when...	tends to 1 when...
RvsE	No relationships or very few relationships	2,5 relationships per entity	Very many relationships per entity
DA	No derived attributes	Half of attributes are derived	All attributes except one are derived
CA	No composite attributes	Half of attributes are composite	All attributes are composite
RR	No redundant relationships	Half of relationships are redundant	All relationships are redundant (impossible in practice)
M:NRel	No M:N relationships	Half of relationships are M:N	All relationships are M:N
IS_ARel	Each subtype has about one parent	All IS_A hierarchies are binary trees	Very bushy tree: a complex hierarchy with multiple inheritance

Table 14.3

Values of the Metrics for the Example in Figure 14.5

Metrics	Values
RvsE	0.5357
DA	0.0740
CA	0.1071
RR	0
M:NRel	0.0666
IS_ARel	0.2975

The Kiviat diagram shown in Figure 14.6 is a graphical representation of the values of the metrics shown in Table 14.3 This diagram is useful because it allows designers to evaluate the overall complexity of an E/R schema at a glance. It also serves to compare different conceptual schemas and then to improve their quality.

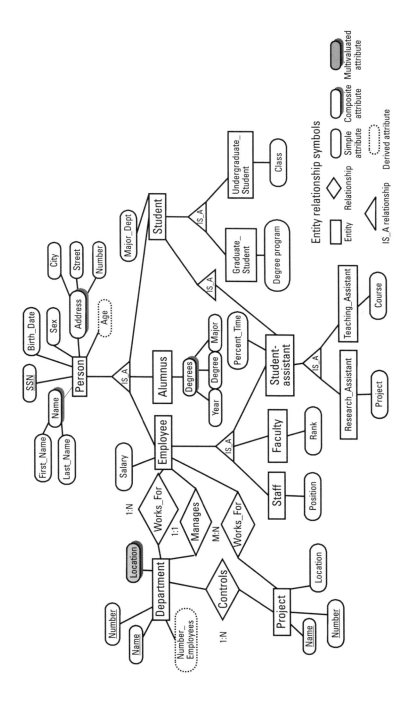

Figure 14.5 An E/R schema.

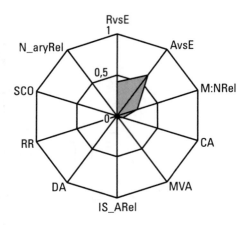

Figure 14.6 A Kiviat diagram.

14.2.6 Weighting

Weighting defines the relative importance of different quality factors in a particular problem environment. It is impossible to say in absolute terms that one data model is better than another, irrespective of context. Values can be assessed only in the light of project goals and objectives. If the system under development will be used as a basis for competing in the marketplace (e.g., a product development system), then flexibility will be paramount. If the system is used internally and the requirements are stable (e.g., a payroll system), then flexibility will be less important. The concept of weightings helps to define what is important and what is not important in the context of the project.

Finding the best representation generally involves tradeoffs among different qualities, and an understanding of project priorities is essential to making those tradeoffs in a rational manner. Depending on users' needs, the importance of different qualities will vary greatly from one project to another. Weightings provide the means to explicitly incorporate user priorities into the evaluation process. An understanding of the relative importance of different quality dimensions can highlight those areas where improvement efforts will be most useful. The project team should come to a common understanding of what is most important to the user as early as possible in the modeling process. Ideally, the user sponsor should define the weightings prior to any data modeling taking place. Analysts can then focus their efforts on maximizing quality in the areas of highest value to the customer.

14.3 Data Quality

DB quality has to deal not only with the quality of the DB models but also with the quality of the data values. There are different relevant dimensions for data quality values, as listed next.

- *Accuracy* sometimes reflects the nearness of the data values to the values considered "correct." Obviously, the problem in this dimension is that correct values are not always known, making it difficult to quantify accuracy.

- *Completeness* refers to the portion of the values (of the real world) that are present in the DB. DB null values reflect sometimes unknown values.

- *Currency* reflects the degree to which data are up to date. There is an inevitable lag between when a data value changes and when it is updated in the DB.

- *Value consistency* means that values do not contradict each other. Consistency is a crucial factor for decision making.

All these and other dimensions (e.g., [44]) help to measure data quality. Three different types of measures can be distinguished [45].

- *Subjective measures* depend upon the subjective assessment of data quality, for example, expressed using a questionnaire with a Likert-type scale from 0 to 7, where 0 indicates "not at all" and 7 "completely" for each question as "The data are correct."

- *Objective, application-independent measures*, for example, in relational DB systems can measure the number of violations of referential integrity present in the DB.

- *Objective, application-dependent measures* require domain expert participation (the percentage of incorrect addresses in the DB).

Several aspects should be addressed by companies in order to achieve good data quality and have "good" marks in these measures: management responsibilities, operation and assurance costs, research and development, production, distribution, personnel management, and legal functions [46]. This section makes reference to only two of them: management and design issues.

14.3.1 Management Issues

Companies must, on the one hand, define a quality policy that establishes the duties of each function to ensure data quality in all its dimensions. But on the other hand, they must implement an information quality assessment process.

Regarding the first issue, Redman [47] has proposed a policy covering four types of roles that can be summed up in five points:

- All the employees of the company have to assume that data, information, and the business processes that create, store, process, and use data are company properties. Data sharing must be restricted to legal or privacy considerations.

- The chief information officer (CIO) will be responsible for keeping an updated data inventory and its availability and for informing others about data quality.

- Data providers and creators both need to understand who uses data and for what purpose. They can then implement data quality measures to ensure that users' requirements are fulfilled, and implement data process management.

- People who store and process data must provide architectures and DBs that minimize unnecessary redundancy, save data from damages or unauthorized access, and design new technologies to promote data quality.

- Users must work with data providers—providing feedback, ensuring that data are interpreted correctly and used only for legitimate company purposes, and protecting clients' and employees' privacy rights.

The data quality policy must be developed by top management and be aligned with the overall quality policy and system implemented in the organization. The CIO's role will become increasingly important in the assurance of the organization's information quality. Miller [48] poses four interesting questions about information quality that must be answered by the heads of information technology (IT):

- Are yesterday's perceptions of our quality needs still valid?

- How do quality needs translate into technology requirements?

- Is our technology strategy consistent with our quality needs?

- Do internal information collection, dissemination, and verification procedures measure up to quality requirements?

Data quality training and awareness programs must be carried out jointly with the data quality policy. Personnel involvement is a prerequisite to quality program success.

In addition, an information quality assessment process must be implemented. English [49] puts forward a methodology called TQdM (*Total Quality data Management*), which allows the assessment of an organization's information quality. The methodology consists of the following steps:

1. Identify an information group that has a significant impact in order to give more added value.

2. Establish objectives and measures for information quality, for example, assess the information timeliness and measure the span that passes from when a datum is known until it is available for a specific process.

3. Identify the "information value and cost chain," which is an extended business value chain focused on a data group. This chain covers all the files, documents, DBs, business processes, programs, and roles related to the data group.

4. Determine the files or processes to assess.

5. Identify the data validation sources to assess data accuracy.

6. Extract random samples of data, applying appropriate statistical techniques.

7. Measure information quality to determine its reliability level and discover its defaults.

8. Interpret and inform others about information quality.

A crucial aspect for carrying out this process is the definition of significant metrics that allow for the analysis and improvement of quality. In [45], three kinds of metrics are given: subjective (based on user opinion about data); objective, application-independent (e.g., accuracy); and objective, application-dependent (specific to a particular domain).

Companies must also measure the value of the information, both information produced by operational systems and information produced by decision-support systems. The way of measuring both kinds of information varies considerably. In Due [50], three different approaches (normative, realistic, and subjective) to the measurement of decision support systems information can be found.

14.3.2 Design Issues

Unfortunately, few proposals consider data quality to be a crucial factor in the DB design process. Works like [17] and [51] are the exception in this sense. The authors of these works provide a methodology that complements traditional DB methodologies (e.g., [22]). At the first stage of this methodology (see Figure 14.7), in addition to creating the conceptual schema using, for example, an extended E/R model, we should identify quality requirements and candidate attributes. Thereafter, the "quality parameter view" must be determined, associating a quality parameter with each conceptual schema element (entity, relationship, ...). For example, for an academic mark, two parameters can be accuracy and timeliness. Next, subjective parameters are objectified by the addition of tags to conceptual schema attributes. For example, for the academic mark we can add the source of the mark (to know its accuracy) and the date (to know its timeliness). Finally, different quality views are integrated.

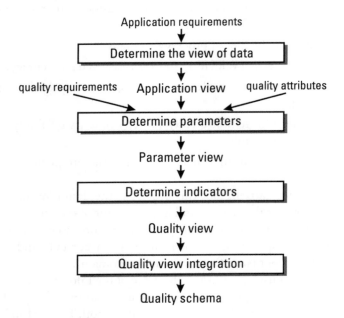

Figure 14.7 Considering data quality in DB design.

These authors also propose to extend relational DBs with indicators, allowing the assignment of objective and subjective parameters to the quality of DB values [51]. For example, in Table 14.4, for each DB value, the source and the date of the data are stored. The source credibility should be known (e.g., in the case of the Department of Education, it could be "high") to help "knowledge workers" in making decisions.

14.4 Summary

If we really consider information to be "the" main organizational asset, one of the primary duties of IT professionals must be ensuring its quality. Traditionally, the only indicator used to measure the quality of data models has been normalization theory; Gray [52], for example, has proposed a normalization ratio for conceptual schemas.

This chapter presented some elements for characterizing and ensuring DB quality. Further research about quality in conceptual modeling can be found in [23, 29, 31, 53–58]. More research is necessary on this subject as well as on the quality of the associated processes: data modeling, data procurement and load, and data presentation.

For data modeling to progress from a craft to an engineering discipline, formal quality criteria and metrics need to be explicitly defined [30]. We affirm that in the next decade information quality will be an essential factor for company success, in the same way as product and service have been in the past. In this sense, measuring data and data model quality will become increasingly important, and more metrics need to be researched. As in other aspects of software engineering, proposing techniques, metrics, or procedures is not enough; it is also necessary to put them under formal and empirical validation to ensure their utility.

Table 14.4
Table Extended With Quality Indicators

Student	Secondary School Final Mark	Entrance Examination Mark
William Smith	8 <30/10/90, Education Ministry>	7 <30/7/95, UCLM Univ.>
Gene Hackman	9 <30/10/90, Education Ministry>	6 <10/9/96, UCLM Univ.>
	...	...

References

[1] Van Vliet, J. C., *Software Engineering: Principles and Practice*, New York: Wiley, 1993.

[2] Zultner, R., "QFD for Software: Satisfying Customers," *American Programmer*, Feb. 1992.

[3] Gillies, A., *Software Quality: Theory and Management*, London, UK: Chapman & Hall, 1993.

[4] Crosby, P., *Quality Is Free*, New York: Penguin Group, 1979.

[5] Juran, J. M., *Quality Control Handbook*, 3rd ed., New York: McGraw-Hill, 1974.

[6] ISO 8042, *Quality Vocabulary*, 1986.

[7] English, L., *Information Quality Improvement: Principles, Methods, and Management Seminar*, 5th ed., Brentwood, TN: Information Impact International, 1996.

[8] Deming, W. E., *Out of the Crisis*, Cambridge, MA: MIT Center for Advanced Engineering, 1986.

[9] ISO 9126, *Software Product Evaluation—Quality Characteristics and Guidelines for Their Use*, ISO/IEC Standard 9126, Geneva, Switzerland, 1998.

[10] Barry, D., *The Object Database Handbook*, New York: Wiley, 1996.

[11] Arthur, L., *Improving Software Quality*, New York: Wiley, 1993.

[12] Oskarsson, Ö., and R. Glass, *An ISO 9000 Approach to Building Quality Software*, Upper Saddle River, NJ: Prentice-Hall, 1996.

[13] Jones, C., *Software Quality: Analysis and Guidelines for Success*, Boston, MA: International Thomson Computer Press, 1997.

[14] Ginac, F., *Customer Oriented Software Quality Assurance*, Upper Saddle River, NJ: Prentice-Hall, 1998.

[15] Sneed, H. and O. Foshag, "Measuring Legacy Database Structures," *Proc. European Software Measurement Conf. FESMA'98*, 1998, pp. 199–210.

[16] Wang, R. Y., H. B. Kon, and S. E. Madnick, "Data Quality Requirements Analysis and Modeling," *Proc. 9th Intl. Conf. on Data Engineering*, Vienna, Austria, 1993, pp. 670–677.

[17] Zultner, R. E., "The Deming Way: Total Quality Management for Software," *Proc. Total Quality Management for Software Conf.*, Washington, DC, Apr. 1992.

[18] Simsion, G. C., "Creative Data Modelling," *Proc. 10th Intl. Entity Relationship Conf.*, San Francisco, CA, 1991.

[19] Meyer, B., *Object Oriented Software Construction*, New York: Prentice-Hall, 1988.

[20] Sager, M., "Data Centred Enterprise Modelling Methodologies: A Study of Practice and Potential," *Australian Computer J.*, Aug. 1988.

[21] Moody, L., and G. Shanks, "What Makes a Good Data Model? Evaluating the Quality of Entity Relationships Models," *Proc. 13th Intl. Conf. on Conceptual Modelling (E/R '94)*, Manchester, England, Dec. 14–17, 1994, pp. 94–111.

[22] Batini, C., S. Ceri, and S. Navathe, *Conceptual Database Design: An Entity Relationship Approach*, Redwood City, CA: Benjamin/Cummings, 1992.

[23] Boman, M., et al., *Conceptual Modelling*, New York: Prentice-Hall, 1997.

[24] Reingruber, M., and W. Gregory, *The Data Modeling Handbook: A Best-Practice Approach To Building Quality Data Models*, New York: Wiley, 1994.

[25] Roman, G., "A Taxonomy of Current Issues in Requirements Engineering," *Computer IEEE*, Apr. 1985, pp. 14–22.

[26] Levitin, A., and T. Redman, "Quality Dimensions of a Conceptual View," *Information Processing and Management*, Vol. 31, 1994, pp. 81–88.

[27] Simsion, G., *Data Modeling Essentials*, New York: Van Nostrand Reinhold, 1994.

[28] Lindland, O., G. Sindre, and A. Solvberg, "Understanding Quality in Conceptual Modelling," *IEEE Software*, Vol. 11, No. 2, 1994, pp. 42–49.

[29] Moody, D., "Metrics for Evaluating the Quality of Entity Relationship Models," *Proc. 17th Intl. Conf. on Conceptual Modelling (E/R '98)*, Singapore, Nov. 16–19, 1998, pp. 213–225.

[30] Krogstie, J., O. I. Lindland, and G. Sindre, "Towards a Deeper Understanding of Quality in Requirements Engineering," *Proc. 7th Intl. Conf. on Advanced Information Systems Engineering (CAISE)*, Jyväskylä, Finland, June 1995, pp. 82–95.

[31] Melton, A., *Software Measurement*, London, UK: International Thomson Computer Press, 1996.

[32] Fenton, N., and S. Pfleeger, *Software Metrics: A Rigorous and Practical Approach*, 2nd ed., Boston, MA: PWS Publishers, 1997.

[33] McCabe, T., "A Complexity Measure," *IEEE Trans. on Software Engineering*, Vol. 2, No. 5, 1976, pp. 308–320.

[34] MacDonell, S., M. Shepperd, and P. Sallis, "Metrics for Database Systems: An Empirical Study," *Proc. 4th Intl. Software Metrics Symp.—Metrics'97*, Albuquerque, NM, 1997, pp. 99–107.

[35] Briand, L., S. Morasca, and V. Basili, "Property-Based Software Engineering Measurement," *IEEE Trans on Software Engineering*, Vol. 22, No. 1, Jan. 1996.

[36] Graham, I., *Migrating to Object Technology*, Reading, MA: Addison-Wesley, 1995.

[37] DeChampeaux, D., *Object-Oriented Development Process and Metrics*, Upper Saddle River, NJ: Prentice-Hall, 1997.

[38] Pfleeger, S., "Assessing Software Measurement," *IEEE Software*, Vol. 14, No. 2, Mar./Apr. 1997, pp. 25–26.

[39]   Meyer, B., "The Role of Object-Oriented Metrics," *IEEE Computer*, Vol. 31, No. 11, Nov. 1998, pp. 123–125.

[40]   Fenton, N., "Software Measurement: A Necessary Scientific Basis," *IEEE Trans. on Software Engineering*, Vol. 20, No. 3, 1994, pp. 199–206.

[41]   Morasca, S., and L. Briand, "Towards a Theoretical Framework for Measuring Software Attribute," *Proc. 4th Intl., Software Metrics Symp.*, 1997, pp. 119–126.

[42]   Lethbridge, T., "Metrics for Concept-Oriented Knowledge Bases," *Intl. J. Software Engineering and Knowledge Engineering*, Vol. 8, No. 2, 1998, pp. 161–188.

[43]   Elmasri, R., and S. Navathe, *Fundamentals of Database Systems*, 2nd ed., Reading, MA: Addison-Wesley, 1994.

[44]   Wand, Y., and R. Wang, "Anchoring Data Quality Dimensions in Ontological Foundations," *Comm. ACM*, Vol. 39, No. 11, 1996, pp. 86–95.

[45]   Huang, K. -T., Y. Lee, and R. Wang, *Quality Information and Knowledge*, Upper Saddle River, NJ: Prentice-Hall, 1999.

[46]   Wang, R., V. Storey, and C. Firth, "A Framework for Analysis of Data Quality Research," *IEEE Trans. on Knowledge and Data Engineering*, Vol. 7, No. 4, 1995, pp. 623–637.

[47]   Redman, T., *Data Quality for the Information Age*, Norwood, MA: Artech House, 1996.

[48]   Miller, H., "The Multiple Dimensions of Information Quality," *Information Systems Management*, Spring 1996, pp. 79–82.

[49]   English, L., *Improving Data Warehouse and Business Information Quality*, New York: Wiley, 1999.

[50]   Due, R., "The Value of Information," *Information Systems Management*, 1996, pp. 68–72.

[51]   Wang, R., M. Reddy, and H. Kon, "Toward Quality Data: An Attribute-Based Approach," *Decision Support Systems*, Vol. 13, 1995, pp. 349–372.

[52]   Gray, R., et al., "Design Metrics for Database Systems," *BT Technology J.*, Vol. 9, No. 4, 1991, pp. 69–79.

[53]   Eick, C., "A Methodology for the Design and Transformation of Conceptual Schemas," *Proc. 17th Intl. Conf. on Very Large Data Bases*, Barcelona, Spain, 1991.

[54]   Pohl, K., "The Three Dimensions of Requirements Engineering: A Framework and Its Applications," *Information Systems*, Vol. 19, 1994, pp. 243–258.

[55]   Kesh, S., "Evaluating the Quality of Entity Relationship Models," *Information and Software Technology*, Vol. 37, No. 12, 1995, pp. 681–689.

[56] Moody, L., G. Shanks, and P. Darke, "Improving the Quality of Entity Relationship Models—Experience in Research and Practice," *Proc. 17th Intl. Conf. on Conceptual Modelling (E/R '98)*, Singapore, Nov. 16–19, 1998, pp. 255–276.

[57] Shanks, G., and P. Darke, "Quality in Conceptual Modelling: Linking Theory and Practice," *Proc. Pacific Asia Conf. on Information Systems (PACIS'97)*, Brisbane, Australia, 1997, pp. 805–814.

[58] Schuette, R., and T. Rotthowe, "The Guidelines of Modeling—An Approach to Enhance the Quality in Information Models," *Proc. 17th Intl. Conf. on Conceptual Modelling (E/R '98)*, Singapore, Nov. 16–19, 1998, pp. 240–254.

Selected Bibliography

Huang, K. -T., Y. W. Lee, and R. Y. Wang, *Quality Information and Knowledge*, Upper Saddle River, NJ: Prentice-Hall, 1999.

This book can be divided in two different but related parts. The first part deals with information quality; it explains how to manage information as a product and how to measure and improve information quality. The second part focuses on the creation and management of organizational knowledge. Companies must address both of these critical issues if they are to survive and prosper in the digital economy.

Reingruber, M. C., and W. W. Gregory, *The Data Modeling Handbook: A Best-Practice Approach To Building Quality Data Models*, New York: Wiley, 1994.

In a clear and straightforward way, this book on building quality data models offers rules and guidelines for building accurate, complete, and useful data models. It also offers detailed guidance to establishing a continuous quality-evaluation program that is easy to implement and follow.

Zuse, H., *A Framework of Software Measurement*, New York: Walter de Gruyter, 1997.

This book on software measurement provides basic principles as well as theoretical and practical guidelines for the use of numerous kinds of software measures. It is written to enable scientists, teachers, practitioners, and students to define the basic terminology of software measurement and to contribute to theory building. It includes the main proposed metrics so far.

About the Authors

David A. Anstey is a custom solutions practice manager for the Aris Corporation. He is a 1982 graduate of the United States Military Academy, West Point, New York. His 12 years of computer science experience include consulting as well as designing and developing Oracle-based applications. His current technological focus is on UML and e-business solutions. His e-mail address is danstey@airmail.net.

Elisa Bertino is a professor of computer science in the Department of Computer Science at the University of Milan. She is or has been on the editorial boards of the following scientific journals: *ACM Transactions on Information and Systems Security, IEEE Transactions on Knowledge and Data Engineering, Theory and Practice of Object Systems Journal, Journal of Computer Security, Very Large Database Systems Journal, Parallel and Distributed Database,* and *International Journal of Information Technology.* She is currently serving as program chair of ECOOP 2000. Her e-mail address is bertino@dsi.unimi.it.

Mokrane Bouzeghoub is a professor at the University of Versailles in France. He is the director of the database group in the PRiSM laboratory. His research interests are in database design, data integration, data warehouses, workflows, and software engineering. He is the co-editor in chief of the *International Journal on Networking and Information Systems.* He has published different books on databases and object technology. His e-mail address is Mokrane.Bouzeghoub@prism.uvsq.fr.

511

Coral Calero is an assistant professor in the Department of Computer Science at the University of Castilla–La Mancha, in Ciudad Real, Spain. Her research interests include metrics for advanced databases and formal verification and empirical validation of software metrics. Her e-mail address is ccalero@inf-cr.uclm.es.

Hugh Darwen is a database specialist for IBM United Kingdom Limited. He is an active participant in the development of the international standard for SQL. His current special interests are in temporal databases and object/relational databases. His most recently published work, in collaboration with C. J. Date, is *Foundation for Future Database Systems: The Third Manifesto* (Addison-Wesley, 2000). He has honorary degrees from two British universities. His e-mail is Hugh_Darwen@uk.ibm.com.

Chris J. Date is an independent author, lecturer, researcher, and consultant who specializes in relational database technology. He is best known for his book *An Introduction to Database Systems* (7th edition published in 2000). His current research interests include type inheritance and temporal data.

Adoración de Miguel is a professor in the Department of Computer Science at Polytechnic School (Universidad Carlos III de Madrid). She received her B.S. and M.S. in physics from the Universidad Complutense de Madrid and her B.S., M.S., and Ph.D. in computer science from Universidad Politécnica de Madrid. She has been the computing center director and data bank director at INE (the Spanish Statistical Office). Her current research areas include database modeling and design and object-oriented, data warehouse, and multidimensional data models. Her e-mail address is admiguel@inf.uc3m.es.

Oscar Díaz is a professor of computer science at the University of the Basque Country. He received a B.Sc. in 1985 from the University of the Basque Country and a Ph.D. in 1992 from the University of Aberdeen, both in computer science. His current research interests include application servers, active DBMS, conceptual modeling, and requirement engineering. His e-mail address is jipdigao@si.ehu.es.

Klaus R. Dittrich is a professor of computer science at the University of Zurich. He received a B.S. in computer science in 1977 and a Ph.D. in computer science in 1982, both from the University of Karlsruhe. His current research interests include object-oriented, active, engineering, and federated database systems, and database security. His e-mail address is dittrich@ifi.unizh.ch.

Elena Ferrari received her Ph.D. in computer science from the University of Milano, Italy, in 1998. She is now an assistant professor in the Department of Computer Science at the University of Milano, Italy. Her main research interests include database security, access control models, multimedia databases, and temporal object-oriented data models. She has published several papers in refereed journals and conference proceedings. Her e-mail address is ferrarie@dsi.unimi.it.

Marcela Genero is an associate professor in the Department of Computer Science at the University of Comahue, in Neuquén, Argentina, and a Ph.D. candidate at the University of Castilla–La Mancha, in Ciudad Real, Spain. Her research interests are advanced databases design, software metrics, object-oriented metrics, conceptual data model quality, and database quality. Her e-mail address is mgenero@inf-cr.uclm.es.

Andreas Geppert is a senior researcher at the Department of Information Technology at the University of Zurich. He received a B.S. in computer science from the University of Karlsruhe in 1989 and a Ph.D. in computer science from the University of Zurich in 1994. His current research interests include object-oriented and active database systems, workflow management, database middleware, and construction of database management systems and information systems. His e-mail address is geppert@acm.org.

Alfredo Goñi is an assistant professor in the Computer Science Department at the Basque Country University, Spain. His research interests are databases, mobile computing, interoperable data systems, and software engineering. His e-mail address is alfredo@si.ehu.es.

Arantza Illarramendi is a professor in the Computer Science Department at the Basque Country University, Spain. Her research interests are databases, interoperable data systems, and mobile computing. Her e-mail address is jipileca@si.ehu.es.

Zoubida Kedad is an associate professor at the University of Versailles in France. She received a Ph.D. from the University of Versailles in 1999. Her works mainly concern database design, specifically schema integration issues and the design of multisource information systems and datawarehouses. Her e-mail address is Zoubida.Kedad@prism.uvsq.fr.

Esperanza Marcos received a Ph.D. in computer science from the Polytechnical University of Madrid in 1997. She is now an associate professor at the Escuela Superior de Ciencias Experimentales y Tecnolgía in the Rey Juan Carlos University (Madrid). She teaches courses on advanced databases and database design and information security. Her research interests include object-oriented database design, conceptual modeling, and methodologies for software engineering research. Her e-mail address is cuca@escet.urjc.es.

Paloma Martínez has a B.S. in computer science from the Universidad Politécnica de Madrid in 1992. Since 1992, she has been working at the Department of Computer Science at the Universidad Carlos III de Madrid. In 1998 she obtained a Ph.D. in computer science from Universidad Politécnica de Madrid. She is currently teaching advanced databases and natural language processing. She has been working in several European and national research projects on natural language techniques, advanced database technologies, and software engineering. Her e-mail address is pmf@inf.uc3m.es.

Peter McBrien is a lecturer at the Department of Computing at Imperial College in London. He lectures in databases and computer communications. His research areas include the design and analysis of distributed information systems and temporal databases. His e-mail address is pjm@doc.ic.ac.uk.

Elisabeth Métais is an associate professor at the University of Versailles in France and a researcher in the PRiSM Laboratory at the University of Versailles. She participated in the definition of SECSI, the first expert system on database design, and is currently interested in applying natural language techniques to database design. Her e-mail address is Elisabeth.Metais@prism.uvsq.fr.

Antoni Olivé is a professor of Information Systems in the Software Department at the Universitat Politécnica de Catalunya in Barcelona, Spain. His research interests include conceptual modeling, requirements engineering, and information systems design. His e-mail address is olive@lsi.upc.es.

Norman W. Paton is a senior lecturer in computer science at the University of Manchester, England. He received a B.Sc. in 1986 and a Ph.D. in 1989, both in computing science, from Aberdeen University, where he worked as a research assistant from 1986 to 1989. From 1989 to 1995, he was a lecturer at Heriot-Watt University. His principal research interests are in databases, including active, spatial, and deductive-object-oriented databases. He also works on distributed information systems, visual interfaces, and bioinformatics. His e-mail address is norm@cs.man.ac.uk.

Mario Piattini holds M.Sc. and Ph.D. degrees in computer science from the Polytechnical University of Madrid. He is certified as an information system auditor by the Information System Audit and Control Association (ISACA), an associate professor at the Escuela Superior de Informática of the Castilla–La Mancha University, and the author of several books and papers on databases, software engineering, and information systems. He also leads the ALARCOS research group in the Department of Computer Science at the University of Castilla–La Mancha, in Ciudad Real, Spain. His research interests are advanced database design, database quality, software metrics, object-oriented metrics, and software maintenance. His e-mail address is mpiattin@ inf-cr.uclm.es.

Macario Polo is an assistant professor in the Department of Computer Science at the University of Castilla–La Mancha in Ciudad Real, Spain. He received his M.S. in computer science from the University of Seville, Spain, in 1996. His current research areas include software maintenance and metrics for databases. His e-mail address is mpolo@inf-cr.uclm.es.

Alexandra Poulovassilis is a reader in computer science in the Department of Computer Science at Cirkbeck College, University of London. Her research interests are active databases, database programming languages, graph-based data models and languages, heterogeneous databases and database integration, intelligent networks, and query optimization. Her e-mail address is ap@dcs.bbk.ac.uk.

Francisco Ruiz is an associate professor in the Department of Computer Science at the University of Castilla–La Mancha, in Ciudad Real, Spain. His current research interests include metrics for object-oriented databases, software maintenance, and methodologies for information systems. Currently, he is Dean of the Faculty of Computer Science. His e-mail address is fruiz@inf-cr.uclm.es.

Timos Sellis is a professor in the Department of Electrical and Computer Engineering at the National Technical University of Athens. His research interests include extended relational database systems, data warehouses, and spatial, image, and multimedia database systems. He is a recipient of the Presidential Young Investigator (PYI) award for 1990–1995 and of the VLDB 1997 10-Year Paper Award. His e-mail address is timos@dbnet.ece.ntua.gr.

Ernest Teniente is an associate professor in the Software Department at the Universitat Politécnica de Catalunya in Barcelona, Spain. He teaches courses on information systems and database technology. His research interests include database updating, database schema validation, and data warehousing. His e-mail is teniente@lsi.upc.es.

Bhavani Thuraisingham, chief scientist in data management at the MITRE Corporation, is the recipient of the IEEE Computer Society's 1997 technical achievement award and the author of several books on data mining: technologies, techniques, tools, and trends; and data management evolution, and interoperation. She has published more than 40 journal articles and serves on the editorial board of *IEEE Transactions on Knowledge and Data Engineering.* Her e-mail address is thura@mitre.org.

Michalis Vazirgiannis is a lecturer in the Department of Informatics of Athens University of Economics and Business. His research interests and work range from interactive multimedia information systems to spatio-temporal databases, uncertainty, and data mining. His e-mail address is mvazirg@aueb.gr.

Index

= (equal sign), 214
== (two equal signs), 214

ABC Corporation example, 203–8
  defined, 204
  logical relationship of components, 205
  logical representation, 207
  See also Object-relational DBMSs
    (ORDBMSs)
Abstract architecture, 46–51
Abstract data types (ADTs), 198, 200
Access control
  concepts, 354–55
  content-based, 395
  discretionary (DAC), 356–59, 362–75
  lists (ACLs), 385
  mandatory (MAC), 359–60
  models, 354
  policies, 355–60
  role-based, 396
  See also Secure databases
Active databases, 19, 61–88
  advantages, 62
  analysis, 64–68
  authorization models, 369–70
  behavior, 76–78
  change computation in, 112
  condition monitoring in, 112–13
  defined, 62

design, 69–78
  execution model, 78
  implementation issues, 78–85
  information passing, 78
  language expressiveness, 78
  rule maintenance, 85–87
  summary, 87–88
  university database example, 63–64
  See also Databases
Active documents, 341
Active function, 30–31
  defined, 27
  example, 30
  modes, 30
  performing, 30
  See also Information systems (IS)
Active rules, 69
  auditing, 81–82
  components, 69
  computation model, 69
  evaluation, 77, 78
  maintenance, 85–87
  in Oracle, 79–81
  processed, 76–77
  supporting causal business policies
    with, 73–76
  supporting recovering business policies
    with, 69–73

Active rules (continued)
    transition granularity of set, 78
    transition granularity of tuple, 78
    in use, 81–85
    view materialization, 82–85
Actors
    defined, 261–62
    spatiotemporal composition of, 261–65
Administration
    DBA, 360–61
    delegation, 361
    joint, 362
    object "curator," 361
    object-owner, 361
    policies, 360–62
    policy taxonomy, 363
    tools, 443
    transfer, 361–62
Advanced mobile phone service
    (AMPS), 334
Advanced radio data information system
    (ARDIS), 335
Agents, 343–44
    implementation in mobile
        systems, 343–44
    profile, 343
    system, 343
Aggregate operators, 160–62
Aggregations, 213, 216–17
    member-collection, 239, 240
    part-whole, 240
    tree, 239
    UML support, 239–40
Algebraic composition, 260
Allen's operators, 159, 160, 183
    defined, 159
    list of, 159–60
Analog cellular networks, 334
Analysis, 64–68
    casual business policies, 67–68
    defined, 64
    recovering business policies, 64–67
    See also Active databases
ANSI/SPARC architecture, 47
ANSI standard, 191
AnyLan, 13

Application programming interfaces
    (APIs), 11
Array type, 241
Associations, 235–37
    with attributes, 237
    binary, 235, 237
Asynchronous communications, 343–44
Atomicity, consistency, isolation, durability
    (ACID), 16, 292
Atoms, 94
Authorization models
    for active DBMSs, 369–70
    comparative analysis, 370–72
    Iris, 368–69
    for object DBMSs, 366–69
    Orion, 367–68
    for relational DBMSs, 363–66
    Starburst, 369–70
    See also Discretionary access control
Authorizations
    content-based, 359
    explicit, 357–58
    implicit, 357–58
    negative, 356–57, 365
    objects, 354
    positive, 356–57
    privileges, 355
    propagated, 358
    strong, 357
    subjects, 354
    weak, 357
Autonomous communications, 344

Backman, C. W., 5
Bag type, 240–41
Base station (BS), 333
Binary associations, 235, 237
Binary large objects (BLOBs), 198
Binary relvars, 180
Bitemporal tables, 186
Booch method, 10
Bottom-up design, 301
    local DBs and, 307
    schema conformance, 307
    schema improvement, 307
    schema merging, 307

semantic schema integration
example, 308
See also Distributed databases
Bottom-up query evaluation, 103–5
defined, 102
drawbacks, 104–5
example, 104
steps, 103–4
See also Query processing
Boyce-Codd normal form (BCNF), 469
Broadcasting, 339–40
defined, 339
methods, 340

CAD/CAM/CIM, 13, 211
Canonical forms, 183
CASE tools, 10, 13, 211, 439–80
communication between, 444–45
conceptual design, 447–68
creative design, 451
database design, 442
framework for database design, 445–47
functional classification of, 440–44
functionalities, 440
history of, 439–40
ideal toolset, 441
integration approaches, 444
intelligent, 458
introduction to, 439–45
logical design, 469–79
maintenance and administration, 443
mapping process support, 477–79
process modeling, 443
project management, 441–42
repository and metadata, 443–44
reverse engineering, 452
summary, 479–80
types of, 440
Causal business policies, 67–68
defined, 73
graphical representation, 75–76
supporting, through active rules, 73–76
Cellular digital packet data (CDPD), 335
Change computation, 109–14
in active DBs, 112
applications, 111–13
aspect related to, 110–11

example, 109–10
methods for, 113–14
problem definition, 109
treatment of multiple transactions, 111
See also Update processing
Character large objects (CLOBs), 198
Chief information officer (CIO), 502
Classes, 218–19
defined, 213
persistent, 230, 233
subclasses, 219
superclasses, 219
See also Object-oriented DBMSs
(OODBMSs)
Classification, 36
Closed intervals, 154
Closed world assumption (CWA), 97
Coalesced form, 183
COALESCE operator, 160–62
Codasyl DBTG language, 6
Codasyl sets, 5
Codd, Dr. E. F., 5, 9
Code-division multiple access
(CDMA), 334–35
Collection types, 196–97, 198, 199–200
array type, 241
bag type, 240–41
dictionary type, 241
list type, 241
nested tables, 196–97
ODMG support of, 224
POET-supported, 244
set type, 241
VARRAYs, 196
Commitment, concurrency, and recovery
(CCR) protocol, 319
Common Object Request Broker
Architecture (CORBA), 12
Complex objects, 217
Component DBMSs (CDBMSs), 403–31
architecture, 409–13
categories, 430
component development, 427–28
configurable, 416
database design for, 426–27
defined, 296, 405
development of, 424–28

Component DBMSs (CDBMSs) (continued)
  extensions, 409
  full-fledged, building, 429
  introduction to, 403–5
  middleware, 414–15
  model classification, 424
  models, 416–24
  motivation, 405–9
  plug-in style, 413–14
  principles, 409–16
  roots of, 428–29
  service-oriented architectures, 415–16
  summary, 430–31
  typology of, 413–16
  See also Databases
Component Object Model (COM), 420
Composite objects, 216, 217
Composition
  algebraic, 260
  defined, 262
  spatiotemporal, 257, 260, 261–65
Computer-aided software/system
    engineering (CASE).
    See CASE tools
Computer-supported cooperative work
    (CSCW), 362
Concept queries, 277
Concepts, 35–36
Conceptual design, 9
  based on reusable components, 467–68
  by schema integration, 463–66
Conceptual design tools, 447–68
  creative design, 449–52
  modeling, 449–54
  verification and validation, 455–63
  See also CASE tools
Conceptual modeling, 33–46
  creative design, 449–50
  defined, 35
  languages, 35, 37
  model choice, 448–49
  natural language understanding, 453–54
  purposes, 26
  reverse engineering, 450–52
  tools, 449–54
Conceptual schemas, 35
  100% principle, 53–54

  of the behavior, 39–43
  of chess-playing example, 48
  completeness of, 54–55, 459
  consistency, 455–57
  correctness, 54
  defined, 37
  design independent, 55
  desirable properties of, 53–55
  ease of understanding, 55
  information base and, 38
  irredundancy of, 457–59
  mapping, to logical schema, 473–79
  principle of conceptualization, 55
  readability of, 460–61
  reusability of, 461
  stability property, 55
  of the state, 34–38
  validation, 55, 461–63
Concurrency control
  approaches, 316
  defined, 315
  distributed, 316–19
Condition activation, 127–28
Condition monitoring, 114
Configurable DBMSs, 416, 423–24
  defined, 416
  KIDS project, 423
  principle, 146
  unbundled DBMS tasks, 423
Constraints
  current snapshot database, 146
  encapsulation vs., 202
  first temporal database, 151–53
  involving intervals, 170–74
  semitemporal database, 147–48
Content-based access control, 395
Content-based authorizations, 359
Content-based retrieval, 276–80
  comparative presentation of, 283–84
  future directions and trends, 282–85
  image retrieval, 276–79
  video retrieval, 279–80
CORBAservices, 422
Coupling modes
  deferred, 77
  defined, 77
  intermediate, 77, 79

Creative design, 449–50

Data abstraction, 445
Database design
    CASE framework for, 445–47
    conceptual, 9
    logical, 10
    methodologies, 8–10
    physical, 10
    stages, 9
    tools, 442
Databases
    active, 19, 61–88
    advances, foundations of, 7
    architecture, 409–12
    changes impact on, 11–13
    component, 296, 403–31
    current, problems of, 11
    deductive, 20, 22, 91–131
    dictionary-catalog, 18
    distributed, 17, 22, 291–325
    evolution, 4–10
    extensional part of, 95
    external, 47
    federated, 17
    first generation, 4
    fuzzy, 20, 22
    historical overview, 4–8
    inconsistent, 127
    intensional part of, 95
    internal, 50
    layered architecture, 410–11
    modeling, 8
    monolithic, 408
    multilevel, 20
    multimedia, 19, 251–86
    nontraditional applications, 13–15
    object-oriented, 19, 190,
        191–92, 211–47
    object-relational, 19, 189–208
    parallel, 22
    parallel evolution of, 92
    performance, 16–17
    promotion of, 5
    quality, 485–505
    real-time, 16
    relational (RDBMSs), 5

research and market trends, 15–20
    secure, 20, 353–99
    semantic, 19
    snapshot, 137–38
    temporal, 19, 137–87
    Web, 13
Database technology
    dimensions in evolution of, 15
    evolution and trends, 3–22
    maturity of, 20–22
    synergy, 22
Data definition language (DDL), 5, 100
Datalog
    in deductive DBs, 100
    defined, 92
DATAMAN group, 331
Data manipulation language (DML), 5
Data model quality, 488–500
    concepts, 492–93
    factors, 490
    improvement strategies, 493
    metrics, 493–500
    process, 489
    stakeholders, 490–91
    weighting, 500
Data quality, 501–5
    design issues, 504–5
    management issues, 502–4
    measurement types, 501
    policy, 502
    value dimensions, 501
    See also Quality
Data warehousing (DW), 14–15
DB2
    authorities, 374
    DAC in, 374
    privileges, 374
DB administrators (DBA), 17
    administration, 360–61
    in federated multi-DBMS, 294
    multiple, 294
    role, 17
DB-Main, 468
DB management systems (DBMSs).
        See Databases
DBTG model, 5
Deadlocks, 318–19

Decision support systems (DSS), 20
Decomposition, 177–81, 183
   horizontal, 177–79
   vertical, 179–81
Deduction rules, 471–72
Deductive databases, 20, 22, 91–131
   base predicates, 100
   basic concepts of, 93–102
   Datalog, 92, 100
   defined, 91–92, 93–96
   derived predicates, 101
   historical perspective, 92
   interpretation, 96
   introduction to, 91–93
   prototype summary, 129
   query processing, 102–8, 128
   relational databases vs., 100–102
   semantics of, 96–98
   stratified, 98
   summary, 130–31
   system prototypes, 128–30
   update processing, 108–28, 130
   views in, 98
Deductive rules, 92
   existential, translation of, 116–17
   intensional information definition, 94
   representation, 94
   See also Databases
DELETE operator, 175, 176
Denials, 94
Derivation rules, 45–46
   defined, 45
   inclusion of, 46
   in practice, 46
Dictionary type, 241
Digital cellular networks, 334–35
Digital libraries (DLs), 394–96
   content-based access control to
      multimedia, 395
   copying and usage, 396
   distributed, 395–96
   flexible subject specification
      mechanism, 394–95
Digital publication, 14
Direct mappings, 475–76
Disconnections, mobile computing, 337

Discretionary access control
   (DAC), 356–59, 362–75
   authorization models, 363–72
   in commercial DBMSs, 370–75
   content-based authorizations, 359
   DB2, 374
   explicit and implicit
      authorizations, 357–58
   GemStone, 374–75
   Oracle, 370–73
   positive and negative
      authorizations, 356–57
   strong and weak authorizations, 357
   TRUDATA, 385
   See also Access control
Distributed commit, 319–22
   three-phase, 321–22
   two-phase, 319–21
Distributed Common Object Model
   (DCOM), 12
Distributed concurrency control, 316–19
   deadlocks, 318–19
   locks, 316–18
   two-phase locking, 316
Distributed databases, 22, 291–325
   alternative transaction models, 323–24
   architecture, 293–300
   architecture taxonomy, 293
   areas, 17
   bottom-up design, 301, 307–10
   client/server system, 300
   data fragmentation, 301–4
   data independence, 299–300
   data replication, 304
   defined, 291
   design, 301–10
   elements, 294
   federated, 294, 295
   global query processing, 292
   global transactions in, 293
   introduction to, 291–93
   mediator architectures, 324–25
   parallel system, 300
   top-down design, 301, 304–7
   trends and challenges, 323–25
   unfederated, 294, 295

World Wide Web and, 325
  See also Databases
Distributed digital libraries, 395–96
Distributed locks, 316–18
  read-write conflict, 317
  write-write conflict, 318
Distributed query processing, 310–14
  in heterogeneous DDBs, 314
  in relational DDBs, 310–14
  See also Query processing
Distributed queue dual bus (DQDB), 13
Distributed recovery, 322
Distributed transaction
        management, 315–23
  commit, 319–22
  concurrency control, 316–19
  in heterogeneous DDBs, 322–23
  recovery, 322
Domains, 35
Downward interpretation, 122–24
  computing, 123
  defined, 122
  example, 123–24
  result, 123
  See also Event rules
Dyadic operators, 160
Dynamic URLs, 341

Education and training, 14
Electronic commerce, 14
Encapsulation, 197
  constraints vs., 202
  strict, 217
Enterprise resource planning packages, 14
Entities
  defined, 36
  as instances of concepts, 36
  types, 36, 37
Entity relationship (E/R) model, 9, 73, 448
E/R schema, 499
Event rules, 120–24
  defined, 120
  downward interpretation, 122–24
  examples, 120–21
  interpretation of, 121–24
  upward interpretation, 121–22

Events
  algebraic composition of, 260
  cause, 258
  classification, 258–59
  conjunction, 261
  defined, 40, 258
  disjunction, 260
  duration, 40
  external, 41
  generated, 41, 43
  IMD, 257–61
  inclusion, 261
  interobject, 259
  intra-object, 259
  modeling and composition of, 259–60
  modeling interaction with, 257–61
  negation, 261
  user-defined, 259
  user interaction, 258–59
Event types
  defined, 42
  generated, 43
  sets of, 42
Executive information systems (EIS), 20
Explicit authorization, 357–58
Extended-kernel architecture, 379–80
Extended markup language (XML), 325
EXTENDS relationship, 223
Extensibility, 253–54
  in access methods, 253–54
  logical, 253
  physical, 253
  in storage mechanisms, 254
Extensional part of DB
        (EDB), 95, 102, 114
Extents, 223
External DBs, 47
External processor, 49
External schemas, 49

Fast Ethernet, 13
Federated multi-DBMS, 17, 294
  component schema, 296
  defined, 295
  export schemas, 296
  external schemas, 297–98
  five-level model for, 296–98

Federated multi-DBMS (continued)
   global schemas, 296–97
   local schema, 296
   query processing in, 314
   transaction management in, 322–23
   See also Databases
Fiber distributed data interface (FDDI), 13
Fixed host (FH), 333
Formal verification, 455–59
   completeness of schema, 459
   irredundancy of schema, 457–59
   schema consistency, 455–57
   See also Verification and validation tools
Fourth normal form (4NF), 469
Fragmentation, 301–4
   advantages, 303
   disadvantages, 303–4
   horizontal, 301–3
   hybrid, 302, 303
   vertical, 302, 303
Functional dependency acquisition, 470–73
   attribute combination avoidance, 471
   deduction rule application, 471–72
   learning from small examples, 472
   mining dependencies, 472–73
   universal relation assumption
      removal, 470–71
   See also Logical design tools
Future Public Land Mobile
      Telecommunications in 2000
      (FPLMTS/IMT 2000), 334
Fuzzy DBs, 20, 22

Gateway support nodes (GSNs), 345–47
   defined, 345
   model services, 346, 347
GemStone system, 225–27
   DAC in, 374–75
   defined, 225
   features, 225–26
   methods, 226–27
   privileges, 374–75
   queries, 227
   segments, 374
Generalizations
   defined, 205
   hierarchy transformation, 477

POET support, 244
UML support, 238
General packet radio service (GPRS), 335
Generated events, 41, 43
Geographical Information System
      (GIS), 14, 194
Geostationary satellites (GEOS), 335
Global queries, 292
   DDB vs. centralized system, 292
   processing, in relational DDBs, 310–11
   See also Queries
Global query processor (GQP), 310
Global transaction manager (GTM), 315
Granularity, 145
Graphical user interfaces (GUIs), 17
Groups
   defined, 354
   organization, 355
Guard functions, 369

Hashing, 340
Herbrand interpretation, 96, 97
Horizontal decomposition, 177–79, 183
Horizontal fragmentation, 301–3
   defined, 301
   derived, 301
   top-down design and, 305–6
   See also Fragmentation
Hybrid fragmentation, 302, 303
Hypergraph data model (HDM), 309
Hypertext markup language (HTML), 325
Hypertext transfer protocol (HTTP), 17

IDEA methodology, 10
Image retrieval, 276–79
   defined, 276
   query categories, 276–77
Implicit authorization, 357–58
Improvement strategies, 493
Inconsistent databases, 127
Indexing
   efficient, mechanisms, 269
   spatial/temporal scheme, 269–70
   techniques for large IMDs, 268–69
   unified spatiotemporal scheme, 270–71
   visual features, 278
Inference rules, 471–72
Information base, 38–39

conceptual schema and, 38
consistency, 44
defined, 38
integrity, 44
Information processor, 49, 50
Information systems (IS)
abstract architecture of, 46–51
active function, 27, 30–31
architecture alignment, 11
conceptual modeling of, 25–55
defined, 25–27
engineering, 26
examples of, 31–33
executive (EIS), 20
functions of, 25–31
geographical, 194
informative function, 27, 28–30
kinds of knowledge required by, 33–34
memory function, 27, 28
process-oriented, 18
real-time, 32, 33
Informative function, 28–30
defined, 27
execution modes, 30
extensional queries, 29
intensional queries, 29
performing, 29
See also Information systems (IS)
Informix multimedia asset management
technology, 280–81
Inheritance, 192, 197
concept, 205, 219
defined, 201
multiple, 219
POET support, 244
See also Object-oriented DBMSs
(OODBMSs)
INNOVATOR, 468
INSERT operator, 174–75
Instances, 223
Instantiation, 36, 218–19
Integrated services digital network
(ISDN), 334
Integrity constraint
enforcement, 108, 117–19
defined, 117
example, 118

performance of, 118–19
problem definition, 117
satisfiability checking vs., 126
view updating and, 118–19
See also Deductive databases
Integrity constraints, 43–45, 92, 99
advantages provided by, 98–100
checking, 112, 113, 117
defined, 44, 64
in denial form, 94
falsification of, 99–100
heads of, 95
maintenance, 117, 118
program development and, 100
redundancy of, 126–27
references, 45
representation, 94
unfulfillment of, 69
violated, 64–65
Integrity lock architecture, 378–79
Intelligent integration of information
(I3), 324
Intensional part of DB (IDB), 95, 102
Interactive multimedia document
(IMD), 252
actors, 261–65
authoring, 273
complex, 257
composition of events, 260
events, 257
framework, 257
indexing techniques, 268–69
modeling, 256–61
rendering, on the Web, 285
retrieval, based on spatiotemporal
structure, 267–74
retrieval issues, 266–74
retrieval requirement, 256
sample, 254–56
scenario, 256, 257, 265–66
spatiotemporal composition, 257
synchronization and presentation, 267
See also Multimedia DBMSs
(MM-DBMSs)
Interface definition language (IDL), 222
Internal DBs, 50
Internal schema, 50–51

Internal schema (continued)
    defined, 50
    using, 51
Interobject events, 259
Interpretations
    defined, 96
    Herbrand, 96, 97
Intervals, 154–56
    aggregate operators on, 160–62
    canonical forms, 183
    closed, 154
    comparison operators, 159
    constraints involving, 170–74
    defined, 182
    denoting, 155
    dyadic operators on, 160
    open, 154
    relational operators with, 162–70
    scalar operators and, 159–60
    update operators involving, 174–76
    value, 158
Interval types, 155, 156–59
    defined, 156–57
    point type of, 157, 183
    type generator, 157
Intra-object events, 259
Iris authorization model, 368–69
    defined, 368–69
    guard functions, 369
    proxy functions, 369
    See also Authorization models
Is-a relationship, 204, 223
Is-a-type-of relationship, 204

Jajodia-Kogan model, 390–91
Java Database Connectivity (JDBC), 298
Joins, 211
Joint administration, 362

Keys, 224
    temporal candidate, 173
    temporal foreign, 174
KIDS project, 423, 429
Kiviat, 498, 500
Knowledge acquisition, 445
Knowledge base, 39
Knowledge reuse and fusion/transformation
    (KRAFT), 324–25

Layered DBMS architecture, 410–11
    illustrated, 411
    layers, 410–11
List type, 241
Local query processor (LQP), 310
Local transaction manager (LTM), 315
LOCK Data Views (LDV) system, 382–83
    defined, 382
    design concepts, 383
    security policy, 382
    type-enforcement mechanism, 383
Logical design, 10, 479
Logical design tools, 469–79
    functional dependency
        acquisition, 470–73
    mapping, 473–79
    See also CASE tools
Logical extensibility, 253
Low earth orbit satellites (LEOS), 335

Magic sets, 107–8
    defined, 107
    example, 107–8
Maintenance
    adaptive, 86
    corrective, 85–86
    rule, 85–87
    tools, 443
Mapping
    CASE support of, 477–79
    conceptual object-oriented schema into
        relational schema, 476–77
    conceptual schema to logical
        schema, 473–79
    direct, 475–76
    E/R schema into relational
        schema, 473–76
    intermediate, rules, 474–75
Massively parallel processing (MPP), 12
Materialized view
        maintenance, 112, 113–14
Mediator architectures, 324–25
Medical systems, 14
Medium earth orbit satellites (MEOS), 336
MEGA, 468
Memory function, 28
    defined, 27

modes, 28
objective, 28
See also Information systems (IS)
MetaEdit+, 468
Methods, 217–18
  GemStone/S, 226–27
  implementation, 217
  signature, 217
Middleware DBMSs, 414–15, 419–22
  defined, 414
  illustrated, 415
  OLE DB, 420–21
Millen-Lunt model, 389–90
  defined, 389
  security properties, 389–90
  See also Multilevel object data models
Minimum bounding rectangles
    (MBRs), 271, 272
Mining algorithms, 473
Mobile computing, 329–47
  agents, 343–44
  AMPS, 334
  architecture, 332–34
  base station (BS), 333
  battery power limitation, 338
  caching, 341
  client/agent/server model, 342–43
  client/intercept/server model, 342, 343
  communication models, 342–43
  database interfaces, 341–42
  design features for accessing data
    services, 344–47
  digital cellular networks, 334–35
  disconnections, 337
  environment, 333
  environment with GSN elements and
    mobile agents, 346
  fixed host (FH), 333
  handoff, 333
  impact on data management, 338–42
  mobile unit (MU), 333
  mobility, 336
  motivation, 331–32
  portability of mobile elements, 337–38
  query processing, 340–41
  satellite networks, 335–36
  size/capability limitations, 337

  software systems, 330–31
  summary, 347
  technological aspects, 334–36
  transactions, 338–39
  wireless local-area networks, 335
  wireless medium, 336–37
  wireless wide-area networks, 335
Mobile unit (MU), 333
Monolithic DBMSs
  implementation, 408
  information system on top of, 407
Morgenstern's model, 391
Multidatabases, 17
Multilevel object data models, 387–92
  Jajodia-Kogan model, 390–91
  Millen-Lunt model, 389–90
  Morgenstern's model, 391
  SODA model, 388
  SORION model, 388–89
  UFOS model, 391–92
Multilevel secure DBMSs (MLS/DBMS),
    20, 359, 360, 375–92
  architectures, 376–80
  commercial products, 384–87
  distributed architecture, 377–78
  extended-kernel architecture, 379–80
  integrity lock architecture, 378–79
  LOCK Data Views (LDV)
    system, 382–83
  object data models, 387–92
  prototypes, 380–83
  relational data model, 375–76
  SeaView, 380–82
  Secure Sybase, 385–86
  single-kernel architecture, 377
  TRUDATA, 384–85
  Trusted Informix, 387
  Trusted Oracle, 386–87
  trusted-subject architecture, 378
  See also Secure databases
Multimedia DBMSs
    (MM-DBMSs), 19, 251–86
  achievements of, 274–80
  commercial products and research
    prototypes, 280–82
  commercial systems, 280–81
  conclusions, 274–86

Multimedia DBMSs (MM-DBMSs)
        (continued)
    content-based
            retrieval, 276–80, 282–85
    design goals, 253
    development of, 253
    directions and trends, 282–86
    extensibility, 253–54
    integrity, 275–76, 282
    introduction to, 251–54
    modeling, 274–75, 282
    research systems, 280
    retrieval, 254
    systems for the World Wide
            Web, 281–82
    See also Databases
Multimedia objects, 251–52
    real-time requirements, 252
    size, 252

Negative authorization, 356–57, 365
Nested tables, 196–97, 201
Networks
    analog cellular, 334
    digital cellular, 334–35
    satellite, 335–36
    wireless local-area, 335
    wireless wide-area, 335
Noncascading revocation, 364
Nonevents, 68
Nontraditional applications, 13–15

Object composition petri nets
        (OCPN), 275
Object "curator" administration, 361
Object Database Management Group
        (ODMG), 192
    binary association support, 237
    collection type support, 224
    data model, 223, 224
    maximum multiplicity, 235–36
    objective, 222
    ODMG-93, 222
    standard, 221–24
    two-way relationship support, 236
Object database management system
        (ODMS), 16
Object definition language (ODL), 222

class definition in, 234
conceptual schema, 234
disjoint and incomplete generalization
        in, 238
relationships in, 235
schema, 243
self-association definition in, 237
Objectering, 468
Object identifiers
        (OIDs), 192, 193, 214–16
    building approaches, 215
    logical, 214
    mapping, 215
Object Management Group (OMG), 222
Object modeling technique (OMT), 10
Object-oriented DBMSs
        (OODBMSs), 19, 190,
        191–92, 211–47
    authorization models, 366–69
    classes, 218–19
    conceptual design, 232–33
    conceptual schema, 231
    data model concepts, 212–20
    defined, 213
    design, 230–46
    design process, 232
    drawbacks, 193–95, 247
    feature comparison, 192–93
    graphical notation, 220–21
    implementation schema design, 242–46
    industry standard, 192
    inheritance, 192, 219–20
    introduction to, 211–12
    joins, 211
    methods, 217–18
    objects, 213, 214–16
    OIDs, 192, 193, 214–16
    origins, 192
    RID, 215–16
    schema example, 221
    standard schema design, 233–42
    subtyping, 219
    summary, 246–47
    technology, 225–30, 247
    uses, 211
    See also Databases

Object-oriented software engineering
  (OOSE), 10
Object-owner administration, 361
Object privileges, 373
Object-relational DBMSs
  (ORDBMSs), 19, 189–208
  ABC Corporation example, 203–8
  behaviors, 196
  built-in types support, 198
  characteristics, 190
  collection types, 196–97, 198, 199–200
  defined, 190
  design issues, 201–3
  drawbacks, 193–95
  encapsulation, 197
  feature comparison, 192–93
  inheritance, 192, 197
  introduction to, 189–91
  physical implementation, 198–200
  polymorphism, 197
  reference types, 198, 199
  row types, 198–99
  summary, 208
  See also Databases; Object-oriented
    DBMSs (OODBMSs)
Objects, 214–16
  aggregations, 213
  authorization, 354
  classes, 213
  complex, 216, 217
  composite, 217
  defined, 213
  detection, 278
  indexing, 267
  instances, 213
  media, 251–52
  persistent, 222
  state, 213
  transient, 222
  types, 222–23, 252
  See also Object-oriented DBMSs
    (OODBMSs)
ObjectStore, 227–29
  defined, 227–28
  features, 228
  relationships, 228–29
OLE DB, 420–21

  components, 420
  query execution, 421
  rowsets, 420
One-way relationships, 236
On-line analytical processing
  (OLAP), 14–15
On-line transactional processing (OLTP), 6
Ontology, 35
Open Database Connectivity
  (ODBC), 298
Open intervals, 154
Open Server, 298
OPENTOOL, 468
Operators, 182
  aggregate, 160–62
  Allen's, 159–60
  comparison, 159
  dyadic, 160
  relational, 162–70
  TAC, 262–63
  update, 174–76
Optimization, 447
Oracle
  DAC in, 370–73
  Designer/2000, 468
  object privileges, 373
  Oracle8, 280
  system privileges, 373
Oracle active rule language, 79–81
  defined, 79
  features, 79–80
ORCA, 468
Orion authorization model, 367–68
  defined, 367
  extensions, 368
  propagation rules, 367
  See also Authorization models

Pacbase, 468
Paradigm, 468
Parallel DBs, 22
Perceived semantic quality, 492
Performance
  DBMS, 16–17
  integrity constraint
    enforcement, 118–19
  three-phase commit, 322

Persistent objects, 222
Persistent storage, 201
Personal digital assistants (PDA), 12
Photobook system, 280
Physical design, 10
Physical extensibility, 253
PICQUERY+, 278
Platinum ERwin, 468
Plug-in components, 417–19
Plug-in style DBMSs, 413–14
POET system, 229–30
    collection types support, 244
    database schema, 247
    data types, 242
    defined, 229
    features, 229–30
    generalization support, 244
    inheritance support, 244
    OQL use, 242
    schema definition, 245
    type system, 242
Point type, 157, 183
Polyinstantiation, 375, 386
Polymorphism, 197
Positive authorization, 356–57
PowerDesigner, 468
Pragmatica, 468
Pragmatic quality, 492
Principle of conceptualization, 55
Privileges, 355
    DB2, 374
    GemStone system, 374–75
    object, 373
    Oracle, 370, 373
    system, 373
Process
    modeling tools, 443
    quality, 486, 487
    systems, 18
Product quality, 486, 487
Project management tools, 441
Propagation policies, 358
Proxy functions, 369

QBIC, 267, 281
Quality, 485–505
    concepts, 492–93

data, 501–5
data model, 488–500
definitions, 486
factors, 490
information, 487
perceived semantic, 492
pragmatic, 492
process, 486, 487
product, 486, 487
semantic, 492
social, 492
summary, 505
syntactic, 492
See also Databases
Quality assessment, 460–63
    conceptual schema readability, 460–61
    schema reusability, 461
    schema validation, 461–63
    See also Verification and validation tools
Quality metrics, 493–500
    CA, 495
    DA, 494–95
    defined, 493
    example values, 498
    IS_ARel, 496
    M:NRel, 496
    measurement interpretation, 498
    PR, 495
    RvsE, 494
Queries, 218, 219
    atomic, 285
    combination, 277
    concept, 277
    current snapshot database, 146–47
    extensional, 29
    feature combination, 276
    first temporal database, 153–54
    GemStone/S, 227
    global, 292, 310–11
    intensional, 29
    localized feature, 276
    object relationship, 277
    semitemporal database, 148–49
    simple visual feature, 276
    spatial, 271
    uncertainty, handling of, 285
    user-defined attribute, 277

Query by icons, 342
Query optimization
  defined, 291
  illustrated, 312
Query plans
  alternative set of, 312
  defined, 291
  good, 291–92
Query processing, 102–8, 128
  bottom-up, 102, 103–5
  distributed, 310–14
  in heterogeneous DDBs, 314
  magic sets, 107–8
  mobile computing, 340–41
  in relational DDBs, 310–14
  top-down, 103, 105–7
  See also Deductive databases

Rational Rose, 468
Record identifier (RID), 215–16
Recovering business policies, 64–67
  defined, 69
  graphical representation, 73
  supporting, through active rules, 69–73
Reference relationships, 36
Reference types, 198, 199
  importance, 199
  values, 199
Referential integrity (RI), 191
Relational data interface (RDI), 412
Relational data system (RDS), 412
Relational DBMSs (RDBMs), 5
  authorization model for, 363–66
  constraints role, 191
  data integrity enforcement, 191
  deductive databases vs., 100–102
  migrating, toward object
    orientation, 194–95
  SQL, 100
  table structure modification, 191
  See also Databases
Relational DDBs
  query processing in, 310–14
  top-down design in, 304–7
  See also Distributed databases
Relational design, 469–70
Relational operators

COALESCE, 165, 166
GROUP, 164
involving intervals, 162–70
overloading, 164
UNION, 178
Relational storage system (RSS), 412
Relationships
  as instances of concepts, 37
  in ODL, 235
  one-way, 236
  reference, 36
  two-way, 236
  types, 36, 37
Remote communications, 344
Replication, 304
Repository and metadata tools, 443–44
Representation conflict, 463–64
Requirements engineering, 51–53
  defined, 52
  phases, 52
  requirements determination, 52
  requirements specification, 52
  requirements validation, 53
Reusability, 461, 467–68
Reverse engineering, 450–52
RIDL, 468
RoboCASE, 468
Roles, 355
Row triggers, 85
Row types, 198–99
R-trees, 271–74
  3D, spatial/temporal layout retrieval
    with, 274
  defined, 271–72

Sagas, 323
Satellite networks, 335–36
Satisfiability checking, 125–26
Scalar operators, 159–60
Scenario model, 256, 257, 265–66
  defined, 265
  tuple attributes, 265–66
  verbal description, 266
  See also Interactive multimedia
    document (IMD)
Schemas
  comparison, 465

Schemas (continued)
   conceptual, 35, 39–43, 53–54
   conflict between, 463–64
   conforming, 466
   E/R, 499
   external, 49
   integration, 447, 463–66
   internal, 50–51
   merging, 466
   restructuring, 466
   standard design, 233–42
   validation, 461–63
Scientific applications, 14
SeaView, 380–82
   components, 381–82
   data model, 382
   defined, 380–81
   reference monitor concept, 381
Secure databases, 20, 353–99
   access control, 354–62
   administration policies, 360–62
   basic concepts, 354–55
   DAC, 356–59, 362–75
   design issues, 392–93
   digital libraries, 394–96
   introduction to, 353–54
   MAC, 359–60
   MLS/DBMS, 359, 360, 375–92
   multilevel secure, 359
   research trends, 393–98
   summary, 398–99
   WFMS, 396–97
   World Wide Web, 397–98
   See also Databases
Secure Sybase, 385–86
   defined, 385
   polyinstantiation support, 386
Security
   levels, 359
   mandatory, 360
   multilevel, 360, 375–92
Semantic DBs, 19
Semantic quality, 492
Semijoin operator, 301–3
Sequenced operations, 186
Service-oriented DBMSs, 422–23
   architectures, 415–16

CORBAservices, 422
   strawman architecture, 422–23
   See also Databases
Set type, 241
Side effects
   defined, 116
   prevention, 127
Single-kernel architecture, 377
Snapshot databases, 137–38
   defined, 137
   snapshot time, 138
   See also Databases
Social quality, 492
SODA model, 388
Software through Picture, 468
SORION model, 388–89
   defined, 388
   security policy, 388–89
   system implementation, 389
   See also Multilevel object data models
Spatial queries, 271
Spatiotemporal composition, 257, 260
   of actors, 261–65
   EBNF definition of, 264–65
   model, 263–65
   of multimedia applications, 264
   See also Composition
Spatiotemporal indexing scheme, 270–71
Specialization, 206, 213
SQL
   relational databases, 100
   SQL2, 101
   SQL3, 198
   SQL: 1999, 85
SQLNet, 299
Stakeholders, 490–91
Standard schema design, 233–42
   aggregation, 239–40
   associations, 235–37
   collection and structured types, 240–42
   generalizations and realizations, 238–39
   object types translation, 233–35
   See also Object-oriented DBMSs
      (OODBMSs); schemas
Starburst authorization model, 369–70
Statement triggers, 80–81
   access from, 81

for auditing, 81–82
defined, 80
example, 80
features, 80–81
SQL: 1999, 85
for view materialization, 82–85
State transition diagrams (STD), 67
Statistical systems, 14
Stratification, 98
Strawman architecture, 422–23
Strict 2PL, 316
Strong authorization, 357
Structural conflict, 463–64
Structured type, 224, 241
Subclasses, 219
    defined, 213
    instances, 219
    See also classes
Subqueries, 105, 106
Successor function, 158, 183
Superclasses, 213, 218
Sybase Adaptive Server Enterprise, 421
Symmetric multiprocessing (SMP), 12
Syntactic quality, 492
System privileges, 373
System R authorization model, 363–66
    defined, 363
    extensions, 364–66
    recursive revocation, 364
    See also Authorization models

Temporal candidate key, 173
Temporal databases, 20, 137–87
    aggregate operators on intervals, 160–62
    concepts, 142–46
    constraints, 146, 147–48, 151–53
    constraints involving intervals, 170–74
    data, 140–46, 154
    decomposition, 177
    defined, 137
    design considerations, 176
    horizontal decomposition, 177–79
    intervals, 154–56
    interval types, 156–59
    introduction to, 137–40
    queries, 146–47, 148–49, 153–54

relational operators involving
    intervals, 162–70
research issues, 139
scalar operators on intervals, 159–60
summary, 182–83
terminology, 143
update operators involving
    intervals, 174–76
vertical decomposition, 179–81
See also Databases
Temporal difference, 167
Temporal elements, 185
Temporal foreign key, 174
Temporal projection, 166
Temporal relations, 182–83
Temporal relvars, 183
Temporal support, 185
Temporal upward compatibility, 186
Textual information, 14
Third normal form (3NF), 469
Three-phase commit, 321–22
    performance, 322
    phases, 321
Time
    transaction, 143
    valid, 143, 178
Time-division multiple access
    (TDMA), 334, 335
Timepoints, 144
Timestamps, 140, 182, 185
Top-down design, 301, 304–7
    horizontal fragmentation and, 305–6
    issues, 304
    vertical fragmentation and, 306–7
    See also Distributed databases
Top-down query evaluation
    defined, 103
    drawbacks, 106–7
    example, 105–6
    process, 105
    repetitive subqueries, 106
    See also Query processing
Total quality management (TQM), 488
TQdM, 503
Transaction manager, 292
Transaction proxies, 339

Transactions
    defined, 292
    global, 293
    isolation-only, 339
    mobile computing, 338–39
    weak, 339
Transaction time, 143
Transient objects, 222
Triggered procedures, 178
Triggers
    row, 85
    SQL: 1999, 85
    statement, 80–81
    temporarily deactivating, 87
    tracking, 87
TRUDATA, 384–85
    ACLs, 385
    DAC, 385
    defined, 384
    objects in, 384
Trusted Informix, 387
Trusted Oracle, 386–87
Trusted-subject architecture, 378
Tutorial D, 162
    defined, 141
    type generator, 157
Two-phase commit, 319–21
    failures, 320
    phases, 319–20
Two-way relationships, 236
Types, 222–23
    array, 241
    bag, 240–41
    collection, 196–97, 198, 199–200,
        224, 240–41
    dictionary, 241
    extents, 223
    external specification, 223
    implementations, 223
    list, 241
    set, 241
    structured, 224, 241
    subtypes, 223

UFOS model, 391–92
Unfederated multi-DBMS, 294
    defined, 295

four-level model for, 298
Unfolded form, 183
UNFOLD operator, 160–62
Unified Modeling Language (UML), 231
    aggregation support, 239–40
    aggregation tree, 239
    conceptual schema, 243
    generalization support, 238
    interfaces, 234
    persistent classes, 233
    realization, 239
UNION operator, 178
Universal Mobile Telecommunication
        System (UMTS), 334
Universal relation assumption, 470–71
UPDATE operator, 174–75
Update operators
    DELETE, 175, 176
    INSERT, 174–75
    involving intervals, 174–76
    UPDATE, 175, 176
    See also Temporal databases
Update processing, 108–28, 130
    change computation, 109–14
    condition activation enforcement, 127
    condition activation prevention, 128
    database inconsistency
        maintenance, 127
    event rules, 120–24
    inconsistent database repair, 127
    problem classification, 124–28
    problem framework, 119–28
    redundancy of integrity
        constraints, 126–27
    satisfiability checking, 125–26
    side effect prevention, 127
    view liveliness, 126
    view updating, 114–17
    See also Deductive databases
Upward interpretation, 121–22
    defined, 121
    example, 122
    result, 121
    See also Event rules
User-defined events, 259
User interaction events, 258–59

Validation
    defined, 446
    schema, 461–63
    See also Verification and validation tools
Validator, 468
Valid time, 178
    defined, 143
    event tables, 186
    state tables, 186
Verification
    defined, 446
    formal, 455–59
Verification and validation tools, 455–63
    formal verification, 455–59
    quality assessment, 460–61
    schema validation, 461–63
Vertical decomposition, 179–81, 183
Vertical fragmentation, 302, 303
    defined, 303
    top-down design and, 306–7
    See also Fragmentation
Video retrieval, 279–80
Views
    advantages, 98–100
    in deductive DBs, 98
    defined, 95
    integration, 447
    liveliness, 126
    materialized maintenance, 112, 113–14
    power of, 99
View updating, 108, 114–17
    aspects related to, 115–17
    defined, 114
    example, 115

integrity constraint enforcement
        and, 118–19
    methods for, 117
    multiple translations, 115
    multiple update treatment, 116
    performance of, 118–19
    problem definition, 114–15
    process illustration, 114
    side effects, 116
    translation of existential deductive
        rules, 116–17
    See also Deductive databases
Virage system, 281
VIS, 468

Weak authorization, 357
Web
    data protection for, 397–98
    distributed databases and, 325
    growth of, 285
    IMD rendering on, 285
    retrieval, QoS issues, 285–86
WebSEEk, 281
WebSeer project, 281–82
Weighting, 500
Wireless local-area networks, 335
Wireless wide-area networks, 335
Workflow Management Coalition
        (WfMC), 397
Workflow management systems (WFMSs)
    access control, 396–97
    authorization constraint modeling, 397
    defined, 396
Workflow models, 324
World Wide Web. *See* Web

Recent Titles in the Artech House Computing Library

Advanced ANSI SQL Data Modeling and Structure Processing, Michael M. David

Advanced Database Technology and Design, Mario Piattini and Oscar Díaz, editors

Business Process Implementation for IT Professionals and Managers, Robert B. Walford

Data Modeling and Design for Today's Architectures, Angelo Bobak

Data Quality for the Information Age, Thomas C. Redman

Data Warehousing and Data Mining for Telecommunications, Rob Mattison

Distributed and Multi-Database Systems, Angelo R. Bobak

Electronic Payment Systems, Donal O'Mahony, Michael Peirce, and Hitesh Tewari

Future Codes: Essays in Advanced Computer Technology and the Law, Curtis E. A. Karnow

Global Distributed Applications With Windows® DNA, Enrique Madrona

A Guide to Programming Languages: Overview and Comparison, Ruknet Cezzar

A Guide to Software Configuration Management, Alexis Leon

Guide to Standards and Specifications for Designing Web Software, Stan Magee and Leonard L. Tripp

How to Run Successful High-Tech Project-Based Organizations, Fergus O'Connell

For further information on these and other Artech House titles, including previously considered out-of-print books now available through our In-Print-Forever® (IPF®) program, contact:

Artech House
685 Canton Street
Norwood, MA 02062
Phone: 781-769-9750
Fax: 781-769-6334
e-mail: artech@artechhouse.com

Artech House
46 Gillingham Street
London SW1V 1AH UK
Phone: +44 (0)20 7596-8750
Fax: +44 (0)20 7630-0166
e-mail: artech-uk@artechhouse.com

Find us on the World Wide Web at:
www.artechhouse.com